Business Plans Handbook

Business Plans Handbook

A COMPILATION OF BUSINESS PLANS DEVELOPED BY INDIVIDUALS THROUGHOUT NORTH AMERICA

VOLUME

15

**Lynn M. Pearce,
Project Editor**

GALE
CENGAGE Learning

Detroit • New York • San Francisco • New Haven, Conn • Waterville, Maine • London

GALE
CENGAGE Learning™

Business Plans Handbook, Volume 15

Project Editor: Lynn M. Pearce

Product Manager: Jenai Mynatt

Product Design: Jennifer Wahi

Composition and Electronic Prepress: Evi Seoud

Manufacturing: Rita Wimberley

Editorial: Erin Braun

Gale
27500 Drake Rd.
Farmington Hills, MI, 48331-3535

ISBN-13: 978-1-4144-1910-7
1084-4473

Printed in the United States of America
1 2 3 4 5 6 7 12 11 10 09

Contents

BUSINESS PLANS

CONTENTS

Highlights

Business Plans Handbook, Volume 15 (BPH-15) is a collection of business plans compiled by entrepreneurs seeking funding for small businesses throughout North America. For those looking for examples of how to approach, structure, and compose their own business plans, *BPH-15* presents 20 sample plans, including plans for the following businesses:

- Air Brushing Services
- Art Easel Manufacturer
- Bicycle Shop
- Comedy Club
- DVD Kiosk Rental Business
- Energy Consultant
- Environmentally–Friendly Greenhouse
- Furniture Resale Shop
- Furniture Restoration Company
- Healthcare Marketing Agency
- Low–Cost Home Decorating Service
- Music Store
- Natural Gas Home Filling Station Provider
- Photography Studio
- Plus–Sized Children's Clothing Store
- Real Estate Brokerage
- Real Estate Renovation and Resale
- Rental Defibrillator Service
- Windmill Distributor
- Yoga Studio

FEATURES AND BENEFITS

BPH-15 offers many features not provided by other business planning references including:

- Twenty business plans, each of which represent an attempt at clarifying (for themselves and others) the reasons that the business should exist or expand and why a lender should fund the enterprise.
- Two fictional plans that are used by business counselors at a prominent small business development organization as examples for their clients. (You will find these in the Business Plan Template Appendix.)
- A directory section that includes: listings for venture capital and finance companies, which specialize in funding start-up and second-stage small business ventures, and a comprehensive listing of Service Corps of Retired Executives (SCORE) offices. In addition, the Appendix also contains updated listings

of all Small Business Development Centers (SBDCs); associations of interest to entrepreneurs; Small Business Administration (SBA) Regional Offices; and consultants specializing in small business planning and advice. It is strongly advised that you consult supporting organizations while planning your business, as they can provide a wealth of useful information.

- A Small Business Term Glossary to help you decipher the sometimes confusing terminology used by lenders and others in the financial and small business communities.

- A cumulative index, outlining each plan profiled in the complete Business Plans Handbook series.

- A Business Plan Template which serves as a model to help you construct your own business plan. This generic outline lists all the essential elements of a complete business plan and their components, including the Summary, Business History and Industry Outlook, Market Examination, Competition, Marketing, Administration and Management, Financial Information, and other key sections. Use this guide as a starting point for compiling your plan.

- Extensive financial documentation required to solicit funding from small business lenders. You will find examples of: Cash Flows, Balance Sheets, Income Projections, and other financial information included with the textual portions of the plan.

Introduction

Perhaps the most important aspect of business planning is simply doing it. More and more business owners are beginning to compile business plans even if they don't need a bank loan. Others discover the value of planning when they must provide a business plan for the bank. The sheer act of putting thoughts on paper seems to clarify priorities and provide focus. Sometimes business owners completely change strategies when compiling their plan, deciding on a different product mix or advertising scheme after finding that their assumptions were incorrect. This kind of healthy thinking and re-thinking via business planning is becoming the norm. The editors of *Business Plans Handbook, Volume 15 (BPH-15)* sincerely hope that this latest addition to the series is a helpful tool in the successful completion of your business plan, no matter what the reason for creating it.

This fifteenth volume, like each volume in the series, offers business plans used and created by real people. *BPH-15* provides 20 business plans. The business and personal names and addresses and general locations have been changed to protect the privacy of the plan authors.

NEW BUSINESS OPPORTUNITIES

As in other volumes in the series, *BPH-15* finds entrepreneurs engaged in a wide variety of creative endeavors. Examples include a proposal for a air brushing services company, an art easel manufacturer, a comdy club, and a music store. In addition, several other plans are provided, including a DVD Kiosk Rental Business, a healthcare marketing agency, a windmill distributor, a plus-sized childrens clothing store, and a yoga studio.

Comprehensive financial documentation has become increasingly important as today's entrepreneurs compete for the finite resources of business lenders. Our plans illustrate the financial data generally required of loan applicants, including Income Statements, Financial Projections, Cash Flows, and Balance Sheets.

ENHANCED APPENDIXES

In an effort to provide the most relevant and valuable information for our readers, we have updated the coverage of small business resources. For instance, you will find: a directory section, which includes listings of all of the Service Corps of Retired Executives (SCORE) offices; an informative glossary, which includes small business terms; and a cumulative index, outlining each plan profiled in the complete Business Plans Handbook series. In addition we have updated the list of Small Business Development Centers (SBDCs); Small Business Administration Regional Offices; venture capital and finance companies, which specialize in funding start-up and second-stage small business enterprises; associations of interest to entrepreneurs; and consultants, specializing in small business advice and planning. For your reference, we have also reprinted the business plan template, which provides a comprehensive overview of the essential components of a business plan and two fictional plans used by small business counselors.

SERIES INFORMATION

If you already have the first fourteen volumes of *BPH*, with this fifteenth volume, you will now have a collection of over 320 business plans (not including the one updated plan in the second volume, whose original appeared in the first, or the two fictional plans in the Business Plan Template Appendix section of the second, third, fourth, fifth, sixth, and seventh volumes); contact information for hundreds of organizations and agencies offering business expertise; a helpful business plan template; a foreword providing advice and instruction to entrepreneurs on how to begin their research; more than 1,500 citations to valuable small business development material; and a comprehensive glossary of terms to help the business planner navigate the sometimes confusing language of entrepreneurship.

ACKNOWLEDGEMENTS

The Editors wish to sincerely thank the contributors to *BPH-15*, including:

- Laura Becker
- BizPlanDB.com
- Heidi Denler
- Paul Greenland
- Merrill Guerra
- Dan Izzo
- Kari Lucke
- Gerald Rekve, Corporate Management Consultants
- Jonathan Rekve
- Lubnah Shomali
- Elliot Smith

COMMENTS WELCOME

Your comments on *Business Plans Handbook* are appreciated. Please direct all correspondence, suggestions for future volumes of *BPH*, and other recommendations to the following:

Managing Editor, Business Product
Business Plans Handbook
The Gale Group
27500 Drake Rd.
Farmington Hills, MI 48331-3535
Phone: (248)699-4253
Fax: (248)699-8052
Toll-Free: 800-347-GALE
E-mail: BusinessProducts@gale.com

Air Brushing Services

Workz of Art

53290 Bliss Blvd.
Philadelphia, Pennsylvania 19131

Gerald Rekve

Workz of Art will strive to provide our clients with high–quality air brushing services and offer quality products/services to the Greater Philadelphia market. While there are many competitors in the market in which we will be operating, we feel that the quality of our artists will provide a stable income for both the owners and the artists we hire.

BUSINESS OVERVIEW

Mission

Our mission is to provide our clients with the best in artist–quality air brushing services. Since art appreciation is very subjective, we will rely on the customer who pays for the art work to determine if what they are paying for is what they like. We will work with our clients until they are happy with the art we provide to them. We will even go the point of not making money on a sale in order to win our customer's approval for the art work. We realize that the clients may use a variety of techniques to get us to reduce the price we charge for our services. Therefore, we will be sure to understand the client's needs before we even start work on the client's order.

Management Summary

Workz of Art will be owned by Eli Thompson and Peter Boge. Both Eli and Peter have been working in the air brush business for over ten years. Eli Thompson will be President and CEO; Peter Boge will be Operations Manager.

Both the owners of the business will run the day–to–day operations. Then they will hire artists who will act as contract agents for the business. Every client who needs work done will go through the business to place the order. The managers will ask one of the artists to paint the project in our painting facility.

Personnel plan	FY 2009	FY 2010	FY 2011
Eli Thompson	$ 51,917	$ 60,000	$ 65,000
Peter Boge	$ 49,114	$ 55,000	$ 60,000
Total payroll	**$101,030**	**$115,000**	**$125,000**

Eli Thompson worked for a major supplier of art supplies in Philadelphia; Peter Boge was a winner of a local art competition—winning an award for Best in Air Brush Work. Peter Boge was a sales consultant for a local telecom business for over five years, and is a close friend of Eli's. Both love this business and hired an accounting firm to do market research in the Greater Philadelphia area.

Highlights

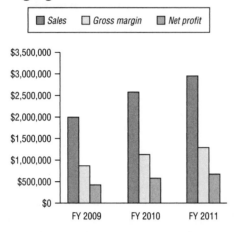

OBJECTIVES

Workz of Art's objectives will be to offer quality products/services to the Greater Philadelphia market. While there are many competitors in the market in which we will be operating, we feel that the quality of our artists will provide a stable income for both the owners and the artists we hire.

Market Analysis

Our objectives can be best broken down into the sectors we operate in.

- Individual Client—This client wants a custom piece of art work or a specific object air brushed.

- Business Client—This client requires some custom art work.

- Government Client—This client requires custom art work.

Keys to Success

The keys to the success of Workz of Art will be the following:

- We are able to hire quality air brush artists

- Our pricing is fair, based on the market

- Our competitors can not give away the products and services in order to compete

- There is no additional growth in the marketplace during our first year of business.

BUSINESS STRATEGY

The studio will sell air brush work to a variety of clients. With the growth of the internet, the need for art work has grown tremendously over the past few years.

Start-up requirements

Start-up expenses	
Payroll	$10,000
Equipment	$15,000
Lease hold improvements	$10,000
Rent	$ 1,300
Inventory start up	$10,000
Other	$ 5,000
Total start-up expenses	**$51,300**
Start-up assets	
Cash required	$10,000
Start-up stock	$ 5,000
Other current assets	$ 0
Fixed assets	$ 0
Total assets	**$15,000**
Total requirements	**$66,300**

Market Analysis

We will target the client that needs air brush work done on their automobiles, motorcycles, etc. We will focus all our sales strategies on these two auto–related markets and will support our business with sales of airbrush supplies to the artist markets. This will ensure we have good cash flow in our business from the start. Any other business will be considered a bonus.

Advertising

Our strategy will be to advertise our products and services using a variety of methods. Here are a few places we will use to promote our products and services to our clients:

- Yellow Pages
- Radio
- Television
- Internet search engines
- Website
- Bus and taxi mobile billboards
- Sponsor sports events and minor league teams on a contract basis
- Newspaper
- Magazine
- Store signage and window
- Small artist credits on completed work

Company Ownership

The company will be owned by Eli Thompson and Peter Boge, according to the following breakdown:

- Eli Thompson: 55 percent
- Peter Boge: 45 percent

PRODUCTS & SERVICES

All Workz of Art products will be related to the art market. Here are a few of the product lines and services we will offer the customers:

- Air brush art work for businesses

- Air brush art work for the consumer market
- Air brush supplies and products for artists
- Classes in air brush art

FINANCIAL ANALYSIS

Marketing & Sales

Our strategy will be to reach a large number of clients on an ongoing basis. Our start–up funding will give us the required operating money.

Sales Forecast

Sales forecast	FY 2009	FY 2010	FY 2011
Unit sales			
Air brush work for cars, trucks, vehicles	537	700	800
Air brush work for helmets, motorcycles etc	577	700	800
Air brush supply sales	681	800	800
Total unit sales	**1,794**	**2,200**	**2,400**
Unit prices			
Air brush work for cars, trucks, vehicles	$ 3,500.00	$ 3,500.00	$ 3,500.00
Air brush work for helmets, motorcycles etc	$ 250.00	$ 250.00	$ 250.00
Air brush supply sales	$ 65.00	$ 65.00	$ 65.00
Sales			
Air brush work for cars, trucks, vehicles	$ 1,878,256	$ 2,450,000	$ 2,800,000
Air brush work for helmets, motorcycles etc	$ 144,151	$ 175,000	$ 200,000
Air brush supply sales	$ 44,278	$ 52,000	$ 52,000
Total sales	**$2,066,685**	**$2,677,000**	**$3,052,000**
Direct unit costs			
Air brush work for cars, trucks, vehicles	$ 1,995.00	$ 1,995.00	$ 1,995.00
Air brush work for helmets, motorcycles etc	$ 142.50	$ 142.50	$ 142.50
Air brush supply sales	$ 24.05	$ 24.05	$ 24.05
Direct cost of sales			
Air brush work for cars, trucks, vehicles	$ 1,070,606	$ 1,396,500	$ 1,596,000
Air brush work for helmets, motorcycles etc	$ 82,166	$ 99,750	$ 114,000
Air brush supply sales	$ 16,383	$ 19,240	$ 19,240
Subtotal direct cost of sales	**$ 1,169,155**	**$ 1,515,490**	**$ 1,729,240**

Sales Monthly

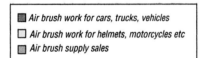

☐ Air brush work for cars, trucks, vehicles
☐ Air brush work for helmets, motorcycles etc
☐ Air brush supply sales

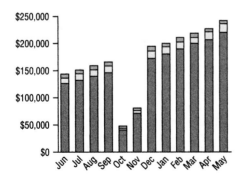

Sales by Year

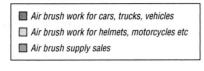
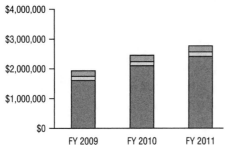

- ■ Air brush work for cars, trucks, vehicles
- □ Air brush work for helmets, motorcycles etc
- ■ Air brush supply sales

Operations

Eli Thompson will invest $30,000 and Peter Boge will invest $20,000 in the company. Based on this information, the company will have an operating base of $50,000 in cash. We will also retain an operating line of credit of $25,000 to handle the setup of the studio for lease hold and other startup expenses. The total start–up expenses are $66,300, with total assets of $23,700.

Start-up funding	
Start-up expenses to fund	$51,300
Start-up assets to fund	$15,000
Total funding required	**$66,300**
Assets	
Non-cash assets from start-up	$ 5,000
Cash requirements from start-up	$10,000
Additional cash raised	$ 8,700
Cash balance on starting date	$18,700
Total assets	**$23,700**
Liabilities and capital	
Liabilities	
Current borrowing	$25,000
Fixed liabilities	$ 0
Accounts payable (outstanding bills)	$ 0
Other current liabilities	$ 0
Total liabilities	**$25,000**
Capital	
Planned investment	
Owner	$30,000
Investor	$20,000
Additional investment requirement	$ 0
Total planned investment	**$50,000**
Loss at start-up (start-up expenses)	$51,300
Total capital	**$ 1,300**
Total capital and liabilities	**$23,700**
Total funding	**$75,000**

The return on investment is based on an average of 16 percent ROI for the first year of operation. The ROI in subsequent years will be 21 percent.

Financial Assumptions

Our assumptions are that we will be able to achieve the sales amounts we are predicting; this will allow for us to make the money we are projecting. We, as business owners, will take out dividends as they become available.

Break–Even Analysis

Break-even analysis

Monthly units break-even	43
Monthly revenue break-even	$ 49,548

Assumptions:

Average per-unit revenue	$ 1,152.00
Average per-unit variable cost	$ 651.70
Estimated monthly fixed cost	$21,517.83

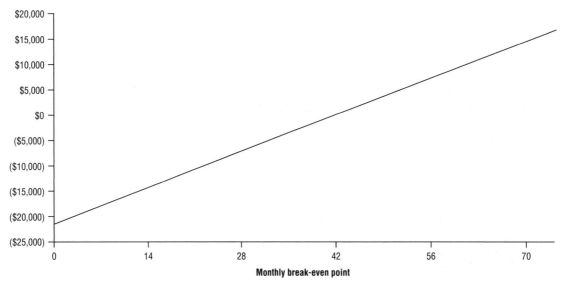

Monthly break-even point

Break-even point = where line intersects with 0

Projected Profit and Loss

Pro forma profit and loss	FY 2009	FY 2010	FY 2011
Sales	$2,066,685	$2,677,000	$3,052,000
Direct costs of goods	$1,169,155	$1,515,490	$1,729,240
Other costs of goods	$ 0	$ 0	$ 0
Cost of goods sold	$1,169,155	$1,515,490	$1,729,240
Gross margin	$ 897,530	$1,161,510	$1,322,760
Gross margin %	43.43%	43.39%	43.34%
Expenses			
Payroll	$ 101,030	$ 115,000	$ 125,000
Marketing/promotion	$ 10,265	$ 13,000	$ 15,000
Depreciation	$ 0	$ 0	$ 0
Rent	$ 8,760	$ 9,000	$ 10,000
Utilities	$ 5,752	$ 6,000	$ 7,000
Advertising	$ 20,259	$ 25,000	$ 30,000
Payroll	$ 82,483	$ 88,050	$ 98,750
Inventory ongoing	$ 29,664	$ 40,000	$ 50,000
Total operating expenses	**$ 258,214**	**$ 296,050**	**$ 335,750**
Profit before interest and taxes	$ 639,316	$ 865,460	$ 987,010
Interest expense	$ 2,500	$ 2,500	$ 2,500
Taxes incurred	$ 191,045	$ 258,888	$ 295,353
Net profit	$ 445,771	$ 604,072	$ 689,157
Net profit/sales	21.57%	22.57%	22.58%

Projected Cash Flow

Pro forma cash flow	FY 2009	FY 2010	FY 2011
Cash received			
Cash from operations			
Cash sales	$2,066,685	$2,677,000	$3,052,000
Subtotal cash from operations	$2,066,685	$2,677,000	$3,052,000
Additional cash received			
GST/HST received (output tax)	$ 0	$ 0	$ 0
GST/HST repayments	$ 0	$ 0	$ 0
New current borrowing	$ 0	$ 0	$ 0
New other liabilities (interest-free)	$ 0	$ 0	$ 0
New fixed liabilities	$ 0	$ 0	$ 0
Sales of other current assets	$ 0	$ 0	$ 0
Sales of fixed assets	$ 0	$ 0	$ 0
New investment received	$ 0	$ 0	$ 0
Subtotal cash received	$2,066,685	$2,677,000	$3,052,000
Expenditures			
Expenditures from operations			
Cash spending	$ 101,030	$ 115,000	$ 125,000
Bill payments	$1,475,405	$1,961,726	$2,234,715
Subtotal spent on operations	$1,576,436	$2,076,726	$2,359,715
Additional cash spent			
GST/HST paid out (input tax)	$ 0	$ 0	$ 0
GST/HST payments	$ 0	$ 0	$ 0
Principal repayment of current borrowing	$ 0	$ 0	$ 0
Other liabilities principal repayment	$ 0	$ 0	$ 0
Fixed liabilities principal repayment	$ 0	$ 0	$ 0
Purchase other current assets	$ 0	$ 0	$ 0
Purchase fixed assets	$ 0	$ 0	$ 0
Dividends	$ 0	$ 0	$ 0
Subtotal cash spent	$1,576,436	$2,076,726	$2,359,715
Net cash flow	$ 490,250	$ 600,274	$ 692,285
Cash balance	$ 508,950	$1,109,224	$1,801,509

Projected Balance Sheet

Pro forma balance sheet	FY 2009	FY 2010	FY 2011
Assets			
Current assets			
Cash	$508,950	$ 1,109,224	$ 1,801,509
Stock	$138,336	$ 179,315	$ 204,606
Other current assets	$ 0	$ 0	$ 0
Total current assets	**$647,286**	**$1,288,538**	**$2,006,115**
Fixed assets			
Fixed assets	$ 0	$ 0	$ 0
Accumulated depreciation	$ 0	$ 0	$ 0
Total fixed assets	**$ 0**	**$ 0**	**$ 0**
Total assets	**$647,286**	**$1,288,538**	**$2,006,115**
Liabilities and capital			
Current liabilities			
Accounts payable	$ 23,620	$ 214,995	$ 243,414
Current borrowing	$ 25,000	$ 25,000	$ 25,000
Other current liabilities	$ 0	$ 0	$ 0
Subtotal current liabilities	$ 48,620	$ 239,995	$ 268,414
Fixed liabilities	$ 0	$ 0	$ 0
Total liabilities	**$ 48,620**	**$ 239,995**	**$ 268,414**
Paid-in capital	$ 50,000	$ 50,000	$ 50,000
Retained earnings	$ 51,300	$ 394,471	$ 998,543
Earnings	$445,771	$ 604,072	$ 689,157
Total capital	**$444,471**	**$1,048,543**	**$1,737,700**
Total liabilities and capital	**$493,092**	**$1,288,538**	**$2,006,115**
Net worth	$598,665	$ 1,048,543	$ 1,737,700

Business Ratios

Ratio analysis	FY 2009	FY 2010	FY 2011	Industry profile
Sales growth	0.00%	29.53%	14.01%	5.46%
Percent of total assets				
Other current assets	0.00%	0.00%	0.00%	59.37%
Total current assets	100.00%	100.00%	100.00%	81.29%
Fixed assets	0.00%	0.00%	0.00%	18.71%
Total assets	100.00%	100.00%	100.00%	100.00%
Current liabilities	7.51%	18.63%	13.38%	35.74%
Fixed liabilities	0.00%	0.00%	0.00%	11.32%
Total liabilities	7.51%	18.63%	13.38%	47.06%
Net worth	92.49%	81.37%	86.62%	52.94%
Percent of sales				
Sales	100.00%	100.00%	100.00%	100.00%
Gross margin	43.43%	43.39%	43.34%	100.00%
Selling, general & administrative expenses	21.86%	20.82%	20.76%	78.24%
Advertising expenses	0.00%	0.00%	0.00%	0.79%
Profit before interest and taxes	30.93%	32.33%	32.34%	2.95%
Main ratios				
Current	13.31	5.37	7.47	1.55
Quick	10.47	4.62	6.71	1.16
Total debt to total assets	7.51%	18.63%	13.38%	57.56%
Pre-tax return on net worth	106.37%	82.30%	56.66%	6.34%
Pre-tax return on assets	98.38%	66.97%	49.08%	14.93%
Additional ratios				
Net profit margin	21.57%	22.57%	22.58%	n.a.
Return on equity	74.46%	57.61%	39.66%	n.a.
Activity ratios				
Accounts payable turnover	69.99	9.30	9.30	n.a.
Total asset turnover	3.19	2.08	1.52	n.a.
Debt ratios				
Debt to net worth	0.08	0.23	0.15	n.a.
Current liab. to liab.	1.00	1.00	1.00	n.a.
Liquidity ratios				
Net working capital	$598,665	$1,048,543	$1,737,700	n.a.
Interest coverage	255.73	346.18	394.80	n.a.
Additional ratios				
Assets to sales	0.31	0.48	0.66	n.a.
Current debt/total assets	8%	19%	13%	n.a.
Acid test	10.47	4.62	6.71	n.a.
Sales/net worth	3.45	2.55	1.76	n.a.
Dividend payout	0.00	0.00	0.00	n.a.

Art Easel Manufacturer

Art Easels and Supplies, Inc.

421 Ferne St.
Traverse City, Michigan 49684

Gerald Rekve

Art Easels and Supplies, Inc. is a company that will produce and sell art easels. The owner is a woman with an lifelong love for wood products and their production.

EXECUTIVE SUMMARY

Art Easels and Supplies, Inc. is a start–up company that will produce artist easels and other related items. Art Easels and Supplies, Inc. will be owned 100 percent by Sharon Armitage.

Sharon Armitage will invest $240,000 into the business and will secure a loan of $270,000 to start the business. The growth of this market segment has grown by 14 percent year after year from 2001–2007. With the trend reversing from offshore manufacturing to USA–based manufacturing of wood products, we feel we are well–positioned to take advantage of this market shift.

The artist easel business is a growing business. With the aging boomer population retiring, our products are well designed to target this market. Our market research has discovered people in the USA are wanting to support USA–based manufacturing companies. These same people have said they know the cost of the product may be 4–12 percent more in cost; however, they are more than happy to buy these products.

With the downturn in the housing market, we are very confident that we will be able to secure very competitive prices on wood products. Also, the downturn in the employment situation should lead to more incentives to hire people from local and national governments; this will reduce our employee costs. These incentives offered by governments will most likely be tax reductions, actual per–hour shared wage payments.

Highlights

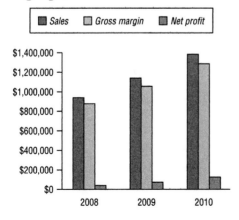

BUSINESS OVERVIEW

Art Easels and Supplies, Inc. will be owned by Sharon Armitage. Sharon was a lawyer working for a local company. She has a long love for wood products and how they are made. When Sharon was laid off by the company she was working for, she decided to manufacture items instead of working in the legal field.

Objectives

We will put together a strong business that will focus on manufacturing artist easels. Our main objective is to produce quality products that will sell themselves.

Mission

Our mission is to provide our market with the best products, at prices that are comparable to the market products being sold today. While there are many competitors, we feel with the internet we will be able to sell to a larger market through mail order.

Keys to Success

- Manufacture products that the market will buy

- Build using the best in quality

- Find a good supply of wood at reasonable prices

- Hire staff that can be easily trained to build easels

- Find a building that will be the startup place we work from

- Design a great website that will be easy to use and navigate

FINANCIAL ANALYSIS

Company Ownership

Art Easels and Supplies, Inc. will be owned 100 percent by Sharon Armitage. She will be targeting to secure $270,000 from investors and banks in addition to her investment of $240,000.

Start–up Summary

Art Easels and Supplies, Inc. start–up money will be financed by lenders and investors. The total cash required will be $510,000. This will get the company to the position of producing products. Then, once

Start-up requirements	
Start-up expenses	
Legal	$ 3,000
Stationery etc.	$ 1,000
Insurance	$ 1,000
Rent	$ 5,000
Office equipment	$ 5,000
Manifacturing equipment	$ 75,000
Shipping equipment	$ 20,000
Vehicals	$ 20,000
Production supplies	$ 50,000
Staffing payroll	$ 30,000
Management Payroll	$ 25,000
Shipping costs	$ 2,000
Total start-up expenses	**$237,000**
Start-up assets	
Cash required	$250,000
Start-up stock	$ 20,000
Other current assets	$ 0
Fixed assets	$ 0
Total assets	**$270,000**
Total requirements	**$507,000**

the products are in the warehouse, we will have the website up and running. While we will focus on selling our products over the internet, we will also sell to third party retailers.

Start-up

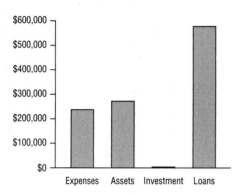

Start-up funding

Start-up expenses to fund	$237,000
Start-up assets to fund	$270,000
Total funding required	**$507,000**
Assets	
Non-cash assets from start-up	$ 20,000
Cash requirements from start-up	$250,000
Additional cash raised	$ 63,000
Cash balance on starting date	$313,000
Total assets	**$333,000**
Liabilities and capital	
Liabilities	
Current borrowing	$400,000
Fixed liabilities	$150,000
Accounts payable (outstanding bills)	$ 20,000
Other current liabilities	$ 0
Total liabilities	**$570,000**
Capital	
Planned investment	
Owner	$ 0
Investor	$ 0
Additional investment requirement	$ 0
Total planned investment	**$ 0**
Loss at start-up (start-up expenses)	$237,000
Total capital	**$237,000**
Total capital and liabilities	**$333,000**
Total funding	**$570,000**

Break-even Analysis

Break-even analysis

Monthly units break-even	634
Monthly revenue break-even	$ 66,982
Assumptions:	
Average per-unit revenue	$ 105.59
Average per-unit variable cost	$ 7.39
Estimated monthly fixed cost	$62,293.25

Projected Profit and Loss

Pro forma profit and loss	2008	2009	2010
Sales	$927,0933	$1,120,000	$1,358,100
Direct costs of goods	$ 64,897	$ 78,400	$ 95,067
Other costs of goods	$ 0	$ 0	$ 0
Cost of goods sold	$ 64,897	$ 78,400	$ 95,067
Gross margin	$ 862,196	$1,041,600	$1,263,033
Gross margin %	93.00%	93.00%	93.00%
Expenses			
Payroll	$ 185,100	$ 197,000	$ 216,000
Marketing/promotion	$ 42,936	$ 55,000	$ 65,000
Depreciation	$ 15,732	$ 20,000	$ 24,000
Building rent	$ 15,732	$ 16,000	$ 18,000
Utilities	$ 8,442	$ 9,000	$ 10,000
Insurance	$ 6,816	$ 7,500	$ 8,500
Management payroll	$ 12,957	$ 13,790	$ 15,120
Production materials	$ 20,736	$ 18,000	$ 20,000
Office supplies	$ 5,472	$ 6,000	$ 7,000
Auto	$ 8,976	$ 9,000	$ 10,000
Manufacturing equipment maintenance	$ 15,084	$ 18,000	$ 20,000
Staff payroll	$ 409,536	$ 500,000	$ 600,000
Total operating expenses	**$ 747,519**	**$ 869,290**	**$1,013,620**
Profit before interest and taxes	$ 114,677	$ 172,310	$ 249,413
Interest expense	$ 59,056	$ 69,612	$ 80,662
Taxes incurred	$ 16,686	$ 30,810	$ 50,625
Net profit	$ 38,935	$ 71,889	$ 118,126
Net profit/sales	4.20%	6.42%	8.70%

Projected Cash Flow

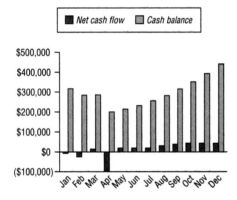

Pro forma cash flow	2008	2009	2010
Cash received			
Cash from operations			
Cash sales	$231,773	$ 280,000	$ 339,525
Cash from receivables	$541,029	$ 807,896	$ 978,949
Subtotal cash from operations	$772,802	$1,087,896	$1,318,474
Additional cash received			
GST/HST received (output tax)	$ 0	$ 0	$ 0
GST/HST repayments	$ 0	$ 0	$ 0
New current borrowing	$106,622	$ 120,000	$ 130,000
New other liabilities (interest-free)	$ 0	$ 0	$ 0
New fixed liabilities	$ 0	$ 0	$ 0
Sales of other current assets	$ 0	$ 0	$ 0
Sales of fixed assets	$ 0	$ 0	$ 0
New investment received	$120,000	$ 140,000	$ 140,000
Subtotal cash received	$999,424	$1,347,896	$1,588,474
Expenditures			
Expenditures from operations			
Cash spending	$185,100	$ 197,000	$ 216,000
Bill payments	$683,702	$ 842,120	$1,002,983
Subtotal spent on operations	$868,802	$1,039,120	$1,218,983
Additional cash spent			
GST/HST paid out (input tax)	$ 0	$ 0	$ 0
GST/HST payments	$ 0	$ 0	$ 0
Principal repayment of current borrowing	$ 13,506	$ 14,000	$ 15,000
Other liabilities principal repayment	$ 0	$ 0	$ 0
Fixed liabilities principal repayment	$ 0	$ 0	$ 0
Purchase other current assets	$ 0	$ 0	$ 0
Purchase fixed assets	$ 0	$ 0	$ 0
Dividends	$ 0	$ 0	$ 0
Subtotal cash spent	$882,308	$1,053,120	$1,233,983
Net cash flow	$117,117	$ 294,775	$ 354,491
Cash balance	$430,117	$ 724,892	$1,079,383

Projected Balance Sheet

Pro forma balance sheet	2008	2009	2010
Assets			
Current assets			
Cash	$ 430,117	$724,892	$ 1,079,383
Accounts receivable	$ 154,291	$186,395	$ 226,020
Stock	$ 55,103	$ 76,703	$ 93,010
Other current assets	$ 0	$ 0	$ 0
Total current assets	**$639,511**	**$987,991**	**$1,398,413**
Fixed assets			
Fixed assets	$ 0	$ 0	$ 0
Accumulated depreciation	$ 15,732	$ 35,732	$ 59,732
Total fixed assets	**$ 15,732**	**$ 35,732**	**$ 59,732**
Total assets	**$ 623,779**	**$952,259**	**$1,338,681**
Liabilities and capital			
Current liabilities			
Accounts payable	$ 58,728	$ 69,319	$ 82,616
Current borrowing	$493,116	$599,116	$ 714,116
Other current liabilities	$ 0	$ 0	$ 0
Subtotal current liabilities	$551,844	$668,435	$ 796,732
Fixed liabilities	$150,000	$150,000	$ 150,000
Total liabilities	$701,844	$818,435	$ 946,732
Paid-in capital	$120,000	$260,000	$ 400,000
Retained earnings	$237,000	$198,065	$ 126,176
Earnings	$ 38,935	$ 71,889	$ 118,126
Total capital	**$ 78,065**	**$133,824**	**$ 391,950**
Total liabilities and capital	**$623,779**	**$952,259**	**$1,338,681**
Net worth	**$ 78,065**	**$133,824**	**$ 391,950**

PRODUCTS

Art Easels and Supplies, Inc. will manufacture a variety of products, using a variety of woods.

Oil & Acrylic Artists Easels

Watercolor Artists Easels

Table Top Easels

Deluxe Easels

Academy Art Easels

Tote Easels

Artists Taborets

2–in–1 Easels

Studio Furniture

Smart Easels

Pro Easels

French Easels

Painter Easels

Clinton Artists's Easels

Clinton Watercolor Easels

French Easels

Art Easels and Accessories

Dean Martin Easels

Mills Steel Easels

California Easels

Eileen's Watercolor Stations

Steel Art Easels

Standard Easels

Mars Desk Easels

Watercolor Easels

Danter Easels

Turntable Easels

Windsor Easels

MARKET ANALYSIS

Art Easels and Supplies, Inc.'s target market segmentation strategy will be to get our production facility up and running. When this is done, we will have gotten our website up and running. We will send samples of our products to various wholesalers and also attend trade shows to target retailers. With all these various strategies in place, it will allow us to build our business in three key market segments—Mail Order, Wholesale, and Retail Clients.

Mail Order from our Website: We will have a website built with a state–of–the–art shopping cart. This will allow buyers to purchase via the website using a credit card, checking account, or money order. The website will be very functional. The buyer just has to click on the *Purchase Now* icon and the item will be placed in the shopping cart of the buyer. When the buyer has finished shopping, they simply have to check out and verify their purchase. There will be at least four system checks to confirm that the buyer wants to purchase these products. This will also be a check system for the buyer to confirm what they are buying. Having these check systems in place will protect both us and the buyer from any unwanted charge backs. We will also place ads in national newspapers and magazines, directing potential buyers to go to our website or call our toll free hotline to purchase our products.

Wholesale Commercial: We will sell our products to larger wholesalers who resell to large department stores. We realize the margins will be smaller; however this will get our products to the end–users hands and allow us to increase our market share. The shipments and orders to these clients will be large. We also realize that this will eat into our cash flow as we build these orders and have to wait up to sixty days to get paid.

Retail Clients: We will sell directly to art supply stores across the country. This will insure our products get into the hands of artists. The benefit will be the large market we will be going into. We know that we will be getting less profit on these orders, but in the end, this will result in larger dollar orders.

Market analysis	Growth	2008	2009	2010	2011	2012	CAGR
Potential customers							
Mail order—off website & other	35%	1,000	1,350	1,823	2,461	3,322	35.01%
Wholesale—commercial sales	25%	25	31	39	49	61	24.98%
Retail clients sales (# of retailers)	40%	5,000	7,000	9,800	13,720	19,208	40.00%
Other	0%	0	0	0	0	0	0.00%
Total	**39.15%**	**6,025**	**8,381**	**11,662**	**16,230**	**22,591**	**39.15%**

Market Analysis

OPERATIONS

Our manufacturing process will be such that the ramp–up to full product can be one of a staged production. The products we produce do not require specialized equipment. We will be able to start our business from buying all of our equipment from a local home supply company. As we roll ahead, we can add equipment in stages as sales volumes increase. In the future, we will buy necessary equipment from a company that sells production line products; this will allow us to reduce the downtime due to breakdowns, etc.

Competition

Competitive Advantages

> We will offer just–in–time delivery
>
> We will manufacture in the USA; therefore offering all our customers homemade products
>
> We will hire USA–based people, therefore be a client–based friendly buyer program
>
> Our suppliers will be USA–based, therefore allowing us to give back to the USA. This will also attract customers that know when they buy our products they are employing USA–based people

MARKETING & SALES

Growth Strategy

For the company to compete in the market, we need to build quality products. The main focus for us will be to use streamlined technologies to manufacture the easels.

In the mail order market segment, we will promote the products by advertising in newspapers, magazines, and on the company website. The website will be designed to draw traffic by means of keyword searches. Another draw for the website will be to have industry key links agreements with other like business groups. An example of this would be an artist group association website. We will also use the variety of classified websites which allow free ad posting. This will allow us to get exposure without incurring the advertising cost.

In the wholesale industry, our focus is to sell our products to wholesalers with just–in–time delivery. We will also provide a drop shipments backroom order service for our wholesalers. Specifically, when a retailer orders twenty easels from the wholesaler, an order will electronically be sent to us for the order. We will then package the order using the wholesaler's shipping labels and box markings, and then ship the order to the retailer. When the retailer gets the order, they will know the order was shipped from us. This saves the wholesalers money for shipping, allows them to be more effective, and allows them to make more money on the order.

The retail clients's sales strategy will be focused on the mom and pop stores, which include craft stores, hobby stores, artist shops, galleries, and so on. We will find these clients by attending trade shows, and by the advertising we do in trade magazines.

Sales Forecast

Art Easels and Supplies, Inc.'s 2009 sales strategy will be to sell $724,114 worth of products. Then for 2010 and 2011 the sales levels will be $875,000 and $1,061,300, respectively.

We have only projected very conservative increases. The great down turn in October 2008 was the reason for our low numbers. Based on all we know about the USA economic recession, the recovery will not take real effect till 2011. By this point we will have had the opportunity to get all the bugs out of the systems.

Sales forecast	2008	2009	2010
Unit sales			
Artist easels	6,042	7,000	8,090
Furniture for studios	2,738	3,500	4,500
Total unit sales	**8,780**	**10,500**	**12,590**
Unit prices			
Artist easels	$ 90.00	$ 90.00	$ 90.00
Furniture for studios	$ 140.00	$ 140.00	$ 140.00
Sales			
Artist easels	$543,809	$ 630,000	$ 728,100
Furniture for studios	$383,284	$ 490,000	$ 630,000
Total sales	**$927,093**	**$1,120,000**	**$1,358,100**
Direct unit costs			
Artist easels	$ 6.30	$ 6.30	$ 6.30
Furniture for studios	$ 9.80	$ 9.80	$ 9.80
Direct cost of sales			
Artist easels	$ 38,067	$ 44,100	$ 50,967
Furniture for studios	$ 26,830	$ 34,300	$ 44,100
Subtotal direct cost of sales	$ 64,897	$ 78,400	$ 95,067

Sales by Month

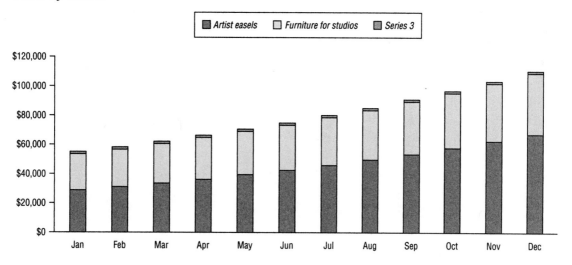

Sales by Year

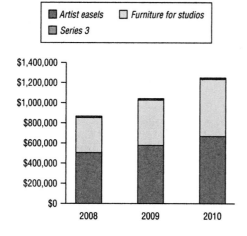

MANAGEMENT SUMMARY

The owner of the company will be Sharon Armitage who will own 100 percent of the company. Sharon's background is in furniture manufacturing. She will hire other managers, such as:

Production Manager

Shipping Manager

Accountant

HR Manager

Sales & Marketing Manager

Personnel Plan

Personnel plan	2008	2009	2010
Owner	$ 41,088	$ 44,000	$ 47,000
Production manager	$ 32,544	$ 34,000	$ 36,000
HR manager	$ 23,406	$ 25,000	$ 27,000
Accountant	$ 33,984	$ 35,000	$ 37,000
Sales & marketing manager	$ 32,256	$ 35,000	$ 40,000
Shipping manager	$ 21,822	$ 24,000	$ 29,000
Total people	**21**	**25**	**30**
Total payroll	**$185,100**	**$197,000**	**$216,000**

Bicycle Shop

Wheelies

1245 Main St.
De Pere, Wisconsin 54115

Gerald Rekve

The main objectives of Wheelies are to provide our customers with the best products and services that will ensure all our clients a long and happy motorcycling experience.

EXECUTIVE SUMMARY

Wheelies was formed in 2008 by Thomas Ritche. After spending over 20 years working for a motorcycle shop, Thomas was offered a franchise for a new line of super bikes. The new franchise was located just on the outside perimeter where Thomas was working and the shop owner that Thomas worked for did not want to invest in another shop in this market. Knowing that this second market would have little impact on the shop owner's sales, the shop owner offered the opportunity to Thomas. The shop owner even offered financial assistance to Thomas to open this shop.

Thomas opened the new super bike sales franchise in De Pere, Wisconsin. The population of De Pere is just below 20,000; however, there is a trading area within 100 miles of over 1,000,000 people. The company will be set up a LLB allowing for protection for Thomas Ritche if there are any legal issues related to the products being sold.

FINANCIAL SUMMARY

The start up funding of Wheelies will be as follows: Thomas will invest $200,000 and in exchange for 20 percent share in the company, Thomas's former boss will invest $30,000. Additional financing will come from the manufacturer, the bank in De Pere, the state government, and the federal government.

Our profit and loss summary for Wheelies is as follows:

- 2010 Net profit is $502,895 on sales of $2,507,070
- 2011 Net profit is $412,685 on sales of $3,160,000
- 2012 Net profit is $492,688 on sales of $3,770,000

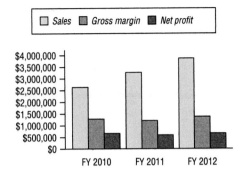

Here is a breakdown of the financing:

- The Manufacturer will carry $500,000 worth of inventory for 180 days interest–free. After that, any inventory left over from the original opening day will incur a 1 percent carrying charge. Then any reorders or new inventory purchased will be carried free for 90 days, after which a 1 percent carrying charge will be added.

- The Bank will offer an operating line of credit of $250,000 at 3 percent charged for the portion used. This means the interest charge will only apply to the amount of money drawn on.

- The city of De Pere, as part of their new business opening incentive, will offer a two year tax holiday, then after that will charge the going rate for business taxes.

- The state government, as part of their job creation program, will pay new businesses a $2.00 per hour hiring incentive for the first 6 months. This means for every new employee hired, $2.00 per hour of their salary will be paid to the employer as an incentive.

- The federal government will pay the employer a $5,000 tax credit per new employee in job training.

Company Ownership

Wheelies will be owned 80 percent by Thomas Ritche and 20 percent by his former boss. This will only last for 5 years when the final repayment will be made by Thomas's former boss.

Start–up Summary

Wheelies's start–up requirements are $787,500; however the manufacturer is going to carry $475,000 worth of inventory for free for 6 months. This means Thomas Ritche will only need to secure $287,500 in funding to start the business. Thomas and his partner will invest $120,000. This means that $147,500 will be funded by bank loans and lines of credit from either banks or vendors that Wheelies will be buying the products from.

Start-up requirements

Start-up expenses

Leasehold improvements	$ 30,000
Fixtures—store	$ 20,000
Insurance	$ 1,000
Rent	$ 4,000
Office equipment	$ 5,000
Grand opening advertising	$ 10,000
Staff	$ 15,000
Legal	$ 2,500
Inventory other than bikes	$ 75,000
Shipping	$ 10,000
Total start-up expenses	**$172,500**

Start-up assets

Cash required	$120,000
Start-up stock	$475,000
Other current assets	$ 0
Fixed assets	$ 20,000
Total assets	**$615,000**
Total requirements	**$787,500**

Start-up funding

Start-up expenses to fund	$172,500
Start-up assets to fund	$615,000
Total funding required	$787,500

Assets

Non-cash assets from start-up	$495,000
Cash requirements from start-up	$120,000
Additional cash raised	$182,500
Cash balance on starting date	$302,500
Total assets	**$797,500**

Liabilities and capital

Liabilities

Current borrowing	$400,000
Fixed liabilities	$ 0
Accounts payable (outstanding bills)	$ 20,000
Other current liabilities	$ 0
Total liabilities	**$420,000**

Capital

Planned investment

Owner	$250,000
Investor # 1	$150,000
Investor # 2	$150,000
Total planned investment	**$550,000**
Loss at start-up (start-up expenses)	$172,500
Total capital	**$377,500**
Total capital and liabilities	**$797,500**
Total funding	**$970,000**

OBJECTIVES

The main objectives of Wheelies are to provide our customers with the best products and services that will ensure all our clients a long and happy motorcycling experience. Having said this, we will work closely with all the stake holders in order to ensure we provide our customers with a safe and enjoyable time spent on our super bikes.

Mission

Similar to our objectives, Wheelies's mission is to provide our customers with the best in service, parts, and motorcycles. We will offer riding training so our customers will be safe on their super bikes.

We want to make sure 100 percent of our customers are never seriously injured in a car accident, while at the same time being able to win our share of the super bike sales in our region.

Keys to Success

1. We meet our monthly sales targets.

2. Our products meet our customers expectations.

3. We will be able to hire the best mechanics.

4. Our staff in the sales, parts counter and safety bike training is of high caliber resulting in happy customers.

PRODUCTS

Wheelies will sell a variety of products related to the motorcycling industry. Because the product line is going to be restricted to the Super Bike type of products, this means we will not be selling dirt bikes or touring bikes commonly found in other motorcycle shops.

Here is a breakdown of the products we sell:

- Super Bikes, all sizes of engine type

- Custom Super Bikes built by local and regional custom bike builders

- Helmets, both standard and custom types

- Custom paint jobs for bikes in our in–house paint shop

- Custom modifications to bikes by our trained tech staff

- Other parts to support the bikes from our parts department

- Clothing, including: jackets, pants, and shirts

- Misc. decals, cups, hats, etc. from our promotional imprinted products

- Courses in safety riding, stunt driving, etc.

- Autobody shop department. We will repair damaged bikes. This sports has lots of bike accidents.

- Finally, we will sell touring packages for our clients and others to take trips together. We handle complete bookings of hotels, etc.

MARKET ANALYSIS

Market Segmentation

Wheelies market segmentation is two distinct areas:

- Sale of motorcycles and the related products like clothing, helmets and other directly related items

- Non product–related sales, like motorcycle safety training and special holiday touring trips around the USA.

Market analysis	Growth	2009	2010	2011	2012	2013	CAGR
Potential customers							
Super Bike sales and related	5%	100,000	105,000	110,250	115,763	121,551	5.00%
Training & touring	5%	20,000	21,000	22,050	23,153	24,311	5.00%
Total	**5.00%**	**120,000**	**126,000**	**132,300**	**138,916**	**145,862**	**5.00%**

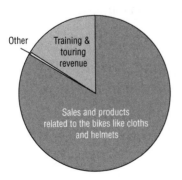

Target Market Segment Strategy

The product lines that we will be selling are not new to the industry. They are, however, a new concept in bike riding. In the past motorcycle riders were choosing either touring bikes or dirt bikes. The new Super Bike is just what it says it is, a bike that is fashioned around a jet on wheels.

There are riding contests for these bikes, i.e. trick riding, stunt riding and so on. The customers for these bikes consume everything about these bikes.

For example, a Super Bike sells for about $15,000. Along with this, the customer will buy about $1,200 worth of protective clothing. Then will most likely enroll in a safety riding training course with us. The cost of the training course is $495 with updates every 3 months that sell for $95.

Then there is the touring program, where Super Bike customers can travel around USA and enter riding shows and riding contests. This touring program sells for on average $39 for entry. The $39 is payable to our bike stores and we pass on $12 to the show organizer and keep the rest.

Competition

Our competitive edge will be the fact that we will sell all the products in line with Super Bikes as well as both stunt training and safety training. This is a huge advantage over most of our competitors because they do not offer this to their customers. The fact that we are offering training to our customers keeps our customers coming back. Also they see all the products we sell related to the Super Bike business.

Having said this, it seems most businesses offer these products/services as a normal part of business. However, our business is the Super Bike business which is totally different than most other businesses. Therefore, we create loyal customers and if you keep them happy they will spend every dollar possible with us.

MARKETING & SALES

Advertising

We will use the following medium to sell and promote our products and services:

- Newspapers
- Yellow Pages
- Radio
- Internet
- YouTube

Our products will be promoted with a non–traditional form of advertising; we will use the stunting events as a way to promote our bikes to our clients. These stunting events will be offered by trained professionals to events that are promoted by a variety of end users, like fairs, trade associations, retail associations, and so on. We then will video tape these events and post them on YouTube.

Sales

Wheelies's sales strategy will be to focus on the customer's wants and needs in a non–traditional manner. Never before will motorcycle owners be targeted in the way our type of bikes will target our clients.

The growth of the super bike sales in the USA has grown by leaps and bounds. Our sales strategy is to be more than a traditional motorcycle shop. We will offer safety training, we will offer stunt riding training, and we offer touring packages where riders can travel to contests located across USA for stunt riding of Super Bikes.

We will open our store for seven days a week, allowing customers total access to our parts as well service departments. All our products that can be found in the USA will be sold in our shop.

Our sales forecast is based on market averages for the cities our size, factoring in the number of competitors and the type of bikes we are selling.

Monthly Sales

Monthly sales forecast	GST/HST rate	Mar	Apr	May	Jun	Jul	Aug
Sales							
Motorcycles	7.00%	$ 42,840	$ 50,032	$123,240	$268,440	$414,200	$297,600
Products related to bikes	7.00%	$ 12,704	$ 15,376	$ 20,368	$ 20,880	$ 28,048	$ 22,064
Touring packages		$ 3,257	$ 7,168	$ 12,480	$ 17,040	$ 29,008	$ 22,718
Training for safety & stunting	7.00%	$ 5,562	$ 5,562	$ 15,592	$ 33,144	$ 35,280	$ 33,840
Total sales		**$ 64,362**	**$ 78,138**	**$171,680**	**$339,504**	**$506,536**	**$376,222**
Direct cost of sales							
Motorcycles	7.00%	$100,000	$100,000	$100,000	$100,000	$100,000	$100,000
Products related to bikes	7.00%	$ 9,230	$ 9,230	$ 9,230	$ 9,230	$ 9,230	$ 9,230
Touring packages		$ 1,589	$ 1,589	$ 1,589	$ 1,589	$ 1,589	$ 1,589
Training for safety & stunting	7.00%	$ 856	$ 856	$ 856	$ 856	$ 856	$ 856
Subtotal direct cost of sales		$111,675	$111,675	$111,675	$111,675	$111,675	$111,675

		Sep	Oct	Nov	Dec	Jan	Feb
Sales							
Motorcycles	7.00%	$266,000	$114,880	$105,600	$225,280	$ 35,660	$ 21,910
Products related to bikes	7.00%	$ 20,128	$ 18,256	$ 6,714	$ 25,014	$ 2,208	$ 13,376
Touring packages		$ 13,456	$ 7,408	$ 1,872	$ 9,488	$ 2,068	$ 4,049
Training for safety & stunting	7.00%	$ 27,312	$ 14,948	$ 11,160	$ 10,000	$ 8,280	$ 5,562
Total sales		**$326,896**	**$155,492**	**$125,346**	**$269,782**	**$ 48,216**	**$ 44,896**
Direct cost of sales							
Motorcycles	7.00%	$100,000	$100,000	$100,000	$100,000	$100,000	$100,000
Products related to bikes	7.00%	$ 9,230	$ 9,230	$ 9,230	$ 9,230	$ 9,230	$ 9,230
Touring packages		$ 1,589	$ 1,589	$ 1,589	$ 1,589	$ 1,589	$ 1,589
Training for safety & stunting	7.00%	$ 856	$ 856	$ 856	$ 856	$ 856	$ 856
Subtotal direct cost of sales		$111,675	$111,675	$111,675	$111,675	$111,675	$111,675

Yearly Sales

Yearly sales forecast	FY 2010	FY 2011	FY 2012
Sales			
Motorcycles	$ 1,965,682	$ 2,500,000	$ 3,000,000
Products related to bikes	$ 205,136	$ 250,000	$ 320,000
Touring packages	$ 130,012	$ 150,000	$ 170,000
Training for safety & stunting	$ 206,241	$ 260,000	$ 280,000
Total sales	**$2,507,070**	**$3,160,000**	**$3,770,000**
Direct cost of sales			
Motorcycles	$ 1,200,000	$ 1,900,000	$ 2,300,000
Products related to bikes	$ 110,765	$ 125,000	$ 155,000
Touring packages	$ 19,063	$ 25,000	$ 30,000
Training for safety & stunting	$ 10,272	$ 15,000	$ 19,000
Subtotal direct cost of sales	$ 1,340,100	$ 2,065,000	$ 2,504,000

MANAGEMENT SUMMARY

Yearly Personnel Plan

Personnel plan	FY 2010	FY 2011	FY 2012
CEO	$ 62,285	$ 75,000	$ 85,000
Sales manager	$ 27,638	$ 30,000	$ 40,000
Service manager	$ 23,712	$ 25,000	$ 26,000
Parts manager	$ 19,546	$ 22,000	$ 24,000
Training & touring manager	$ 25,162	$ 26,000	$ 27,000
Sales & office staff	$ 27,206	$ 28,000	$ 28,000
Mechanics & parts staff	$ 69,864	$ 70,000	$ 80,000
Total people	**14**	**20**	**23**
Total payroll	**$255,413**	**$276,000**	**$310,000**

Monthly Personnel Plan

Personnel plan	Mar	Apr	May	Jun	Jul	Aug
CEO	$ 5,190	$ 5,190	$ 5,190	$ 5,190	$ 5,190	$ 5,190
Sales manager	$ 2,303	$ 2,303	$ 2,303	$ 2,303	$ 2,303	$ 2,303
Service manager	$ 1,976	$ 1,976	$ 1,976	$ 1,976	$ 1,976	$ 1,976
Parts manager	$ 1,629	$ 1,629	$ 1,629	$ 1,629	$ 1,629	$ 1,629
Training & touring manager	$ 2,097	$ 2,097	$ 2,097	$ 2,097	$ 2,097	$ 2,097
Sales & office staff	$ 2,267	$ 2,267	$ 2,267	$ 2,267	$ 2,267	$ 2,267
Mechanics & parts staff	$ 5,822	$ 5,822	$ 5,822	$ 5,822	$ 5,822	$ 5,822
Total people	**14**	**14**	**14**	**14**	**14**	**14**
Total payroll	**$21,284**	**$21,284**	**$21,284**	**$21,284**	**$21,284**	**$21,284**

	Sep	Oct	Nov	Dec	Jan	Feb
CEO	$ 5,190	$ 5,190	$ 5,190	$ 5,190	$ 5,190	$ 5,190
Sales manager	$ 2,303	$ 2,303	$ 2,303	$ 2,303	$ 2,303	$ 2,303
Service manager	$ 1,976	$ 1,976	$ 1,976	$ 1,976	$ 1,976	$ 1,976
Parts manager	$ 1,629	$ 1,629	$ 1,629	$ 1,629	$ 1,629	$ 1,629
Training & touring manager	$ 2,097	$ 2,097	$ 2,097	$ 2,097	$ 2,097	$ 2,097
Sales & office staff	$ 2,267	$ 2,267	$ 2,267	$ 2,267	$ 2,267	$ 2,267
Mechanics & parts staff	$ 5,822	$ 5,822	$ 5,822	$ 5,822	$ 5,822	$ 5,822
Total people	**14**	**14**	**14**	**14**	**14**	**14**
Total payroll	**$21,284**	**$21,284**	**$21,284**	**$21,284**	**$21,284**	**$21,284**

Comedy Club

The Comedy Corner

1414 Greeway Blvd.
East Lansing, Michigan 48823

Dan Izzo

Comedy Corner will provide the audience with a unique interactive comedy entertainment experience. Comedy Corner will feature improvised comedy competitions in a game show setting.

BUSINESS OVERVIEW

Comedy Corner is a new live entertainment venue opening on College Avenue in downtown East Lansing, Michigan. Improv is comedy created spontaneously and without a script. Improv is extremely interactive. The actors take the audience's suggestions, however mundane or innocent, and create funny, interesting and comic scenes.

Interactive and spontaneous entertainment is extremely appealing to our two primary markets: college students and entertainment seeking young adults. For evidence of this, one need only look to movies and television where the focus has shifted to two genres which are unscripted: reality shows, such as *Survivor* or *The Bachelor*, and on–the–spot sitcoms and movies, such as FOX's *Arrested Development*, HBO's *Curb your Enthusiasm*, and the films, *A Mighty Wind* and *Best in Show*.

Products
Comedy Corner will provide the audience with a unique interactive comedy entertainment experience. Comedy Corner will feature improvised comedy competitions in a game show setting. The shows will feature a high degree of audience interaction. Interaction generates not only entertainment, but also positive word of mouth, which is crucial to an entertainment enterprise. We have produced this show in Chicago to excellent sized audiences and rave reviews. New City, a Chicago based alternative weekly newspaper recommended the show as one of its "Top 5 Shows to See Now."

MARKET ANALYSIS

East Lansing is a unique location, given the substantial college population as well as its presence as part of the Greater Detroit Metropolitan Area. Enrollment at Michigan State University is 46,000. Our location in downtown East Lansing is close enough to campus to attract college students, and offers a convenient downtown location for the year–round residents of Lansing.

Market Segmentation
Comedy Corner will appeal to two major market segments. These segments have compatible tastes in entertainment such that Comedy Corner will be able to strongly appeal to both segments.

1. Entertainment–Seeking Young Adults. This market segment would include couples out on a date, a group of friends out for an evening, bachelor parties, etc. These people fall into the 21–44 year old age range, have a high disposable income and tend to spend a high percentage of this on entertainment.

2. College Students. College students fall into the 18–22 year old age range and similarly have a high degree of disposable income which is disproportionately spent on entertainment. While some students are below the legal drinking age, they still can be an active part of our audience base and prime candidates for our training program.

Target Market Segment Strategy

Comedy Corner will use a multi–pronged marketing strategy to capture our target market. We will utilize print and radio advertisement to capture the Entertainment–Seeking Young Adult market. These advertisements would be placed in outlets that specifically serve this market, such as entertainment oriented alternative newspapers. We will also place ads in smaller targeted publications, which will allow us to target specific segments of the Entertainment–Seeking Young Adult market (i.e., bachelor and bachelorette parties).

With regard to college students, the marketing will include advertisements in student publications, strategically placed posters, postcards, and directed mailings. The idea is to create a constant presence on campus and generate a buzz regarding Comedy Corner. Consistent–looking weekly ads will be placed in the college newspaper. Posters reinforcing the basic marketing message of Comedy Corner (e.g. "You Are The Show!" or "It's What You're Doing this Weekend") will be placed and maintained at strategic locations on campus (e.g., informational kiosks, coffee shops and other establishments frequented by students). Postcards, again with this consistent message, will be placed at similar locations on campus as well as being distributed in campus welcome kits and by hand to students at larger functions (football and basketball games, campus events, etc.). Directed mailings will be sent to fraternities, sororities and other campus social organizations offering Comedy Corner as a potential outing with a group discount. Theme nights, such as Greek Night, Senior Night, etc. will be organized to drive sales. We will not only target Michigan State University, but also surrounding colleges and universities.

Our radio campaign will utilize Lansing–based stations to maximize local impact and minimize costs. We will place strategically timed radio spots to coincide with theater events. We will also look to sponsor station promotions and events that target our target markets. Again, the radio advertisements would be used to drive traffic for specific events as well as to reinforce our basic marketing message of "It's What You're Doing this Weekend."

The overall marketing strategy will be a combination of long–term consistent advertising and short–term targeted advertising. Our long–term consistent message will be built on the "It's What You're Doing this Weekend" campaign. This advertising campaign will appeal directly to people seeking out entertainment options and offer Comedy Corner as the solution to their weekend entertainment needs. Short–term promotions will be centered on city–wide and campus–wide events to capture the attention of members of the target market that might not otherwise be exposed to the long–term campaign. A combination of long–term and short–term marketing campaigns will generate a sense of consistency through the long–term campaign, and a sense of vibrancy and activity through the short–term campaigns. Our overall marketing strategy will successfully capture enough of our target market to provide a revenue stream sufficient to cover operating expenses and generate profits.

MISSON

Comedy Corner, which will open in East Lansing, Michigan, will be a one–hundred–seat live theater venue which will provide the public with improvised comedy shows which are not only entertaining to the audience, but also performed with the highest degree of artistic proficiency.

Comedy Corner grew out of our desire to integrate and apply our artistic knowledge and talents as producers, directors and actors with our proven business talents. Comedy Corner will unify our proven business acumen with our artistic success and drive. Our goal is to operate a financially successful lounge/comedy theater which is well received critically and generates a loyal customer base.

OPERATIONS

Comedy Corner will be a privately held Michigan LLC. The LLC will consist of two members, Brett Shaw and Katy Miller. This form of ownership will provide maximum tax benefits for an entity of our size as well as providing protection against any direct liabilities incurred in conjunction with the operation of the business.

Management Summary

Comedy Corner will have a dedicated and strong management team. Brett Shaw, the majority partner, who will serve as Managing Director and Artistic Director, has been improvising for over ten years in Philadelphia. Brett has produced or directed over a dozen shows in Philadelphia, and has been an instructor in improvisation at a comedy club and a university. In addition, he ran a training center for improvisation for two years in Philadelphia. Brett is an attorney having successfully run his own residential real estate practice for the past seven years. Katy Miller, who will serve as Operations Manager, has a wide array of relevant experience necessary for the successful operation of Comedy Corner. Katy has been the box office manager for a comedy club, has helped in the construction and management of a theater in Indianapolis, has co-produced an improv festival, and has bartended both in Boston and Detroit.

Brett Shaw, who will act as Managing Director and Artistic Director, has been both a successful entrepreneur and an accomplished actor and director. As a lawyer, Brett has owned and operated a successful legal practice specializing in residential real estate since 1997. He received his B.A., cum laude, in Psychology from the University of Chicago in 1989 and his J.D., magna cum laude, from the University of Michigan in 1992. He was a senior member of the Law Journal, and had an article published in a law journal.

As an actor and director, Brett has taught improvisation. Brett was responsible for marketing the training center, scheduling instructors and classes, negotiating space for classes, and coordinating the registration of several hundred students. Brett also has directed several improvised features that were critically–acclaimed.

Katy Miller, who will serve as the Operations Manager, has over ten years of Management and Administrative experience, and a huge love for the creative arts. She is currently employed at a music company in Philadelphia. Her position as Administrative Coordinator in this fast–paced environment requires the marriage of good communication, technical and organizational skills. She has broad experience including bartending, catering, box office management, stand–up, improvisation, writing and directing.

Katy was born in Indianapolis and is a graduate of Butler College with a BA in English. During her time in Indianapolis, she was part of the stand–up community and box office manager at an improve theater for five years. She then moved back to Indianapolis and attended bartending school, earning a certificate in Bartending & Beverage Management. Upon graduation, she had a full understanding of bar tools and equipment, staffing, cost control and marketing. This enabled her to bartend in Boston for over a year and half.

In the past twelve years, Katy has consulted and been involved with various creative arts spaces in Indianapolis, Boston, and Michigan, all of which have added to her personal growth—creatively, administratively and technologically.

She has excellent communication skills and most recently co–produced for a comedy theatre in downtown Boston. She also aided in the construction and management of a small theatre in Grosse Pointe, Michigan.

Brett Shaw will serve as the Managing Director and Artistic Director of Comedy Corner. The Managing Director will be directly responsible for the financial aspects of the business, including: book keeping, marketing, setting sales goals, budgeting and long term planning. The Artistic Director will be directly responsible for the artistic aspects of the enterprise, including: casting, scheduling shows, content and production quality.

Katy Miller will be serving as the Operations Manager of Comedy Corner. The Operations Manager will be responsible for the day–to–day operations of the enterprise, including inventory management, hiring and supervising wait staff and other personnel, daily accounting and similar functions.

A minimal wait staff would be needed, insofar as alcohol will be sold more in the manner of a bar and less in the manner of a restaurant.

Personnel plan

FY 2005	
Brett Shaw	$15,000
Katy Miller	$15,000
Wait staff	$36,868
Performers	$15,600
Total payroll	**$82,468.00**

FINANCIAL ANALYSIS

Equipment investment and site modification costs will be the primary expenses incurred by Comedy Corner during its initial operational phase. Theatrical lighting and sound equipment will need to be purchased and professionally installed in the space. The space itself will need to be converted into a useable space for a theater. These costs would include material and labor costs for construction of the stage, the seating area and the lobby. Initial marketing costs will include allocations for radio and print ads as well as costs for informational postcards to be distributed via direct mail and strategic placement throughout the community.

Start up

Initial liquor inventory	$ 6,000
Ice machine	$ 2,000
Glassware	$ 2,000
Misc. bar equipment	$ 2,000
Cash register systems	$ 3,000
Color printer	$ 1,000
Electrician	$ 2,000
Lighting designer	$ 1,500
Television systems	$ 2,000
Sound system	$ 1,600
Light board	$ 1,000
Stage light fixtures	$ 2,000
Seating	$ 5,000
Dimmer packs	$ 2,000
Stage	$ 2,500
Outside signage	$ 6,000
Interior painting	$ 1,500
Exterior painting	$ 1,500
Promotional materials	$ 5,000
Advertising	$ 5,000
Security deposit	$ 10,400
Tax reserve	$ 5,000
Insurance reserve	$ 12,000
Operating reserve	$ 18,000
Total funds needed at start up	**$100,000.00**

Start–up Funding Requirements

The initial funding required by Comedy Corner will be equal to the start–up expenses and operating expenses that will be incurred during the first year of operations. This will require total funding of approximately $100,000. These funds will be provided as set forth in the table below.

Start up funding requirements

Brett Shaw	$ 50,000
Loan	$ 50,000
Total start up funding	**$100,000.00**

BUSINESS STRATEGY

Comedy Corner's main business and revenue source will be the production of live theater events. Significant additional revenue will come from alcohol sales to the audience. With a start–up expenditure of just under $50,000, Comedy Corner will generate over $200,000 in sales in year one, and over $300,000 in sales in year two. Profitability will be reached in year two.

Comedy Corner will feature improvised comedy competitions in a game show setting. These shows have actors competing against one another in a series of improv games (similar to the television show *Whose Line is it Anyway?*) in a context that is evocative of a traditional television game show (i.e. *Let's Make a Deal*). The audience will be central to the presentation. They will provide suggestions that the performers will use in the games and ultimately have the chance to win prizes themselves. We have produced this show in Boston to excellent sized audiences and rave reviews. A Boston–based alternative weekly newspaper recommended the show as one of its "Top 5 Shows to See Now."

Most unique for this type of performance, the shows will feature a high degree of audience interaction. At various points during the show, members of the audience will be brought on stage to interact with the game show host, and actually participate with the performers in some of the games. This will serve not only to entertain the audience, but also to turn the audience into advocates for the show.

The direct participation by audience members will give the audiences an easy hook for describing the show (i.e., "They brought this guy on stage during the show…") when they discuss it with their friends and acquaintances. Interaction generates not only entertainment, but also positive word of mouth. This interactive element will be featured prominently in our marketing campaigns. The central message of our marketing will be based upon the themes "You are the show!" and "It's What You're Doing This Weekend."

Ancillary Business Opportunities

While the main business of Comedy Corner will be producing shows in the theater, there are areas of natural growth and expansion for the company. The company will be looking to exploit these opportunities immediately.

Alternative Productions

In addition to the basic comedy game show product, Comedy Corner would be able to feature other theatrical and comedy products. Holiday–themed productions (such as a Christmas show) can be developed as a means of generating audiences and revenue on off–peak and off–night times. Comedy Corner would also be ideal for hosting stand–up comedy events. We have already received a commitment from a local stand–up comedian to host and book talent for a Stand–Up Comedy Open Mike Night every Sunday.

Educational Opportunities

The audience participation elements of the main product provided by Comedy Corner will instill in some patrons the desire to learn more about improvisational techniques and learn how to improvise. Classes in improvisation can be offered as a way of exploiting this captured market. Classes can be offered at any time and thus provide a way in which the facility can generate revenue during non–weekend and non–peak times.

Corporate Events

Additional revenue can be realized from applying the Comedy Corner product in a corporate setting. In addition to revenue to the company itself, these opportunities can help keep personnel costs low by creating additional revenue streams for the performers and staff of Comedy Corner. These corporate applications break down into two basic types.

Creativity Training

The techniques of improvisational theater are utilized by corporations in creativity training programs for their employees. We have experience in teaching these types of programs for corporations and non-profit organizations across the country.

Remote Performance

Corporations often bring in outside entertainment, either as an incentive or in conjunction with internal training programs. Again, we have experience in providing entertainment of this type at corporate functions.

COMPETITION

Comedy Corner will have two main competitors in the comedy entertainment market. We will also have several indirect competitors in the more general entertainment market.

FunnyLaughs, located at 192 Truse Rd. in Lansing, is our closest direct competitor. The FunnyLaughs features stand–up comedy performances on Thursday, Friday and Saturday. On Wednesday night, they have a hosted improv jam and open mike. FunnyLaughs's primary strength is its status as the first entrant in the market. It's been open since 1987 in the same location, with a management change in 2001. As a result they presumably have an advantage in terms of already having an audience base and a reputation in the market. The main weakness of the Comedy Corner would be its low profile location (it is located underneath a restaurant). This gives them low visibility and curb–appeal. It also limits their ability to capture any walk–by or drive–by audience. If you don't know it's there, it can be difficult to find.

Second City Detroit is an offshoot of the main Second City production company located in Chicago. Second City Detroit puts on sketch comedy shows Wednesdays through Sundays. Second City Detroit also offers classes in improvisation and does corporate training. Their strengths include name recognition as well an extensive marketing budget. Their main weakness is their location. Their theater is currently in the process of relocating from downtown Detroit to Novi, which is a more suburban and family oriented location than East Lansing. They also have a nominal focus on improvisation, rather than putting improvisation forward as their primary product.

Comedy Corner will be competing in the broader entertainment market, which would include movies, restaurants, bars and other forms of evening entertainment.

Competition Analysis

Comedy Corner will be able to effectively compete in the East Lansing entertainment market. With respect to both direct competitors, our primary advantage will be a focus on improvised comedy, rather than stand–up or sketch comedy. Our shows will feature a degree of audience participation far in excess of those offered by our direct competitors. Without drastically altering their business models, our direct competitors will not be able to provide the same product we provide. Stand–up and sketch comedy do not offer much, if any, audience participation. Improvisation, particularly as we do it, has a high degree of audience participation. This focus will help to distinguish Comedy Corner from its competition and establish us as a unique entertainment option. With regard to the FunnyLaughs, our venue will be much more high profile and aggressively marketed. Our above ground location will allow for a much more impressive street presence, and our marketing will be targeted in a way which will truly appeal to our core market. With regard to Second City Detroit, Comedy Corner will offer a more intimate and accessible experience. The fact that Second City Detroit already offers improv classes will actually help us. First, we will be an alternative class program for those people who have completed the Second City program and want to continue their studies. Second, we can feed off of the market for improvised comedy which Second City has started to develop. With regard to our indirect competitors, we will be more of a complementary offering to their services rather than a replacement for it. We can be something that someone does in addition to going to a bar or restaurant, not merely a substitution for the same. Similarly, with regard to other forms of entertainment (movies, music clubs, etc.), Comedy Corner will offer a live and highly interactive experience, rather than the prefabricated, passive experience typical at an entertainment event.

MARKETING & SALES

Important Assumptions

1. Audience revenues and performance costs are based on five full–price shows and three half–price shows per week with a ticket price of $10.00 and $5.00, respectively.

2. Revenues on alcohol sales are based on 3 drinks for a bar patron, and 2.5 drinks for theater patrons, at an average drink price of $3.50.

3. Non–alcohol concession cost will be 14 percent of non–alcohol sales.

4. Alcohol cost will be 20% of alcohol sales.

Sales Projections

The following table sets forth the sales projections for Comedy Corner.

Sales Forecast	FY 2005	FY 2006	FY 2007
Ticket sales	$ 93,700.00	$141,300.00	$149,600.00
Alcohol sales	$121,517.50	$174,037.50	$183,820.00
Class income	$ 13,500.00	$ 23,700.00	$ 27,000.00
Total gross sales	**$229,831.50**	**$340,687.50**	**$362,164.00**
Alcohol costs	$ 24,303.50	$ 34,807.50	$ 36,764.00
Subtotal direct cost of sales	$ 24,303.50	$ 34,807.50	$ 36,764.00
Gross profit	$205,528.00	$305,880.00	$325,400.00

Projected Profit and Loss

Pro forma profit and loss	FY 2005	FY 2006	FY 2007
Ticket sales	$ 93,700.00	$141,300.00	$149,600.00
Alcohol sales	$121,517.50	$174,037.50	$183,820.00
Miscellaneous concessions	$ 1,114.00	$ 1,650.00	$ 1,744.00
Class income	$ 13,500.00	$ 23,700.00	$ 27,000.00
Total gross sales	**$229,831.50**	**$340,687.50**	**$362,164.00**
Alcohol costs	$ 24,303.50	$ 34,807.50	$ 36,764.00
Miscellaneous concession cost	$ 154.72	$ 229.17	$ 242.22
Subtotal direct cost of sales	$ 24,458.22	$ 35,036.67	$ 37,006.22
Gross profit	$205,373.28	$305,650.83	$325,157.78
Expenses			
Payroll	$ 82,468.00	$112,468.00	$112,468.00
Marketing	$ 6,000.00	$ 6,000.00	$ 6,000.00
Rent	$ 52,000.00	$ 64,272.00	$ 66,200.16
Utilities	$ 12,000.00	$ 12,000.00	$ 12,000.00
Management fee	$ 19,200.00	$ 19,200.00	$ 19,200.00
Ongoing maintenance	$ 3,000.00	$ 3,000.00	$ 3,000.00
Waste management	$ 6,000.00	$ 6,000.00	$ 6,000.00
Insurance	$ 12,000.00	$ 12,000.00	$ 12,000.00
Payroll taxes	$ 12,370.20	$ 12,370.20	$ 12,370.20
Real estate taxes	$ 5,000.00	$ 5,000.00	$ 5,000.00
Debt service	$ 15,000.00	$ 15,000.00	$ 15,000.00
Total expenses	**$225,038.20**	**$267,310.20**	**$269,238.36**
Net profit	**($ 19,664.92)**	**$ 38,340.63**	**$ 55,919.42**

DVD Kiosk Rental Business

RENT DVDS NOW

100 Soundview Lane
Seattle, Washington 98101

Laura Becker

RENT DVDS NOW (www.rentdvdsnow.com) is a independent DVD kiosk rental business. The kiosk will contain movies and/or video games with kiosks strategically located in high traffic locations such as supermarkets, convenience stores and apartment buildings.

EXECUTIVE SUMMARY

This is a business opportunity to become an independent–owner of a DVD Kiosk Rental Business/ Franchise for movies and/or games.

There are currently several players in the industry who provide kiosks to corporate entities directly such as supermarket chains, convenience stores, apartment complexes and college campuses. These corporate distributors work with very high traffic locations (usually a minimum of 15,000 customers per week).

There is another distributor, DVDNow Kiosks which sells kiosks directly to independent operators/ entrepeneurs. The business opportunity is to run your own DVD rental kiosk in select locations. It is a fairly simple business to set up. The most important component is selecting a high traffic, return customer location; purchasing the kiosk; setting up Internet access and credit card processing capability; and reaching a deal with the location owner. Then the operator needs to have an agreement to obtain all movies (new releases usually are the best sellers; with some older classics). The owner can also sell advertising to local vendors which will display on the kiosk.

The owner can rent these movies for $1/night which is a very attractive price.

Depending on revenue and expense predictions, the average profit per kiosk can average in the mid $30,000 range.

INDUSTRY ANALYSIS

The DVD rental market is a nearly $10 billion North American market. DVD and video rentals totaled $8.16 billion in 2008. This number is very consistent with the 2007 figures which were $8.18 billion in rental revenue. This is seen as encouraging given that the sales of DVDS and Blu–ray discs fell 23.4% during the same period according to Adams Media Research (New York Times, March 2, 2009). There is an emerging trend toward consumer rentals rather than outright purchases, particularly in a difficult economy.

According to *Video Rental 2009: Innovations Halt Long Decline*, a report from Adams Media Research, "Though consumers put the brakes on most discretionary spending during the second half of the year [2008], the video rental segment wasn't hit as hard as other retail businesses. The main reason: new and attractive forms of rental—online subscriptions and $1/night kiosks—are making up for continued declines in traditional specialty–store rentals."

The reports conclusion is that "As the rental business reached its 30th birthday, it is still the most popular way to watch movies at home, with a total of 2.5bn rental turns in the U.S. last year. Coming in virtually flat in a year when everything else was down, the video rental market continues to be the target of innovative business plans ranging from Netflix and Redbox to iTunes and the Xbox Live Marketplace."

According to Adams Media Research, kiosks average 49.1 rentals per day and $37,457 a year in revenue (*The Washington Post*, April 28, 2007).

Facts about the Home Video Market:

- DVD players are found in 81.2% of United States households (2006 Nielsen Media Research). According to The Digital Entertainment Group, 33 million DVD players were sold to U.S. consumers in 2007.

- Blockbuster forecased 2 million subscribers to Blockbuster Online by Q1/06. Blockbusinter intends to invest $120 million in their online business.

- Netflix had 3.2 million subscribers by end of June 2005.

- Video rental is a $8 billion industry, on 3.2 billion transactions. DVD sales totalled 1.1 billion transactions. VOD and PPV totalled fewer than 350 million purchases.

- Redbox machines are made by Flextronics (based in Singapore). In 2008, they doubled their machine count to 9,600 machines.

- McDonald's reported that they estimate each Redbox machine yields $2,000 to $4,000 per square foot per year and each unit is profitable 3 months of launch. McDonald's charges $1 a day per title and offers top 40 DVD titles. McDonald's has 30,000 stores.

Outlook for DVD Rental Kiosks

In a recent interview, Chuck Berger of DVDPlay told Video Business that he estimates that by 2010 or 2011 DVD kiosks will grow to more than 20 percent of the market (it was between 2 and 5 percent in 2008).

The formula for success for a DVD kiosk is a mix of high–traffic locations and lower prices for rentals than the traditional brick and mortar stores charge. "The person we are going to attract is the person who is not motivated to go out of her way to rent a DVD—or to take back a DVD," said Chuck Berger of DVDPlay (www.kioskmarketplace.com).

Russ Crupnick, a senior industry analyst at consumer research firm NPD, said that the kiosks target impulse shoppers. (The Washington Post, April 28, 2007). The question of evolving technologies will not affect the efficacy and success of the kiosks because they will be able handle all technologies (including Blu–Ray discs and DVD to burn downloading).

A recent conference on the Future of Packaged Media found that according to retail participants physical discs (DVDs) make consumers feel more comfortable than movie downloading. At this point in time, there are too many steps to have a seamless movie downloading experience; therefore, physical discs will have a place for sometime in the future.

As the economy falters, inexpensive DVD rentals become even more attractive. Consumers are feeling more and more at ease using self–service kiosks. Rebecca Chan, Director of Marketing at MovieMate, said that "consumer attitudes towards these kinds of purchases have changed to the point that kiosks can be viable in just about any location with enough customer traffic to support a reasonable volume of sales." (www.kioskmarketplace.com). DVD rental kiosks can be located almost anywhere. They are relatively small and they are idea for supermarkets, malls, gas stations and other retail outlets. College campuses and corporate offices also have kiosks.

The Internet provides a backbone for servicing kiosks. Kiosks can be monitored and serviced 24 hours a day. Real–time inventory updating and rental trends/reports can be monitored constantly. From a customer perspective, web sites can be used for online reservations and advance decision–making.

Market Analysis for DVD Rental Kiosks

The market for kiosk rentals is booming. In 2007 the market for Kiosk Rentals doubled according to the Entertainment Merchant Association, 2008 Annual Report from 1% of the market to 2% of the overall video market. The forecast by 2009 for kiosks can be as high as 20% of the overall rental market.

The growth has been significant as one can see below, in 2006 kiosks represented about .9 percent of the DVD rental market according to Adams Media Research. Chain video stores had approximately 43% of the market, while online companies such as Netflix were at about 16% of the market.

Video Rental Market Share by Type of Outlet—2006

The following facts were reported from Adams Media Research, Online DVD Subscription: Reinventing Video Rental

- There were approximately 10,000 DVD rental kiosks operational in the U.S. at the end of 2007.

- Traditional rental stores, dominated by Blockbuster, accounted for 73% of the rental business in 2007. Online subscription rental (such as Netflix and Blockbuster's Total Access) were 25% of the market. Kiosk rental doubled its market share to 2%.

- Redbox has now surpassed Blockbuster in its number of locations. Blockbuster is testing express kiosks at various Papa John's and Family Dollar locations in the Lexington, KY area. The company plans to roll out the kiosks to other rural areas. The Blockbuster kiosk holds 250 titles.

- Over the last three years, Redbox has averaged 300 percent annual growth.

- The market for Interactive Game Sales showed considerable and stead growth over the last 11 years.

Interactive Game Sales 1995—2006

According to data from The NPD Group, Inc. sales of entertainment software included 65.3 million units in 1995 equating to a total of $2.4 billion in sales. This number steadily increased since that time, and rose to a high of 241.0 million unites, or $7.4 billion in sales, in 2006. Adams Media Research reported similar findings with rentals and sell–through spending, a market that increased from $0.5 billion in 1981 to $24.9 billion in 2006.

INDUSTRY PLAYERS

The DVD Rental Kiosk industry is dominated by companies who sell to corporate entities such as Redbox. There are a few companies, DVDNow a leading one, who sell directly to independent operators. This is the business opportunity for the entrepreneur to create an independently–owned DVD rental kiosk franchise.

The competitive landscape in the movie and game rental business includes traditional video stores such as the Blockbuster chain, online players such as Netflix and the kiosks located in high traffic areas.

Kiosks will generally attract impulse shoppers who are looking for a good deal and when they see they can rent a movie for $1 they are drawn in.

Players in the DVD Rental Kiosk Industry

Company–Operated Kiosk Vendors

Redbox Automated Retail, LLC (Redbox)

Redbox is the leading renter of DVDs through self–service kiosks in the United States. Redbox currently has 35 million customers and 12,000 locations. Redbox rents movies for $1 per night. Customers can rent in one location and return in another location. Redbox kiosks can be found in grocery stores (including Giant Food and Stop & Shop), McDonald's restaurants, Walmart and Walgreen's stores. There is tremendous competition among these company–operated kiosk vendors for the large chain stores. Redbox generally looks to place kiosks in businesses who have at least 15,000 customers each week.

Coinstar, Inc. used its option to purchase their remaining stake in Redbox in February 2009 because they feel so strongly about the growth potential of the DVD rental market.

"Redbox has been a great addition to our 4th Wall product portfolio, and we are very enthusiastic about the DVD rental kiosk market having seen tremendous growth and acceptance over the past few years," said Paul David, Chief Operating Officer of Coinstar, Inc. (Reuters, Februrary 12, 2009).

TNR Entertainment Corp.—The New Release (moviecube)

The New Release is a Houston–based company with approximately 2,100 kiosk locations in the United States and Canada. The company currently has deals with grocery chains including Albertson's, Dillon's, Kroger, Publix, Ralph's, Schnuck's and Overwaitea and Sobey's in Canada.

TNR is backed by an institutional investor group led by MCG Capital Corporation.

DVDPlay

DVDPlay established its first kiosk in the Silicon Valley in 2002. The company is based in San Jose, California; and has several venture capital partners including El Dorado Ventures, Emergence Venture Partners, Palo Alto Venture Partners and Vanguard Ventures.

DVDPlay has kiosks located in supermarket chains including Safeway, Albertson's, Kroger, Von's, and others thoughout the United States and Canada. There are currently 1,400 kiosk locations.

DVDXpress

DVDXpress has been operating since 2001. They are headquartered in Manhattan, NY. They currently have deals with A&P, Pathmark, and King Kullen, among others. They also have machines in residential buildings, office buildings, and college campuses. In 2006, DVDXpress operated about 250 kiosks in the United States.

The company has experimented with an online subscription model similar to Netflix where a customer can subscribe for $12.99 per month and rent unlimited movies during the month with no due dates and no late fees.

Manufacturers

The information provided below is on the DVD Kiosk manufacturers; however, they generally sell to a distributor such as Redbox or DVDNow and not directly to an individual.

iMOZI

iMOZI, a Vancouver, British Columbia based company, is offering DVD kiosks for direct ownership. The kiosks are state–of–the–art technology that allow for rentals of physical discs but also on–demand DVD burning and downloading to a portable flash–memory storage devise. Each kiosk holds 1,000 DVDs.

iMOZI is a leader in providing automated and digital media self–service solutions. With an end–to–end offering that merges traditionally packaged media with digitally delivered content, iMOZI offers "best of best" kiosks to enable automated DVD rental and sales, as well as DVD–on–Demand, video games, music downloads, digital photo print and mobile content. As innovators, our experienced management team continues to develop the concept with the integration of future technologies that leverage new delivery methods and revenue channels. As a technology development and distribution company, iMOZI's automated DVD kiosks are currently distributed in USA, Canada and Australia.

iMOZI currently has a deal with United Supermarkets in Texas.

MovieMate

MovieMate is a New York–based manufacturer of automated DVD vending and rental machines. MovieMate is a leading developer of DVD Rental Kiosks, Digital Signage, and Cashless Technology for the out–of–home self–service and retail market. The company specializes in the development of reliable DVD kiosks systems that are designed, verified and manufactured to perform optimally in the retail environment, delivering a superior customer experience. With a proven track record of technical excellence, superior quality and on–time delivery, the market is turning to MovieMate to deliver selfservice retail solutions that must perform reliably in the field. Working since 2004 with the focus on self–service DVD Rental technology, MovieMate has developed the engineering and software capability, vendor relationships and valuable manufacturing partnerships and can support a manufacturing capability of myriad of products. Today MovieMate's expertise extends across the full breadth of internet connected retail technologies, from remote device management, self–service retail kiosk, smart digital signage and electronic payment software.

Flextronics

Flextronics is based in Singapore and manufactures machines for Redbox.

Independently–Operated Kiosk Opportunities

Own your own DVD Kiosk Rental Business Opportunity

To date, only a handful of large operators have led the explosion of DVD kiosks sprouting up at the front of stores and quick–service franchises across America. In fact, the overwhelming majority of all installed DVD kiosks are currently owned and operated by such companies (predominately Redbox) through standard "hosting placement agreements" with the retailer or restaurant, which receives a small portion of the revenue. ("Enabling the Solution: The Benefits of Owning and Operating a DVD Kiosk" by Christopher Hall, www.KioskMarketplace.com).

Direct–Owned, Independently–Operated DVD Rental Kiosks

DVDNow, Kiosks Inc. based in North Vancouver, BC sells rental kiosks for movie and/or video game rentals to corporate as well as independent entrepeneurs.

There are other DVD rental kiosk distributors who sell directly to independent operators such as DVmatic Kiosks by ELO Media. ELO Media is based in Piscataway, NJ and is a smaller distributor than DVDNow.

As an entrepreneur you can not own a Red Box or DVDPlay distributorship for any amount of money, just like you can't buy a Starbucks franchise they are almost wholly corporately owned. However, there is a way that you can participate in and profit from this massive rental paradigm shift and be on the forefront of the DVD rental kiosk revolution. The DVDNow automated rental kiosk enables entrepreneurs to capitalize on the over $20 billion DVD industry by allowing them to participate in this exploding market. With our program, independent operators are able to establish a network of state of the art DVD rental kiosks in locations such as grocery and convenience stores, fast food restaurants and large apartment/condo complexes.

DVDNow kiosks generate revenue through four primary sources.

1. The rental of DVDs and video games

2. Late fees from overdue movies

3. The sale of advertisements (onscreen and positioned within the DVD jewel case)

4. The sale of previously viewed DVDs

PRODUCT AND SERVICES

DVDNow Rental Kiosk

Each DVDNow kiosk can hold 150 movie/game titles. DVDNow kiosks provide transparent glass doors so customers can easily pick titles and see the physical package before selecting. Movies are rented in their original packaging minimizing labor and maximizing sell–through potential.

The owner of the kiosk can price movies however he/she deems fit; but generally, $1 for the first day is customary in a high traffic, return customer setting such as a supermarket. The owner may be able to charge a higher fee such as $2 if the kiosk is in a setting such as an apartment complex where the customer may pay up a little for the convenience of not having to leave home.

Kiosk Specifications

*   Dimensions: 26' x 19' x 69'

*   Weight: 363 pounds

*   Capacity: 110 DvDs

*   Payment: VISA, Mastercard, American Express, or Discover

*   Electrical Requirements: 120 VAC

*   Environment: Indoor

*   Communication: Any broadband connection

How To Set Up A DVD Kiosk

1. Locate a high traffic, return customer location. This is usually a supermarket, convenience store or apartment building complex.

2. Negotiate price per machine with distributor such as DVDNow Kiosk. The price of a DVD Kiosk is generally between $18,000 and $19,000. If you buy multiple machines you may be able to negotiate better pricing.

3. Negotiate agreement with a movie distributor such as VPD.

4. Set up a web site (the distributor supplies a template) so that customers can see inventory online. Operator can then also manage reports and machines online.

5. Set up a merchant account (with company like First Data Corp.) to process credit card transactions. You will also need back–end processing with a company like 3C International.

6. Set up an Internet Hookup which can be either a DSL or a cable connection.

7. Negotiate deal with location owner. The usual deal is that the location owner receives 10%—20% of net revenue.

8. Purchase RFID (radio frequency identification) tags that will be put on each DVD for tracking purposes.

9. Usually operators buy about 6 new releases for the kiosk each week which will need to be loaded.

10. As movies get less use and get older, the operator will try to sell the DVDs outright to customers for reasonable prices.

11. Movies that don't get sold through the kiosk can be returned through a buy–back program with VPD or sold on EBay or other sites.

REVENUE

Revenue from the kiosk is generated from rentals and late fees. The monthly average generated between these two revenue streams is $1,369 per kiosk. An additional $433 can be generated from the sale of previously used DVDs, and $100 per month can be earned from the DVDs that are returned to the movie distributor. Advertising is another significant revenue opportunity. Sales of kiosk side panel ad space and multimedia advertising can amount to $1,600 per month. All of these sources of revenue total $3,502 per month per kiosk.

Monthly expenses per kiosk total $692 and include such costs as location commission, inventory costs, and the price of the internet connection for the kiosk.

The net income per kiosk is expected to be $2,810 per month, or $33,720 per year.

CUSTOMER SERVICE

The independent operator will likely provide customer service instructions clearly on the actual kiosk. There will be references to the operator's web site where further information is available. In addition, there should be a toll–free customer support number.

MARKETING AND SALES

The operator will need to "get the word out" that the kiosk exists. This can be done by placing flyers around the location and in local stores; or by purchasing local newspaper ads. In addition, the operator may place flyers or special coupons (for free nights for example) in the supermarket circulars and in other locations.

ADVERTISING REVENUE

The DVDNow kiosk provides slots on the kiosk for advertising. As the operator, you can seek local businesses to a buy advertising rights for either print or video ads.

RESALE MARKET FOR USED KIOSKS

If the operator decides to opt out of the business, there is a generally strong resale market for the kiosks. Particularly in a weak economy, there are people looking to buy the kiosks used rather than new ones. Used kiosks may sell for about $13,000—$15,000 depending on the age and condition of the kiosk.

Energy Consultant

Jacobs Consulting

5420 Brown Ave.
Palo Alto, California 94302

Gerald Rekve

The major component of Jacobs Consulting will be the ability to centralize the contact points for business customers to contact a firm that specializes in energy consultation.

EXECUTIVE SUMMARY

Jacobs Consulting was formed by James Jacobs as a result of increased requests from clients who needed consultants that focused on energy–related services and advice.

During the past five years, businesses have started thinking more about the energy sector on a daily basis. In 2008, oil hit $140 per barrel and this left a lot of businesses' budgets and profits in the sink. The price of energy immediately hit the bottom line of the balance sheet in ways never seen before. Jacobs Consulting saw a way to fill this market need by setting up a consulting firm that provides advisory services to businesses in all sectors and in all regions of North America and the world. The business of Jacobs Consulting will be established to allow consultants in any region or country to join as a co–consultant or affiliate. It will also allow existing consulting firms to brand our services into their business and act as an extension to us and the services that we offer.

MARKETING & SALES

Jacobs Consulting's Sales Forecasts for 2009–2011

- 2009 = $2,301,969 with net cash flow of $720,048

- 2010 = $2,764,524 with net cash flow of $320,006

- 2011 = $2,975,439 with net cash flow of $61,041

Total borrowing of $900,000 and an investment by the owner of $100,000.

Highlights

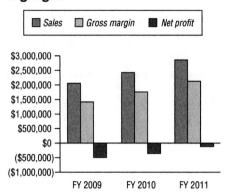

OBJECTIVES

Jacobs Consulting will be set up to sell *green technology services* to business customers. Our objective is to make money by selling our *green advisory services* to business customers. Using our advice will allow business owners to save money in their businesses by using green power and technologies.

We will position our business to be the industry leader within five years of operation.

Mission

Jacobs Consulting's mission will be to provide the best–in–class consulting services to our customers. We will hire the best–in–class consultants to work closely with our business customers.

Our goal, as well our mission, is to be profitable in our first year of operation.

Keys to Success

The keys to success for Jacobs Consulting are as follows:

- Hiring the right consultants who have the background that meets the needs of our business customers.

- Contracting with government agencies who have the responsibility to manage the green technology and promoting it.

- Insuring business decision–makers have the correct information that will allow for them to make correct decisions when it comes to green business and profit.

OPERATIONS

Jacobs Consulting will be 100 percent owned by James Jacobs, while each consultant that works for Jacobs Consulting will be an independent consultant and be paid based on the work they do for the company. None of the consultants or firms who contract with Jacobs Consulting will be an employee. Jacobs Consulting will be set as a corporation with limited liability to protect them. Each consultant hired will be an independent consultant and not an employee of the company; this reduces the payroll for our company, yet allows for us to have in–depth market reach.

Start–up Summary

The major component of Jacobs Consulting will be the ability to centralize the contact points for business customers to contact a firm that specializes in energy consultation.

The start–up expenses are mostly related to the set–up of the firm, research and development, and marketing expenses for advertising the message to business customers.

Also, the hiring of consultants will be done from various regions of North America that specialize in all areas of energy consultation.

Start-up Costs

Start-up requirements	
Start-up expenses	
Legal	$ 5,000
Accounting	$ 2,000
Insurance	$ 2,500
Office equipment	$ 10,000
Travel	$ 20,000
Advertising	$ 30,000
Consultant fees	$ 20,000
Research staff	$ 25,000
Printing office stationary	$ 10,000
Website setup & design	$ 5,000
Total start-up expenses	**$129,500**
Start-up assets	
Cash required	$150,000
Other current assets	$ 10,000
Fixed assets	$ 5,000
Total assets	**$165,000**
Total requirements	**$294,500**

Start-up Summary

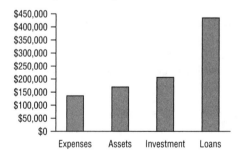

SERVICES

The complexity of today's energy markets requires an energy industry base of knowledge that stretches from the wellhead and generating station to your plant. This base of knowledge is critical in effectively developing and executing energy strategies that will save your company money and time.

We provide customized energy solutions to industrial/manufacturing companies in North America. We are a comprehensive energy management consulting company. We create an energy environment for our customers, generating justifiable energy savings and a seamless flow of energy information to all levels of the organization.

We manage our customer's energy requirements with the perspective of an end–user and the knowledge of a marketer and utility. We will effectively manage your energy, so you can manage your business.

Our customized energy solutions approach allows the customer to sculpt a service level that best fits its specific internal energy objectives.

Examples of services are:

- Request for proposal management
- Invoice reconciliation
- Energy Solutions advice
- Basic Energy reporting
- Customized reporting
- Risk management
- Tax management
- Budgeting and forecasting
- Any and all other energy–related activities
- Wholesale and retail electricity price forecasts
- Wholesale natural gas price forecasts
- Energy risk management analysis and advice
- Electricity and natural gas buying and selling advice and services
- Electricity market training courses
- Natural gas market training courses
- Electricity and gas market modelling and information
- Electricity and gas contracts, generation projects and energy market player valuations
- Related consultancy and advisory services
- Agency services for entry of offers and bids in the wholesale electricity spot market
- Electricity and gas market models

MARKET ANALYSIS

Market Segmentation

Jacobs Consulting will sell to a number of sectors, all of which are in the commercial segments. Jacobs Consulting does not plan on selling to the homeowner sectors.

Customer segments are as follows:

- Mining Customers: With the huge input costs for mining, our advisory services can be very helpful to reduce, as well focus, costs for ongoing mining projects and new projects that are being planned now.

- Manufacturing Customers: Similar to that of the Mining sector.

- Aviation Customers: Aviation energy costs can put a company out of business. Without planning for these costs properly, investors and owners of aviation companies can end up in the red. We allow these companies to plan and profit.

- Transportation Customers: This area is a direct link to the economy; every dollar that is added to the cost of a product due to shipping will result in a cost increase for that item in order to cover the shipping/energy costs. In some cases our services reduced the cost of a product by 5 percent because of shipping.

- Retail Business Customers: Similar to that of the Transportation sector.

- State Government: This area is where we can help develop policy that, in the end, will help all sectors if managed correctly.

- Federal Government: This area is where we can help develop policy that, in the end, will help all sectors if managed correctly.

Market Analysis

Market analysis	Growth	2008	2009	2010	2011	2012	CAGR
Potential customers							
Mining customers	5%	50	53	56	59	62	5.53%
Aviation customers	5%	20	21	22	23	24	4.66%
Transportation customers	5%	150	158	166	174	183	5.10%
Manufacturing customers	5%	500	525	551	579	608	5.01%
Retail business customers	5%	1,000	1,050	1,103	1,158	1,216	5.01%
State government	5%	50	53	56	59	62	5.53%
Federal government	0%	10	10	10	10	10	0.00%
Total	**5.02%**	**1,780**	**1,870**	**1,964**	**2,062**	**2,165**	**5.02%**

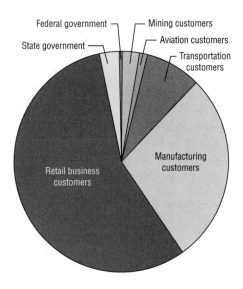

Service Business Analysis

Geographic area: United States

NAICS code: 54

Meaning: Professional, scientific, & technical services

Number of establishments: 2,904,089

Receipts ($1,000): $124,236,645

This number of professional, scientific, and technical service consultants includes the entire USA, and includes everyone from one–man shops to large Fortune 500 companies.

BUSINESS STRATEGY

Jacobs Consulting's strategy will be to hire all the key management, then roll out an hiring of consultants across all sectors. Once the consultants are trained in our business policies and fundamentals, we will let the consultants do what they know best—finding and securing clients.

Competition

Jacobs Consulting's major competitive advantage will be our vast regional market penetration by our consultants. We will be operating in every market in North America. This will allow us to target large Fortune 500 companies with multiple locations. This is very critical to our success and our ability to win contracts. Being able to drawn on various markets and then compare the results will help both our clients and our consultants. We can look at one market and see what is working. Then we can go to other markets and see if this business tactic works in that market. The ability to compare markets for us and our clients will give us a unique competitive advantage over our competitors both regionally and nationally.

With this reach, we will deliver excellent services for a fraction of what other firms will be charging. It is not that we are giving our services away. The reverse will be true—we will be paid top dollar for products that we have been able to keep our costs down on.

Marketing & Sales

Jacobs Consulting's marketing strategy is very simple and, for this reason, it will be easy to monitor and achieve. Our marketing strategy is to place our name in front of key decision makers when they are in the market to buy our type of services. We will be able to monitor the success of these by the reach of our consultants in the field; the reach will be our success factor.

Sales Strategy

Our sales strategy will be to offer as much information on our website. This will allow our customers the ability to find key information, which will lead them to call us to request more information or our assistance.

In each of the segments, we will have consultants who specialize in those areas. We will also have our consultants spread all around USA and Canada, and this will allow for easy access. Our focus will be an advisor to all our clients' needs; this allows Jacobs Consulting to be in the forefront of all our clients' requests.

We will also attend tradeshows for all sectors and have a booth so attendants can ask us questions.

Specific Marketing Plans by Customer Sector

- Mining Customers: We will attend trade shows and place advertisements in industry trade publications.
- Aviation Customers: We will attend trade shows and place advertisements in industry trade publications.
- Transportation Customers: We will attend trade shows and place advertisements in industry trade publications.
- Retail Business Customers: We will attend trade shows and place advertisements in industry trade publications.
- State Government: We will send letters to local officials in all related departments.
- Federal Government: We will send letters to local officials in all related departments.
- Manufacturing Customers: We will attend trade shows and place advertisements in industry trade publications.

Sales Forecast

We will be able to achieve these sales results based on the fact that we will be hiring consultants to work for us across North America. Each one of these consultants will go out and grow their regions' revenue. We understand that not all the consultants we hire will attain the same levels of sales revenue for us; therefore we have budgeted doubling up on our consultants in some regions, in order to achieve our sales results. Then the consultant that draws the most revenue from these key regions will allow us to meet our sales projections.

Sales forecast	FY 2009	FY 2010	FY 2011
Sales			
Mining customer	$ 424,435	$ 445,000	$ 475,000
Aviation customer	$ 461,350	$ 546,000	$ 566,000
Transportation customer	$ 119,069	$ 130,000	$ 150,000
Manufacturing customer	$ 518,465	$ 575,000	$ 600,000
Retail customer	$ 180,437	$ 210,000	$ 240,000
State government customer	$ 25,432	$ 140,000	$ 255,000
Federal government customer	$ 249,612	$ 300,000	$ 500,000
	$ 0	$ 0	$ 0
Total sales	**$1,978,801**	**$2,346,000**	**$2,786,000**
Direct cost of sales			
Consultants fee	$ 519,721	$ 550,000	$ 600,000
Our expenses	$ 55,873	$ 65,000	$ 75,000
	$ 0	$ 0	$ 0
Subtotal direct cost of sales	$ 575,594	$ 615,000	$ 675,000

MANAGEMENT SUMMARY

Because Jacobs Consulting will be built with independent consultants, we will have a streamlined employee payroll.

- CEO: James Jacobs

- CFO: TBD

- Marketing Director: TBD

- Sales Director: TBD

- IT Director: TBD

- Eastern USA Consultant Manager: TBD

- Western USA Consultant Manager: TBD

- Canada Consultant Manager: TBD

- Mexico Consultant Manager: TBD

- Europe Consultant Manager: TBD

- Asia Consultant Manager: TBD

- Middle East Consultant Manager: TBD

Personnel Plan

While we will have a large number of consultants working for us, most likely over one hundred in the first year, we will only have twelve key management personnel and an additional ten in support staff. For the purpose of this business plan, we have only counted the salaried employees.

Personnel plan	FY 2009	FY 2010	FY 2011
CEO	$ 60,000	$ 60,000	$ 60,000
CFO	$ 48,000	$ 50,000	$ 52,000
Marketing director	$ 48,000	$ 55,000	$ 55,000
Sales director	$ 48,000	$ 53,000	$ 53,000
IT director	$ 40,800	$ 44,000	$ 44,000
Eastern USA consultant manager	$ 48,000	$ 53,000	$ 53,000
Western USA consultant manager	$ 48,000	$ 53,000	$ 53,000
Canada consultant manager	$ 48,000	$ 54,000	$ 54,000
Mexico consultant manager	$ 48,000	$ 52,000	$ 52,000
Europe consultant manager	$ 48,000	$ 53,000	$ 53,000
Asia consultant manager	$ 48,000	$ 54,000	$ 54,000
Middle east consultant manager	$ 48,000	$ 54,000	$ 54,000
Total people	**25**	**35**	**35**
Total payroll	**$580,800**	**$635,000**	**$637,000**

FINANCIAL ANALYSIS

Start-up Funding

Start-up funding	
Start-up expenses to fund	$129,500
Start-up assets to fund	$165,000
Total funding required	**$294,500**
Assets	
Non-cash assets from start-up	$ 15,000
Cash requirements from start-up	$150,000
Additional cash raised	$335,500
Cash balance on starting date	$485,500
Total assets	**$500,500**
Liabilities and capital	
Liabilities	
Current borrowing	$300,000
Fixed liabilities	$100,000
Accounts payable (outstanding bills)	$ 20,000
Other current liabilities	$ 10,000
Total liabilities	**$430,000**
Capital	
Planned investment owner	$100,000
Investor	$100,000
Additional investment requirement	$ 0
Total planned investment	**$200,000**
Loss at start-up (start-up expenses)	$129,500
Total capital	**$ 70,500**
Total capital and liabilities	**$500,500**
Total funding	**$630,000**

Break-even Analysis

Break-even analysis	
Monthly revenue break-even	$ 220,819
Assumptions:	
Average percent variable cost	29%
Estimated monthly fixed cost	$156,587.47

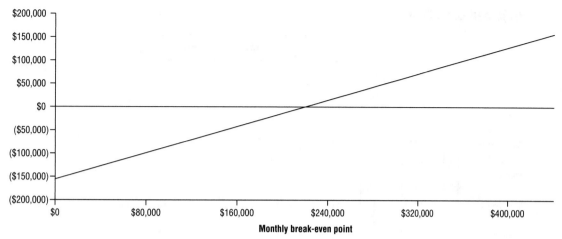

Break-even point = where line intersects with 0

Projected Profit and Loss

Pro forma profit and loss	FY 2009	FY 2010	FY 2011
Sales	$1,978,801	$2,346,000	$2,786,000
Direct cost of sales	$ 575,594	$ 615,000	$ 675,000
Other costs of sales	$ 36,000	$ 40,000	$ 45,000
Total cost of sales	**$ 611,594**	**$ 655,000**	**$ 720,000**
Gross margin	$1,367,207	$1,691,000	$2,066,000
Gross margin %	69.09%	72.08%	74.16%
Expenses			
Payroll	$ 580,800	$ 635,000	$ 637,000
Marketing/promotion	$ 20,000	$ 30,000	$ 40,000
Depreciation	$ 0	$ 0	$ 0
Office lease	$ 24,000	$ 30,000	$ 35,000
Utilities	$ 12,000	$ 14,000	$ 16,000
Insurance	$ 1,594	$ 2,500	$ 2,700
Payroll—support staff	$ 40,656	$ 44,450	$ 44,590
Payroll—consultants	$1,200,000	$1,300,000	$1,400,000
Total operating expenses	**$1,879,050**	**$2,055,950**	**$2,175,290**
Profit before interest and taxes	$ 511,843	$ 364,950	$ 109,290
Interest expense	$ 54,350	$ 63,050	$ 83,550
Taxes incurred	$ 0	$ 0	$ 0
Net profit	$ 566,193	$ 428,000	$ 192,840
Net profit/sales	−28.61%	−18.24%	−6.92%

Projected Cash Flow

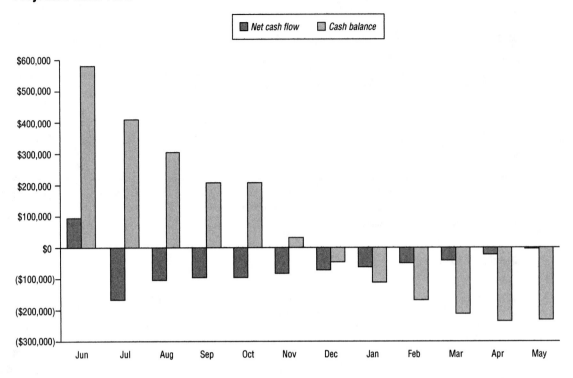

Pro forma cash flow	FY 2009	FY 2010	FY 2011
Cash received			
Cash from operations			
Cash sales	$ 494,700	$ 586,500	$ 696,500
Cash from receivables	$ 937,221	$1,658,017	$1,967,897
Subtotal cash from operations	$1,431,921	$2,244,517	$2,664,397
Additional cash received			
GST/HST received (output tax)	$ 0	$ 0	$ 0
GST/HST repayments	$ 0	$ 0	$ 0
New current borrowing	$ 150,000	$ 200,000	$ 250,000
New other liabilities (interest-free)	$ 0	$ 0	$ 0
New fixed liabilities	$ 0	$ 0	$ 0
Sales of other current assets	$ 0	$ 0	$ 0
Sales of fixed assets	$ 0	$ 0	$ 0
New investment received	$ 0	$ 0	$ 0
Subtotal cash received	$1,581,921	$2,444,517	$2,914,397
Expenditures			
Expenditures from operations			
Cash spending	$ 580,800	$ 635,000	$ 637,000
Bill payments	$1,709,169	$2,114,524	$2,313,439
Subtotal spent on operations	$2,289,969	$2,749,524	$2,950,439
Additional cash spent			
GST/HST paid out (input tax)	$ 0	$ 0	$ 0
GST/HST payments	$ 0	$ 0	$ 0
Principal repayment of current borrowing	$ 12,000	$ 15,000	$ 25,000
Other liabilities principal repayment	$ 0	$ 0	$ 0
Fixed liabilities principal repayment	$ 0	$ 0	$ 0
Purchase other current assets	$ 0	$ 0	$ 0
Purchase fixed assets	$ 0	$ 0	$ 0
Dividends	$ 0	$ 0	$ 0
Subtotal cash spent	$2,301,969	$2,764,524	$2,975,439
Net cash flow	$ 720,048	$ 320,006	$ 61,041
Cash balance	$ 234,548	$ 554,555	$ 615,596

Projected Balance Sheet

Pro forma balance sheet	FY 2009	FY 2010	FY 2011
Assets			
Current assets			
Cash	$234,548	$ 554,555	$ 615,596
Accounts receivable	$546,880	$ 648,363	$ 769,965
Other current assets	$ 10,000	$ 10,000	$ 10,000
Total current assets	**$322,331**	**$ 103,808**	**$ 164,369**
Fixed assets			
Fixed assets	$ 5,000	$ 5,000	$ 5,000
Accumulated depreciation	$ 0	$ 0	$ 0
Total fixed assets	**$ 5,000**	**$ 5,000**	**$ 5,000**
Total assets	**$327,331**	**$ 108,808**	**$ 169,369**
Liabilities and capital			
Current liabilities			
Accounts payable	$275,024	$ 299,500	$ 327,902
Current borrowing	$438,000	$ 623,000	$ 848,000
Other current liabilities	$ 10,000	$ 10,000	$ 10,000
Subtotal current liabilities	$723,024	$ 932,500	$1,185,902
Fixed liabilities	$100,000	$ 100,000	$ 100,000
Total liabilities	**$823,024**	**$1,032,500**	**$1,285,902**
Paid-in capital	$200,000	$ 200,000	$ 200,000
Retained earnings	$129,500	$ 695,693	$1,123,693
Earnings	$566,193	$ 428,000	$ 192,840
Total capital	**$495,693**	**$ 923,693**	**$1,116,533**
Total liabilities and capital	**$327,331**	**$ 108,808**	**$ 169,369**
Net worth	$495,693	$ 923,693	$1,116,533

Business Ratios

Ratio analysis	FY 2009	FY 2010	FY 2011	Industry Profile
Sales growth	0.00%	18.56%	18.76%	6.75%
Percent of total assets				
Other current assets	3.06%	9.19%	5.90%	47.90%
Total current assets	98.47%	95.40%	97.05%	73.42%
Fixed assets	1.53%	4.60%	2.95%	26.58%
Total assets	**100.00%**	**100.00%**	**100.00%**	**100.00%**
Current liabilities	220.88%	857.02%	700.19%	32.60%
Fixed liabilities	30.55%	91.91%	59.04%	15.44%
Total liabilities	251.43%	948.92%	759.23%	48.04%
Net worth	−151.43%	−848.92%	−659.23%	51.96%
Percent of sales				
Sales	100.00%	100.00%	100.00%	100.00%
Gross margin	69.09%	72.08%	74.16%	100.00%
Selling, general & administrative expenses	97.71%	90.32%	81.08%	82.46%
Advertising expenses	0.00%	0.00%	0.00%	1.09%
Profit before interest and taxes	−25.87%	−15.56%	−3.92%	0.73%
Main ratios				
Current	0.45	0.11	0.14	1.72
Quick	0.45	0.11	0.14	1.39
Total debt to total assets	251.43%	948.92%	759.23%	65.13%
Pre-tax return on net worth	114.22%	46.34%	17.27%	1.20%
Pre-tax return on assets	−172.97%	−393.35%	−113.86%	3.44%
Additional ratios				
Net profit margin	−28.61%	−18.24%	−6.92%	n.a
Return on equity	0.00%	0.00%	0.00%	n.a
Activity ratios				
Accounts payable turnover	7.14	7.14	7.14	n.a
Total asset turnover	**6.05**	**21.56**	**16.45**	**n.a**
Debt ratios				
Debt to net worth	0.00	0.00	0.00	n.a
Current liab. to liab.	0.88	0.90	0.92	n.a
Liquidity ratios				
Net working capital	$400,693	$828,693	$1,021,533	n.a
Interest coverage	−9.42	−5.79	−1.31	n.a
Additional ratios				
Assets to sales	0.17	0.05	0.06	n.a
Current debt/total assets	221%	857%	700%	n.a
Acid test	−0.31	−0.58	−0.51	n.a
Sales/net worth	0.00	0.00	0.00	n.a
Dividend payout	0.00	0.00	0.00	n.a

Environmentally–Friendly Greenhouse

Green Greenhouse

90 Appian Blvd.
Auburn, Indiana 46706

Gerald Rekve

Our mission is to grow products using environmentally–friendly methods, offering products that are competitively priced while maintaining quality. We also want to position our greenhouse as a quality producer of products, with a quick delivery time of our products to our major retail clients, who will resell our products to their clients.

EXECUTIVE SUMMARY

Opening Green Greenhouse in Auburn, Indiana in 2009 was a result of over twelve months of planning and research. We have been able to build this business plan factoring in the stock market crash of 2008. Our concept will be that one of building a business using the most energy efficient equipment and technologies to do so.

The main purpose of this business plan is to show the potential for a new–state–of–the–art greenhouse that will be operated at lower cost than anyone else in the market today.

While the start–up investment is over one million dollars, we want to remind the reader that the repayment will take place over a 12 year period, therefore reducing our monthly costs. Our cash flow for 2009 will be $316,775; for 2010 it will be $164,065. Our sales for 2009 will be $1,606,069; for 2010 is will be $1,955,650. Our total loan requirements for 2009 and the following twelve years will be $1,900,000.

Highlights

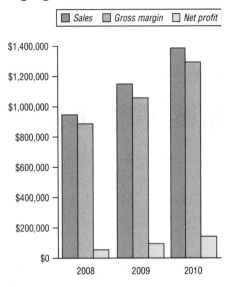

OBJECTIVES

It will be our objective to operate a greenhouse that can focus on selling products that are grown using green technology where possible. We will offer a wide variety of products ensuring to reach the most possible cliental. In our market there are a number of competitors selling similar products. Our objective is to use streamline technology allowing us to produce our products at a lower cost, and then pass on these savings to our clients and consumers.

Green Greenhouse has specific objectives, including:

- Secure financing for our business
- Have facilities built on time and on budget
- Secure key staff
- Secure key commercial clients
- Ensure facilities are operating efficiently

MISSION

Our mission is to grow products using environmentally–friendly methods, offering products that are competitively priced while maintaining quality. We also want to position our greenhouse as a quality producer of products, with a quick delivery time of our products to our major retail clients, who will resell our products to their clients.

BUSINESS OVERVIEW

Keys to Success

The keys to our Green Greenhouse success will be the following:

- Our ability to offer quality products
- Our ability to be competitive

- Secure land required to build infrastructure

- Secure loans to hire contractors to build buildings

- Hire staff that are well–educated in horticulture

Business Strategy

Green Greenhouse will be a retail/commercial greenhouse located in Auburn, Indiana. We will sell to the retail sector as well the commercial sector. The retail sector will include a walk–in greenhouse that allows people to buy our products. They can buy single items or groups of products at reasonable, competitive prices. The commercial sector will include big retailers like Wal–Mart, Target and other major retailers in our trading area.

Organization

Our company will be owned by two people. Fred Paco will own 60 percent of the company and Herb Bunn will own 40 percent of the company. Each partner has been in the greenhouse business for over 15 years.

Green Greenhouse will be setup as a limited liability company and incorporated as Green Greenhouse Inc. The operations of the company will be setup in the Jurisdiction of Indiana with the name registered in all 52 United States.

OPERATIONS

Start–up Summary

Green Greenhouse will have a great startup position. The shareholders will have an investment of $420,000 with an additional funding requirement of $1,674,000. The purchasing of the land as well as the construction of the buildings required to house the production facilities are the reason for the high startup expenses.

The acquisition of the land and the construction of the production facilities will take approximately six months from start to finish. We already have placed a refundable deposit on the land based on successfully attaining financing for the whole project. The land seller agreed to these terms because our business fits in with desired types of businesses in the area where they own other land.

We will have up to six months to get funding; if we fail to win funding for our business, then we will get the deposit back. If we decide not to pursue this property for any reason other than failing to get funding, we will lose the deposit. We set this up this way in order to insure we have the land once we win financing. Additionally we have also hired a contractor to draw up blueprints. This cost is only $40,000; we did this only to insure we have everything ready to go once we get funding. We realize that normally we will wait to get funding before we secure the land and hire a contractor to get the blueprints ready. However by doing it our way we save about four months in the planning stages; therefore, all that will need to be done is to have the buildings built which will take about three to six months.

Start-up requirements

Start-up expenses

Legal	$ 4,500
Stationery etc.	$ 500
Insurance	$ 2,000
Land	$ 120,000
Building	$ 500,000
Fertilizer	$ 40,000
Seeds	$ 55,000
Equipment—heavy tractors etc	$ 300,000
Equipment—light lawnmowers etc	$ 60,000
Bedding materials	$ 120,000
Contractors	$ 340,000
Advertising	$ 12,000
Auto expense	$ 5,000
Hydro	$ 14,000
Gas—natural	$ 21,000
Employee's salary	$ 50,000
Management salary	$ 20,000
Travel	$ 10,000
Total start-up expenses	**$1,674,000**

Start-up assets

Cash required	$ 200,000
Start-up stock	$ 20,000
Other current assets	$ 100,000
Fixed assets	$ 100,000
Total assets	**$ 420,000**
Total requirements	**$2,094,000**

PRODUCTS

Our products will include everything you can find in a greenhouse

- Bedding plants

- All types of flowers

- Vegetables

- Cedar–built yard products

- Marble and cement yard ornaments

- Trees

- Fertilizers

- Planters

- Hanging plants

- More products as they are identified

MARKET ANALYSIS

Market analysis	Growth	2008	2009	2010	2011	2012	CAGR
Potential customers							
Commercial—bedding plants	5%	25	26	27	28	29	3.78%
Commercial—hanging plants	5%	34	36	38	40	42	5.42%
Commercial—trees	5%	12	13	14	15	16	7.46%
Commercial—potting plants	5%	16	17	18	19	20	5.74%
Commercial—cedar products	5%	5	5	5	5	5	0.00%
Retail—bedding plants	15%	2,100,000	2,415,000	2,777,250	3,193,838	3,672,914	15.00%
Retail—hanging plants	15%	2,100,000	2,415,000	2,777,250	3,193,838	3,672,914	15.00%
Retail cedar products	15%	2,100,000	2,415,000	2,777,250	3,193,838	3,672,914	15.00%
Other	0%	2,100,000	2,100,000	2,100,000	2,100,000	2,100,000	0.00%
Total	**11.79%**	**8,400,092**	**9,345,097**	**10,431,852**	**11,681,621**	**13,118,854**	**11.79%**

Target Market Segment Strategy

Green Greenhouse will target major retailers for our commercial division like Wal–Mart, Target, and smaller stores who want to sell greenhouse–related products. While we will sell to the commercial market, we will also have a retail store set up at our greenhouse. We will be careful to price our products at about 3 percent higher than the price our retailers will resell our products for. By doing this we will protect our wholesale client base.

Industry Analysis

Nursery Crop Outlook–2008

National Situation and Outlook USDA/ERS reported in *Floriculture and Nursery Crops Yearbook (Dec. 2007)* that value of production of greenhouse and nursery crops had increased from $12.4 billion in 1997 to an estimated value of $16.8 billion for 2006, for an average growth rate of about 3.6%. This was considerably lower than estimated growth rates for the 1980s and 1990s, and the estimated change from 2005 to 2006 was only 0.3%. Changes in the larger economy in terms of income growth and rising interest rates probably have been responsible for these declines. The demand for plants and flowers as ornaments depends on consumer discretionary income and consumer preferences, and to levels of other household expenses. Energy costs in particular probably have affected sales of ornamental plants and added to the cost structure of growers in production and transportation.

In 2006, an important factor in the economy was declining growth rates (in some cases, actual declines) in prices of residential housing. This trend continued and might have been more pronounced in 2007, and early in 2008 there are few signs of abatement. Forecasts of recession are common. In this environment, reduced growth rates for expenditures on nursery and floriculture products should be expected. Our outlook a year ago was that it "might be expected that sales at the national level again would increase in the range of 2 percent to 3 percent." That apparently did not happen. Further, economic reports and declines in consumer confidence as measured by polls suggest that consumers might lower spending. However, the National Gardening Association reported that in 2006 "Home-owners spent a record $44.7 billion . . . to hire lawn care and landscape maintenance services, landscape installation and construction services, tree care services, and landscape design services. Thirty percent of all households nationwide, or an estimated 34.5 million households, currently hire at least one type of lawn and landscape service. And the market for residential lawn and landscape services has increased at a compound annual growth rate of more than 10 percent a year for the past five years." In addition, lawn and garden participation rates have not declined. So, factors suggest market weaknesses are evident, but other pieces of evidence suggest any decline in expenditures on gardening may be moderate. Overall, conservative planning based on the expectation that sales level as measured by dollars would be no higher than 2007 seems to be appropriate.

COMPETITION

Green Greenhouse's competitive advantages are:

- We will use new technologies to produce our products.

- These technologies will be solar/Geothermal.

- Our input costs will be—on average—14 percent less than our competitors.

- Our setup costs will only be about 7 percent more than our competitors, based on future dollar calculation.

- We will still sell similar products to our competitors; however we will offer more quantity for the same dollar value.

- Our new state–of–the–production facility will be more efficient than that of our competitors, therefore allowing us to produce more products for less cost than our competitors. This means our profit will be greater because more product will be produced for less dollars.

MARKETING & SALES

Marketing Strategy

Green Greenhouse's marketing strategy will be to use the media to get the message out about our state–of–the–art environmentally friendly production facility. While we will send out the normal press releases, we will also make phone calls to the media to tell them our story. Our story is one that is in tune with today's world of worry about our climate.

We believe this will benefit us, because we are building our business using 2008 technologies, the greener and cleaner way. We are certain our customers, who also want to promote they are buying green companies, can use our products as an example of how their clients are being green.

Therefore this is a dual green benefit. We are seen by the media as a green company, and our commercial clients will like us because they can benefit from buying our products. Our competitors cannot promote themselves in the same way, unless they invest a great deal in improvements to their production facilities and infrastructure.

Sales Strategy

We will hire two sales consultants. Their job will be to make sales calls to local and national commercial accounts like Wal–Mart, Home Depot and so on. They will set up accounts so we will have a base from which to operate from.

Our second sales strategy will be to sell to the retail sector. This means we will have a full retail setup.

Sales Forecast

Our sales forecast is based on the ability of our sales consultants to secure retail stores to resell our products to national, as well as local, retail stores like Wal–Mart, Home Depot, and Target stores in the region. This will allow us to grow our wholesale clientele levels needed to secure the market share we are attempting to attain in the first three years of operation.

The retail sales we are budgeting is based on the ability to have the products our retail consumers want to buy. We are set up in the central region of all our competitors; this allows our retail clients to come to our greenhouse as it is located closer than others. Our pricing will reflect the ease of access to our store.

Sales Forecast	FY 2009	FY 2010	FY 2011
Sales			
Garden products	$ 157,948	$ 220,000	$ 240,000
Yard products	$ 829,762	$ 950,000	$1,100,000
Greenery	$ 706,523	$ 800,000	$ 900,000
Total sales	**$1,694,233**	**$1,970,000**	**$2,240,000**

MANAGEMENT SUMMARY

CEO—Fred Paco: 60 Percent Ownership

Fred Paco has 15 years of experience working in a variety of positions for a national greenhouse chain. When Fred left the company, he was the Regional Manager in charge of Operations. Fred will oversee the loan applications and the hiring of an outside consulting firm to research and write the business plan. He will also work with the other parts of the management team to implement the business plan as well the ongoing operations of the business.

General Manager—Herb Bunn: 40 Percent Ownership

Herb will support Fred in all aspects of the business start–up. Herb has over 15 years of experience working in the same national greenhouse chain as Fred worked. Herb was in charge of Production.

Other positions include:

- Sales Manager
- CFO/Accountant
- Production Manager
- Floor Manager
- Distribution Manager
- Retail Store Manager
- Production Supervisor
- HR Manager

Our schedule for hiring for these positions is noted in the schedule below.

Milestone	Start Date	End Date	Manager	Department
CEO	11/17/2008	12/17/2008	Owner	Office
Gen manager	11/17/2008	12/17/2008	Owner	Office
Sales manager	11/17/2008	12/17/2008	TBD	Marketing
CFO accountant	11/17/2008	12/17/2008	TBD	Office
Production manager	11/17/2008	12/17/2008	TBD	Production
Floor manager	11/17/2008	12/17/2008	TBD	Production
Distribution manager	11/17/2008	12/17/2008	TBD	Production
Retail store manager	11/17/2008	12/17/2008	TBD	Office
Production supervisor	11/17/2008	12/17/2008	TBD	Production
HR manager	11/17/2008	12/17/2008	TBD	Office

Salaries for the various position are noted in the following chart.

Personnel plan	FY 2009	FY 2010
CEO	$ 60,000	$ 60,000
General manager	$ 52,800	$ 52,800
Sales manager	$ 16,056	$ 16,056
CFO	$ 43,248	$ 43,248
Production manager	$ 15,084	$ 15,084
Floor manager	$ 16,380	$ 16,380
Distribution manager	$ 16,380	$ 16,380
Retail store manager	$ 15,894	$ 15,894
HR manager	$ 21,426	$ 21,426
Production manager	$ 1,338	$ 1,338
Total people	**24**	**452**
Total payroll	**$258,606**	**$258,606**

We will grow our employee base as we need them. Our start up period as well the construction phase will only require a handful of staff. However, once we are open we will hire staff to fill positions on an ongoing basis. There will be the months of February thru July where we will require maximum staff levels. During the other months, we will only require minimal staff levels.

FINANCIAL ANALYSIS

Our financial projections are based on the assumption that 2009 will be in an extreme recession, but not a depression. We used very conservative numbers to determine our market share target, as well our market penetration ratio. We do feel there are competitors in the market we are moving into that have poor financial positions. We feel that one, or possibly two, of these competitors will close in 2009 due to the current market conditions.

Start–up Funding

Both the investors and the same ongoing owners will be responsible for their investment. Both will also manage the start–up and the ongoing operations of the business.

Start-up funding	
Start-up expenses to fund	$1,674,000
Start-up assets to fund	$ 420,000
Total funding required	**$2,094,000**
Assets	
Non-cash assets from start-up	$ 220,000
Cash requirements from start-up	$ 200,000
Additional cash raised	$ 140,000
Cash balance on starting date	$ 340,000
Total assets	**$ 560,000**
Liabilities and capital	
Liabilities	
Current borrowing	$ 674,000
Fixed liabilities	$1,000,000
Accounts payable (outstanding bills)	$ 120,000
Other current liabilities	$ 0
Total liabilities	**$1,794,000**
Capital	
Planned investment	
CEO	$ 240,000
General manager	$ 200,000
Additional investment requirement	$ 0
Total planned investment	**$ 440,000**
Loss at start-up (start-up expenses)	$1,674,000
Total capital	**$1,234,000**
Total capital and liabilities	**$ 560,000**
Total funding	**$2,234,000**

Important Financial Assumptions

It is important to assume that due to the current economic situation in the USA, borrowing may be somewhat hampered. We need to wonder how the recession is going to change the assumptions in the business plan. For 2009, 2010, and so on, we have factored in this in the assumptions. The major factor supporting our business model and type is the fact that, in this economic climate, the homeowners would improve their home rather than buying a new home.

Break–Even Analysis

Break-even analysis	
Monthly revenue break-even	$ 165,708
Assumptions:	
Average percent variable cost	0%
Estimated monthly fixed cost	$165,707.98

Break–Even Analysis

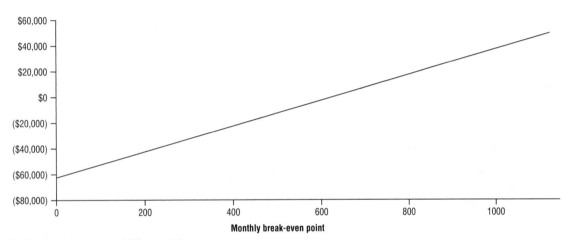

Break-even point = where line intersects with 0

Projected Profit and Loss

Pro forma profit and loss	FY 2009	FY 2010	FY 2011
Sales	$ 1,694,233	$ 1,970,000	$ 2,240,000
Direct costs of goods	$ 0	$ 0	$ 0
Other costs of goods	$ 0	$ 0	$ 0
Cost of goods sold	$ 0	$ 0	$ 0
Gross margin	$ 1,694,233	$ 1,970,000	$ 2,240,000
Gross margin %	100.00%	100.00%	100.00%
Expenses			
Payroll	$ 258,606	$ 0	$ 0
Marketing/promotion	$ 15,325	$ 17,000	$ 18,000
Depreciation	$ 18,673	$ 27,000	$ 35,000
Management salary	$ 242,850	$ 270,000	$ 290,000
Utilities	$ 44,921	$ 55,000	$ 65,000
Insurance	$ 12,286	$ 13,000	$ 14,000
Payroll taxes	$ 51,386	$ 55,000	$ 65,000
Employee salary	$ 582,849	$ 650,000	$ 700,000
Marketing—advertising	$ 82,672	$ 90,000	$ 95,000
Office exp	$ 34,945	$ 40,000	$ 50,000
Materials used for production	$ 480,262	$ 500,000	$ 550,000
Equipment leases	$ 110,721	$ 120,000	$ 130,000
Training	$ 32,801	$ 35,000	$ 40,000
Supplies	$ 20,201	$ 24,000	$ 27,000
Total operating expenses	**$1,988,496**	**$1,896,000**	**$2,079,000**
Profit before interest and taxes	$ 294,263	$ 74,000	$ 161,000
Interest expense	$ 280,399	$ 281,488	$ 300,488
Taxes incurred	$ 0	$ 0	$ 0
Net profit	$ 574,662	$ 207,488	$ 139,488
Net profit/sales	−33.92%	−10.53%	−6.23%

Projected Cash Flow

Pro forma cash flow	FY 2009	FY 2010	FY 2011
Cash received			
Cash from operations			
Cash sales	$1,270,675	$1,477,500	$1,680,000
Cash from receivables	$ 335,395	$ 478,150	$ 545,950
Subtotal cash from operations	$1,606,069	$1,955,650	$2,225,950
Additional cash received			
GST/HST received (output tax)	$ 0	$ 0	$ 0
GST/HST repayments	$ 0	$ 0	$ 0
New current borrowing	$1,200,000	$ 300,000	$ 400,000
New other liabilities (interest-free)	$ 0	$ 0	$ 0
New fixed liabilities	$ 0	$ 0	$ 0
Sales of other current assets	$ 0	$ 0	$ 0
Sales of fixed assets	$ 0	$ 0	$ 0
New investment received	$ 0	$ 0	$ 0
Subtotal cash received	$2,806,069	$2,255,650	$2,625,950
Expenditures			
Expenditures from operations			
Cash spending	$ 258,606	$ 0	$ 0
Bill payments	$1,976,567	$2,139,715	$2,331,333
Subtotal spent on operations	$2,235,173	$2,139,715	$2,331,333
Additional cash spent			
GST/HST paid out (input tax)	$ 0	$ 0	$ 0
GST/HST payments	$ 0	$ 0	$ 0
Principal repayment of current borrowing	$ 134,121	$ 150,000	$ 170,000
Other liabilities principal repayment	$ 120,000	$ 130,000	$ 140,000
Fixed liabilities principal repayment	$ 0	$ 0	$ 0
Purchase other current assets	$ 0	$ 0	$ 0
Purchase fixed assets	$ 0	$ 0	$ 0
Dividends	$ 0	$ 0	$ 0
Subtotal cash spent	$2,489,294	$2,419,715	$2,641,333
Net cash flow	$ 316,775	$ 164,065	$ 15,383
Cash balance	$ 656,775	$ 492,710	$ 477,327

Projected Balance Sheet

Pro forma balance sheet	FY 2009	FY 2010	FY 2011
Assets			
Current assets			
Cash	$ 656,775	$ 492,710	$ 477,327
Accounts receivable	$ 88,164	$ 102,514	$ 116,564
Stock	$ 20,000	$ 20,000	$ 20,000
Other current assets	$ 100,000	$ 100,000	$ 100,000
Total current assets	**$ 864,939**	**$ 715,224**	**$ 713,891**
Fixed assets			
Fixed assets	$ 100,000	$ 100,000	$ 100,000
Accumulated depreciation	$ 18,673	$ 45,673	$ 80,673
Total fixed assets	**$ 81,328**	**$ 54,328**	**$ 19,328**
Total assets	**$ 946,266**	**$ 769,551**	**$ 733,218**
Liabilities and capital			
Current liabilities			
Accounts payable	$ 135,049	$ 145,821	$ 158,976
Current borrowing	$1,739,879	$1,889,879	$2,119,879
Other current liabilities	$ 120,000	$ 250,000	$ 390,000
Subtotal current liabilities	$ 1,754,928	$1,785,701	$1,888,855
Fixed liabilities	$ 1,000,000	$ 1,000,000	$ 1,000,000
Total liabilities	**$2,754,928**	**$2,785,701**	**$2,888,855**
Paid-in capital	$ 440,000	$ 440,000	$ 440,000
Retained earnings	$1,674,000	$2,248,662	$2,456,149
Earnings	$ 574,662	$ 207,488	$ 139,488
Total capital	**$1,808,662**	**$2,016,149**	**$2,155,637**
Total liabilities and capital	**$ 946,266**	**$ 769,551**	**$ 733,218**
Net worth	$ 1,808,662	$ 2,016,149	$ 2,155,637

Furniture Resale Shop

St. Patrick Furniture Supply

BEGIN New Venture Center
St. Patrick Center
St. Louis, Missouri 63101

Elliot Smith

St. Patrick Furniture Supply is a social enterprise dedicated to furniture resale. Our mission is to provide a retail outlet for repaired and refinished furniture as well as new furniture pieces to the St. Louis area, while offering homeless and impoverished individuals a unique career path leading to sustainable employment opportunities.

EXECUTIVE SUMMARY

St. Patrick Furniture Supply is a social enterprise dedicated to furniture resale. Our mission is to provide a retail outlet for repaired and refinished furniture as well as new furniture pieces to the St. Louis area while offering homeless and impoverished individuals a unique career path leading to sustainable employment opportunities. St. Patrick Furniture Supply is a venture of a non–profit group for the homeless (St. Patrick Center) located in downtown St. Louis.

St. Patrick Furniture Supply's customer base is anticipated to include high–end consumers seeking to acquire newly–refinished furniture products, for whom a social value premium approximating 20% may be expected. We will also market to price–conscious customers for whom a discount to retail would be acceptable and clients who will receive, at no cost, lower–end yet functional pieces not otherwise suitable for sale.

We will employ current St. Patrick Center clients and provide them with expert training and supervision in all aspects of furniture resale. Employees will also learn the skills necessary to succeed in a professional work environment, and will be assisted by a case manager/job coach throughout the process, with the objective of securing a sustainable job opportunity following their time with St. Patrick Furniture Supply.

St. Patrick Furniture Supply is presently in its start–up stage. Our financial objectives include profitability within the first year of operations, and achieving above–average industry profit margins by year two. All profits will support the long–term financial sustainability of the non–profit organization. Our social value objectives include 80% placement and 70% 1–year retention of employees into higher–wage sustainable jobs after no more than two years of work at St. Patrick Furniture Supply.

Several areas of resale will be explored, all utilizing furniture pieces that have been refurbished or made by another, related organization, Furniture Restoration Business. Warehouse space will be utilized to house ready pieces, which will be sold through a number of different outlets, including: local antique dealers and other furniture outlets, flea markets, internet shopping forums, our own online store, and, eventually, a store–front retail location.

BUSINESS OVERVIEW

Market Analysis

Furniture resale is classified as part of the Used Merchandise Sales industry in major industry reports. A 2007 industry report indicates a used merchandise market in the U.S. comprising approximately 70 to 80 thousand firms with average yearly revenues of $10.6 billion during the last five years. The Census also indicates that the sale of used furniture, sleep equipment and outdoor/patio furniture amounted to 11.36 percent of industry sales. This would correspond, roughly, to a local market of $201 million in used merchandise sales and $22.9 million in used furniture sales annually.

For the St. Louis metropolitan area, the 2002 Census report indicates the presence of 152 establishments generating $63 million in revenues in the used merchandise industry, with an employee base of 1,086 and annual payroll of $14.2 million. General industry averages suggest a 2–3 percent profit margin for firms in this industry, with a larger margin potential for those firms who are able to acquire used goods through donations instead of purchases. A typical cost breakdown is shown below, from national industry averages:

Cost structure

Year: 2007

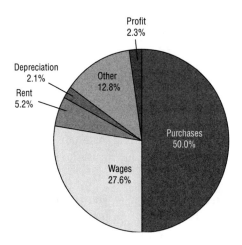

Mission

St. Patrick Furniture Supply will support the efforst of Furniture Restoration Business by providing retail outlets for the high-quality furniture pieces that they have repaired and refinished.

Company History

Because of the lack of a reliable life structure and a corresponding difficulty in fully assuming responsibility in a professional workplace, the homeless and impoverished population has a significant need for meaningful transitional jobs training. In fact, in an October 2006 employment report of the St. Louis area by the Public Policy Research Center, employers listed the top four employee shortcomings for the workforce at large as: a lack of positive attitude, a poor work ethic, poor customer service skills and poor communication skills. Development of these skills, along with marketable technical skills and a demonstrated work history through transitional jobs training, becomes especially critical to the long–term employment success of these clients.

St. Patrick Center (SPC) is a 25–year old social service agency, and the largest provider of homeless services in Missouri with 22 separate programs and housing for 13 social service and healthcare partner agencies. Collectively, SPC and its partners assist approximately 9,000 persons annually who are homeless or at risk of becoming homeless. They facilitate permanent, positive changes in people's lives through affordable housing, sound mental health, employment, and financial stability. Our clients are at the center of all decisions and we work with them in a holistic manner: honoring their dignity and human rights; listening to each individual; providing for emotional, physical, and spiritual needs; and creating an environment that encourages all to be the best they can be.

Located in downtown St. Louis, SPC and its partners are able to serve clients collaboratively in one building, providing services which range from emergency response to stabilization to employment to housing to mental health. This center is a national model for best practices in addressing homelessness, and SPC is recognized for its innovation and successful outcomes.

SPC had operating revenues of $11.4 million in 2007. Currently, unrestricted donations, government grants and other funding are each approximately one–third of total revenues. Within the latter category, SPC currently operates a number of social enterprises. Profits from these enterprises help sustain operating costs throughout the agency.

St. Patrick Furniture Supply is a new social enterprise initiative conceived through SPC. The concept originated in 2008 as a way to provide employment opportunities for SPC clients and to financially contribute to the long–term sustainability of SPC, a community partnership program incorporating a small business incubator, an education and training center, and a multipurpose conference center. In particular, St. Patrick Furniture Supply seeks to address the need for meaningful transitional jobs training for SPC clients, and the gap that exists in the furniture resale market, especially for a community–oriented, socially driven repair and refinishing services provider.

BUSINESS STRATEGY

St. Patrick Furniture Supply will seek out furniture donations and utilize the furniture repair and refinishing facilities of Furniture Restoration Business to salvage untenable furniture pieces. As the project's capacity grows, St. Patrick Furniture Supply will develop a furniture donation and acquisition process to source larger numbers of furniture for resale and expand into new market venues. St. Patrick Furniture Supply will actively engage local furniture outlets, antique shops, flea markets, and local internet forums in an effort to increase visibility for our used furniture products. Eventually, if demand is sufficient for our products, we may expand to our own retail location.

Growth Strategy

St. Patrick Furniture Supply will leverage St. Patrick Center's affiliation with Catholic Charities as a source for new business prospects and cultivate new relationships with vendors offering complimentary products and services. This could include furniture stores, storage companies, and housewares and construction materials retailers in the St. Louis area. These relationships will function as referral sources for new business.

St. Patrick Furniture Supply will also attempt to gain retail floor space with an initial pilot furniture shop partnership. Our intent is to mitigate the organization's lack of a retail store by building retail outlet partnerships to market our used and salvaged furniture products. Retailers will benefit from the public exposure generated by supporting social consciousness, community development, and environmental stewardship. They will also benefit materially by attaching an in–kind donation value to the retail space occupied by St. Patrick Furniture Supply's products in place of a lease. Besides yielding a significant donation tax deduction, furniture retailers might also find that an on–site used furniture option increases both foot traffic and sales of new furniture. Finally, we will also attempt to negotiate a commission percentage payable to the retailer if needed.

Educational partnerships will also be vital to success of the venture. The St. Louis University Service Leadership Certificate Program will function as a conduit for energetic and enthusiastic student volunteers committed to using their business acumen for social change. The venture might also benefit from continuing involvement with educational institutions. Students will be actively engaged in helping to run the business operations of the enterprise on a volunteer basis with support of St. Patrick Center staff.

OPERATIONS

Client Impact and Training

In keeping with the social goals of the enterprise and the mission of St. Patrick Center, St. Patrick Furniture Supply will commit to employing SPC clients for its staffing needs. Jack Hayden will oversee the supervision and training of client–employees through his capacity as manager of SPC's BEST program.

St. Patrick Furniture Supply will build on the integrated model employed by SPC's other social ventures. St. Patrick Furniture Supply will serve as an extension of SPC's current training and education programs offering clients an additional pathway to self–sufficiency. SPC's network of wrap–around social services provides a much–needed holistic approach to clients's unique needs. St. Patrick Furniture Supply will add an additional layer of soft skills training to that support network, providing clients who are ready, willing, and able a pathway to higher–paying sustainable work opportunities.

Management Summary

St. Patrick Furniture Supply will function as a distinct for–profit social venture under the umbrella of SPC and the direct support of BEGIN staff. The four SPC executive officers, the Director of BEGIN and the proposed St. Patrick Furniture Supply Manager are as follows:

- Dan Buck, Chief Executive Officer. Dan spent 18 very successful years in the broadcasting industry, during which he founded his own video production company that helped non–profit organizations across the country in their fundraising efforts. He subsequently made the choice to leave this career in order to dedicate his professional life to service, becoming the Chief Executive Officer of SPC on St. Patrick's Day of 2003. He is recognized as a national authority on issues facing the homeless and serves as a change–agent for ending chronic homelessness.

- Greg Vogelweid, Chief Operating Officer. Greg is a veteran of thirty years of experience in financial and operational functions. He has been with SPC since 1993. The Governor of Missouri appointed Greg to the Governor's Committee on Ending Chronic Homelessness in 2003. He was also appointed to the Restructuring Committee for the city's Homeless Network Board in 2005. Greg has consulted with numerous social service agencies on Best Practices for the administration and financial management of an agency.

- Jan Rasmussen, Chief Development Officer. Jan has more than 20 years of senior management and development experience, and started with SPC in 2000. Prior, she functioned in leadership, strategic planning, program development and team building roles for the American Red Cross and the St. Louis Science Center. Once at SPC, she established the Board of Trustees, an active group of leadership volunteers with two core programs: the Key Player Initiative (a high–profile fundraising program) and the Speakers Bureau. Jan was selected as the 2006 Outstanding Fundraising Executive by the Association of Fundraising Professionals.

- Elaine St. Clemens, Chief Program Officer. Elaine joined SPC in 2005 to provide leadership, oversight and strategic direction to the 22 programs providing supportive services to the homeless and those at risk of becoming homeless. For over 12 years, she has worked with organizations whose missions dealt with empowering underserved families and communities through comprehensive counseling, affordable housing, community advocacy and outreach programs. Elaine holds a Master's degree in Public Administration from Troy State University and a Bachelor of Arts in Urban Studies from the University of Tennessee.

- Jan DeYoung, Executive Director of Project BEGIN. Jan joined SPC in October 2007 after serving for seven years as Executive Director of the St. Louis County Economic Council's enterprise Centers Program, a network of four small business incubators which supported approximately 85 start-up companies.

- Jack Hyden, Manager of St. Patrick Furniture Supply. Jack has worked for SPC for several years as Assistant Coordinator for the BEST Program, which prepares and employs SPC clients for jobs in the janitorial, maintenance, and guard security sectors, while providing substance abuse counseling and general case management. Jack has extensive expertise in the restoration and construction of furniture and has worked with crew members in selling repair and refinishing services as well as the completed pieces on an informal basis for several years. Her experience and existing client base make him ideally suited to lead St. Patrick Furniture Supply general management and training operations. He will report to Mr. DeYoung, who will provide daily business management assistance.

MARKETING & SALES

St. Patrick Furniture Supply will increase visibility for Furniture Restoration Business's refurbished furniture products. As new products are designed and built, our business will market those products as well. Outlets for marketing and selling these items include the following, along with timelines for implementing them:

- Regular booths will be set up a local flea markets by September 1, 2009

- Items will be placed in local consignment shops by September 1, 2009

- Items notices will be placed on internet shopping sites by September 1, 2009

- Local furniture outlets will be engaged by February 1, 2010

- Partnerships with local antique shops will be complete by February 1, 2010

- Our own online store will be established by August 15, 2010

- Our own retail location will be open—TBD

An online store will experience greatest success when the business is better established and able to provide a steady supply of a given particular line of items.

Competition

There are a number of firms in the St. Louis area which offer similar resale services as those proposed by St. Patrick Furniture Supply. Furthermore, there is a large local market of second–hand sales. Despite significant competition and a volatile industry outlook, the social value inherent to St. Patrick Furniture Supply's activities and its association with St. Patrick Center provide a unique and compelling competitive advantage in the market.

Major Resale Competitors, from the 2007 IBIS Report:

"The total market for used merchandise is competitive; this has been aided by low barriers to entry, which in turn has intensified competition. Used merchandise retailers operate in a highly fragmented market with non–employers (self employed individuals, partnerships or businesses that have no paid employees) accounting between 70%–80% of the industry's total establishments in 2007."

"The industry's major players, Goodwill Industries, The Salvation Army, Cash America and EZCORP together are estimated to account between 15.0 percent–21.0 percent of the total industry revenue in 2007, which identifies this industry to have a low concentration level in the US. Recently the major players have also begun retailing used merchandise over the internet via their own websites."

There are a large number of independent small businesses dedicated to the sale of used furniture and other goods in the St. Louis metropolitan area. The local market is made up mostly of small businesses, although there are some major players to be considered.

Furniture Resale Competitors

Name	Location(s)	Activities/Services	Competitive advantage
Goodwill Industries	4140 Forest Park Ave St Louis, MO 63108 (314) 371-1296 *7 other locations in MO	• National franchise model • Sale of donated goods, inc. furniture • Proceeds go to job training/career placement services provided by agency	• National reach/brand equity • Multiple local locations • Reputation/expertise
Home Renew Forest Park	5617 Pershing Ave St Louis, MO 63112: (314) 367-3366	• Consignment store	• "Green reputation" • Conveniently located near complementary service providers
Salvation Army	3949 Forest Park Ave. St. Louis, MO 63108 (314) 535-0057	• Sale of donated furniture and other goods • Limited home pick-up service	• National reach/band equity • Multiple local locations
Online stores	Ebay.com Craigslist.com Backpage.com Locanto.com	• Forum for easy exchange of items between parties—both locally & nationally	• Accessibility to both individual & organizational vendors • National reach • Ease of use

Competitive Advantage

Costs

While St. Patrick Furniture Supply will provide many of the same services and benefits as its competitors, it will do so at a significant cost savings relative to traditional restoration services. Since St. Patrick Furniture Supply will carry a non–profit legal status under SPC, it will not be subject to the same tax liability as its competitors and will benefit from significantly reduced expenses through solicitation of in–kind and material donations. The venture will also benefit from lower labor costs relative to competitors. St. Patrick Furniture Supply's employees will be St. Patrick Center clients hired at minimum wage for the duration of their training. This transitional training will expand employment opportunities for SPC clients as they gain the soft skills necessary to transition to higher paying permanent employment. These cost savings will ultimately yield higher profit margins relative to the industry average and/or lower prices for customers.

Marketing Plan

Target Market

Prior to entering full operations, St. Patrick Furniture Supply seeks to engage in a "soft" marketing thrust that will target furniture owners involved with St. Patrick Center in various capacities, including employees, supporters, donors, and friends.

After this initial marketing step, St. Patrick Furniture Supply's customer base is anticipated to include high–end consumers seeking to acquire newly–refinished furniture products, for whom a social value premium approximating 20 percent may be expected. We will also market to price–conscious customers for whom a discount to retail would be acceptable and to SPC clients who will receive, at no cost, lower–end, yet functional, pieces not otherwise suitable for sale. The mechanisms through which we will tailor our services to each of those populations will develop during the various stages of the business as we evaluate the overall effect of the initial marketing methods described below.

Advertising

St. Patrick Furniture Supply will seek to brand itself as a unique provider of furniture resale services in the St. Louis area. We will showcase our commitment to building permanent, positive change in the lives of many homeless and impoverished individuals by offering them a transitional job training experience through which they can develop personal and professional skills and provide services of high quality to their community. St. Patrick Furniture Supply branding will be both unique and also consistent with current SPC brand identity.

The SPC Chief Development Officer, the SPC Director of Communications and the BEGIN Director will be directly involved in developing all branding for St. Patrick Furniture Supply, along with appropriate collateral material, media strategy to promote our services, and a SPC–consistent website. By the end of the first year of operations, the website is expected to include the online store featuring major products and services.

Internal staff–level discussions and conversations with members of the antique and furniture sales and restoration sector suggest that word of mouth is the most effective marketing device for service providers in this industry. To that end, our initial marketing efforts will seek to take advantage of several existing avenues of communication in order to cultivate a client base that can deeply benefit St. Patrick Furniture Supply in the short and long run through extensive word–of–mouth advertising.

First, we will seek to spread the news about our newly–inaugurated enterprise to all SPC donors and supporters through the Development and Communications departments at SPC. This has a considerable potential to attract customers who may request St. Patrick Furniture Supply's services as a new and innovative way of supporting SPC's mission. A more ambitious yet promising approach may seek the assistance of the Catholic Charities communications network as a larger venue through which we can contact new customers, including churches and other organizations who may decide to use our services in a larger scale.

In addition to direct and electronic mail communications, St. Patrick Furniture Supply will seek to market its services in two additional outlets during these first stages of operations. Selected pieces of donated or salvaged furniture that have been refinished through the enterprise will be made available for sale at consignment stores or local flea markets once or twice per month, in a similar fashion to the farmer's markets visits already being performed every weekend by SPC. Refinished, manufactured, or resale products for sale will also be posted in free online retail venues including Craigslist and Backpages, with a full description of St. Patrick Furniture Supply and SPC's work attached to every posting.

St. Patrick Furniture Supply will also seek to develop formal and informal relationships with various local businesses that provide services complimentary to those provided by our enterprise, such as furniture stores, and storage companies among others. As part of these relationships, partner businesses will give referrals about St. Patrick Furniture Supply to customers who inquire about furniture restoration and resale services. Their collaboration will be reciprocated in various capacities on an individual basis.

Finally, St. Patrick Furniture Supply will establish its own online store to promote its products. If this venture is successful, operations may expand into our own retail location.

FINANCIAL ANALYSIS

Conservative Financial Assumptions

Projected Sales—Furniture Resale

Furniture Social Enterprise (Conservative)
Projected Sales Forecast

Products and services	Assumptions	%	Jul	Aug	Sept	Oct	Nov	Dec
Furniture resale								
Price per unit	$120.00	100.00%						
Variable cost per unit	$ 24.00	20.00%						
Gross margin per unit	$ 96.00	80.00%						
Projected unit sales								
Seasonality factor			8.33%	8.33%	8.33%	8.33%	8.33%	8.33%
Year one			1	1	1	1	1	1
Year two growth	5.00%		1	1	1	1	1	1
Year three growth	5.00%		1	1	1	1	1	1
Fixed expense allocation	16.67%							
Projected revenue	$ 1,440							
Variable costs	288							
Gross margin	1,152							

Products and services	Assumptions	%	Jan	Feb	Mar	Apr	May	Jun	Totals
Furniture resale									
Price per unit	$120.00	100.00%							
Variable cost per unit	$ 24.00	20.00%							
Gross margin per unit	$ 96.00	80.00%							
Projected unit sales									
Seasonality factor			8.33%	8.33%	8.33%	8.33%	8.33%	8.33%	100.00%
Year one			1	1	1	1	1	1	12
Year two growth	5.00%		1	1	1	1	1	1	13
Year three growth	5.00%		1	1	1	1	1	1	13
Fixed expense allocation	16.67%								
Projected revenue	$ 1,440								
Variable costs	288								
Gross margin	1,152								

The total St. Louis area market for used furniture, sleep equipment, and outdoor/patio furniture is assumed to be roughly $7.3 million in revenues. This is calculated using total recorded revenues for the metro area in "used merchandise" ($63 million) and the percentage of national industry sales attributed to the above named product segment within the "used merchandise" category (11.36 percent) (U.S. Census). A .002 percent (1/50th of 1 percent) market penetration is assumed for year one with modest increases of 5 percent for each subsequent year. This is due to limited space capacity at SPC. The lease, purchase, or donation of additional warehousing and/or retail space would dramatically raise the level of projected sales in this category.

Net Income—Furniture Resale

**Retail Furniture Social Enterprise
(Conservative)
Year End Summary**

	Year one	Year two	Year three
Income	1,440	1,512	1,588
Costs of sales	288	302	318
Gross margin	1,152	1,210	1,270
Wage expense	72	76	79
Operating expense	288	302	318
Net income	792	832	873

Costs associated with furniture resale activities are based in small part on industry averages, but take into account the lack of a retail space and low–cost "virtual" nature of the proposed resale operations as well as the use of volunteers to market furniture. Purchasing costs are therefore estimated at 20 percent, wages at 5 percent, and operating expenses at 20 percent.

Aggressive Financial Assumptions

Projected Sales—Furniture Resale

**Furniture Social Enterprise (Aggressive)
Projected Sales Forecast**

Products and services	Assumptions	%	Jul	Aug	Sept	Oct	Nov	Dec
Furniture resale								
Price per unit	$ 120.00	100.00%						
Variable cost per unit	$ 12.00	10.00%						
Gross margin per unit	$ 108.00	90.00%						
Projected unit sales								
Seasonality factor			1.64%	3.28%	4.92%	4.92%	6.56%	6.56%
Year one			1	2	3	3	4	4
Year two growth	35.00%		1	3	4	4	5	5
Year three growth	35.00%		2	4	5	5	7	7
Fixed expense allocation	16.67%							
Projected revenue	$ 7,320							
Variable costs	732							
Gross margin	6,588							

Products and services	Assumptions	%	Jan	Feb	Mar	Apr	May	Jun	Totals
Furniture resale									
Price per unit	$ 120.00	100.00%							
Variable cost per unit	$ 12.00	10.00%							
Gross margin per unit	$ 108.00	90.00%							
Projected unit sales									
Seasonality factor			9.84%	9.84%	11.48%	13.11%	13.11%	14.75%	100.00%
Year one			6	6	7	8	8	9	61
Year two growth	35.00%		8	8	9	11	11	12	82
Year three growth	35.00%		11	11	13	15	15	16	111
Fixed expense allocation	16.67%								
Projected revenue	$ 7,320								
Variable costs	732								
Gross margin	6,588								

In this scenario, a .01 percent market penetration is assumed for year one with annual increases of 35 percent. This scenario takes into account significant numbers of used furniture being housed off–site through retail outlets or furniture store partnerships.

Net Income—Furniture Resale

**Retail Furniture Social Enterprise
(Aggressive)
Year End Summary**

	Year one	Year two	Year three
Income	7,320	9,882	13,341
Cost of sales	732	988	1,334
Gross margin	6,588	8,894	12,007
Wage expense	366	494	667
Operating expense	732	988	1,334
Net income	**5,480**	**7,412**	**10,006**

Furniture Restoration Company

Furniture Restoration Business

BEGIN New Venture Center
St. Patrick Center
St. Louis, Missouri 63101

Elliot Smith

Furniture Restoration Business is a social enterprise dedicated to furniture restoration. Our mission is to provide high–quality furniture repair and refinishing services to the St. Louis area while offering homeless and impoverished individuals a unique career path leading to sustainable employment opportunities. FRB is a venture of BEGIN, located on the fourth floor of the St. Patrick Center (SPC) facilities in downtown St. Louis.

EXECUTIVE SUMMARY

Furniture Restoration Business is a social enterprise dedicated to furniture restoration. Our mission is to provide high–quality furniture repair and refinishing services to the St. Louis area while offering homeless and impoverished individuals a unique career path leading to sustainable employment opportunities. FRB is a venture of BEGIN, located on the fourth floor of the St. Patrick Center (SPC) facilities in downtown St. Louis.

FRB will provide furniture restoration services for antique and used furniture. These will involve primarily the repair and restoration of wooden furniture based on the needs of customers and the capabilities of our staff and facilities. Our services will incorporate environmentally friendly and sustainable products and practices whenever possible. Our main offerings will include furniture repair, cleaning, stripping, refinishing, painting, staining, and polishing. We will also offer very limited reupholstery for wood pieces incorporating upholstered seating or backing.

FRB's customer base includes current furniture owners requesting restoration services. Data from the 2002 U.S. Economic Census indicates the presence of a local St. Louis market for furniture restoration services of at least $11 million in annual sales.

Compared to the majority of furniture restoration companies in the St. Louis area, FRB offers a unique opportunity for customers to receive a product of fine quality at a competitive price while supporting a focused effort to reengage the homeless and impoverished as agents of economic growth. Our competitive advantage lies in the social value we are able to create as a transitional jobs program without sacrificing the quality of our service.

We will employ current SPC clients and provide them with expert training and supervision in all aspects of furniture repair and refinishing. Employees will also learn the skills necessary to succeed in a professional work environment, and will be assisted by an SPC case manager/job coach throughout the process, with the objective of securing a sustainable job opportunity following their time with FRB. Backed by significant experience in the restoration and construction of furniture, our training coordinator will work directly with every employee to ensure that all services provided meet customer expectations.

Jack Hyden, Assistant Coordinator of SPC's BEST (Building Employment Skills for Tomorrow) Program, will be managing enterprise activities. Mr. Hyden has extensive expertise in furniture restoration and has been providing repair and refinishing services through the BEST Program on an informal basis for several years. He will also be in charge of developing and delivering all training to new employees. Mr. Hyden will continue to report to Nancy Box, but will coordinate all FRB activities with Jan DeYoung, Director of The BEGIN Center.

Mr. DeYoung has more than ten years of experience advising small businesses, most recently as the Director of the St. Louis County Economic Council's Enterprise Centers Program, a network of four small business incubators which supported approximately 85 start–up companies. In addition to coordinating all initial efforts to create FRB, Mr. DeYoung has overseen the development of the newly–inaugurated BEGIN New Venture Center business incubator, located adjacent to the FRB on the fourth floor of the SPC facilities.

FRB is presently in its start–up stage. The space currently being considered is the training and education space on the southeast corner of the fourth floor of the SPC facility. This space includes a large work area, an office and a storage room. The enterprise has already benefitted from a significant estate donation of woodworking equipment made by a private SPC contributor. Essential capital improvements to the existing space might include the creation of a refinishing/paint room with exhaust fan, an air purifying system, and a dust collection system.

Our financial objectives include profitability within the first year of operations, and achieving above–average industry profit margins by year two. All profits will support the long–term financial sustainability of The BEGIN Center and St. Patrick Center. Our social value objectives include 100% placement and 75% 1–year retention of employees into higher–wage sustainable jobs after no more than two years of work in FRB.

BUSINESS STRATEGY

Market Penetration

The proposed furniture social venture serves as an extension of activities already conducted by St. Patrick Center in the past. The BEST program Assistant Coordinator, Jack Hyden, has engaged St. Patrick Center clients in small refinishing projects for St. Patrick Center staff and facilities with great success and quality results in the past. Moreover, Jack brings years of both restoration and client management experience to the table. This venture will initially serve as an extension of his duties under the BEST program, and will involve a maximum 12 hours of his time on a weekly basis, essentially managing the furniture crew in a similar manner as the BEST crew, though with closer supervision.

In addition, the proposed social venture has benefitted from a generous donation (in excess of $25,000 in value) of industrial–grade tools and equipment more than suited to the types of restoration and repair activities outlined in this plan.

A Proven Model

The proposal outlined in this business plan was derived from exhaustive research performed on the area market, potential competitors, and similar ventures operating around the world within a social service context. In addition, many St. Louis area furniture business owners, antiques dealers, restoration crafts-men, internal stakeholders, and operators of similar furniture social ventures stretching across a dozen or more countries were consulted in development of this model. While this plan assumes an extremely modest commitment of agency resources, the potential for future growth is evidenced by the success of many other agencies (see *Existing Social Enterprises in the Furniture Restoration Industry*).

This plan assumes a commitment to two related activities initiated in phases: furniture repair and restoration and furniture manufacture of various items. The benefit of this model is that conducting a diversity of related activities broadens the pool of potential customers, partners, collaborators, and client participants. This further dilutes the amount of risk involved by allowing the market to dictate which niche St. Patrick Center can ultimately fill most efficiently, broadening the potential revenue stream, and adding to potential future growth.

Synergy with The BEGIN Center and St. Patrick Center

This social venture serves the interest of The BEGIN Center and St. Patrick Center by operating as a working example to both potential employer partners and incubator companies, by contributing to a valid work history for client participants, and by adding to the financial sustainability of St. Patrick Center.

Community Outreach and Media Opportunities

The proposed collaboration with area universities for operation of the venture (including St. Louis University's Service Leadership Certificate Program) presents a unique opportunity to add to the efficiency of the overall operation while simultaneously creating a golden opportunity for media coverage and a unique human interest story that touts both the social mission and innovative nature of St. Patrick Center.

BUSINESS OVERVIEW

Mission

FRB will provide high quality furniture repair and refinishing services to the St. Louis area while offering homeless and impoverished individuals a unique career path leading to living–wage, sustainable employ-ment opportunities.

Operations

Because of the lack of a reliable life structure and a corresponding difficulty in fully assuming responsi-bility in a professional workplace, the homeless and impoverished population served by St. Patrick Center (SPC) has a significant need for meaningful transitional jobs training. In fact, in an October 2006 employment report of the St. Louis area by the Public Policy Research Center, employers listed the top four employee shortcomings for the workforce at large as a lack of positive attitude, a poor work ethic, poor customer service skills and poor communication skills. Development of these skills, along with marketable technical skills and a demonstrated work history through transitional jobs training, becomes especially critical to the long–term employment success of SPC clients.

SPC is a 25–year old social service agency, and the largest provider of homeless services in Missouri with over 20 separate programs and 13 on–site social service and healthcare partner agencies. Collectively, SPC and its partners assist approximately 9,000 persons annually who are homeless or at risk of becoming homeless. SPC facilitates permanent, positive changes in their lives through affordable housing, sound mental health, employment, and financial stability. SPC clients are at the center of all decisions and are engaged in a holistic manner: honoring their dignity and human rights; listening to each individual; providing for emotional, physical, and spiritual needs; and creating an environment that encourages all to be the best they can be.

Located in downtown St. Louis, SPC and its partners are able to serve clients collaboratively in one building, providing services which range from emergency response to stabilization to employment to housing to mental health. This Partnership Center today is a national model for best practices in addressing homelessness, and SPC is recognized for its innovation and successful outcomes.

SPC had operating revenues of $11.4 million in 2007. Currently, unrestricted donations, government grants and other funding are each approximately one–third of total revenues. Within the latter category, SPC currently operates a number of social enterprises, including McMurphy's Grill, the City Seeds Urban Farm, and the BEST (Building Employment Skills for Tomorrow) Program. Profits from these enterprises help sustain operating costs throughout the agency.

FRB is a new social enterprise which would function as a component of The BEGIN Center. The concept originated in 2008 as a way to provide employment opportunities for SPC clients and to financially contribute to the long–term sustainability of SPC and The BEGIN Center, a community partnership program incorporating a small business incubator, an education and training center, and a multipurpose conference center. In particular, FRB seeks to address the need for meaningful transitional jobs training for SPC clients, and the gap that exists in the furniture restoration market for a community–oriented, socially driven repair and refinishing services provider.

FRB is presently in its start–up stage. The space currently being considered for operations is the training and education space on the southeast corner of the fourth floor of the SPC facility. This space includes a large work area, an office and a storage room. Essential capital improvements to the existing space will include an above–window exhaust fan and double doors for this room, an air purifying system and dust collection system for the woodworking portion of the work area, an air compressor, and 220 circuits run to the central columns. It is anticipated that some or all of these capital improvements will qualify for Missouri incubator tax credits.

In addition, the enterprise has already benefitted from a significant estate donation of woodworking equipment including hardware tools, cabinets, benches, and other materials. The donation was made by a private contributor identified by Leo Paradis, former SPC Executive Director. Identification and acquisition of necessary upgrades to this donated equipment will be a priority during the initial months of the enterprise based upon the overall scope of operations. New equipment additions may include a high quality band saw and wood lathe.

Whereas furniture repair and refinishing will be the initial focus of the enterprise, a potential early expansion may explore new furniture construction, particularly of unique product line offerings such as Adirondack–style chairs.

PRODUCTS & SERVICES

Furniture Repair and Refinishing

SPC's Furniture Restoration Business will provide furniture repair and refinishing services for antique and used furniture. In Phase I of the project, FRB will offer repair and restoration of wooden furniture based on the needs of customers and capabilities of our staff and facilities. These services will incorporate environmentally friendly and sustainable practices/products whenever possible. As part of our service, we will provide pickup and delivery upon request with pricing based on proximity to St. Patrick Center. We will also provide customers with a pricing estimate of the work to be done prior to commencement and engage customers from the very beginning to ensure customer satisfaction and set reasonable expectations. Our service offerings will include furniture repair, cleaning, stripping, refinishing, painting, staining, and polishing. We will also offer very limited reupholstery for wood pieces incorporating upholstered seating or backing. The following are example products which FRB might restore for customers:

Dining Room Sets

- Tables
- Chairs
- China cabinets
- Buffets
- Corner cabinets

Bedroom Sets

- Beds
- Dressers
- Chest of drawers
- Night stands
- Armoires

Kitchen/Dinette Sets

- Kitchen/dinette tables
- Kitchen chairs
- Kitchen cabinets

Furniture Manufacture

Phase II of the project will also include limited furniture manufacturing activities. This will begin with the initial production of Adirondack style chairs, outdoor patio furniture, and indoor novelty items. Furniture manufacture activities will include a limited amount of experimentation to gauge the tastes of consumers and serve as a base for future production. FRB will actively engage local furniture outlets, antique shops, flea markets, and local internet forums in an effort to increase visibility and market our furniture products.

GROWTH STRATEGY

FRB will leverage St Patrick Center's affiliation with Catholic Charities as a source for new business prospects and cultivate new relationships with vendors offering complimentary products and services.

This could include furniture stores, storage companies, and houseware and construction materials retailers in the St. Louis area. These relationships will function as referral sources for new business.

FRB will also attempt to gain retail floor space with an initial pilot furniture shop partnership. Our intent is to mitigate the organization's lack of a retail store by building retail outlet partnerships to market manufactured and salvaged furniture products. Retailers will benefit from the public exposure generated by supporting social consciousness, community development, and environmental stewardship. They will also benefit materially by attaching an in-kind donation value to the retail space occupied by FRB's products in place of a lease. Besides yielding a significant donation tax deduction, furniture retailers might also find that an onsite used furniture option increases both foot traffic and sales of new furniture. Finally, we will also attempt to negotiate a commission percentage payable to the retailer if needed.

Educational partnerships will also be vital to success of the venture. The Saint Louis University Service Leadership Certificate Program will function as a conduit for energetic and enthusiastic student volunteers committed to using their business acumen for social change. The venture might also benefit from continuing involvement with Washington University or other educational institutions. Students will be actively engaged in helping to run the business operations of the enterprise on a volunteer basis with support of St. Patrick Center staff.

ORGANIZATION

In keeping with the social goals of the enterprise and the mission of St. Patrick Center, FRB will commit to employing St. Patrick Center clients for its staffing needs. Jack Hyden will oversee the supervision and training of client–employees in furniture repair and refinishing through his capacity as Assistant Coordinator of SPC's BEST program.

FRB will build on the integrated model employed by SPC's other social ventures including McMurphy's Grill and the BEST program. FRB will serve as an extension of SPC's current training and education programs offering clients an additional pathway to self–sufficiency. St Patrick Center's network of wrap–around social services provides a much needed holistic approach to clients' unique needs. FRB will add an additional layer of soft skills training to that support network, providing clients who are ready, willing, and able a pathway to higher–paying sustainable work opportunities.

Significant Milestones

Milestone	Completion date
Phase I	
Development of a refinishing training schedule and plan	May 15, 2009
Identification of 1 or 2 client participants	June 10, 2009
Acquisition of initial refinishing training pieces	June 10, 2009
Initiate furniture refinishing for employees and offices	June 15, 2009
Phase II	
Development and implementation of marketing plan	July 15, 2009
Implement a furniture refinishing waiting list	December 15, 2009
Initiate furniture manufacture operations	December 15, 2009
Establish pilot retail furniture partnership	January 15, 2010

Phase I

A refinishing training and schedule plan will be an important component of a successful training program. Mr. Hyden will be in charge of ensuring that all client employees undergo an initial training on basic techniques before being allowed to work on any customer–submitted piece.

The process towards completion of facilities outfitting for the fourth floor will include all necessary capital investment considerations as well as a study of compliance with regulations and safety equipment. This will be a key component of initial operations.

Client participants will be current participants of the BEST Program, selected by Mr. Hyden based on an appraisal of the candidate's willingness and potential to succeed in this program.

Please refer to the *Marketing & Sales* section below for details on the donation acquisition and startup operations process.

Phase II
Please refer to the *Marketing & Sales* section below for details on marketing and advertising.

By the end of calendar year 2010, we will attempt to reach a volume of operations to support a waiting list for future service orders. The creation of this list will therefore serve as a business performance measure.

Furniture manufacture operations will initially focus on wood–related household furniture such as Adirondack style chairs and patio furniture.

Years Two to Five
Following the first year of activity, FRB will seek continued growth focused on core strengths and competencies. Possible expansion/investment opportunities include the acquisition of new equipment, storage space, and a separate storefront location; increasing the number of trainers, client employees and their rate of circulation through the program; and concentrating a larger portion of operations towards a particular area (e.g. having a stronger focus on manufacturing new items), among others.

All decisions will be made following conversations between the FRB management staff, the proposed FRB board of advisors, The BEGIN Center Director and the SPC Executive Officers. Emphasis will be placed on how the proposed expansion or investment can serve the mission of FRB and SPC as well as increase the efficiency and self-sufficiency of the operations of both the enterprise and our agency.

COMPANY HISTORY

History of St. Patrick Center

SPC was founded in 1983 and celebrates its 25th anniversary in 2008. SPC is the largest provider of homeless services in Missouri, serving approximately 9,000 persons annually who are homeless or at risk of becoming homeless. Its more than twenty existing programs in the areas of emergency services, intake and assessment, stabilization, education, employment and housing are comprehensive and reflect the agency's goal of helping individuals and families move from homelessness to independence. Recognizing that the comprehensive nature of its mission requires partnership with other organizations, SPC has a long history of forming partnerships in order to supplement its own best practices. Among its network of community partners are thirteen partners with a physical presence within the existing SPC facility:

- Birthright Counseling, St. Louis
- BJC Behavioral Health
- Catholic Charities Housing Resource Center
- Criminal Justice Ministry of Society of St. Vincent de Paul
- Gateway Greening City Seeds Urban Farm
- Grace Hill Health Services
- Greater St. Louis Dental society
- Logan Chiropractic Clinic
- Missouri Career Works
- Missouri Department of Corrections

- Presbyterian Children's Services

- St. Louis Community College

- St. Louis Public Schools

FRB also rests on this essential component of partnership building and a holistic approach to serving both clients and customers.

MANAGEMENT SUMMARY

FRB will function as a distinct for–profit social venture under the umbrella of SPC and the direct support of The BEGIN Center staff. The four SPC executive officers, the Director of The BEGIN Center, and the proposed FRB Manager are as follows:

- Dan Buck, Chief Executive Officer: Dan spent 18 very successful years in the broadcasting industry, during which he founded his own video production company that helped non–profit organizations across the country in their fundraising efforts. He subsequently made the choice to leave this career in order to dedicate his professional life to service, becoming the Chief Executive Officer of SPC on St. Patrick's Day of 2003. He is recognized as a national authority on issues facing the homeless and serves as a change–agent for ending chronic homelessness.

- Greg Vogelweid, Chief Operating Officer: Greg is a veteran of thirty years of experience in financial and operational functions. He has been with SPC since 1993. The Governor of Missouri appointed Greg to the Governor's committee on Ending Chronic Homelessness in 2003. He was also appointed to the Restructuring Committee for the St. Louis city Homeless Network Board in 2005. Greg has consulted with numerous social service agencies on Best Practices for the administration and financial management of an agency.

- Jan Rasmussen, Chief Development Officer: Jan has more than 20 years of senior management and development experience, and started with SPC in 2000. Prior thereto, she functioned in leadership, strategic planning, program development and team building roles for the American Red Cross and the St. Louis Science Center. Once at SPC, she established the Board of Trustees, an active group of leadership volunteers with two core programs: the Key Player Initiative (a high–profile fundraising program) and the Speakers Bureau. Jan was selected as the 2006 Outstanding Fundraising Executive by the Association of Fundraising Professionals.

- Elaine St. Clemmons, Chief Program Officer: Elaine joined SPC in 2005 to provide leadership, oversight and strategic direction to the 22 SPC programs providing supportive services to the homeless and those at risk of becoming homeless. For over 12 years, she has worked with organizations whose missions dealt with empowering underserved families and communities through comprehensive counseling, affordable housing, and community advocacy and outreach programs. Elaine holds a Master's degree in Public Administration from Troy State University and a Bachelor of Arts in Urban Studies from the University of Tennessee.

- Jan DeYoung, Director of The BEGIN Center: Jan joined SPC in October 2007 after serving for seven years as Executive Director of the St. Louis County Economic Council's Enterprise Centers Program, a network of four small business incubators which supported approximately 85 start–up companies. He has been involved in structuring, launching and overseeing the ongoing operations of The BEGIN Center, including the creation of the BEGIN New Venture Center small business incubator. Jan works closely with each of the SPC executive officers and senior managers to ensure that The BEGIN Center functions cohesively and effectively within the comprehensive mission of SPC. He reports directly to Greg Vogelweid, SPC Chief Operating Officer, and serves as the primary champion of The BEGIN Center.

- Jack Hyden, Manager of FRB: Jack has worked for SPC for several years as Assistant Coordinator for the BEST (Building Employment Skills for Tomorrow) Program, which prepares and employs SPC clients for jobs in the janitorial, maintenance, and guard security sectors, while providing substance abuse counseling and general case management. Jack has extensive expertise in the restoration and construction of furniture and has worked with BEST Program crew members in selling repair and refinishing services on an informal basis for several years. His experience and existing client base make him ideally suited to lead FRB general management and training operations. Jack will oversee and engage in the furniture restoration process, and will work closely with client–employees to ensure that they are receiving all the assistance necessary and that all services meet consumer expectations. He will receive daily business management assistance from Mr. DeYoung.

Collaborative Partners

In order for FRB to succeed, it must be an enterprise endorsed by the local and regional community as a sound mechanism to help SPC's mission and to provide a service of finest quality for customers. Success will be based as well on FRB's ability to leverage the support of already–existing businesses in the furniture sector—to brand itself as a complement rather than a substitute for them and consequently make partners out of otherwise–competitors. Several of these partners will be asked to serve on a volunteer FRB advisory board that will contribute invaluable expertise and business acumen to our enterprise. This effort is already in steady progress; collaborations currently underway in support of FRB include the following:

- St. Louis Restoration: St. Louis Restoration is a 55–year–old family–owned local restoration and refinishing business. Mr. Derek Puleo, business manager, has expressed interest in getting involved with SPC as a charitable effort on behalf of his company. Collaboration could include on–site training and employment opportunities as well as retail space availability, among other possibilities.

- R–n–R Restoration: R–n–R Restoration is a local refinishing business operated by Mr. Randy Miles. Mr. Miles is an acquaintance of Mr. Hyden, and has already engaged in conversations with BEGIN staff concerning the feasibility of FRB's initiative. Mr. Miles has expressed willingness to continue to be available on this advising role at our request.

- A Light Above: A Light Above is an antique furniture and vintage lighting store located on Antique Row (Cherokee Street, St. Louis, MO). BEGIN staff visited the store and had a conversation with Mr. John Ottwell, owner and manager, as part of the feasibility study for FRB. Mr. Ottwell was supportive of the initiative and expressed willingness to collaborate on it in an advising role, as well as to consider offering employment opportunities to FRB's graduates.

- Browser's Welcome: Browsers Welcome is a successful refinishing, repair and re–upholstery business and entrepreneurship program in Columbus, Ohio, operated by formerly–homeless furniture craftsman Melvin Satterfield (described below). During a recent conference call with Mr. Satterfield; initiated by BEGIN for consulting and feasibility study purposes, Mr. Satterfield expressed enthusiasm for FRB's concept, and extended an offer to further collaborate with the initiative through continued advising and a self–funded speaking engagement at FRB/SPC's location at our request. Mr. Satterfield is to be a key partner for FRB, not only for his 45 years of expertise, but also for the close connection between his outstanding life story and the mission of SPC.

- Betel International: BEGIN staff has engaged in conversation with Ms. Naomi Tepper, co–operator of Betel America, (described below), and Mr. Nathan Marriot from Betel UK concerning FRB's concept. Along with several of the other international social ventures described above, Betel is expected to serve as an outside advisor–at–large for our enterprise.

MARKET ANALYSIS

Re–upholstery and Furniture Repair Industry

According to the 2002 U.S. Economic Census, Missouri's re–upholstery and furniture repair industry is comprised of 113 firms with an aggregate of over $17.3 million in annual revenue. The Economic Census also records 318 Missouri employees within the industry and over $6 million in industry–wide yearly payroll. In addition, there are close to 600 independent and informal providers within Missouri (without employees) with aggregate annual revenues of over $13 million. Listed below is a market share breakdown of the various industry segments (nationally).

Products and service segmentation

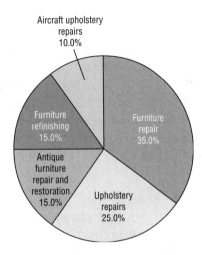

The Census also records approximately 46 St. Louis metro area firms with an employment base of 144 employees for 2006. St. Louis area payroll in this industry amounted to a total of over $3.5 million in 2006. There are at least 200 metro area independent providers (with no employees) with total annual receipts of over $5.2 million in 2005. This is in addition to the $6.4 million in St. Louis area revenues recorded for the industry. All of this translates into a local metro market of close to *$11 million in revenue annually*. General industry averages also suggest a three–four percent net profit margin potential for firms in this industry. An average cost structure is listed below for the industry nationally.

Cost structure

Year: 2004

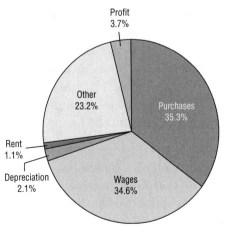

Barriers to entry in this industry are quite low. The industry is dominated by highly fragmented, local firms and independent providers. While barriers to entry might be low, the industry as a whole is currently in a state of contraction. According to the latest IBIS Industry Report, this industry is in the decline stage of its life cycle as observed by the following:

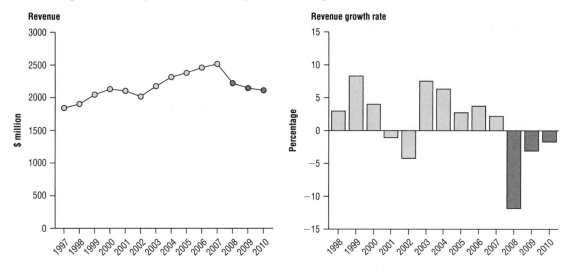

While industry trends seem to present a challenging market environment, there is still a significant (though declining) demand for furniture repair and refinishing services and there are many profitable players in the St. Louis metro area.

Furniture Manufacturing Industry

The industry–specific category for which the U.S. Census records data and which most closely aligns with manufacturing activities proposed in the business plan is **Nonupholstered Wood Household Furniture Manufacturing**. In the St. Metro Area, the Census records 20 formal firms that are operating with close to 1000 employees and $81 million in revenues in this manufacturing category. St. Louis Metro Area data is not available for non–employer firms. The non–employer market is the most relevant to the activities proposed by this plan, as any furniture manufacturing done by St. Patrick Center clients will more closely align with a craftsman or hobbyist market than a capital–intensive production level firm. In light of this, it should be noted that any data used in financial projections are based solely on data collected for larger firms with employees.

Products and service segmentation

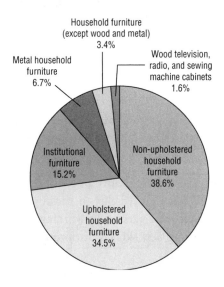

Existing Social Enterprises in the Furniture Restoration Industry

The following are excerpts from descriptions of several existing social enterprises in the furniture restoration industry nationally and internationally.

Furniture REHA—Odyssey House Louisiana (New Orleans, LA): "Furniture REHAB is a furniture restoration and rehabilitation business, restoring antiques and damaged furniture items. However, Furniture REHAB is truly unique from other furniture businesses in a very distinct way. The individuals restoring the furniture items are residents of Odyssey House's residential substance abuse treatment program, and are in the process of addiction recovery.

All participants are trained by a professional carpenter in all aspects of furniture repair and refinishing. Furniture REHAB displays one–of–a–kind, handcrafted furniture items and antiques, as well as eclectic and original art pieces available for resale to the community."

Project ReNEW—Acadiana Outreach Center (Lafayette, LA): "ReNEW is a social enterprise program designed to empower poor and homeless individuals to rebuild their lives to self–sufficiency, by teaching marketable vocational skills, such as carpentry and construction, through the production of artistic functional furniture made from reclaimed hurricane debris and salvaged building materials.

While clients are actively learning employable skills, their self–confidence, self–respect and sense of dignity increase, making them feel prod and important for the work they are doing."

Browsers Welcome (Columbus, OH): "Browsers Welcome is a highly rated refinishing, repair and re–upholstery business and entrepreneurship program in Columbus, Ohio, operated by formerly homeless furniture craftsman Melvin Satterfield. Participants, mostly young men aged 15–18, attend classes every Saturday where they learn how to refinish and repair furniture.

Six former students are now full–time employees. Browsers Welcome also partners with a local nonprofit to help participants buy new clothes, enroll in school and find employment."

(Recently featured in the front page article of Angie's List Magazine)

Caroline Center Upholstery (Baltimore, MD): "Caroline Center Upholstery is a retail upholstery shop providing services and upholstery fabric sales to residential and commercial customers in the Baltimore metropolitan region. We offer quality workmanship, competitive pricing and turnaround times as well as training and employment of Baltimore City women.

Caroline Center Upholstery began in 2001 as an upholstery training program with a retired master upholsterer and five women. The program has grown over the years and transformed itself into a production shop as well as a training program. Over 25 women have participated in the program since 2001.ÿ Some of them elect to stay on as employees after their training has been completed, while others go on to jobs with other upholsterers in the area or even start their own business. All earned income is used to support all the training programs of Caroline Center."

Good Day Workshop (Ottawa, ON, Canada): "Good Day Workshop Programs Inc. welcomes people who are unemployed because of problems related to addiction, homelessness, mental or physical disability, and teaches them to repair and refinish furniture.

The Program provides a productive and supportive work experience, skills training and social contact for men and women. It enables men and women who are unemployed due to various disabilities to become more holistically healthy, happy and potentially employable persons by working and socializing with peers staff and customers, and by sharing old and learning new skills of furniture refinishing and repair, upholstery and caning."

Betel Furniture (New York, NY; several locations, UK): "Betel Furniture is one of the charitable businesses run by Betel International, a nonprofit community dedicated to restoring homeless and substance dependent people to productive, independent lifestyles. Furniture resale and refinishing services fund approximately 90 percent of Betel's operations worldwide. They currently operate 13 businesses across Europe and North America providing varying degrees of furniture refinishing, restoration, or donation–resale based on cultural preference and local capacity and expertise."

Furniture Resource Center (Liverpool, UK): "The Furniture Resource Centre Group (FRC) is a major social business enterprise which provides low–income households with furniture to enable them to create homes for themselves and their families. Through its varied activities, the Group creates work for some 120 people annually and offers salaried training to long–term unemployed individuals."

COMPETITION

Competitive Landscape

There are a number of firms in the St. Louis area which offer similar restoration services as those proposed by FRB. Furthermore, there is a large local market of independent restoration providers, informal hobbyists, and second–hand sales. Despite significant competition and a volatile industry outlook, the social value inherent to FRB's activities and its association with St. Patrick Center provide a unique and compelling competitive advantage in the market.

The restoration and refinishing market is dominated by many small businesses and informal second–hand transactions. Below is a sampling of some major competitors and their respective strengths.

Furniture Restoration/Repair Competitors

Name	Location(s)	Activities/Services	Competitive advantage
St. Louis Restoration	1831 South Kingshwy, St. Louis, MO 63110	• Antique restoration • Residential and commercial restoration and repair • Large-volume refinishing/repair capability • Pickup/delivery	• (Limited) on-site service • Reputation/expertise • History (since 1950's)
Furniture Medic	4919 Chapel Hill Rd. St. Louis, MO 2022 Grecian Way Court, St. Louis, MO	• National franchise • Residential and commercial services • Specialization in on-site repairs • Enhancement, refinishing, repair, and restoration • Pickup/delivery	• National reach/brand equity • On-site service • Multiple local locations • On-site inspections • Mobile stripping technology
Zollinger Furniture	4821 Fairview Ave., St. Louis, MO 63116	• Refinishing & high-end antique restoration • Custom furniture manufacture	• Custom furniture • History (since 1893) • Expertise/quality of work
Ray's Furniture Restoration	3409 Roger Place St. Louis, MO 63116	• Residential and commercial • Repair, refinishing, and antique restoration • Pickup/delivery • (Limited) custom furniture and hand carvings	• (Limited) custom furniture • Expansion to onsite repairs • (Limited) upholstery servicing • On-site inspections

Competitive Advantage

Costs

While FRB will provide many of the same services and benefits as its competitors, it will do so at a significant cost savings relative to traditional restoration services. Since FRB will carry a non–profit legal status under St. Patrick Center, it will not be subject to the same tax liability as its competitors and will benefit from significantly reduced expenses through solicitation of in–kind and material donations. The venture will also benefit from lower labor costs relative to competitors. FRB's employees will be St. Patrick Center clients hired at minimum wage for the duration of their training. This transitional training will expand employment opportunities for SPC clients as they gain the soft skills necessary to transition to higher paying permanent employment. Since FRB will be housed on the fourth floor of the Partnership Center and will solicit furniture retail space through local partners, capital costs for the enterprise will be minimal relative to the competition. These cost savings will ultimately yield higher profit margins relative to the industry average and/or lower prices for customers.

Brand Equity

The St. Louis Metro Area is home to a number of well–established restoration firms with some degree of name recognition. Firms such as Furniture Medic command national recognition, while others such as Zollinger Furniture benefit from a long local history. St. Patrick Center holds its own unique name recognition within the community which FRB can capitalize on. Customers attuned to the mission of St. Patrick Center may be expected to pay a significant social value premium of at least 20 percent to market. This will of course require significant product positioning, branding, and tagging of finished furniture items.

Servicing

Finally, it is anticipated that the most challenging aspect of the enterprise will be service delivery. Word–of–mouth advertising will be crucial to the early success of the venture so service quality will be critical to the operation. FRB is a new entrant to the industry and works with underserved and inexperienced employees. Training and supervision must be of the utmost quality to successfully compete against established firms with experienced staff. FRB will also follow strict criteria for projects accepted and place great emphasis on customer service in order to manage expectations and deliver a quality product.

MARKETING & SALES

Target Market

Prior to entering full operations, FRB seeks to engage in a "soft" marketing thrust that will target furniture owners involved with St. Patrick Center in various capacities, including employees, supporters, donors, and friends. They will be offered the opportunity to provide the initial restoration service requests for their own furniture and to donate used furniture pieces that will help launch FRB' activities.

After this initial marketing step, FRB's customer base is anticipated to include current furniture owners requesting restoration services but also high–end consumers seeking to acquire newly–refinished furniture products, for whom a social value premium of at least twenty percent to market may be expected.

Branding and Promotion

FRB will seek to brand itself as a unique provider of furniture restoration services in the St. Louis area. We will showcase our commitment to building permanent, positive change in the lives of many homeless and impoverished individuals by offering them a transitional jobs training experience through which they can develop personal and professional skills and provide services of high quality and good craftsmanship to their community. FRB branding will be both unique and also consistent with current SPC brand identity.

The SPC Chief Development Officer, the SPC Sr. Director of Communications, and Director of The BEGIN Center will be directly involved in developing all branding for FRB, along with appropriate collateral material, media strategy to promote our services, and an SPC–consistent website.

Internal staff–level discussions and conversations with members of the antique and furniture sales and restoration sector suggest that word of mouth is the most effective marketing device for service providers in this industry. To that end, our initial marketing efforts will seek to take advantage of several existing avenues of communication in order to cultivate a client base that can deeply benefit FRB in the short and long run through extensive word–of–mouth advertising.

First, we will seek to spread the news about our newly–inaugurated enterprise to all SPC donors and supporters through the Development and Communications departments at SPC. This has a considerable potential to attract customers who may request FRB's services as a new and innovative way of supporting SPC's mission. A more ambitious yet promising approach may seek the assistance of the Catholic Charities communications network as a larger venue through which we can contact new customers, including churches and other organizations who may decide to request our services in a larger scale.

In addition to direct and electronic mail communications, FRB will seek to market its services in two additional outlets during these first stages of operations. Selected pieces of manufactured furniture will be made available for sale at consignment stores or local flea markets once or twice per month, in a similar fashion to the farmer's markets visits already being performed every weekend by SPC's City Seeds urban farm program. Refinished or manufactured products for sale will also be posted in free online retail venues including Craigslist and Backpages, with a full description of FRB and SPC's work attached to every posting.

Lastly, during the first three months of operation FRB will seek to develop formal and informal relationships with various local businesses that provide services complimentary to those provided by our enterprise, such as furniture stores, storage companies, and houseware and construction materials retailers, among others. As part of these relationships, partner businesses will give referrals about FRB to customers who inquire about furniture restoration services. Their collaboration will be reciprocated in various capacities on an individual basis.

Product Design

Every piece of furniture serviced through FRB will be tagged with a company seal containing the FRB logo, meant to remain permanently visible on the wood surface after leaving our location. In addition, every piece will contain a removable tag with information about SPC including brief background information on at least one SPC client who worked on that particular unit.

FINANCIAL ANALYSIS

Key Financial Assumptions

Labor

This plan assumes crews of two to four client employees (similar to a BEST Program crew), working four–hour shifts three times per week—24–48 labor hours/week. This schedule is meant to accommodate the time constraints of the current BEST Assistant Coordinator, Jack Hyden, in accordance with his regular duties. Proper scheduling will allow for a maximum of 12 hours per week devoted on the part of Jack Hyden to supervised production. Labor costs are assumed to be variable and based on units of production. Labor costs associated with any volunteer help from St. Louis University Service Leadership program or other sources will be negligible as no salary will be paid.

Note that both conservative and aggressive scenarios assume wage costs attributable to the enterprise. These costs may be mitigated (especially during start–up) by extending the BEST Program wages to encompass work performed for the furniture enterprise.

Start–up, Fixed, and Operating Expenses

This plan uses input from industry averages, experienced furniture professionals, and Jack Hyden as a baseline for calculating expenses. It is assumed that various basic fixed expenses such as rent, utilities, and equipment expense will be greatly reduced due to the housing of the venture within St. Patrick Center and a significant equipment donation. It is further assumed that startup expenses will be negligible and can be phased in along with sales. All expenses are therefore recorded as variable expenses.

Capital Expenses

Capital improvement expenses are not yet added into either financial scenario. Capital improvements to the existing space under consideration are: an above–window exhaust fan, double doors with window and vent, an air purifying system and dust collection system for the woodworking portion of the work area, an air compressor, and 220 circuits run to the columns. A copy of the proposed activities involved with the social venture, including materials and proposed capital improvements, was given to Fire Marshall Charles Coyle, who expressed tentative support for the proposal.

Notes on Method and Calculation

The base unit used to calculate projected sales and expenses in both scenarios is a low–to–mid tier refinished or manufactured table piece valued at $200 and $150 respectively. As such, sales projections in either scenario may well be conservative considering there is a potential for higher mark–ups based on quality or social value premium.

Conservative Financial Assumptions

Projected Sales—Refinishing

This scenario assumes a modest sales projection of 4 units per month for the first year with subsequent increases of 2 per month in each of the following two years. The total St. Louis Metro Area market for the Re–upholstery and Furniture Repair Industry approximates $11 million in annual sales (U.S. Census Bureau). It is assumed that for purposes of the refinishing component of this enterprise, the total market is further reduced to the "Furniture Refinishing" and "Antique Furniture Repair and Restoration" market segments (IBISWorld Industry Reports). This translates into a total St. Louis Metro Area market size of $3.3 million for refinishing related activities. The projected sales of $9,600 in Year One and $19,200 by Year Three correspond to a modest 0.3% and 0.6% market penetration, respectively.

Projected Sales—Furniture Manufacture

This scenario assumes a modest sales projection of 2 units per month (starting in month 6) with subsequent increases of 2 units per month in years two and three. The total St. Louis Metro Area market for Non–Upholstered Wood Household Furniture is $81 million (U.S. Census Bureau). The market for those items marketed to end–users approximates $2.7 million (IBISWorld Industry Reports) and pro-jected sales of manufactured items translates into a negligible market penetration. The projected sales of $1,800 in Year One and $10,800 by Year Three correspond to a modest .1% and .4% of market penetration, respectively.

Furniture Social Enterprise (Conservative)
Projected Sales Forecast

Products and services	Assumptions	%	Jul	Aug	Sept	Oct	Nov	Dec
Refinishing services								
Price per unit	$ 200.00	100.00%						
Variable cost per unit	$ 30.00	15.00%						
Gross margin per unit	$ 170.00	85.00%						
Projected unit sales								
Seasonality factor			8.33%	8.33%	8.33%	8.33%	8.33%	8.33%
Year one			4	4	4	4	4	4
Year two growth			6	6	6	6	6	6
Year three growth			8	8	8	8	8	8
Projected revenue	$ 9,600							
Variable costs	1,440							
Gross margin	8,160							
Fixed expenses	—							
Profit	8,160	85.00%						
Breakeven sales revenue	$							
Breakeven sales units	—							
Furniture manufacture								
Price per unit	$ 150.00	100.00%						
Variable cost per unit	$ 50.00	33.33%						
Gross margin per unit	$ 100.00	66.67%						
Projected unit sales								
Seasonality factor			0.00%	0.00%	0.00%	0.00%	0.00%	0.00%
Year one			—	—	—	—	—	—
Year two growth			4	4	4	4	4	4
Year three growth			6	6	6	6	6	6
Projected revenue	$ 1,800							
Variable costs	600							
Gross margin	1,200							
Fixed expenses	—							
Profit	1,200	66.67%						

Products and services	Assumptions	%	Jan	Feb	Mar	Apr	May	Jun	Totals
Refinishing services									
Price per unit	$ 200.00	100.00%							
Variable cost per unit	$ 30.00	15.00%							
Gross margin per unit	$ 170.00	85.00%							
Projected unit sales									
Seasonality factor			8.33%	8.33%	8.33%	8.33%	8.33%	8.33%	100.00%
Year one			4	4	4	4	4	4	48
Year two growth			6	6	6	6	6	6	72
Year three growth			8	8	8	8	8	8	96
Projected revenue	$ 9,600								
Variable costs	1,440								
Gross margin	8,160								
Fixed expenses	—								
Profit	8,160	85.00%							
Breakeven sales revenue	$								
Breakeven sales units	—								
Furniture manufacture									
Price per unit	$ 150.00	100.00%							
Variable cost per unit	$ 50.00	33.33%							
Gross margin per unit	$ 100.00	66.67%							
Projected unit sales									
Seasonality factor			16.67%	16.67%	16.67%	16.67%	16.67%	16.67%	100.00%
Year one			2	2	2	2	2	2	12
Year two growth			4	4	4	4	4	4	48
Year three growth			6	6	6	6	6	6	72
Projected revenue	$ 1,800								
Variable costs	600								
Gross margin	1,200								
Fixed expenses	—								
Profit	1,200	66.67%							

Expenses—Refinishing

Variable costs associated with refinishing activities are based on an analysis of recorded industry average cost structure (outlined on pg. 15) and input from refinishing experts including Jack Hyden and Randy Miles. This includes industry average purchases (35%), wages (34%), and other (23%). "Other" expenses are referred to as *operating expenses* and include freight and cartage, office supplies and services, telephone and postage, advertising, accounting and legal services, sub–contract and commission payments. Industry average wage expenses are $12.50 per hour (U.S. Census). With St. Patrick Center paying minimum wage of $6.65, it is assumed that wage expense will be significantly lower than the industry average, but that efficiency assumptions must also take into account the ongoing training of client participants that must occur. **This scenario assumes a conservative wage expense of 40% of revenues.** This figure is based both on a lower assumed wage and production time cited by Jack Hyden. It is further assumed that purchase costs will be significantly lower due to a lack of upholstery service offering and associated material costs. Jack Hyden and Randy Miles have cited a material cost of 10%–15% of revenue. **This scenario assumes a purchase expense of 15% of revenue and uses the industry average for operating expense (23%).**

Expenses—Furniture Manufacture

Costs associated with furniture manufacture activities are assumed based on industry averages and input from Jack Hyden. Purchases are assumed at 33% of revenue, wages at 53%, and operating expense at 8%. Industry average wage expense approximates 22%, however, Jack Hyden has cited a conservative wage expense of 53% (allowing for significant training time). While industry average purchases approximate 55%, this scenario (as well as the latter) assumes a significant amount of otherwise purchased items have been donated along with the tool donation and takes into account the use of reclaimed lumber in the manufacture process. Operating expense is cited using industry averages.

Furniture Social Enterprise (Conservative)
Projected Income Statement—Year One

	Jul	Aug	Sept	Oct	Nov	Dec	Jan	Feb	Mar	Apr	May	Jun	Totals
Income													
Refinishing services	800	800	800	800	800	800	800	800	800	800	800	800	9,600
Furniture manufacture	—	—	—	—	—	—	300	300	300	300	300	300	1,800
Total income	800	800	800	800	800	800	1,100	1,100	1,100	1,100	1,100	1,100	11,400
Cost of sales													
Refinishing services	120	120	120	120	120	120	120	120	120	120	120	120	1,440
Furniture manufacture	—	—	—	—	—	—	100	100	100	100	100	100	600
Total cost of sales	120	120	120	120	120	120	220	220	220	220	220	220	2,040
Gross margin	680	680	680	680	680	680	880	880	880	880	880	880	9,360
Wage expense													
Refinishing wage expense	320	320	320	320	320	320	320	320	320	320	320	320	3,840
Manufacture wage expense	—	—	—	—	—	—	159	159	159	159	159	159	954
Total wage expenses	320	320	320	320	320	320	479	479	479	479	479	479	4,794
Operating expense													
Refinishing services	184	184	184	184	184	184	184	184	184	184	184	184	2,208
Furniture manufacture	—	—	—	—	—	—	24	24	24	24	24	24	144
Total operating expenses	184	184	184	184	184	184	208	208	208	208	208	208	2,352
Net income	176	176	176	176	176	176	193	193	193	193	193	193	2,214

Aggressive Financial Assumptions

Projected Sales—Refinishing

Under this scenario, projected sales are assumed to be eight units per month for the first year with subsequent increases of four per month in each of the following two years. The projected sales of $19,200 in Year One and $28,800 by Year Three correspond to a modest 0.6% and 0.9% of market penetration, respectively.

Furniture Social Enterprise (Aggressive)
Projected Sales Forecast

Products and services	Assumptions	%	Jul	Aug	Sept	Oct	Nov	Dec
Refinishing services								
Price per unit	$ 200.00	100.00%						
Variable cost per unit	$ 20.00	10.00%						
Gross margin per unit	$ 180.00	90.00%						
Projected unit sales								
Seasonality factor			8.33%	8.33%	8.33%	8.33%	8.33%	8.33%
Year one			8	8	8	8	8	8
Year two growth			10	10	10	10	10	10
Year three growth			12	12	12	12	12	12
Projected revenue	$ 19,200							
Variable costs	1,920							
Gross margin	17,280							
Fixed expenses	—							
Profit	17,280	90.00%						
Breakeven sales revenue	—							
Breakeven sales units	—							
Furniture manufacture								
Price per unit	$ 150.00	100.00%						
Variable cost per unit	$ 50.00	33.33%						
Gross margin per unit	$ 100.00	66.67%						
Projected unit sales								
Seasonality factor			0.00%	0.00%	0.00%	0.00%	0.00%	0.00%
Year one			—	—	—	—	—	—
Year two growth			8	8	8	8	8	8
Year three growth			10	10	10	10	10	10
Projected revenue	$ 3,600							
Variable costs	1,200							
Gross margin	2,400							
Fixed expenses	—							
Profit	2,400	66.67%						

Products and services	Jan	Feb	Mar	Apr	May	Jun	Totals
Refinishing services							
Price per unit							
Variable cost per unit							
Gross margin per unit							
Projected unit sales							
Seasonality factor	8.33%	8.33%	8.33%	8.33%	8.33%	8.33%	100.00%
Year one	8	8	8	8	8	8	96
Year two growth	10	10	10	10	10	10	120
Year three growth	12	12	12	12	12	12	144
Projected revenue							
Variable costs							
Gross margin							
Fixed expenses							
Profit							
Breakeven sales revenue							
Breakeven sales units							
Furniture manufacture							
Price per unit							
Variable cost per unit							
Gross margin per unit							
Projected unit sales							
Seasonality factor	16.67%	16.67%	16.67%	16.67%	16.67%	16.67%	100.00%
Year one	4	4	4	4	4	4	24
Year two growth	8	8	8	8	8	8	96
Year three growth	10	10	10	10	10	10	120
Projected revenue							
Variable costs							
Gross margin							
Fixed expenses							
Profit							

Projected Sales—Furniture Manufacture

In this scenario, it is assumed that furniture manufacture activities will commence in the sixth month of operations. Under this scenario projected sales are assumed be four units per month for the first year, eight per month in year two, and ten per month in year three. The projected sales of $3,600 in Year One and $18,000 by Year Three correspond to a modest 0.1% and 0.7% market penetration, respectively.

Expenses—Refinishing

This scenario assumes a more aggressive 10% purchase expense and 20% wage expense as a percentage of revenue.

Expenses—Furniture Manufacture

This scenario assumes a more aggressive 26 percent wage expense as a percent of revenue.

Furniture Social Enterprise (Aggressive)
Projected Income Statement—Year One

	Jul	Aug	Sept	Oct	Nov	Dec	Jan	Feb	Mar	Apr	May	Jun	Totals
Income													
Refinishing services	1,600	1,600	1,600	1,600	1,600	1,600	1,600	1,600	1,600	1,600	1,600	1,600	19,200
Furniture manufacture	—	—	—	—	—	—	600	600	600	600	600	600	3,600
Total income	1,600	1,600	1,600	1,600	1,600	1,600	2,200	2,200	2,200	2,200	2,200	2,200	22,800
Cost of sales													
Refinishing services	160	160	160	160	160	160	160	160	160	160	160	160	1,920
Furniture manufacture	—	—	—	—	—	—	200	200	200	200	200	200	1,200
Total cost of sales	160	160	160	160	160	160	360	360	360	360	360	360	3,120
Gross margin	1,440	1,440	1,440	1,440	1,440	1,440	1,840	1,840	1,840	1,840	1,840	1,840	19,680
Wage expense													
Refinishing wage expense	320	320	320	320	320	320	320	320	320	320	320	320	3,840
Manufacture wage expense	—	—	—	—	—	—	156	156	156	156	156	156	936
Total wage expenses	320	320	320	320	320	320	476	476	476	476	476	476	4,776
Operating expense													
Refinishing services	368	368	368	368	368	368	368	368	368	368	368	368	4,416
Furniture manufacture	—	—	—	—	—	—	48	48	48	48	48	48	288
Total other expenses	368	368	368	368	368	368	416	416	416	416	416	416	4,704
Net income	752	752	752	752	752	752	948	948	948	948	948	948	10,200

Healthcare Marketing Agency

Johnson & Brooks LLC

4126 Sister Bay Ave.
Haddonfield, Illinois 61071

Paul Greenland

Johnson & Brooks is a full-service marketing agency specializing in the healthcare industry. In addition to traditional print, television, and radio advertising, the firm offers special capabilities in the areas of Internet and direct marketing, as well as consulting and strategic planning.

EXECUTIVE SUMMARY

Business Overview

Johnson & Brooks is a full-service marketing agency specializing in the healthcare industry. In addition to traditional print, television, and radio advertising, the firm offers special capabilities in the areas of Internet and direct marketing, as well as consulting and strategic planning.

In many communities throughout the United States, consumers are able to choose between multiple providers of healthcare services. For example, insurance plans often allow participants to choose between several local or regional healthcare systems, each of which may consist of one or more hospitals, networks of clinics that provide family medicine services, home health care agencies, and more.

Although most mid-sized and large healthcare systems employ staff who are dedicated to the disciplines of marketing and public relations, these organizations normally utilize outside marketing and advertising agencies for at least some of the work that they do.

Agencies like ours offer special expertise in areas such as competitive analysis, planning, strategic development, graphic design, and multimedia production. Some healthcare systems seek outside assistance in one or all of these areas.

INDUSTRY ANALYSIS

The healthcare industry is unique in many ways, especially when compared to the manufacturing and retail sectors. There are many specialized variables that healthcare marketers must deal with, including groups of independent doctors who provide services, executive teams that may include doctors and other clinical professionals, boards of directors consisting of local business leaders, government agencies that regulate the delivery of healthcare services, unions that may represent certain types of employees, multiple insurance companies that provide payment for services, as well as individuals with no insurance or limited insurance who require treatment for medical problems.

For these and other reasons, healthcare systems benefit when they employ agencies with experience in the healthcare industry, as opposed to agencies who are more accustomed to working with clients in other sectors.

During the late 2000s, the healthcare industry was filled with both challenge and opportunity. Dire economic conditions were putting additional financial pressure on hospitals and healthcare systems. Healthcare providers contended with higher costs for services and medical supplies, as well as falling levels of reimbursement from private health insurance companies.

As unemployment levels continued to rise, the number of individuals with private health insurance plans—which generally provide the best level of reimbursement—was falling. At the same time, the number of individuals covered by public health programs such as Medicaid and Medicare was increasing. While this was a challenge, it meant that the competition for healthcare consumers with private insurance was more cutthroat than ever. Therefore, healthcare marketing agencies with a proven track record of helping their healthcare provider clients acquire new patients had ample opportunity.

Specifically, great opportunity existed in the area of a new service and facility promotion. According to a construction spending forecast published in the January 1, 2009, issue of *Consulting-Specifying Engineer*, in 2008 healthcare ranked second among all industries for construction spending, second only to education. Spending totaled $45.7 billion that year, and was forecast to reach $46.1 billion in 2009. Specifically, spending among hospitals was forecast to remain steady at $31 billion in 2009.

MARKET ANALYSIS

Johnson & Brooks specializes in working with mid-sized community hospitals in the midwestern United States—namely those organizations located outside the limits of larger metropolitan markets. Specifically, the firm concentrates on working with healthcare systems with 100– to 250–bed hospitals, and operating revenues in the range of $150 million to $500 million.

According to the American Hospital Association's *Trendwatch Chart Book 2009*, some 4,897 community hospitals were in operation as of 2007. Of these, a total of 2,900 were located in urban areas, while 1,997 were located in rural areas. In addition, a total of 2,730 hospitals were part of a larger health care system.

In the Midwest, major metropolitan and suburban markets already include a number of established players within the healthcare marketing agency field. Although some of these agencies serve smaller and mid-sized hospitals and healthcare systems in outlying communities, the potential for new business within this niche remains very promising.

Examples of potential Johnson & Brooks clients, ranked by operating revenue, include:

1. Western Plains Regional Hospital L.L.C., Dodge City, Kan., $145 million
2. North Central Health Services Inc., Lafayette, Ind., $149 million
3. Jackson Purchase Medical Center, Mayfield, Ky., $269 million
4. Ingalls Health System Harvey, Ill., $312 million
5. Via Christi Regional Medical Center Inc., Wichita, Kan., $332 million

OPERATIONS

Personnel

Johnson & Brooks brings more than 35 years of healthcare marketing experience to its clients. The agency's founders, President and CEO Charlene Johnson and Chief Creative Officer Jonathan Brooks, both worked as healthcare marketing executives at large healthcare systems in extremely competitive and progressive markets.

President & CEO: Prior to co-founding Johnson & Brooks, Charlene Johnson worked for several hospitals and healthcare systems on the East Coast, last serving as chief marketing officer at Menley Memorial Healthcare System, where she oversaw a staff of 17 professionals responsible for marketing, strategic planning, public relations, and government relations. A native of Kansas City, Mo., Johnson earned a Masters of Business Administration from Northern Illinois University.

Chief Creative Officer: Jonathan Brooks spent most of his career on the West Coast, working almost exclusively in the Los Angeles area. Like Johnson, he worked for several area hospitals before being promoted to a higher ranking executive role at Freske Memorial Healthcare System, where he oversaw a 10-member staff responsible for marketing and media relations. A native of Cedar Rapids, Iowa, Brooks earned a Masters of Business Administration from the Yale School of Management at Yale University.

Creative Director: Our creative director is responsible for working with the account executive to develop breakthrough creative ideas for our clients. This person is tasked with learning about our customers' goals and objectives, translating them into innovative campaign concepts, and overseeing all of the players on our creative team as they translate concepts into reality. In addition, this position involves identifying and contracting with freelance talent, including writers, graphic designers, Web developers, programmers, videographers, printers, signage vendors, and parties involved in television production.

Account Executive: The account executive has several key responsibilities. In the area of new business development, he or she is responsible for approaching prospective clients and educating them about the services we provide. In addition, as the front-line contact with existing customers, this individual must be able to gain a quick understanding of client needs and connect them with the right individual or blend of services at our agency. In the interest of customer retention, the account executive regularly meets with our customers, in order to stay abreast on what their needs are, the challenges they are facing, and new projects that they may have on the horizon. He or she needs to be a "people person," who can effectively handle criticism and difficult situations, and build and maintain client relationships.

Business Manager: This individual is responsible for handling accounting and bookkeeping for the agency. In addition to maintaining the general ledger, the business manager prepares various financial reports and statements, maintains the agency's bank account, oversees accounts payable and receivable, and handles payroll functions.

Graphic Designers: Two full-time graphic designers are responsible for taking concepts developed by our clients or creative teams and turning them into reality. Using Macintosh computers, they are responsible for developing a wide range of print and electronic materials, including booklets, signage, brochures, postcards, fliers, promotional items, Web sites and more. In addition to performing page layout, designers also come up with brand identities for our clients, including logos, typefaces, and color schemes.

Copywriter: We employ one full-time copywriter who is an integral part of the creative team. This individual works in concert with the creative director, graphic designers, account manager, client, freelance writers, and others to develop attention-getting copy for advertising and promotional campaigns, as well as a wide range of print and electronic media.

Administrative Assistant: This critical front-line position serves as the hub of our agency. He or she is responsible for maintaining schedules, scheduling appointments and meetings, maintaining all electronic and paper files, making copies, ordering supplies and computer software, fielding telephone calls and e-mails, coordinating travel arrangements, assisting with projects, performing general research tasks, coordinating inbound and outgoing U.S. mail and overnight packages, and performing other duties as assigned.

Customers

Johnson & Brooks counts three healthcare organizations in the Midwest among its regular customer base. In addition, the firm performs projects on an as-needed basis for approximately 15 other hospitals and healthcare systems. Our primary customers include:

- Eagles Bluff Health System, Drummond, Ia.: A non-profit healthcare system that operates a community hospital, extended-care facility, and five primary care clinics.

- Desler HealthCare, Gentzel Park, Mich.: This non-profit system is comprised of a regional medical center, two acute-care hospitals, one long-term care facility, a home health agency, and a rehabilitation center.

- Troughton Lake Health Services, Bloomfield Park, Ill.: For-profit Troughton Lake Health operates four outpatient surgery centers throughout Illinois, as well as a bariatric hospital and a behavioral health facility.

SERVICES

Johnson & Brooks provides a wide range of advertising, marketing, and promotion services, including:

- Television advertising
- Radio advertising
- Print advertising
- Printed collateral
- Branding and corporate identity
- Interior and exterior signage
- Tradeshow exhibits
- Presentations
- Videography
- Web site development
- Social Media
- E-mail marketing

GROWTH STRATEGY

Johnson & Brooks believes in a philosophy of slow, measured growth. While we handle short-term projects for a variety of hospitals and healthcare systems, our objective is to add one client per year for whom we provide the majority of their outsourced marketing services.

In order to meet our objective, we will perform quarterly direct mailings to prospective clients that summarize our firm's capabilities. In addition, we also will mail these same prospective clients a quarterly newsletter that contains useful healthcare marketing tips, as well as case studies that outline successful projects we have worked on.

All of our direct marketing materials will direct prospects to our Web site, as well as to our CEO's blog, which provides an insider's perspective on healthcare marketing issues.

Building upon the aforementioned direct marketing efforts, our principals and the account executive will personally call upon key prospects in an effort to schedule Web conferences, conference calls, or in-person meetings where we can share our portfolio and discuss our capabilities.

Johnson & Brooks also is a member of The Society for Healthcare Strategy and Market Development. Consisting of 4,500 healthcare professionals, this organization hosts an annual conference each year that allows us to network with executives and vendors from points throughout the country. In addition, we are members of state associations such as the Illinois Society for Healthcare Marketing and Public Relations and the Wisconsin Healthcare Public Relations & Marketing Society, allowing us to stay visible with key hospitals and healthcare system executives throughout the Midwest.

FINANCIAL ANALYSIS

In 2008, Johnson & Brooks generated net income of approximately $1.3 million. A detailed breakdown can be seen in the following balance sheet, which covers the time period January 1, 2008 to December 31, 2008:

Income

Agency fees	$ 1,458,824
Consulting	$ 785,229
Public speaking	$ 15,487
Royalty income	$ 3,886
Total income	**$2,263,426**

Expenses

Salaries	$ 677,500
Utilities	$ 5,351
Rent	$ 56,220
Insurance	$ 19,854
401 K Contributions	$ 43,228
Office supplies	$ 15,403
Marketing & advertising	$ 23,478
Telecommunications & internet	$ 4,250
Professional development	$ 32,647
Travel & entertainment	$ 65,884
Subscriptions & dues	$ 1,544
Repairs & maintenance	$ 1,547
Taxes	$ 18,423
Total expenses	**$ 965,329**
Net income	$ 1,298,097

Based on our agency's analysis of the market, and factoring in current economic conditions, we are forecasting that our net income will grow at a compound annual rate of 3.5 percent for the next five years:

- 2000—$1,343,530

- 2010—$1,390,554

- 2011—$1,439,223

- 2012—$1,489,596

- 2013—$1,541,732

Low–Cost Home Decorating Service
Your Home Stylists

562 Palm Tree Dr.
Orlando, Florida 38201

Gerald Rekve

Your Home Stylists will work with homeowners to beautify their homes on a low budget.

EXECUTIVE SUMMARY

Your Home Stylists is in the interior design business. However, this being said, we will focus on the new trend of *Interior Re–Design*. The idea to this new trend is working with home owners to beautify their homes on a low budget.

Bonnie Bills is the owner and invested $20,000. She is also securing a loan of $65,000. While the economic conditions of 2008 were very difficult when this plan was being written, we feel that the long–term success of our business will be solid, based on our understanding of the market we are entering. Bonnie Bills has worked in the interior design business for over 15 years for three different firms, with the last firm being the largest. The position that Bonnie Bills held was Branch Manager, in charge of overseeing a staff of seven people.

Objectives

Your Home Stylists' main objective is to provide a low–cost home decorating service to the Orlando area. With the cost of interior designing going through the roof and factoring in the current economic conditions of the country and the home market, our objective is to not be another interior designer, but a re–designer. The definition of a re–designer is to take existing furniture and household items, and reposition them in the home to create a new look.

The major part of our objectives will be to educate our clients on the services we provide and how we can assist our client's requirements for interior designing on a small budget. This will be a key factor in our success.

Mission

Simply put, our mission is to provide a great quality service to the market we work in, or to be the best re–designer in our region. While doing this, we will work toward getting one referral for each client we provide our services to. This referral service will provide increased sales, while reducing our marketing expense.

Business Strategy
Keys to Our Success

- One stop shop for interior design services

- Low price point entry, resulting in larger market share

- Offer one more than all competitors for 20 percent less costs

- The housing market staying flat or less than 2 percent growth over the next 3 years

- Hiring qualified re–design staff

- Reaching market saturation rates that will result in securing a large client pool

BUSINESS OVERVIEW

Your Home Stylists will open as a limited liability company operating at 562 Palm Tree Dr., Orlando, Florida. The company will be operated by Bonnie Bills, who will own 100 percent of the company. She will invest $20,000 to start up the company in the early months of 2009.

Start–up Summary
While our start–up expenses are low, they are still considered a decent amount of investment. The owner, Bonnie Bills, will invest $20,000 into the start–up company.

Start-up requirements

Start-up expenses	
Legal	$ 2,500
Stationery etc.	$ 1,200
Insurance	$ 700
Rent	$ 400
Computer	$ 2,500
Advertising	$10,000
Auto expense	$ 700
Travel & entertainment	$ 1,500
Vehicle lease	$ 600
Total start-up expenses	**$20,100**
Start-up assets	
Cash required	$40,000
Other current assets	$ 5,000
Fixed assets	$ 5,000
Total assets	**$50,000**
Total requirements	**$70,100**

Services
These are the services that Your Home Stylists will provide its clients:

- Interior designs for retail and commercial clients

- Redesign services for the home owner

- Hiring contractors service, where we offer suggestions as to which contractor is best in the field

- General Contractor–type Management for home renovations, etc.

- Low cost due to low per hour rates

MARKET ANALYSIS

Market Segmentation

Our market segmentation is based on the assumption that the majority of our first year clients are going to be coming from the home owner segment. This being said, we will still have a focus on the realtor, as well as developer, sectors. The home owner sector has a shorter sales cycle, while the realtor and developer segments have a longer sales cycle.

The home owner sector we feel will be focused on the facts as indicated here. When in a market slowdown and recession, if people do spend money they spend it on improving their homes that they presently live in. People tend to not buy a new home. However, they do want to change their surroundings. This is primarily done by renovating their homes. But on a larger scale, some will simply hire an interior designer to change their home surroundings. These changes are always done on a very thin budget, anywhere from 5 percent to 15 percent of an actual cost of a total renovation of the same home.

These changes can be anything from moving furniture around, changing a few wall items (pictures), painting the room, to replacing carpet with a newer carpet type or with stone or tile. An average cost of a renovation can cost around $25,000, where the average cost of a home redesign is typically $1,500.

As you can see, the market segmentation as well as the market budget for a redesign can be extensive, therefore increasing the size of potential customers who will buy our services.

Target Market Segment Strategy

Target Market

- *Home Owners*: People just wanting to change their surroundings without spending a lot of money

- *Realtors*: People reselling an existing home, using our services to spruce up the home in order to increase the potential value

- *Developers*: People that are in charge of staging new units being built

Market analysis	Growth	2009	2010	2011	2012	2013	CAGR
Potential customers							
Home owners	15%	1,500	1,725	1,984	2,282	2,624	15.01%
Realtors	7%	450	482	516	552	591	7.05%
Developers	12%	55	62	69	77	86	11.82%
Total	**13.27%**	**2,005**	**2,269**	**2,569**	**2,911**	**3,301**	**13.27%**

Service Business Analysis

While there is a large list of interior designers in the market radius, we must point out that due to the market size, travel time to one location of the market to another can be an 80 minute one–way drive. Once our competitors are broken into regional market segments, there may only be seven or eight competitors that are considered direct competitors to the market in which we operate.

Our services will be more than just an interior design studio; we will also offer staging services as well as interior Re–Design, a new concept that has risen in the past two years.

All of our Interior Designers will be trained as well as certified. This will allow us to charge higher rates for clients looking for qualified designers.

COMPETITION

In the Interior Design business, customers choose the firm that they will hire to work in their home using some of the following factors:

- Image is gold—we need great looking yellow page ad, business cards, etc.

- Trade show booths—we must make sure ours is looking very professional.

- The staff attending the trade shows needs to be very knowledgeable; this is key because people buy knowledge in our business sector.

- Ongoing exposure with sustaining advertising campaigns.

- Happy clients who refer you to more clients; each client will give you a name of a friend if they are happy.

Competitive Edge

Our competitive edge will be the following: We will be the first in the market to offer all three services in one design house. Most interior designers do not offer Re–Design with their other services. They feel this will weaken their sales revenue and try to up–sell the client, rather than take the lower price Re–Design service.

Services Offered:

- *Re–Design*: About 70 percent of our business

- *Staging*: About 20 percent of our business

- *Interior Design*: About 10 percent of our business

MARKETING & SALES

Marketing Strategy

Our marketing strategy will be to position our company as a one stop shop for home design services. The one area we did not put in our business plan is an area where we are going to attempt to secure market share—home renovation business. While we will accept every job that comes to our business, we feel the bigger market for us will the Re–Design Market.

The life cycle for this Re–Design business is in the early stages. The Re–Design business is a relatively newer business. Traditionally it was done by the home owner. However, now the home owner feels that for an investment of anywhere from $500–$1,500, he can have a fresh new look in his home. This is the market we are going after.

We know this strategy is different than that of our competitors, and knowing the economy for 2009 will be difficult. Because of the economic state, there will be fewer $5,000–$10,000 interior design contracts. We will still go after this market; however we will put more focus on the lesser market of $500–$1,500.

Advertising

Our strategy will be to hit the ground running. We will have the Interior Designer staff hired two months prior to the new phonebook ad coming out and will run ads in local media to factor this in. We will tag TV ads on shows in our marketplace that focus on promoting our business.

Sales Forecast

When we put together our sales strategy, we did so using very conservative growth percentages. We also factored in the slowing economy in 2009 and 2010.

Sales forecast	2009	2010	2011
Unit sales			
Home owners—interior design	14,252	17,000	20,000
Realtor developer	15,724	16,000	19,000
Total unit sales	**29,976**	**33,000**	**39,000**
Unit prices			
Home owners—interior design	$ 15.00	$ 15.00	$ 15.00
Realtor developer	$ 12.00	$ 12.00	$ 12.00
Sales			
Home owners—interior design	$213,786	$255,000	$300,000
Realtor developer	$188,683	$192,000	$228,000
Total sales	**$402,469**	**$447,000**	**$528,000**
Direct unit costs			
Home owners—interior design	$ 1.50	$ 1.50	$ 1.50
Realtor developer	$ 1.20	$ 1.20	$ 1.20
Direct cost of sales			
Home owners—interior design	$ 21,379	$ 25,500	$ 30,000
Realtor developer	$ 18,868	$ 19,200	$ 22,800
Subtotal direct cost of sales	**$ 40,247**	**$ 44,700**	**$ 52,800**

MANAGEMENT SUMMARY

We will operate our business with the owner Bonnie Bills taking the General Manager role. Bonnie will hire a team of interior designers to meet the needs of the business.

Personnel Plan

Personnel plan	2009	2010	2011
General Manager	$ 34,022	$ 57,000	$ 67,000
Interior designer #1	$ 27,506	$ 36,000	$ 40,000
Interior designer #2	$ 22,123	$ 28,000	$ 33,000
Interior designer #3	$ 17,128	$ 24,000	$ 27,000
Total people	**4**	**4**	**4**
Total payroll	**$100,780**	**$145,000**	**$167,000**

FINANCIAL ANALYSIS

Start–up Funding

The owner will invest $20,000 in the company. The company will borrow am additional $65,000 to help fund the purchase of equipment and general operating expenses. Additionally, the company will have a line of credit with suppliers for $5,000 and an additional $5,000 for operating expenses.

Start-up funding

Start-up expenses to fund	**$20,100**
Start-up assets to fund	**$50,000**
Total funding required	**$70,100**
Assets	
Non-cash assets from start-up	$10,000
Cash requirements from start-up	$40,000
Additional cash raised	$ 4,900
Cash balance on starting date	$44,900
Total assets	**$54,900**
Liabilities and capital	
Liabilities	
Current borrowing	$65,000
Fixed liabilities	$ 5,000
Accounts payable (outstanding bills)	$ 5,000
Other current liabilities	$ 0
Total liabilities	**$75,000**
Capital	
Planned investment	
Owner	$ 0
Investor	$ 0
Additional investment requirement	$ 0
Total planned investment	**$ 0**
Loss at start-up (start-up expenses)	**$20,100**
Total capital	**$20,100**
Total capital and liabilities	**$54,900**
Total funding	**$75,000**

Important Assumptions

It is important to assume that 2009 will be a difficult year for home sales and the renovations sectors. Both of these sectors will be slow to recover from the financial crisis of 2008 and the sub–prime mortgage debacle of 2006 through 2008.

We are assuming that our competitors who have been in our market for a long period of time are entrenched in their ways, and will not go after the Re–Design market that we will focus on.

Break–even Analysis

Break-even analysis

Monthly units break-even	1,882
Monthly revenue break-even	$ 25,272
Assumptions:	
Average per-unit revenue	$ 13.43
Average per-unit variable cost	$ 1.34
Estimated monthly fixed cost	$22,744.96

Projected Profit and Loss

For the year 2009, we are expecting a net profit of $48,075. For 2010–2011, this number is expected to be $23,065 and $34,657, respectively.

The end result will be a profit that will be turned back into the business to build equity and allow for cash flow issues in the future.

Pro forma profit and loss	2009	2010	2011
Sales	$ 402,469	$ 447,000	$528,000
Direct cost of sales	$ 40,247	$ 44,700	$ 52,800
Other sosts of sales	$ 13,604	$ 16,000	$ 20,000
Total cost of sales	**$ 53,851**	**$ 60,700**	**$ 72,800**
Gross margin	$ 348,617	$ 386,300	$455,200
Gross margin %	86.62%	86.42%	86.21%
Expenses			
Payroll	$ 100,780	$ 145,000	$167,000
Marketing/promotion	$ 6,154	$ 7,500	$ 8,500
Depreciation	$ 0	$ 0	$0
Rent	$ 9,502	$ 10,200	$ 11,000
Utilities	$ 5,758	$ 6,500	$ 7,500
Insurance	$ 2,590	$ 3,500	$ 4,000
Payroll taxes	$ 7,055	$ 10,150	$ 11,690
Sales commissions for designers	$ 94,228	$ 110,000	$130,000
Materials expenses	$ 10,222	$ 13,000	$ 15,000
Advertising	$ 14,576	$ 16,000	$ 17,000
Office expense	$ 5,722	$ 6,500	$ 7,000
Travel & auto expense	$ 16,355	$ 18,000	$ 20,000
Total operating expenses	**$ 272,940**	**$ 346,350**	**$398,690**
Profit before interest and taxes	$ 75,678	$ 39,950	$ 56,510
Interest expense	$ 6,489	$ 5,162	$ 3,612
Taxes incurred	$ 20,757	$ 10,436	$ 15,869
Net profit	$ 48,432	$ 24,351	$ 37,028
Net profit/sales	12.03%	5.45%	7.01%

Projected Cash Flow

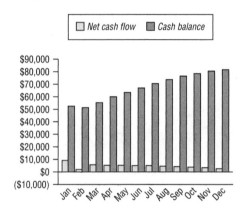

Pro forma cash flow	2009	2010	2011
Cash received			
Cash from operations			
Cash sales	$301,852	$335,250	$396,000
Cash from receivables	$ 78,769	$109,333	$127,603
Subtotal cash from operations	**$380,621**	**$444,583**	**$523,603**
Additional cash received			
GST/HST received (output tax)	$ 0	$ 0	$ 0
GST/HST repayments	$ 0	$ 0	$ 0
New current borrowing	$ 0	$ 0	$ 0
New other liabilities (interest-free)	$ 0	$ 0	$ 0
New fixed liabilities	$ 0	$ 0	$ 0
Sales of other current assets	$ 0	$ 0	$ 0
Sales of fixed assets	$ 0	$ 0	$ 0
New investment received	$ 0	$ 0	$ 0
Subtotal cash received	**$380,621**	**$444,583**	**$523,603**
Expenditures			
Expenditures from operations			
Cash spending	$100,780	$145,000	$167,000
Bill payments	$229,726	$274,901	$318,753
Subtotal spent on operations	**$330,505**	**$419,901**	**$485,753**
Additional cash spent			
GST/HST paid out (input tax)	$ 0	$ 0	$ 0
GST/HST payments	$ 0	$ 0	$ 0
Principal repayment of current borrowing	$ 11,376	$ 14,000	$ 17,000
Other liabilities principal repayment	$ 0	$ 0	$ 0
Fixed liabilities principal repayment	$ 0	$ 0	$ 0
Purchase other current assets	$ 0	$ 0	$ 0
Purchase fixed assets	$ 0	$ 0	$ 0
Dividends	$ 1,078	$ 1,500	$ 2,000
Subtotal cash spent	**$342,960**	**$435,401**	**$504,753**
Net cash flow	$ 37,661	$ 9,182	$ 18,850
Cash balance	$ 82,561	$ 91,743	$110,593

Projected Balance Sheet

Pro forma balance sheet	2009	2010	2011
Assets			
Current assets			
Cash	$ 82,561	$ 91,743	$110,593
Accounts receivable	$ 21,848	$ 24,265	$ 28,662
Other current assets	$ 5,000	$ 5,000	$ 5,000
Total current assets	**$109,409**	**$121,008**	**$144,255**
Fixed assets			
Fixed assets	$ 5,000	$ 5,000	$ 5,000
Accumulated depreciation	$ 0	$ 0	$ 0
Total fixed assets	**$ 5,000**	**$ 5,000**	**$ 5,000**
Total assets	**$114,409**	**$126,008**	**$149,255**
Liabilities and capital			
Current liabilities			
Accounts payable	$ 28,531	$ 31,279	$ 36,498
Current borrowing	$ 53,624	$ 39,624	$ 22,624
Other current liabilities	$ 0	$ 0	$ 0
Subtotal current liabilities	$ 82,155	$ 70,903	$ 59,121
Fixed liabilities	$ 5,000	$ 5,000	$ 5,000
Total liabilities	**$ 87,155**	**$ 75,903**	**$ 64,121**
Paid-in capital	$ 0	$ 0	$ 0
Retained earnings	$ 21,178	$ 25,754	$ 48,105
Earnings	$ 48,432	$ 24,351	$ 37,028
Total capital	**$ 27,254**	**$ 50,105**	**$ 85,134**
Total liabilities and capital	**$114,409**	**$126,008**	**$149,255**
Net worth	$ 27,254	$ 50,105	$ 85,134

Music Store

The Fret Board

6789 Main St.
Mt. Clemens, Michigan 48043

Heidi Denler

The Fret Board will provide friendly, knowledgeable, quality service to experienced and novice musicians through sales, repair, and instruction. The Fret Board will serve a growing market of new bands and established bands, as well as a base of novice musicians.

COMPANY SUMMARY

The Fret Board will be located in Mt. Clemens, Michigan, home to many budding musicians and bands. The area boasts many local and nationally known bands, and before MediaPlay in neighboring Clinton Township closed, shoppers often had the opportunity to meet and talk with members of Insane Clown Posse who liked to shop there. Other well-known area bands are Ethodius and F Street, both from Mt. Clemens, and Gun Shy from nearby St. Clair Shores. Uncle Kracker is often seen shopping locally, and Jack White of White Strips shops locally when he comes home for a visit. The Fret Board will serve a growing market of new bands and established bands, as well as a base of novice musicians.

MANAGEMENT SUMMARY

Three working partners, all of whom have music backgrounds, and one silent partner, who has business management experience, have joined forces to pool their individual talents to serve and promote the local music and band community. The Fret Board has been the dream of the co-owners, who have been friends since middle school.

Aaron Braid has been playing guitar since he was 7 years old, and started played percussion in elementary, middle, and high school band. He formed a band with classmates in middle school that stayed together through high school, playing local gigs. started his music career six years ago on guitar and quickly moved to drums. B was a member of the award-winning high school symphony and jazz bands, as well as Grace Community Church and IHOPE worship bands and various rock groups. He first became interested in rock in middle school, and has pursued that interest ever since.

Joe Waters began playing piano when he was 5, sang in school choral groups, performed in school dramatic productions, played string instruments in school orchestras, including pit orchestras for all school musicals. He began playing acoustic guitar while in middle school and moved to electric and bass guitars in high school. He began playing with Aaron Braid's band in middle school.

Walt Faraday started playing cello in 4th grade, and switched to double bass in 6th grade. In 7th grade at he joined the jazz band and continued to play in the high school jazz band. When not playing with the band he, Aaron Braid, and Joe Waters formed in middle school, he can be seen at local clubs, playing in a band with his brother, sister, his aunt, and his uncle. He became interested in composing rock music when he was in middle school. He was a member of several of his high school and college extracurricular musical ensembles, while continuing to play bass guitar with Aaron Braid and Joe Waters.

Aaron Braid's aunt, Hannah Braid, is the silent partner, providing 25 percent of the proposed start-up costs for The Fret Board. She earned an MBA and JD from the University of Michigan, and is providing legal support until the store is on solid footing, posting profits.

MISSION STATEMENT

The Fret Board will provide friendly, knowledgeable, quality service to experienced and novice musicians through sales, repair, and instruction.

BUSINESS PHILOSOPHY

The Fret Board will provide customer satisfaction through Service, Friendliness, Quality, and Knowledge.

GOALS AND OBJECTIVES

The management team and owners of The Fret Board have determined that they will build their customer base through friendly, high-quality service and instruction. Promotion and advertising will be low-key at the beginning, but as the store becomes successful and profitable, the partners will expand marketing to include advertising in local free and paid publications. They will promote The Fret Board by attending local rock concerts and playing at local clubs where they will distribute flyers with store location, services, hours, web site, and contact information.

A local band, such as Rockaholics or ICP, or individual performers, such as Kid Rock and Uncle Kracker, will perform at the store's Grand Opening and will be approached to come to the store any time they might be in town. At least once a month The Fret Board will invite local cover bands, garage bands, and aspiring musicians to play at regularly scheduled events. Those events will include special promotions on merchandise in stock (not on special orders or repairs).

Guitar and drum lessons will be available to customers. Prices will range from $15 to $25 per session. Each lesson will last between 30 and 45 minutes. Lessons will be taught by the partners, all of whom have experience as musicians, students, and teachers, as well as by local music teachers, who will be hired and paid on a per student basis. Support for lessons will be provided in the form of instruments, supplies, and music for purchase.

Instrument repair is expected to be a primary business function. The majority of repair work will be done onsite by the partners, all of whom have extensive experience in repair and maintenance of guitars and percussion instruments. However, the partners realize that some work might be beyond their scope and will offer shipping service to customers of The Fret Board.

Initially, the partners will staff the store and teach most of the lessons. The silent partner will manage the accounting and legal business of The Fret Board at a reduced cost until such time as the store becomes profitable. Within six to nine months, the partners plan to be in a financial position to hire staff for sales and as teachers. However, repair will be handled exclusively by the partners for the first several years of operation.

ORGANIZATION STRUCTURE

The three partners will share equally in the responsibility and profits of The Fret Board, with the understanding that profits will not be immediately forthcoming. For that reason, the partners are seeking a line of credit from their bank and the Small Business Association. There has been discussion about applying for grants to financially support music lessons.

The silent partner has agreed to seek profit-taking only after The Fret Board is on solid financial ground.

ADVERTISING AND PROMOTION

Initially, advertising and promotion will be word of mouth among fellow musicians, with neighborhood flyers and posters at local clubs, and through the store web site to build a strong customer base. Ads will be placed in alternative Detroit area newspapers, such as *Real Detroit* and *Metro Detroit*. Future plans include advertising in local newspapers, including *The Detroit News*, *The Detroit Free Press*, and *The Macomb Daily*, as well as in magazines popular with local rock musicians.

Press releases announcing the opening of the store and ensuing promotional events will be sent to all local print, radio, and television. Personal phone and e-mail follow-up will be made in an effort to build a relationship with area media personalities, which will result in free positive marketing and promotion.

CUSTOMER BASE

The main customer base for The Fret Board will be aging rockers in their forties and fifties who have been or are members of cover bands and local bands. Customers may be guitar techs, luthiers, music teachers, and even roadies, with a common interest in rock music. They will be able to come in to play display instruments or their own. The common bond among the customers will be an interest in playing or learning to play music.

Customers of The Fret Board will include students from local middle schools, high schools, and colleges, as well as members of professional and cover bands. Friends and family members will be able to access "wish lists" in order to purchase gifts.

The partners expect to broaden the customer base by word of mouth referrals from current friends and associates in the music business. Local bands will be encouraged to "Come Home to Shop" for their music needs.

Middle and high school students will be eligible for a 10 percent discount on purchases (excluding repairs and lessons) when they provide proof of music classes (vocal or instrumental, curricular or extra-curricular) from their schools.

PRODUCTS AND SERVICES

The Fret Board initially will be open Wednesday through Sunday from 11 AM to 9 PM. The store will be closed on Mondays and Tuesdays, but the partners take turns being available to assist customers dealing with emergencies, such as broken strings or repairs, that occur on the days that the store is closed for business.

Future plans call for The Fret Board to host private parties for local bands.

The Fret Board will offer a variety of guitars from entry level for the novice to professional band instruments. Special orders will be placed for high-end instruments, with after-sale service offered at no additional charge. Percussion instruments, keyboards, synthesizers, recording equipment, including but not limited to electric guitars, acoustic guitars, drums, soundboards, tablature, recording software, PA systems, and recording mikes.

Accessories available for customers will include music stands, guitar stands, straps, strings, capos, bottleneck and blues slides, pedals, amp cords, tuners, metronomes, tool kits for simple home repair, music books, and trade publications.

Services will include repair, lessons, special order instruments and parts. A monthly newsletter will be available in the store and online, and will be e-mailed to the customer base as well as to prospective customers and local clubs.

SUPPLIERS

Inventory will be purchased from Gibson, Fender, Dunlop, DigiTech, Boss, Vox, Roland, Wuhan, Tama, Mapex, Zildjian, Simmons, and Yamaha, among other leading brands of guitars, basses, drums, cymbals, and sound systems.

EQUIPMENT

The selling floor will have displays of instruments, accessories, and equipment that are attractive and easily accessible for customers to pick up and use. The partners of The Fret Board believe in "Try Before You Buy." There will be stands for publications and displays of sheet music and tablature. A bulletin board will be near the register/front door area where customers can advertise upcoming gigs.

In the future, customers will be able to trade in or trade up their current gear, which will be sold in a separate area of the store.

LOCATION

The four partners realize that location is important and are committed to opening their proposed retail music store in Mt. Clemens or nearby Clinton Township, Michigan. Aspiring and experienced rock bands are plentiful in both cities. Research in March 2009 has narrowed the search for a location to those two suburbs based on real estate analysis. In addition, The Fret Board would fill a gap in the rock band niche market since the closest similar shops are in Clawson, Royal Oak, Warren, and Roseville.

They have determined that buying a retail facility would be less expensive than leasing in the long run, which also underscores their desire and objective to serve the community for many years to come. In Mt. Clemens, commercial real estate prices range from $79,990 to $195,000, depending on location. A typical downtown retail store would cost between $139,900 and $174,900, with mortgage payments, including taxes and mortgage life insurance, running from $1,060.77 to $1,409.53 per month. The partners considered renting, but with square foot rentals priced between $10 and $20, buying a property makes better business sense.

STORE DESIGN

The store will have the main selling floor at the front with a workroom and office at the back, behind the register. The partners will share one large office. The sides of the store will have a minimum of four (4) soundproofed rooms for music lessons, and one larger room appropriate for a small band to test equipment or "jam." Any of the soundproofed rooms will also be available for testing keyboards, synthesizers, guitars and amps or drum sets. There will be a small display case with picks, strings, and other small supplies next to the register. The register will be a computer that has money management software for a small business installed. The computer in the store front will keep track of sales, repair, special orders, and inventory.

The computer in the store front will be networked with the computer in the office, which will hold the same information. The office computer will also have a password-protected program to keep track of payroll, employee benefits, taxes, and such business expenses as utility bills, mortgage and banking, and insurance.

The workroom will consist of two workbenches and be stocked with necessary tools, including Allen wrenches, wire cutters, copper wire, a soldering iron, interchangeable drills, wrenches, screwdrivers, and any other tools or grips necessary for instrument repair and tuning.

The instrument displays and bookcases for music on the selling floor will be easily movable for special events when local bands and musicians perform.

FINANCIAL

Start-up costs will include purchase of the building, furniture (display, chairs, desks, and workbenches), computers, tools, inventory, and any upgrade to floors and walls deemed necessary, along with the building of soundproof rooms for lessons. Two computers will be purchased, one for a cash register/inventory that will be located in the retail area of the store, and one for company business, including payroll and taxes, that will be in the office near the repair center. These costs will also include any fees for registration of the name and the business with all government authorities.

Overhead will include mortgage payments and taxes, payroll, payroll taxes, key man insurance, property insurance, inventory, telephone and utilities, an alarm system, advertising, wi-fi Internet access from AT&T, two (2) workbenches, and tools for repair.

PROFESSIONAL AND ADVISORY SUPPORT

The Fret Board's silent partner will provide legal and accounting advice and duties pro bono until the store is showing a solid profit. At that time, the silent partner will begin to charge for her services, using a sliding scale rather than a per hour charge, in the interest of maintaining profitability.

The partners will work with J. Denler and Seymour Gill Agency to provide optimal coverage for life, health, and dental insurance and retirement savings. Mr. Denler will work with a local property-casualty agency to cover insurance on the store and its inventory. Any staff hired will be offered low cost benefits at their own expense.

The Fret Board will be banking with Fifth Third, a bank with which three of the four partners established a working relationship while they were in high school. The branch manager and staff are looking forward to supporting The Fret Board with a mortgage and any business needs required by the partners as they build their business.

BUSINESS AND GROWTH STRATEGY

Strengths of the three working partners include their knowledge of music, instruments, bands, and teaching. Strengths of the silent partner include business acumen and legal expertise for running a small start-up business, which offsets the weakness of the working partners in that area. Within one to two years, the partners expect to pay for these services.

COMPETITION

Locally, the nearest competition is about five miles away. The Fret Board expects to fill a niche in Mt. Clemens by offering a place for musicians to play and perform, as well as talk about music and bands. No other music store within 20 miles provides those services. The Fret Board intends to be the place for hometown musicians to come when they need a local music "fix."

WEB SITE

The Fret Board plans an online presence with a store web site that will provide contact information, hours, and a map to the store location. The web site will also provide a list of instruments, supplies, and service offered by the store. However, no online orders will be taken because the partners share the philosophy that music should be shared, and they encourage their customers to come in prepared to "talk shop" with the owners, staff, and other customers.

CONCLUSION

Within two years, the four partners plan to realize their dreams of owning a profitable music store that caters to new and established rock bands. They have solid backing for management and finance, as well as combined decades of experience with music and musicians.

Natural Gas Home Filling Station Provider

Green Fuel Stations

61 Farm Hill Rd.
Spokane, Washington 99201

Gerald Rekve

Green Fuel Stations' business model is that of a company with total focus on the green revolution in automotive industry and transportation. With the greater need to save the environment, along with the need to operate transportation vehicles that are economical, we have developed a home filling station for natural gas automobiles.

EXECUTIVE SUMMARY

Green Fuel Stations' business model is that of a company with total focus on the green revolution in automotive industry and transportation. With the greater need to save the environment, along with the need to operate transportation vehicles that are economical, we have developed a home filling station for natural gas automobiles.

The design as well the concept of the home filling station will allow anyone who owns a vehicle that has been either converted to natural gas or is a hybrid developed by Honda or one of the automakers to fill their tanks at home.

With an investment of $1,277,500 we can roll out products in a timely fashion. We will also have the ability to repeat this production model in other plants around the world. The payback for the investment is based on market conditions—the length of the recession in the USA. We feel that the original investment will be paid back in five years with the caveat that investment in other markets may entice investors to reinvest their original investment into these markets.

OBJECTIVES

Green Fuel Stations' main objective is to provide a support solution to Honda's new natural gas car they have developed. We understand that Honda will focus on building and selling their cars, however we will focus on the infrastructure required to offer a successful backbone to this new form of fuel for automobiles.

While there will be a number of entrants into this field, we feel with our objective to be one of collaboration, we will be able to garner a larger percentage of market share than others.

Mission

Green Fuel Stations' mission is to be the leader in infrastructure support for the natural gas automobile being developed by Honda and other automakers.

BUSINESS OVERVIEW

Keys to Success

- Our ability to partner with Honda as a supplier of the Home Stations required to service their cars.

- Our ability to meet all the environmental standards set forth by states and provinces in which we operate.

- Our ability to garner financing for this new energy form for providing fuel for automobiles.

- The market's acceptance of this form of fuel for automobiles and the market's change from the oil forms used today to fuel cars.

Organization

Green Fuel Stations will be owned by Bradford Thove and other investors who will invest money into the company either through private equity investment or through share–offering on the stock market.

The company will operate as a limited liability company operating in Spokane, Washington. At conception, the company will be owned 100 percent by Bradford Thove. Equality in the company will be offered to investors in exchange for a percentage of the company and or profits.

Operations

Green Fuel Stations' start up will be one of development of the technology to allow for stations to be placed on homes, on garages and so on. With natural gas already used in the majority of homes in North America, it will be easy to add our packaged filling station to the homes.

We will first rent a facility that will be at least 10,000 square feet; this will allow for us to manufacture, as well as produce, the units that will be sold to the market. We have already signed agreements with several universities to help do the research and technology for the units we will be producing.

PRODUCTS

The products that Green Fuel Stations produces are natural gas filling stations for both home and commercial uses. We will also offer service for these units we sell. We will also deploy a network of service companies across North America. These services companies will operate independently of us; we will get a percentage of the revenues once the units have passed the warranty time period. We cover the units for normal repairs and maintenance.

MARKET ANALYSIS

There has been an increase in automobile usage in North America in the past fifty years. It has tripled in most categories. With our conversation kits we are developing along with the new cars coming onto the market we are very confident that even if we win a small percentage of the market we will be able to provide decent profit.

The first market segment we will target is the home market because, once these cars start rolling out, they will need fuel. Therefore the goal will be for us to have an agreement in place with the auto makers. When they sell a new car that is natural gas powered, they can sell the add–on package of our home–installed filling station for the car purchaser.

Market analysis	Growth	2009	2010	2011	2012	2013	CAGR
Potential customers							
Home retail market	10%	20,000,000	22,000,000	24,200,000	26,620,000	29,282,000	10.00%
Commercial market	10%	7,000,000	7,700,000	8,470,000	9,317,000	10,248,700	10.00%
Total	**10.00%**	**27,000,000**	**29,700,000**	**32,670,000**	**35,937,000**	**39,530,700**	**10.00%**

Our target market for the home is just like it states. The market includes anyone who buys a car that is fitted with the natural gas equipment, allowing the driver to fill up using natural gas. It also includes any person who buys a car that does not have the natural gas technology added to the fuelling of the car, because we will sell conversion kits allowing these buyers to use natural gas.

For the commercial market, it will be a little different. We will be selling them the stations for people to use. In some cases we will also sell to these commercial sellers the ability to sell our conversation kits and also have a filling station on site. These commercial sellers will also be able to sell the installation of the home stations.

US Hybrid Sales Down 6 Percent in July 2008

Reported US sales of hybrids in July dropped 6 percent year–on–year to 26,877 units, representing a new vehicle market share of 2.4 percent for the month. Through July, reported 2008 sales of hybrids in the US are down 1.6 percent, compared to the same period in 2007, representing a new vehicle market share for the first seven months of 2008 of 2.5 percent.

Total sales of light duty vehicles in the US dropped 13.2 percent in July, according to figures from Autodata. Through July, total light duty vehicle sales have declined 10.5 percent compared to the same period in 2007.

Toyota. Still challenged by availability, according to Toyota, the Prius posted 14,785 units sold in July, down 8 percent from July 2007. Camry Hybrid sales were down 38.9 percent to 2,645, representing 6.3 percent of all Camry sales, which increased 1.5 percent year–on–year. The Highlander Hybrid posted 1,371 units, up 13.8 percent from the year before, representing 20.3 percent of all Highlander sales. Total Highlander sales dropped 23.7 percent in the month.

The Lexus Rx 400h sold 1,439 units in July, up 3.9 percent from the year before, representing 20.3 percent of all Rx models sold. Sales of all Rx models dropped 15.6 percent in July.

The GS 450h sold 40 units, down 71.8 percent from the year before, representing 3.1 percent of all GX models sold. GX sales were down 42.3 percent in July. The high–end LS 600h sold 83 units, representing 5.7 percent of all LX models sold in the month.

Honda. Sales of the Civic Hybrid reached 3,440 units in July, up 38 percent from the year before, and representing 11.8 percent of all Civic models sold. Sales of all Civic models rose 4.6 percent in July. The Accord Hybrid sold 3 units, down 98.8 percent and representing 0.01 percent of all Accords sold. Sales of all Accord models rose 11.4 percent in the month.

Ford. Combined sales of the Escape and Mariner hybrids dropped 19.8 percent in the month to 1,265 units, representing 10.1 percent of the combined total model sales. Total sales of Escape and Mariner models dropped 16 percent in July.

General Motors. GM posted 351 units for its two–mode hybrid Tahoe and Yukon SUVs, representing 3.2 percent of their sales in July. The Saturn VUE Greenline hybrid with the BAS GM Hybrid System posted 362 units, for 6.7 percent of VUE sales. The Saturn Aura BAS hybrid sold 29 units, for 0.4 percent of total sales, and the Chevy Malibu BAS hybrid sold 349 units for 2.1 percent of all Malibu sales.

Nissan. Nissan sold 715 units of its Altima Hybrid, a 36.8 percent drop compared to last July, and representing 0.8 percent of all Altima sales for the month, which were down 0.1 percent compared to the year before.

MARKETING & SALES

Sales Strategy

Our sales strategy will be to place our commercial refill units in as many service stations in North America as possible. For the home units we will have to resell arrangements with the auto manufacturers, so every time they sell a vehicular driven with natural gas, they can up–sell the home filling station unit to the customer. We will also wholesale the units to a variety of retail chains across North America.

Sales Forecast

We anticipate sales in the first month of operation. This assumption is based on the condition that our prototype will be accepted in the market and we go to product with orders from the auto manufacturers for the products. We will also secure contracts for the placement of the units in the service stations.

MANAGEMENT SUMMARY

The management plan is shown below. We will have key positions filled as we go forward with our company and the required investment is placed in our company.

- CEO—Bradford Thove. Mr. Thove brings a considerable amount of management consulting experience to the business. Mr. Thove has been in the consulting business for over twenty years. In this time he has offered consulting advice to every sector in the business world, from small mom and pop businesses to large Fortune 500 businesses.

- CFO—TBD

- VP of Marketing—TBD

- VP of Manufacturing—TBD

- VP of Research & Development—TBD

- VP of Sales—TBD

- VP of Distribution—TBD

- VP of Channel Management—TBD

Personnel Plan

We will ramp up our product staff as we have our plant where we manufacture the natural gas units we sell. The staff will be added in four month increments.

We will hire staff from the local community college that trains automotive students, in all areas of automotive and agriculture related fields. Each year there is about four hundred students that graduate. These students are highly skilled and will be easy to train for our production lines.

We will offer signing bonuses to the new hires. After three months on the job for every student that stays with our company, the student will be paid a bonus check of 5 percent of their annual pay. This bonus will be paid out over the next nine months in equally divisible amounts.

Personnel plan	Feb	Mar	Apr	May	Jun	Jul
Management	$ 37,440	$ 37,440	$ 37,440	$ 37,440	$ 37,440	$ 37,440
Staff	$233,741	$233,741	$233,741	$233,741	$233,741	$233,741
Total people	**10**	**12**	**14**	**80**	**79**	**92**
Total payroll	**$271,181**	**$271,181**	**$271,181**	**$271,181**	**$271,181**	**$271,181**

Personnel plan	Aug	Sep	Oct	Nov	Dec	Jan
Management	$ 37,440	$ 37,440	$ 37,440	$ 37,440	$ 37,440	$ 37,440
Staff	$233,741	$233,741	$233,741	$233,741	$233,741	$233,741
Total people	**95**	**132**	**134**	**136**	**133**	**135**
Total payroll	**$271,181**	**$271,181**	**$271,181**	**$271,181**	**$271,181**	**$271,181**

FINANCIAL ANALYSIS

Start–up Funding

Start-up funding	
Start-up expenses to fund	$ 522,500
Start-up assets to fund	$ 755,000
Total funding required	**$1,277,500**
Assets	
Non-cash assets from start-up	$ 455,000
Cash requirements from start-up	$ 300,000
Additional cash raised	$1,472,500
Cash balance on starting date	$1,772,500
Total assets	**$2,227,500**
Liabilities and capital	
Liabilities	
Current borrowing	$1,000,000
Fixed liabilities	$1,500,000
Accounts payable (outstanding bills)	$ 50,000
Other current liabilities	$ 0
Total liabilities	**$2,550,000**
Capital	
Planned investment	
Owner	$ 100,000
Investor	$ 100,000
Additional investment requirement	$ 0
Total planned investment	**$ 200,000**
Loss at start-up (start-up expenses)	$ 522,500
Total capital	**$ 322,500**
Total capital and liabilities	**$2,227,500**
Total funding	**$2,750,000**

Sales Forecast

Monthly Sales Forecast

Sales forecast	GST/HST rate	Feb	Mar	Apr	May	Jun	Jul
Unit sales							
Home units	0.00%	345	359	373	388	404	420
Commercial units	0.00%	450	472	496	521	547	574
Total unit sales		**795**	**831**	**869**	**909**	**951**	**994**
Unit prices							
Home units		$ 990.00	$ 990.00	$ 990.00	$ 990.00	$ 990.00	$ 990.00
Commercial units		$ 2,300.00	$ 2,300.00	$ 2,300.00	$ 2,300.00	$ 2,300.00	$ 2,300.00
Sales							
Home units	7.00%	$ 341,847	$ 355,521	$ 369,742	$ 384,531	$ 399,913	$ 415,909
Commercial units	7.00%	$1,034,540	$1,086,267	$1,140,580	$1,197,609	$1,257,490	$1,320,364
Total sales		**$1,376,387**	**$1,441,788**	**$1,510,322**	**$1,582,141**	**$1,657,402**	**$1,736,273**
Direct unit costs							
Home units	27.00%	$ 267.30	$ 267.30	$ 267.30	$ 267.30	$ 267.30	$ 267.30
Commercial units	37.00%	$ 851.00	$ 851.00	$ 851.00	$ 851.00	$ 851.00	$ 851.00
Direct cost of sales							
Home units	7.00%	$ 92,299	$ 95,991	$ 99,830	$ 103,823	$ 107,976	$ 112,295
Commercial units	7.00%	$ 382,780	$ 401,919	$ 422,015	$ 443,115	$ 465,271	$ 488,535
Subtotal direct cost of sales		$ 475,078	$ 497,909	$ 521,845	$ 546,939	$ 573,248	$ 600,830

Sales forecast	GST/HST rate	Aug	Sep	Oct	Nov	Dec	Jan
Unit sales							
Home units	0.00%	437	454	473	491	511	532
Commercial units	0.00%	603	633	665	698	733	769
Total unit sales		**1,040**	**1,087**	**1,137**	**1,189**	**1,244**	**1,301**
Unit prices							
Home units		$ 990.00	$ 990.00	$ 990.00	$ 990.00	$ 990.00	$ 990.00
Commercial units		$ 2,300.00	$ 2,300.00	$ 2,300.00	$ 2,300.00	$ 2,300.00	$ 2,300.00
Sales							
Home units	7.00%	$ 432,546	$ 449,847	$ 467,841	$ 486,555	$ 506,017	$ 526,258
Commercial units	7.00%	$1,386,383	$1,455,702	$1,528,487	$1,604,911	$1,685,157	$1,769,414
Total sales		**$1,818,928**	**$1,905,549**	**$1,996,328**	**$2,091,466**	**$2,191,174**	**$2,295,672**
Direct unit costs							
Home units	27.00%	$ 267.30	$ 267.30	$ 267.30	$ 267.30	$ 267.30	$ 267.30
Commercial units	37.00%	$ 851.00	$ 851.00	$ 851.00	$ 851.00	$ 851.00	$ 851.00
Direct cost of sales							
Home units	7.00%	$ 116,787	$ 121,459	$ 126,317	$ 131,370	$ 136,625	$ 142,090
Commercial units	7.00%	$ 512,962	$ 538,610	$ 565,540	$ 593,817	$ 623,508	$ 654,683
Subtotal direct cost of sales		$ 629,749	$ 660,068	$ 691,857	$ 725,187	$ 760,133	$ 796,773

Yearly Sales Forecast

Sales forecast	FY 2010	FY 2011	FY 2012
Unit sales			
Home units	5,188	7,188	10,000
Commercial units	7,160	8,160	9,000
Total unit sales	**12,348**	**15,000**	**19,000**
Unit prices			
Home units	$ 990.00	$ 990.00	$ 990.00
Commercial units	$ 2,300.00	$ 2,300.00	$ 2,300.00
Sales			
Home units	$ 5,136,527	$ 6,930,000	$ 9,900,000
Commercial units	$ 16,466,904	$ 18,400,000	$ 20,700,000
Total sales	**$ 21,603,431**	**$ 25,330,000**	**$ 25,330,000**
Direct unit costs			
Home units	$ 267.30	$ 267.30	$ 267.30
Commercial units	$ 851.00	$ 851.00	$ 851.00
Direct cost of sales			
Home units	$ 1,386,862	$ 1,871,100	$ 2,673,100
Commercial units	$ 6,092,755	$ 6,808,000	$ 7,659,000
Subtotal direct cost of sales	$ 7,479,617	$ 8,679,100	$ 10,332,100

Profit and Loss Statement

Pro forma profit and loss	GST/HST Rate	Feb	Mar	Apr	May	Jun	Jul
Sales		$1,376,387	$1,441,788	$1,510,322	$1,582,141	$1,657,402	$1,736,273
Direct costs of goods		$ 475,078	$ 497,909	$ 521,845	$ 546,939	$ 573,248	$ 600,830
Other costs of goods	7.00%	$ 12,000	$ 12,000	$ 12,000	$ 14,280	$ 17,874	$ 12,000
Cost of goods sold		$ 487,078	$ 509,909	$ 533,845	$ 561,219	$ 591,122	$ 612,830
Gross margin		$ 889,309	$ 931,878	$ 976,477	$1,020,922	$1,066,281	$1,123,443
Gross margin %		64.61%	64.63%	64.65%	64.53%	64.33%	64.70%
Expenses							
Payroll		$ 271,181	$ 271,181	$ 271,181	$ 271,181	$ 271,181	$ 271,181
Marketing/promotion	7.00%	$ 14,152	$ 14,152	$ 14,152	$ 14,152	$ 14,152	$ 14,152
Depreciation		$ 1,920	$ 1,920	$ 1,920	$ 1,920	$ 1,920	$ 1,920
Rent	0.00%	$ 2,571	$ 2,571	$ 2,571	$ 2,571	$ 2,571	$ 2,571
Utilities	7.00%	$ 2,474	$ 2,474	$ 2,474	$ 2,474	$ 2,474	$ 2,474
Insurance	7.00%	$ 1,639	$ 1,639	$ 1,639	$ 1,639	$ 1,639	$ 1,639
Payroll taxes	7.00%	$ 18,983	$ 18,983	$ 18,983	$ 18,983	$ 18,983	$ 18,983
Other	7.00%	$ 0	$ 0	$ 0	$ 0	$ 0	$ 0
Total operating expenses		$ 312,919	$ 312,919	$ 312,919	$ 312,919	$ 312,919	$ 312,919
Profit before interest and taxes		$ 576,389	$ 618,959	$ 663,558	$ 708,002	$ 753,361	$ 810,524
Interest expense		$ 20,849	$ 20,864	$ 20,879	$ 20,895	$ 20,910	$ 20,925
Taxes incurred		$ 166,662	$ 179,429	$ 192,804	$ 206,132	$ 219,735	$ 236,880
Net profit		$ 388,878	$ 418,667	$ 449,875	$ 480,975	$ 512,716	$ 552,719
Net profit/sales		28.25%	29.04%	29.79%	30.40%	30.93%	31.83%

Pro forma profit and loss	GST/HST Rate	Aug	Sep	Oct	Nov	Dec	Jan
Sales		$1,818,928	$1,905,549	$1,996,328	$2,091,466	$2,191,174	$2,295,672
Direct costs of goods		$ 629,749	$ 660,068	$ 691,857	$ 725,187	$ 760,133	$ 796,773
Other costs of goods	7.00%	$ 17,244	$ 12,000	$ 15,130	$ 12,000	$ 18,714	$ 22,284
Cost of goods sold		$ 646,993	$ 672,068	$ 706,987	$ 737,187	$ 778,847	$ 819,057
Gross margin		$1,171,935	$1,233,481	$1,289,341	$1,354,279	$1,412,327	$1,476,615
Gross margin %		64.43%	64.73%	64.59%	64.75%	64.46%	64.32%
Expenses							
Payroll		$ 271,181	$ 271,181	$ 271,181	$ 271,181	$ 271,181	$ 271,181
Marketing/promotion	7.00%	$ 14,152	$ 14,152	$ 14,152	$ 14,152	$ 14,152	$ 14,152
Depreciation		$ 1,920	$ 1,920	$ 1,920	$ 1,920	$ 1,920	$ 1,920
Rent	0.00%	$ 2,571	$ 2,571	$ 2,571	$ 2,571	$ 2,571	$ 2,571
Utilities	7.00%	$ 2,474	$ 2,474	$ 2,474	$ 2,474	$ 2,474	$ 2,474
Insurance	7.00%	$ 1,639	$ 1,639	$ 1,639	$ 1,639	$ 1,639	$ 1,639
Payroll taxes	7.00%	$ 18,983	$ 18,983	$ 18,983	$ 18,983	$ 18,983	$ 18,983
Other	7.00%	$ 0	$ 0	$ 0	$ 0	$ 0	$ 0
Total operating expenses		$ 312,919	$ 312,919	$ 312,919	$ 312,919	$ 312,919	$ 312,919
Profit before interest and taxes		$ 859,016	$ 920,561	$ 976,421	$1,041,360	$1,099,408	$1,163,696
Interest expense		$ 20,941	$ 20,956	$ 20,971	$ 20,987	$ 21,002	$ 21,017
Taxes incurred		$ 251,423	$ 269,882	$ 286,635	$ 306,112	$ 323,522	$ 342,804
Net profit		$ 586,653	$ 629,724	$ 668,815	$ 714,261	$ 754,884	$ 799,875
Net profit/sales		32.25%	33.05%	33.50%	34.15%	34.45%	34.84%

Cash Flow Projections

Pro forma cash flow		Feb	Mar	Apr	May	Jun	Jul
Cash received							
Cash from operations							
Cash sales		$ 481,735	$ 504,626	$ 528,613	$ 553,749	$ 580,091	$ 607,696
Cash from receivables		$ 0	$ 29,822	$ 896,069	$ 938,647	$ 983,265	$1,030,022
Subtotal cash from operations		$ 481,735	$ 534,447	$1,424,681	$1,492,396	$1,563,356	$1,637,718
Additional cash received							
GST/HST received (output tax)		$ 0	$ 0	$ 0	$ 0	$ 0	$ 0
GST/HST repayments		$ 0	$ 0	$ 0	$ 0	$ 0	$ 0
New current borrowing		$ 3,095	$ 3,095	$ 3,095	$ 3,095	$ 3,095	$ 3,095
New other liabilities (interest-free)		$ 0	$ 0	$ 0	$ 0	$ 0	$ 0
New fixed liabilities		$ 0	$ 0	$ 0	$ 0	$ 0	$ 0
Sales of other current assets	7%	$ 0	$ 0	$ 0	$ 0	$ 0	$ 0
Sales of fixed assets	7%	$ 0	$ 0	$ 0	$ 0	$ 0	$ 0
New investment received		$ 0	$ 0	$ 0	$ 0	$ 0	$ 0
Subtotal cash received		$ 484,831	$ 537,543	$1,427,776	$1,495,491	$1,566,451	$1,640,813
Expenditures							
Expenditures from operations							
Cash spending		$ 271,181	$ 271,181	$ 271,181	$ 271,181	$ 271,181	$ 271,181
Bill payments		$ 114,655	$1,902,272	$ 819,868	$ 860,626	$ 904,919	$ 951,935
Subtotal spent on operations		$ 385,836	$2,173,453	$1,091,049	$1,131,807	$1,176,100	$1,223,116
Additional cash spent							
GST/HST paid out (Input tax)		$ 0	$ 0	$ 0	$ 0	$ 0	$ 0
GST/HST payments		$ 0	$ 0	$ 0	$ 0	$ 0	$ 0
Principal repayment of current borrowing		$ 1,256	$ 1,256	$ 1,256	$ 1,256	$ 1,256	$ 1,256
Other liabilities principal repayment		$ 0	$ 0	$ 0	$ 0	$ 0	$ 0
Fixed liabilities principal repayment		$ 0	$ 0	$ 0	$ 0	$ 0	$ 0
Purchase other current assets	7%	$ 0	$ 0	$ 0	$ 0	$ 0	$ 0
Purchase fixed assets	7%	$ 0	$ 0	$ 0	$ 0	$ 0	$ 0
Dividends		$ 0	$ 0	$ 0	$ 0	$ 0	$ 0
Subtotal cash spent		$ 387,092	$2,174,710	$1,092,305	$1,133,063	$1,177,356	$1,224,372
Net cash flow		$ 97,739	$1,637,167	$ 335,471	$ 362,428	$ 389,096	$ 416,441
Cash balance		$1,870,239	$ 233,072	$ 568,543	$ 930,971	$1,320,067	$1,736,508

Pro forma cash flow		Aug	Sep	Oct	Nov	Dec	Jan
Cash received							
Cash from operations							
Cash sales		$ 636,625	$ 666,942	$ 698,715	$ 732,013	$ 766,911	$ 803,485
Cash from receivables		$1,079,020	$1,130,369	$1,184,180	$1,240,574	$1,299,675	$1,361,613
Subtotal cash from operations		$1,715,645	$1,797,311	$1,882,895	$1,972,587	$2,066,585	$2,165,098
Additional cash received							
GST/HST received (output tax)		$ 0	$ 0	$ 0	$ 0	$ 0	$ 0
GST/HST repayments		$ 0	$ 0	$ 0	$ 0	$ 0	$ 0
New current borrowing		$ 3,095	$ 3,095	$ 3,095	$ 3,095	$ 3,095	$ 3,095
New other liabilities (interest-free)		$ 0	$ 0	$ 0	$ 0	$ 0	$ 0
New fixed liabilities		$ 0	$ 0	$ 0	$ 0	$ 0	$ 0
Sales of other current assets	7%	$ 0	$ 0	$ 0	$ 0	$ 0	$ 0
Sales of fixed assets	7%	$ 0	$ 0	$ 0	$ 0	$ 0	$ 0
New investment received		$ 0	$ 0	$ 0	$ 0	$ 0	$ 0
Subtotal cash received		$1,718,740	$1,800,406	$1,885,990	$1,975,682	$2,069,681	$2,168,194
Expenditures							
Expenditures from operations							
Cash spending		$ 271,181	$ 271,181	$ 271,181	$ 271,181	$ 271,181	$ 271,181
Bill payments		$ 994,959	$1,047,522	$1,095,553	$1,151,589	$1,206,224	$1,270,179
Subtotal spent on operations		$1,266,140	$1,318,703	$1,366,734	$1,422,770	$1,477,405	$1,541,360
Additional cash spent							
GST/HST paid out (Input tax)		$ 0	$ 0	$ 0	$ 0	$ 0	$ 0
GST/HST payments		$ 0	$ 0	$ 0	$ 0	$ 0	$ 0
Principal repayment of current borrowing		$ 1,256	$ 1,256	$ 1,256	$ 1,256	$ 1,256	$ 1,256
Other liabilities principal repayment		$ 0	$ 0	$0	$ 0	$ 0	$ 0
Fixed liabilities principal repayment		$ 0	$ 0	$0	$ 0	$ 0	$ 0
Purchase other current assets	7%	$ 0	$ 0	$0	$ 0	$ 0	$ 0
Purchase fixed assets	7%	$ 0	$ 0	$0	$ 0	$ 0	$ 0
Dividends		$ 0	$ 0	$0	$ 0	$ 0	$ 0
Subtotal cash spent		$1,267,396	$1,319,959	$1,367,990	$1,424,026	$1,478,661	$1,542,616
Net cash flow		$ 451,344	$ 480,447	$ 518,000	$ 551,656	$ 591,019	$ 625,578
Cash balance		$2,187,852	$2,668,299	$3,186,299	$3,737,955	$4,328,974	$4,954,551

Photography Studio

Midwest Studios

710 West Broadway
Columbia, Missouri 65201

Kari Lucke

Midwest Studios is a new photography business based in Columbia, Missouri and founded by Robert Dean. The studio will offer photography services for customers around the mid-Missouri area. Anticipated clients include high school seniors, families, children, and couples that want to preserve memories of their wedding, as well as organizations and schools that need photographs for particular purposes. Products offered will include photographs, albums (both digital and print), and other photography-related items.

INTRODUCTION

Mission Statement

Our purpose is to provide clients with high-quality photographs as well as with a positive and fun experience during photography sessions.

Executive Summary

Midwest Studios is a new photography business based in Columbia, Missouri and founded by Robert Dean. The studio will offer photography services for customers around the mid-Missouri area. Anticipated clients include high school seniors, families, children, and couples that want to preserve memories of their wedding, as well as organizations and schools that need photographs for particular purposes. Products offered will include photographs, albums (both digital and print), and other photography-related items.

Business Philosophy

The most important factor in this business is satisfying the customer. We accomplish this by giving customers what they want and working with their individual desires and interests.

Goals and Objectives

The goal of Midwest Studios is to become a client's family photographer. In other words, we want to photograph a bride's wedding, her sister's children, her parents' fiftieth wedding anniversary, and so on. If people are happy with the product and service, they will pass this recommendation on to family and friends, and often we have found that this is one of the most effective forms of advertising.

Company History

Midwest Studios was originally founded as Northeast Studios in 1980 by Robert Dean in Hannibal, Missouri. In 2005, after 25 years of success in the northern part of the state, Robert moved to Columbia, where he will now continue to serve previous clients as well as residents of Columbia and surrounding areas.

INDUSTRY AND MARKET

Industry Analysis

Although the recent economic recession may have an impact on the professional photography business, there are several factors that show positive trends for the industry. First, the discretionary income of high school seniors has increased, and thus seniors are inclined to place higher-dollar orders. In addition, Columbia continues to produce well-educated and well-paid professionals, who have more income to use toward such luxury items as professional portraits. We have also seen an increase in brides and grooms paying for their own weddings or portions thereof, which also results in an increase in dollar amounts in the orders. Basically, though the economy may cause some people to postpone portrait-taking, as long as people keep getting married and having children, the market for professional photography will exist.

Market Analysis

Our market consists of residents of Columbia, Missouri, and surrounding areas. Columbia is a town of approximately 94,000, not including the student population (Columbia is home to two private four-year colleges and one major state university). The population of Boone County, which includes the towns of Ashland, Centralia, and Hallsville, is around 146,000. The median household income of Columbia residents is $42,163, with a race distribution of 83 percent White, 9 percent Black, and 8 percent other. Our target market consists of middle- and upper-income families with children. Estimates show that this constitutes about 28 percent of the households in the city.

Columbia has grown significantly in the past decade and is expected to see continued growth. It is consistently rated one of the best places to live in America by such well-known entities as *Forbes*, *Money* magazine, and Kiplinger.com due to its excellent educational systems, access to health care, and quality of life. For example, in 2007 *Forbes* ranked Columbia "Third Best Metro for Business and Careers" in its study that factored in the cost of doing business, job growth, and educational attainment.

Due to these factors of demographics and growth trends as well as others, we see significant potential for a photography business in this location. Unlike many small towns in Missouri, which are losing population, Columbia's population is growing. In addition, the location lends itself to current trends in photography, such as more outdoor, onsite (as opposed to in-studio) sessions. With such attractions as Shelter Gardens, the Katy Trail, Rock Bridge State Park, and other outdoor public settings, clients have a wide variety of choices when it comes to selecting a unique and beautiful place in which to have their photographs taken.

Competition

Competitors include other portrait studios in the area such as T. Brown Photography, Lucas Photography, and High Gate Gallery. These studios provide the same services as Midwest Studios, including wedding photography, senior pictures, and family portraits. Photography studios at department store chains such as JC Penney or Sears are not considered competition for private photography studios such as ours due to the common and correct perception that the former do not provide the same range of services or quality of product, environment, or expertise.

The key to rising above the competition in this market, we feel, is a personal touch. The friendly and down-to-earth approach of Robert and the staff at Midwest make clients feel instantly at ease, and all photography is done by Robert himself, not apprentices or other assist staff, as in some other studios. In addition, prices are quoted up front, and there are no hidden fees. Clients appreciate this kind of honesty and transparency and will recommend photographers they feel can be trusted.

PERSONNEL

Management

Robert Dean, who received his bachelor of science degree in photography from Truman State University in Kirksville, Missouri, will act as manager and professional photographer. Robert has 25 years' experience photographing individuals, couples, and families both on location and in the studio. His eye for artistic detail and creative capabilities allow him to shoot memorable and distinctive photographs, and his gregarious and easy-going nature make clients, who are sometimes nervous about having their picture taken, feel at ease.

Staffing

Two other employees will be hired: an administrative assistant and a photography assistant. The administrative assistant will handle phone calls, schedule appointments, receive clients, and manage paperwork, including payroll and taxes. This person will also be in charge of ordering photos from the lab, constructing preview booklets and end-product albums, and managing the physical aspects of the studio. The qualifications for this position will include administrative experience, the minimum of a high school education, strict attention to detail, and an ability to respond appropriately and pleasantly to clients' questions and concerns. The administrative assistant will work 35 hours a week (9 A.M. to 5 P.M. Monday through Friday with a one-hour lunch) at a pay rate of $15 an hour.

The main duty of the photography assistant will be to aid the photographer during photo shoots, which includes but is not limited to transporting and setting up equipment, assisting clients, and other duties deemed necessary by the photographer. The photography assistant will work when clients are scheduled to be photographed, which could include sessions both at the studio and off site (e.g., weddings). This person may also be called upon to help with album preparation or other overflow duties from the administrative assistant. The photography assistant will work varied hours, on average 20 hours a week (sometimes on weekends), at a pay rate of $12 an hour.

Both assistants will be hired after Robert has interviewed the most qualified respondents to a classified ad in the local newspaper, the *Columbia Daily Tribune*. Both assistants will receive on-the-job training from Robert, with the help of written training materials prepared by Robert.

Professional and Advisory Support

Robert is a member of Professional Photographers of America (PPA). With more than 20,000 members, PPA is the world's largest nonprofit association for professional photographers. The organization provides industry standards and resources for photographers, including an annual conference, a monthly publication, and a web site.

GROWTH STRATEGY

We see the most potential for growth in the high school senior and wedding markets. First, the advent of Facebook and other web sites has allowed more exposure as seniors post their portraits online. Often seniors want to know from their friends, "Who took your pictures?" and the resulting word-of-mouth advertising is very effective.

Weddings are also a growth area due to couples waiting longer to get married. Many couples are in their late twenties or early thirties, have already become established in their careers, and have more discretionary income to spend on wedding portraits.

PRODUCTS AND SERVICES

Description

Midwest Studios provides photography services and products for any occasion a family or individual wants to celebrate and remember.

Unique Features/Niche

One of the most significant advantages Midwest Studios offers over competitors is its ability to deal with clients on a personal basis. Whereas some studios have several 'steps' that clients must go through that include various individuals, Robert does all of the consulting and photography himself. This makes the clients feel they are receiving the most professional service and product. In addition, the fact that people can reach Robert almost any time or day of the week is an advantage. Many studios have only an answering machine if clients call on a Sunday or evening, but Midwest Studios provides a human contact at almost any time.

Robert works to build the customers' self-esteem and confidence during photo sessions, which results in higher rates of satisfaction with the product. In addition, we emphasize the 'once in a lifetime' aspect of the photos. In other words, a wedding, a child's first birthday, or a student's senior year occur only once, and we emphasize the idea of 'capturing moments' that will never come again. Parents are especially appreciative of this sentiment regarding portraits of their children.

Pricing

The sitting fee for a wedding is $380. This includes mileage of up to 100 miles (.25 per additional mile), an engagement portrait session, a prebridal studio sitting, formal and candid wedding coverage, and up to two hours of reception coverage. After receiving previews, clients must place an order of a minimum of $600. Thus the minimum cost commitment for a wedding is $980, plus tax. To book a wedding, a retaining fee of $350 is required, which is later applied to the sitting fee.

The sitting fee for individual or family portraits is $55, due at the time of the session.

The cost of the photographs depends on the finish and size desired by the client. There are three types of finishes: (1) Old Masters portraits have a lifetime guarantee and are spray-textured and mounted on canvas. All artwork and retouching is included. (2) Prestige portraits have a 10-year guarantee and are textured, sprayed, and mounted for luster and protection. Some artwork and retouching is included. (3) Machine portraits are quality prints without the additional enhancements found in the other finishes.

Prices for individual portraits are as follows.

- Wall Mural (30x40)—$990.00 for Old Masters; $660.00 for Prestige; $455.00 for Machine

- Large Wall Portrait (24x30)—720.00 for Old Masters; 480.00 for Prestige; 320.00 for Machine

- Wall Portrait (20x24)—455.00 for Old Masters; 305.00 for Prestige; 215.00 for Machine

- Small Wall Portrait (16x20)—285.00 for Old Masters; 155.00 for Prestige; 125.00 for Machine

- Hall Portrait (11x14)—160.00 for Old Masters; 95.00 for Prestige; 75.00 for Machine

- Gift Portrait (8x10)—48.00 for Prestige; 38.00 for Machine

- Desktop Portrait (5x7)—38.00 for Prestige; 26.00 for Machine

- Small Desktop Portrait—24.00 for Prestige; 16.00 for Machine

- 8 Wallets (same pose)—32.00 for Machine

- 24 Wallets (same pose)—49.00 for Machine

- 48 Wallets (same pose)—84.00 for Machine

Because the photos are sent to a lab for processing, the prices are based in part on the cost of production. The markup for photos must be fairly large. For example, a 5 by 7 would typically cost about $5 to print, but we charge the customer $26 because this is the only place profit can occur, and there are many items that must be covered, such as salaries, equipment, rent, and so on.

Photographers price their products and services in different ways, and the range of prices in the Columbia area is wide. However, we feel our wedding package, for instance, offers more flexibility and value than some other studios in the area. For example, T. Brown's smallest wedding package costs $2,000, and High Gate Gallery requires a nonrefundable $500 deposit but is otherwise unclear on its web site regarding minimum order cost. Some studios, such as Lucas Photography, do not advertise their wedding prices, which to most clients is a significant factor.

Regarding individual and family portrait sessions, we are comparable in price to the competition. For senior pictures, T. Brown charges a $49 sitting fee plus a package price of between $250 and $550. High Gate's least expensive package for seniors is $145, although it is not clear whether this includes the sitting fee. Our sitting fee is $55 with no minimum order.

Looking for a photographer for a wedding, senior pictures, or other portraits can be overwhelming for clients because every studio has different policies, packages, and prices. We feel the best way to overcome the confusion often caused when trying to choose a photographer is to keep things simple. We have a set minimum price for weddings and the same sitting fee for families, seniors, and children. The cost is dependent on how many and what type of pictures the client wants, and he or she is not tied in to paying for more than what is really needed or desired.

MARKETING AND SALES

Advertising and Promotion

Midwest Studios' marketing slogan is "Professional portraits aren't expensive; they're priceless" in an effort to convey the idea that the special times (e.g., wedding, child's first birthday, etc.) come only once and it is well worth the investment to document them with beautiful photographs that will last a lifetime.

The studio will use three means of advertising: the yellow pages, a web site, and brochures. This set of media grants good exposure in the area at a minimal cost.

Cost

The cost of the web site is minimal: $35 per year for hosting and $5 a year for the domain. Maintenance and keeping the site up-to-date is performed by the administrative assistant and is included in his or her wages.

There are three main brochures: one for weddings, one for families/children, and one for seniors. These are printed once a year in December, with updated photos from the previous year incorporated. Cost is approximately 50 cents per brochure. Sometimes special brochures may be printed if the studio is running a promotion, and these cost around $1 each to cover extra graphics, higher quality paper, and more color.

Midwest Studios also runs a small box ad in the CenturyTel yellow pages twice a year. Cost depends on the market but runs an average of $500 per ad.

OPERATIONS

Customers

Our customers are mainly high school seniors, families with children, and couples planning a wedding. Columbia, Missouri, is a community with a relatively young population—approximately 30 percent is between 25 and 44 years old—and 51 percent of households are families with children. These demographics make Columbia a good location for a photography studio that focuses on the young adult and family market.

Suppliers

Miller's Professional Imaging is based in Pittsburgh and opened a Columbia lab located at 1712 East Pointe Drive in 2001. All photo orders from Midwest Studios are sent to Miller's via their online order system. Orders are normally delivered to the studio via FedEx within two to three days. Midwest Studios maintains an account with Miller's and pays the balance of a monthly statement.

Equipment

Equipment includes camera, lighting, backgrounds, props, seating, and video display proofing equipment, in addition to Macintosh computers and software. The initial cost is $30,000. Robert has the cash secured for this investment.

The only inventory is packaging materials for mailing photos.

Hours

The studio will be open from 9 A.M. to 5 P.M. Monday through Friday and by appointment. We will take phone calls 24 hours a day, seven days a week. During the hours the studio is not open, the phone will ring in Robert's residence; if no one is available to answer, a recorded message will instruct the caller to leave a name and number for a return call.

Facility and Location

The studio is located in its own building at 710 West Broadway in Columbia, Missouri. Rent on the 1,200 square-foot office space is $1,500 a month, and utilities average $200 a month. The building includes a bathroom but does not have other fixtures; therefore, an investment of about $2,000 in wall partitions, furniture, and office equipment will be necessary. There is a parking lot in front of the building with space for six cars that is for customers of the studio only. The building is located on a main road that runs the length of the city, and it is in a central location one mile from downtown Columbia and two miles from the Columbia Mall.

Legal Environment

One of the major laws that affects the professional photography business is the Federal Copyright Act of 1976 (revised in 1989). Recent technological advances such as high-resolution color printers have made it easier for people to copy photographs and made copyright a more salient issue than it used to be. The so-called 'copyright law' protects photographers from such illegal copying of their work; photographers must be aware of these issues and take steps to protect their work.

FINANCIAL ANALYSIS

Projections below are approximate and based on the following number of bookings per year (order projections include sitting fees):

- 25 weddings (average portrait order, $2,000)

- 75 seniors (average portrait order, $700)

- 50 family/children (average portrait order, $500)

Using these figures, we project total sales of $127,500 for 2009–2010. This includes sales from weddings in the amount of $50,000, sales from seniors in the amount of $52,500, and sales from families and children in the amount of $25,000.

The total cost of these sales for this same period is anticipated to be $97,500 and includes lab costs ($17,500), salaries ($40,000), rent and utilities ($35,000) and miscellaneous costs ($5,000).

These numbers will result in a profit of $30,000 for the 2009–2010 period. With increases in advertising and word-of-mouth business, we expect to see the number of sittings increase substantially in the next five years.

Plus–Sized Children's Clothing Store

Jennifer's Clothing Corner

13 North Main St.
Bangor, Maine 04401

Merrill Guerra

Jennifer's Clothing Corner was born out of founder Jennifer Whittaker's struggle to find well fitting, stylish and age–appropriate clothing for her plus–sized daughter. Market research revealed that there were no attractive, properly–fitting clothes available to this significant and growing market segment. The difficulty of finding age–appropriate, well fitting, and fashionable clothing in a comfortable shopping environment contributes to weight stigma for young plus–size girls. Weight stigma is a burning issue for pre–adolescent girls and their parents, often leading to serious emotional and physical issues.

EXECUTIVE SUMMARY

Jennifer's Clothing Corner addresses the issue of childhood obesity through a unique two–pronged approach of providing clothing to the largely untapped plus–size children's market and balanced healthy lifestyle support to plus–size children and their families.

Jennifer's Clothing Corner was born out of founder Jennifer Whittaker's struggle to find well fitting, stylish and age–appropriate clothing for her plus–sized daughter. Market research revealed that there were no attractive, properly–fitting clothes available to this significant and growing market segment. The difficulty of finding age–appropriate, well fitting, and fashionable clothing in a comfortable shopping environment contributes to weight stigma for young plus–size girls. Weight stigma is a burning issue for pre–adolescent girls and their parents, often leading to serious emotional and physical issues. Jennifer realized that a company offering attractive properly–sized clothing presented in a comfortable shopping environment, when paired with a comprehensive support network, would not only help these young girls but would also provide a tremendous business opportunity.

CUSTOMERS

Of the 16 million pre–adolescent girls in the United States today, approximately 5.5 million are significantly overweight or obese. According to Packaged Facts, this represents a $3.2 billion market. The female plus–size market (which encompasses both women and girls) is growing at 7 percent per year. Plus–size clothing for young girls today is difficult to find and, even when available, is usually unattractive and ill–fitting. A resulting problem is that, out of desperation, 84 percent of these girls find themselves sizing up to teens' and women's clothing, which are often very inappropriate styles for young girls and, ironically, have their own fit issues.

Jennifer's Clothing Corner offers fashionable, age–appropriate, trendy plus–size clothes for girls aged 5 to 12. These clothes are sold through independent style consultants, supported by an ecommerce website and social network. Jennifer's Clothing Corner addresses the self–esteem, health and wellness needs of these children, while promoting the products. The company will also launch the Jennifer's Clothing Corner Parent Network online, providing parents with healthy lifestyle choices for their families and support for dealing with their children's weight stigma, all while promoting the company' clothes.

MARKETING & SALES

A key part of Jennifer's Clothing Corner's marketing strategy is to provide clothes that fit. Jennifer's Clothing Corner offers a proprietary sizing system for the girls in the target demographic. This strategy has been executed using fit models representing the spectrum of girls' body shapes, ensuring an appropriate and comfortable fit. Our sizing system accounts for different body shapes within the plus–size children's market by providing two categories of plus sizes; something no other company does.

The second key strategy is to use direct selling through independent sales consultants. This strategy offers a personal hands–on sales approach. This approach helps girls choose clothes appropriate for them under Jennifer's Clothing Corner's new proprietary sizing system in an environment that is comfortable both for the girls and their parents. This market will support premium pricing to reflect the high–quality and trendy fashion of our line, and the comfort of the personal and private sales environment. Adult plus–sized clothing commands an 8–10 percent premium over "regular" sizes, and this should hold true for the children's market as well.

Clothes Sales Strategy

Go–to–Market Strategy: A Direct Sales (Network Marketing) Model

Jennifer's Clothing Corner is utilizing the direct selling model due to several factors. The relationships our style consultants form with our customers will enable us to receive immediate feedback on the clothing. The networks that the style consultants build of customers and other style consultants whom they recruit will generate exponential growth. The brand loyalty that is generated and sustained through this model is significant. Providing an emotionally safe place for the girls to sample the product in a comfortable home–based setting is another benefit provided by this model.

We recruited our first consultants in June 2008 and anticipate having 62 style consultants by the end of the first full year of sales and over 3800 at the end of five years. Silpada Designs, another network marketing company, grew to over 3000 representatives in its first five years and in its 10th year of operation had over 23,000. We will attract the initial consultants through word–of–mouth, advertisements in local papers that cater to stay–at–home moms, mother's groups, and online mom resource centers such as ClubMom.com and ModernMom.com. The recruiting effort will be led by our Director of Sales and Network Development.

Each style consultant is an independent contractor and is paid only on the revenue she generates. The consultant not only generates her sales through individual consultations and home parties, or trunk shows, she also receives commissions on the sales of other women she recruits to become style consultants thus further expanding the network. As a style consultant builds her network and trains leaders to build their own networks, she is able to significantly increase her income. While the majority of consultants will be "hobbyists" doing only one or two trunk shows a month, there will be a percentage who will be business builders. These consultants will build large networks and receive significant compensation. A chart showing the eight levels of style consultants and the requirements for those levels is listed in Exhibit 7. A more complete explanation of our compensation structure can be found in the "Money Making Slides" and the "Career Plan Booklet".

Jennifer's Clothing Corner is utilizing the services of a consulting firm whose principals have decades of corporate experience in the direct sales industry. This firm has helped us with revenue projections, launch plans, training programs for the consultants, policies and procedures and more. Together with this firm Jennifer's Clothing Corner has built a solid foundation upon with our network of style consultants will grow and prosper.

The Pilot Program for the style consultant network is currently underway in preparation for the official launch of the consultant network in April 2009. We have already doubled the number of style consultants in the network in the few weeks since we have started advertising the Pilot Program.

The online store enables Jennifer's Clothing Corner to generate income from around the country while we concentrate locally in Southeast Michigan on the launch of the consultant network. This will provide a solid foundation of income to support the company while we build the network of independent style consultants which by its nature will start small and local but grow exponentially. We are undergoing search engine optimization and some minor upgrades to the site to draw more traffic to the site.

Social Network Strategy

Building an Online Community of Parents

Jennifer's Clothing Corner is in the process of developing relationships with various content providers such as food coaches, child psychologists, pediatricians, childhood obesity researchers, nutritionists, and child fitness experts. The company will begin development on the social network after funding is achieved. The Founder's Blog is active and the Parent Forum will launch in 2009. The rest of the network features, including the ability to share photos, read articles from experts, find and designate "friends," and, potentially, an online game/forum for children, will follow as funding and development allow. Jennifer's Clothing Corner is currently exploring partnership opportunities with a local hospital.

Further, Jennifer's Clothing Corner could monetize the parent support network by screening and selling ad space for qualified products that fit with Jennifer's Clothing Corner's mission and vision.

BUSINESS OVERVIEW

Jennifer's Clothing Corner will sell to young girls, aged 5 to 12 years old, who need plus–sized apparel. According to Packaged Facts this represents a $3.2B market. The retail apparel industry is expected to see 13 percent growth through 2009. U.S. sales of girls' clothing are forecasted to increase 17 percent through 2008. The percentage of overweight children is projected to reach 50 percent by 2010. Additionally, the plus–sized market is the strongest performing sector in the retail apparel industry and experienced a growth rate of 38 percent for 2000 through 2005 compared to overall retail apparel growth of 2 percent during that period.

Jennifer's Clothing Corner has several competitors in the marketplace. While these companies provide girls plus–size clothing, they typically stock very limited quantities and styles in their stores. Old Navy and Gap don't stock any plus–size clothing in their stores, and customers are forced to go online to purchase these items. Due to these factors, only 16 percent of girls aged 5–12 are able to find styles designed for their age group that fit (according to industry analyst, The NPD Group). Further studies have shown that the fit offered by these companies is unsatisfactory. Jennifer's provides better fit than its competitors. Our fashion and quality are as good as or better than the competition.

While a majority of parents are internet users, the social networks that have been launched typically are focused on teens and 20–somethings. Yet, as venture capitalist and "Infectious Greed" blogger, Paul Kedrosky, states "The older demographic has a bunch of interesting characteristics, not the least of which, is that they hang around." This prospective and relative stickiness is helping drive a wave of new investment into sites that offer like–minded and like–aged individuals discussion forums about diet, fitness and health care, photo–sharing, and news and commentary.

No other company has combined the two models of specialty apparel and a social network for our target market. The synergy resulting from this combination provides Jennifer's Clothing Corner with its unique competitive advantage; namely, providing superior fit and fashion while simultaneously serving the unique physical and emotional needs of our young customers and their parents. This synergy is listed as a success factor by apparel industry analysts when discussing successful specialty retailers.

SERVICES

Clothing Sales Strategy

The online store will enable Jennifer's Clothing Corner to generate income soon after the launch of the clothing line. This will provide a solid foundation of income to support the company while it builds the network of consultants which, by its nature, will start small but will grow exponentially and will eventually surpass the income provided by the online channel. Jennifer's Clothing Corner anticipates having 26 independent sales members by the end of the first year and 2500 at the end of five years. It will attract the initial style consultants through word–of–mouth, advertisements in local papers that cater to stay–at–home moms, mother's groups, and online mom resource centers such as ClubMom.com and Modern Mom.com, and is already receiving inquiries from interested women.

Online Social Network Strategy

Jennifer's Clothing Corner is in the process of developing relationships with various content providers such as food coaches, child psychologists, pediatricians, childhood obesity researchers, nutritionists, and child fitness experts. The company will develop the network after funding is achieved. Once the content providers are secured and the network is designed, Jennifer's will begin approaching various organizations to create strategic partnerships. There are many organizations and celebrities who have childhood health initiatives, and these partnerships will strengthen Jennifer's Clothing Corner Parents Network's credibility and allow it to reach a wider audience.

MANAGEMENT TEAM

Jennifer Whittaker, founder and CEO, earned her MBA from Ohio State University and her BA from Penn State University. She has over ten years experience in project management, direct selling and web marketing. She most recently served as the web marketing manager for an online apparel retailer, where she increased the online conversion rate from .4 percent to 2 percent, bringing them up to the industry average.

Anna Shambline, Director of Sales and Network Development, earned a BA in Social Work from University of Michigan in 1988. She shifted her focus to selling in 1995. Her sales experience includes retailing, insurance, medical devices and direct selling. She has extensive experience training others in consultative sales, networking techniques, business development, and sales presentations.

Wyatt Harric, Interim CFO, has over 25 years in small business management and commercial lending. Wyatt earned an MBA from Duke University and a BA Economics from the University of North Carolina. He serves as Director of Finance of Deeton Technological Services and is financial advisor to a number of early stage companies.

Helena Martin, Director of Marketing, provides Jennifer's Clothing Corner with over twelve years of operational marketing experience. Her experience includes strategic planning and tactical execution across several marketing mediums. She has experience in both global and local grass–roots organizations developing key skills including market research, project management, public relations, graphic design and web development.

FINANCIAL ANALYSIS

The anticipated revenues (net of returns) in the company's first full year of operation are $919K. That number will grow to $42.6M by year five. This growth rate is predicated on the growth of the independent sales force and increased traffic to the website from both web and catalog marketing. The average consultant will have a sales base of 200 children and be able to close sales with 45 percent of their sales base with an average ticket price of $115 by the end of year five. This number takes into account that most consultants will have small clientele numbers and a smaller percentage will have very large clientele numbers.

	Year 1	Year 2	Year 3	Year 4	Year 5
Net Sales ($Mil)	0.92	4.5	8.4	21.7	42.6
Gross Margin	32.5%	37.8%	36.9%	34.3%	32.6%
EBITDA ($Mil)	.02	0.68	1.1	4.5	9.8
Cash Position ($Mil)	0.3	0.7	1.0	3.6	9.2
Headcount (FTE)	4	16	33	53	85
Sales Network Size	62	281	838	1875	3872

In less than five years, the company should be an attractive acquisition target for established "brick and mortar" companies in the adult plus–sized clothing market and in the girls' clothing space. Other potential acquirers include consumer products companies with an interest in online and/or direct sales to the girls' plus–size clothing market. Many direct sales companies have broad lines of products and markets and are continually seeking complimentary or strategic additions to their offerings, for which Jennifer's Clothing Corner may serve as a valuable target. The recent acquisitions of Club Penguin by Disney ($700M), and the purchase of Maya's Mom by Procter & Gamble ($10–20M), confirms that Jennifer's Clothing Corner is in a market space that is actively acquisitive and highly valued.

Jennifer's Clothing Corner will be successful because it is addressing a clear, compelling customer pain in a large, growing, and under–served market and will see strong financial performance due to an effective combination and implementation of direct–to–consumer channels and an online social network for families.

The company will generate strong sales revenues with consistent year–over–year growth and provide handsome returns to its investors. It is projected to achieve breakeven during the first year of sales operations. By year 5, revenue is expected to climb to $29.3M, with gross and net margins of about 34.7 percent and 12.8 percent, respectively. These numbers hinge on certain key assumptions, listed below, each of which is described in detail. Considering the proven strength of the network marketing sales model, which will become the company's most prominent sales channel over time, as well as the strong credentials of the management team and their combined experience, the financial projections are achievable, and relatively conservative.

Key Financial Assumptions

Style Consultants: These are independent contractors who promote and sell the Jennifer's Clothing Corner apparel. Their numbers are projected to increase from 62 at the end of year 1 to 3800 in year 5. By year 5, each sales member is projected to have a clientele of 200 children. Their increasing ability to sell effectively over time, coupled with an attractive portfolio of Jennifer's Clothing Corner products, will help them sell an average of $110 worth of merchandise to 45 percent of their clients by year 5.

Product pricing: Jennifer's Clothing Corner's apparel will be priced competitively in the market in relation to its positioning as a Moderate–to–Better brand with an average retail price of $30. In fashion the pricing structure follows the following format: Popular (Budget or Mass), Moderate, Better, Bridge, Designer, Couture. Examples of Better lines are those found in most high–end department stores such as DKNY and Nautica or some store brands like Banana Republic or Ann Taylor. Gap, Dockers, Guess, and Jones New York Sport are all examples of Moderate lines.

The factors considered when arriving at the average price for apparel include:

- Apparel will be of high quality and provide better fit than comparables currently available.

- Starting out as a more upscale brand allows for expansion down into the Popular category, whereas starting out as a Budget priced brand would make future expansion upward very difficult.

- Currently, the most offerings that can be found for plus–size children reside in the popular category (WalMart, JCPenney, Sears), thus consumers who are willing to pay more and are looking for more fashionable options are in greater need.

- Consultant sale models, in general, typically have premium priced products, due to the personal service and relationships inherent in this business model.

Employees & Compensation: In 2009, Jennifer's Clothing Corner will manage all internal operations between the CEO, CFO, VP, Marketing and Development, and an admin. Jennifer's Clothing Corner will utilize internship programs through Bangor Community College and partnerships with the Maine Technological College for project based work. A design intern is being utilized to create new designs, follow fashion trends, and to assist with product development and production. A Head Designer will be brought on part–time initially and then made full time by the end of the year. Jennifer's Clothing Corner will hire additional employees to keep pace with the company's rapid growth reaching 85 employees in year 5, most of whom are involved in sales support or inventory distribution.

The style consultants are not included in the employee count because they are independent contractors. Each is paid a percentage of the revenue she generates.

Discussion of Financials

The top–line and bottom–line growth of Jennifer's Clothing Corner is strongly dependent on the number of its style consultants and their effectiveness and on the amount of traffic generated by the website. For this, Jennifer's Clothing Corner will train the independent style consultants and give them incentives in the form of financial bonuses and perks. The web marketing initiatives and search engine optimization techniques will continue to increase traffic to the site as well. These and other factors, discussed above, were included in the financial model for Jennifer's Clothing Corner. Projections made for the first five years revealed that Jennifer's Clothing Corner will become profitable at the end of the first year of sales operations and maintain a healthy gross margin in the 35 percent range thereafter.

The company's revenues are expected to grow strongly and consistently, and by year 5 are projected to be $42.6M. This rapid growth can be explained by the corresponding increase in the number of sales members during the same period, productivity improvements, increased site traffic from both web and catalog marketing, and improved click through and conversion rates. Revenue growth is expected to continue at this pace due a combination of the following factors:

- Increases in the number of sales members to over 3800 members by year 5 and increased site traffic and conversion rates.

- A wider array of product offerings and increased brand recognition will increase the effectiveness of the sales force to 45 percent and average ticket prices to $110 by year 5. These projections take into account that most representatives will have small clientele numbers and a smaller percentage will have very large clientele numbers. By offering a wider array of apparel, Jennifer's Clothing Corner will be able to get a bigger share of the customer's annual apparel expenditure.

The network marketing related projections are in line with growth seen in other network marketing companies. Silpada Designs started in 1997 with 14 representatives by the end of their first year. By 2007, Silpada had over 23,000 representatives and revenue of over $237M. Silpada has seen average annual growth rates of around 100 percent and is projecting growth rates into the future over 30 percent per year. Mary Kay was started in 1963 with 9 representatives. By 1973, they had over 21,000 reps and by 1983, they had $300M in revenue. In 2007, Mary Kay had over $2B in revenue with over 1 million representatives in the United States. Further, they have been generated by our consultants, Tetley USA based on their experience with the industry. A chart of our compensation structure is located in the exhibits. Network marketing compensation structures are complex and not easily explained. Tetley USA will be glad to make available the documents we utilized to explain the structure of the compensation plan. The margin that has been allocated to accommodate all compensation paid out through the plan is 40 percent of retail.

The growth in revenue will drive increases in the company's bottom line at a much faster rate. The acceleration in the increase of net income can be ascribed to cost structure, wherein key sales drivers such as bonuses to associates, facility rents, marketing and advertising, and overheads do not rise proportionately with revenue.

The sales growth will follow a general upward trend but will have peaks in key purchasing times for children's clothing at back–to–school (August/September), Christmas (November/December), and spring time (April/May). There is usually a fairly significant drop in early February which begins to rebound by March.

It is important to note in these challenging financial times that the Network Marketing business model we are utilizing performs stronger in true recessions. In a Nov. 2, 2008 article of *Advertising Age*, Amy Robinson of the Direct Selling Association is quoted as saying that the DSA "has seen anecdotal evidence for the third quarter that that bump is beginning to happen." This is due to more people looking for alternative and supplemental forms of income through direct sales opportunities and more customers looking for convenient, in–home, personal service for generally affordable products.

Funding Needs

Jennifer' Clothing Corner closed its first round of funding in November 2008 during the worst financial crisis to affect our country in decades. This round of $142,000 will enable the company to implement its go–to–market strategies and develop a track record of successful growth in both revenue and numbers of style consultants. The matching funds will enable us to produce additional inventory required by the growth of the consultant network and online store as well as providing the means to focus on launching the social network which will be a key factor in building and maintaining our competitive advantage. A final round of funding will be raised in mid–2009 which will be used to implement a major upgrade on the website focusing principally on the backend operations for the style consultants, manufacture inventory, and bring staffing on board to manage our future growth. Jennifer's Clothing Corner expects to fund all subsequent future growth from cash flow. Jennifer's Clothing Corner can miss its revenue projections by 20 percent and still be self–funding.

COMPANY HISTORY

The idea for Jennifer's Clothing Corner was born out of Jennifer's struggles to find clothing for her daughter, Patti. As Jennifer talked with other moms, she found this difficulty in shopping for clothes was a common theme. Given the national attention to the obesity epidemic, it seemed amazing to her that no one was out there trying to address the need to clothe this growing segment of the population.

Not only does Jennifer's vision include providing clothing for this neglected segment of the population, she also wants to provide parents with an online community where they can support one another and find information to help them incorporate healthy lifestyle choices into their families. As a mother who has experienced the pain and challenge of both growing up as an overweight child and seeing her daughter follow that path, Jennifer's blog will become a point of emotional connection and will provide a human and personal face to the business.

As a college student, Jennifer was able to participate in numerous programs to help her refine the business model and pave the way to launching the business. She has been awarded over $35,000 in grants and awards.

MARKET ANALYSIS

In the U.S., childhood obesity is an obvious problem, and the epidemic is steadily growing among U.S. children. In the United States, 30 percent of children ages 5–12 are overweight and 15.5 percent are obese, as reported by the American Obesity Association and MayoClinic.com. In the United States, there are approximately 16M 5 to 12 year–old females. Thus, the number of children in the plus–sized 5–12 year old girl market is estimated to be approximately 5M and the expected revenue from this market is $3.2B. The total clothing market for girls in this age group is $10.6B. The latest data from the Center for Disease Control reports that the number of children considered overweight has tripled since 1980 (Exhibit 1).

The pain these children are facing is that of weight stigma. Weight stigma is a weight bias or discrimination resulting from obesity. A recent study from Yale and the University of Hawaii, Manatoa found that childhood obesity has far reaching emotional and physical health consequences. "The childhood obesity epidemic is rapidly accelerating," said lead author Rebecca Puhl of the Rudd Center for Food Policy & Obesity at Yale. "That means thousands of children in North America are at risk for serious emotional and physical health consequences that science shows are connected to weight stigma. We cannot overestimate the urgency of combating stigma."

The severe lack of clothing available to these children contributes to this stigma. In fact, The NPD Group reports that 74 percent of overweight boys and 84 percent of overweight girls in the 5–12 year–old age group are "sizing up," or buying sizes other than those made for their age. As chief industry analyst for The NPD Group, Marshal Cohen, states, "When kids have to size up to men's and women's sizes it can be challenging to find clothes that are age–appropriate." This is especially true for pre–adolescent girls who are forced to purchase teen clothing that is often suggestive in order to find clothing that fits.

This market pain is more than just the difficulty of finding clothes that fit. The current shopping experience has a powerful negative emotional impact on families. Shopping for clothes is a painful and unpleasant experience for both parent and child and can result in adding to weight stigma.

While there is a perception that this is a "disease of the poor," the research does not completely support that view. The research–to–date investigating factors that lead to obesity, whether among adults or children, suggests a multifaceted and complex picture according to Mintel Reports. The fact that overall obesity rates have risen among higher income earners/families as well as low suggests that other factors are implicated in addition to income. One factor that has been identified is the rising commute times resulting in parents looking for time–saving convenience solutions to feed hungry families.

Ethnicity is another factor in overweight and obesity which should be noted. While white women seem to have stabilized their rate of weight gain, Hispanics and African–Americans are continuing to see increases in their rates of overweight and obesity according to Packaged Facts.

According to Mintel Reports, some demographic groups shop more and spend more on children's clothing than other groups in the population. Approximately half of parents between the ages of 25–44 spend $400 or more per year on children's clothing. (Exhibit 3) Blacks and Hispanics are more likely than whites and Asians to spend in excess of $400 per year on kids' clothing. (Exhibit 4) Therefore the increasing multi-cultural landscape of the U.S. has some positive implications on the children's clothing market.

Parents are still heavily involved in the apparel purchasing decisions for girls ages 5–12 (Exhibit 2) which is a good indicator for the Jennifer's Clothing Corner brand to find acceptance among children and parents in this age group. Additionally, according to Mintel Reports, while pre-teen girls are strongly influenced by wanting to fit in with their peers, their level of brand recognition is still quite low. They are more influenced by the style than the brand name attached to the style.

Apparel Purchaser Internet Acceptance

Excerpt from "The Posh Payoff," *Revenue*, Nov/Dec 2006—"The conventional wisdom about e-commerce was that apparel never would sell well online because people want to try things on before they buy. But more familiarity with a brand's size and quality expectations as well as easier return policies are causing consumers to buy more apparel online every year. People are becoming more and more comfortable buying apparel online,"—Carol Hearon, eLuxury.com's marketing and affiliate manager.

The latest Shop.org e-commerce study, called *The State of Retailing Online 2007*, found that online apparel retailers surpassed computer equipment, long the front-runner, in online sales. In 2007, 10 percent of all clothing sales are expected to occur online. Scott Silverman, executive director of Shop.org, said, "Apparel becoming the top category really is a milestone in evidence of online retail becoming mainstream."

Jennifer's Clothing Corner's positioning as a "better" clothing line will take advantage of the comfort more affluent shoppers have with online shopping. In March 2006, Time magazine found that of adult internet users with household incomes of at least $150,000, 12 percent of respondents said that the internet was their primary place to shop for apparel and 18 percent said it was their secondary place. Luxury buyers, in fact, are 36 percent more likely to be comfortable with online transactions involving their credit cards. "I think a lot of it is time constraint," says American-Luxury's Olsen, "The sophisticated customer is increasingly very, very busy and they don't have time to go to the mall." Forrester found that convenience-driven consumers make up approximately 31 percent of all online shoppers and represent nearly 35 percent of all online spending.

Further, *Packaged Facts*, in their *Plus-Size and Big and Tall Clothing in the U.S.* report, notes that direct sales strategies such as internet retail and catalog marketing have been particularly successful in the plus-size market. *Packaged Facts* expects that "more and more plus-size and big & tall people will order apparel from e-tailers in the future."

Social Networking Making Strides with Parents & Boomers

While a majority of parents are internet users, the social networks that have been launched typically are focused on teens and 20-somethings. Yet, as stated above, there has been a population boom for sites that offer like-minded and like-aged individuals discussion forums about diet, fitness and health care, photo-sharing, and news and commentary. As Susan Ayers Walker, a freelance technology journalist, reports "Not only do [parents and older people] have a lot more money, [they] pay a lot more attention to advertisers." In August 2007, Johnson & Johnson spent $10–$20 million to acquire Maya's Mom, a social networking site for parents that has been in existence for about a year, which is an indication of the value that major companies place on developing online communities for this important market.

Further, while there has been explosive growth of Web 2.0 and user-generated content maturing at a consumer level (sites like Wikipedia, MySpace, Blogger), there's plenty of room for growth in the business environment. Social media and participative technologies can allow for greater collaboration among employees, customers, suppliers and business partners. According to a recent McKinsey Global Survey on how businesses are using Web 2.0 technologies, nearly three–quarters say that their companies plan to maintain or increase investments in Web 2.0 in the coming years. Among the popular technologies/tools that North American executives are using or plan to use are peer–to–peer networks, blogs, collective intelligence (wikis) and social networking. The participatory Web today is all about empowering users to collaborate and share ideas, thoughts, and opinions as well as build communities and socialize with like–minded individuals through these technologies.

GROWTH STRATEGY

Future Market Growth and Attractiveness: Children's Clothing

- 13% projected growth through 2009 in the retail apparel industry (Mintel)

- 23% growth since 2002 for girls' clothing sales with growth projected at a similar rate

- U.S. sales of girls' clothing forecast to increase 17% through 2008 (Mintel)

- Women's and girls' plus–size category to near the $65B in retail by 2012

- Even if the trend toward overweight and obesity reverses, the plus–size market should see annual advances of 4–7% through 2012. (Packaged Facts)

- Total population of children between 0–12 years is projected to increase by 1.7M or 3.3% between 2005 and 2010.

Future Market Growth and Attractiveness: Social Networks

- Use of social networks grew 108% from 2005 to 2006, rising from 3.8 million households to 7.9 million.

- Blog reading saw an increase of 121% and 5.1 million households to a total of 9.2 million households in 2006.

- 15% of online adults use social networking sites monthly. Further, 15% of adults (27% of gen Yers and gen Xers) who have been diagnosed with a medical condition use social networking sites.

- Health–oriented social networks are gaining traction such as CarePages.com—a social network site where friends and family can follow the progress of loved ones receiving care for an illness via profile pages—which now has one–fifth the unique audience of Yahoo.

Forrester 2007 North American Benchmark Study

For this analysis the industry is defined as the children's plus–sized clothing industry. There are several forces which would change if the industry is defined more broadly as the children's clothing industry and could potentially make this a less attractive industry. Given the limited options and the size of the potential market though, it is appropriate to consider only the plus–sized children's market and is similar to market analysis on adult clothing where plus–sized, petite and maternity wear are considered separately from the adult clothing market.

A Porter's Five Forces analysis indicates that the plus–sized children's clothing industry is an attractive industry to enter. Four of the five forces are positive and while there will always be a high threat of entry, Jennifer's Clothing Corner will be able to grow and maintain market share through superior fit, meeting the needs of our target market better than our competitors through ongoing market research, and brand loyalty generated by our superior fit and the parent social network.

OPERATIONS

Vendors

Traditionally the channel for adult plus–size apparel shopping has been conducted through "brick and mortar" retail stores. However online plus–size apparel shopping is becoming increasingly popular. The apparel vendors for children's plus–sizes include JC Penney, Sears, Lands End, Gap, Old Navy, Wal–Mart, jeenybeans.com, and webclothes.com. These vendors' limitations will be discussed in the competition section.

Suppliers

Suppliers receive the designs and source the appropriate fabric and materials to tailor clothing that meet the specifications provided by clothing designers. Fabric wholesalers and manufacturers and sewing contractors can be located throughout the world. While much of clothing production occurs internationally, domestic production is beginning to see a bit of a revival. High end designers have found significant problems with quality producing overseas which makes the cost savings negligible given the impact to their brands.

Jennifer'Clothing Corner will source the fabrics and manufacturing from domestic producers. The main benefits to the company will be:

*   Ability to oversee and monitor quality which is vital to branding and positioning

*   Ability to order small production runs

*   Ability to utilize resources contractors provide such as pattern–making and sample–making.

Value Chain

Products in the clothing industry typically flow in the following manner.

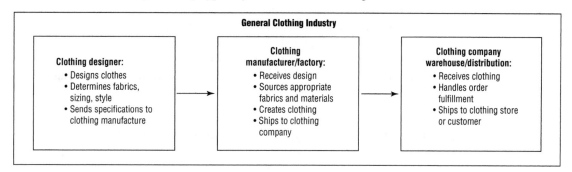

The Margins in the Apparel Industry

Based on independent research, a majority of the cost associated with producing apparel is in sourcing of raw materials (Exhibit 5). The next largest cost is associated with labor and capital expenditures. This production cost is the cost of goods sold and typically represents $0.27 of an MSRP (Manufacturer's Suggested Retail Price) of $1.00. In the figure below, the margin structures between the different apparel industry channels are compared. In a bricks–and–mortar, or traditional retail, model typically the clothing manufacturer/designer sells at a wholesale price to a retailer. The retailer expects MSRP to be a "keystone" figure which is at least 2x the wholesale price, so if the MSRP of the product is $1 the price the retailer is willing to pay is at most $0.50. In the network marketing model, an average of 40 percent of the MSRP is used for the commission structure which gives the network of sales people an incentive to sell both the product and grow the network. Between the immediate mark up (commission) and additional bonuses which can be earned based on volume (both personal and network), the average across all representatives will earn an average 40 percent of each $1 sold. The direct–to–consumer model cuts out all middle people and, in turn, nets the company a higher percentage of the end price to the consumer. Given the need for discounts/incentives in any retail situation, about 10 percent of the MSRP will be given back to the purchaser.

Margin Structures: Apparel Industry Channels

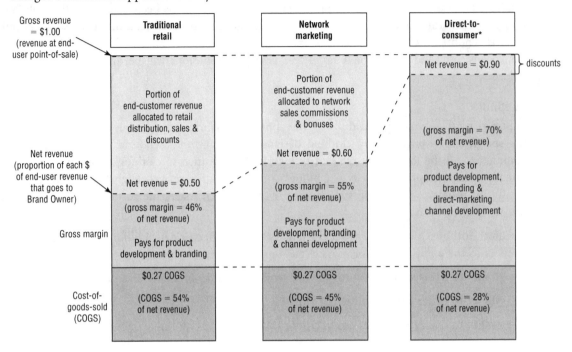

*e-tail, catalog, infomercials, etc.

Hoover's groups all apparel retailers in the same industry and shows the industry median gross profit margin as 34.9 percent. Looking more specifically at specialty retailers within children's apparel, The Children's Place has a GPM of 35.9 percent and Gymboree's is 47.1 percent. Network marketing companies that Hoover's reports on typically see much higher margins. Avon realizes a gross profit margin of 60.8 percent and USANA Health Sciences' GPM sits at 76.3 percent. Charming Shoppes, parent company for women's plus–size industry leader Lane Bryant, shows a GPM of 30.2 percent.

Standard and Poor's *Apparel & Footwear Industry Survey* notes that "retailers are successfully rolling out new stores that cater to various demographics. The new concepts should benefit by tapping into age groups that may not feel well served by stores already out there. Stores that cater to multiple age groups are losing ground. Department stores have lost sales to specialty retailers for years, while the flagship chain of the Gap Inc. is suffering monthly same–store sales declines as it struggles to define who its customer base is. In Standard & Poor's opinion, the specialty retail format holds numerous advantages including: better customer knowledge, more targeted merchandise assortments based on that knowledge, and superior customer service levels."

Chico's is an example of this trend and its gross profit margin sits at an impressive 58.9 percent.

Jennifer's Clothing Corner will use "better" pricing to reflect the high–quality and fashion–forwardness of our line. This pricing is supported by several factors. Adult plus–sized clothing commands an 8–10 percent premium over "regular" sizes due to the reduced need for promotional sales. This will hold true for the children's market as well because children need clothes that fit and their parents are less price–sensitive due to the limited options they have. As Mintel Reports on Children's Clothing says, "appealing to parents on an emotional level can be successful" because many parents and gift givers of children's clothes "buy more to communicate a style and/or lifestyle" rather than on price. The line will include several basic items in reach for mid–income families at price points around the $15–20 range and will incorporate more fashion–forward items commanding as much as $60–80 for a dress or outfit.

Online Parent Social Network

The parent social network will be a key point of differentiation for the Jennifer's Clothing Corner line. It will be a gathering place and support network for any family that is searching for ways to help their children learn that balancing act, recommended by doctors and psychologists, of pursuing a healthy lifestyle and being happy with the way they are. Dr. Tracie Miller, University of Miami professor of pediatrics states, "I think the message should be you should be comfortable with yourself and life is a balance…between your strengths and weaknesses."

The presence of this network will afford Jennifer Clothing Corner the opportunity to create strategic partnerships with the many different organizations and influential individuals who are concerned about children's health, in general, and the obesity epidemic, in particular. One of our potential partners is the William J. Clinton Foundation which supports initiatives aimed at addressing childhood obesity because of President Clinton's childhood (and lifelong) struggle with weight issues. Others include the American Academy of Pediatrics, the American Academy of Child and Adolescent Psychiatry, the NFL, Rachel Ray, Shaquille O'Neil (of Shaq's Big Challenge), Alliance for a Healthier Generation, and many more.

The company will begin to build these strategic partnerships and work to build its content provider list over the next six months. Jennifer's Clothing Corner plans to develop and launch the parent network after funding is complete, while the blog has been active since August 2007 and provides a point of contact and communication with the community.

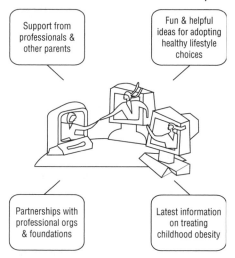

Value Proposition

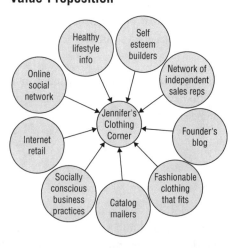

Manufacturing is provided by Snap and Zipper, which has over two decades of experience in cut and sew manufacturing. By contracting with a clothing manufacturer not only are capital costs be reduced, but the sample–making and production preparation services of the manufacturer will also reduce the need for staffing these services in–house. Initially, order fulfillment will take place at the Jennifer's Clothing Corner's offices. As volume grows, Jennifer's Clothing Corner will lease warehouse space and provide order fulfillment from this facility. All orders are received online or via fax and are paid by credit card.

The combined value proposition of convenience, stylish clothes that fit and flatter, and the support network for parents and families is currently unmatched in the industry.

The Jennifer's Clothing Corner value chain is divided into two separate processes: internal and external operations. Internal operations consist of clothing design, production, and inventory control and development of the parent social network. Initially, Jennifer's Clothing Corner will manage all internal operations between the CEO, the CFO, and an administrator. As Jennifer's Clothing Corner grows, staff will be added to support that growth. Jennifer's Clothing Corner will continue to add personnel, growing into a 84 person company by 2012.

External sales and distribution will be largely controlled in the network marketing model by independent Jennifer's Style Consultants. These independent consultants are not included in the employee count because they are independent contractors, yet they are important to remember when considering revenue "per employee." They will be recruited and trained by our Director of Sales and Network Development.

MISSION

Jennifer's Clothing Corner addresses the issue of childhood obesity through a unique two–pronged approach of providing clothing to the largely untapped plus–size children's market and balanced healthy lifestyle support to plus–size children and their families. It aims to address the self–esteem, health and wellness needs of the child. The company through the Jennifer's Clothing Corner Parents Network will provide parents with healthy lifestyle support and through Jennifer's Clothing Corner will provide fashionable clothing that fits the plus–sized child. This flattering and fashionable clothing will help to reduce weight stigma and enable children to meet their need to belong, fit in, and have a positive self–esteem.

Maslow's Hierarchy of Needs places the Love/Belonging/Social needs just above the need for Safety. Humans need to feel a sense of belonging and acceptance. They need to love and be loved by others. In the absence of these elements, many people become susceptible to loneliness, social anxiety, and depression. This need for belonging can often overcome the physiological and security needs, depending on the strength of the peer pressure, e.g. an anorexic ignores the need to eat and the security of health for a feeling of belonging. Therefore, providing clothing that fits and looks great is an important component of meeting the needs of these children.

Further, Jennifer's Clothing Corner has made the commitment to operate the business in a socially, ethically, and environmentally–responsible fashion. This will be evidenced in the sourcing of contractors and materials and treatment of its employees and will influence all strategic decisions.

ORGANIZATION

The Jennifer' Clothing Corner solution provides fashionable clothing that fits the unique needs of the plus–sized child and that can be purchased in a comforting environment and a parent support network to help parents incorporate healthy lifestyle choices in their families. The revenue from the apparel line will support this online network which will be a give back to this community of parents, although over time it will begin to generate revenue as well through ads and business development deals.

The multi–channel model combining internet retail, and network marketing will allow parents and children to find the shopping experience to fit their lifestyle and needs. The online store will take advantage of consumers' increasing comfort with shopping for clothing on the internet. The network of independent style consultants will allow families to shop in a home–based, comfortable, friendly, fun and supportive atmosphere.

The business model will be supported by a website with three main components: an online store, an online parent network, and style consultant management tools. The parent network will provide information on healthy lifestyle choices and a forum for parents to support one another and find ways to reduce weight stigma. This network will be a community of people who are helping their children and families to feel great about who they are and to adopt healthy lifestyle choices. When the children wear our clothing, the will benefit in the short term from improved self esteem. While the clothing addresses the short–term self esteem needs, the social network will address their long term physical and emotional health needs.

ADVERTISING

Jennifer's Clothing Corner will develop a strong web presence utilizing web marketing and search engine optimization. Jennifer's Clothing Corner will use tools such as pay–per–click advertising, blogs, search engine optimization, press releases, and affiliate marketing to drive traffic to the site and create a significant web presence. The presence of the parent network will be beneficial in increasing the traffic, due to increasing the natural search rankings and attracting customers to the site. This will in turn help conversion rates and drive sales.

The catalog mailers will both provide additional revenue and drive increased sales on the website. The E–Tailing Group, Chicago, a consultant for online merchants, noted that "the internet is moving up as the preferred channel for sales spurred by catalogue recipients and that cross–channel shoppers actually constitute the majority of all online consumers, including 65 percent of shoppers in 2004."

The network marketing channel will involve a central management team recruiting, training and motivating a team of independent style consultants. The consultants will purchase a sample line of clothing with a selection of sizes and styles. They will meet with customers to introduce them to the clothing and take orders. The sales members will then place the orders online. The business management tool on the website will enable the independent consultants to track their personal sales and their down–line network sales. It will provide them with access to additional marketing tools, such as forums for sharing marketing and sales ideas, sample invitations, links to helpful sites such as those that sell clothing displays, etc.

The channels will be rolled out in stages to better control growth. The online store launched in May 2008. The first style consultants signed up in June 2008. The official launch of the consultant network will happen in April 2009.

COMPETITION

Jennifer's Clothing Corner currently has several competitors in the marketplace. While these companies provide plus–size clothing, they typically stock very limited quantities and styles in their stores. Old Navy and Gap don't stock any plus–size clothing in their stores, and customers are forced to go online to purchase these items. Due to these factors only 16 percent of girls ages 5–12 are able to find styles designed for their age group that fit according to industry analyst, The NPD Group. Further studies have shown that the fit offered by these companies does not adequately fit. Jennifer's Clothing Corner provides a better fit than the other competitors in the marketplace and fashion and quality in line with the top performers.

Finally, while there are apparel companies and there are social networks, no company has combined the two models. It is the synergy which results from this combination from which Jennifer's Clothing Corner derives its competitive advantage of being able to continue to provide superior fit and of knowing and serving our customers better. This is listed as a success factor by apparel industry analysts when discussing successful specialty retailers such as Chico's, a clothing store targeted to 35–55 year old women.

Jennifer's Clothing Corner enjoys a competitive advantage by:

- Providing fashionable clothing that offers superior fit

- Creating an online community for parents

- Providing a proprietary sizing model

- Utilizing a direct selling (network marketing) model

Fashionable Clothing with Superior Fit: Jennifer's Clothing Corner will provide clothes to these young girls that fit, flatter and look stylish. Jennifer's Clothing Corner will be able to continue to provide superior fit due to its close relationship with its customers through both the style consultants and the online social network. As Kathleen Fasanella, sewn manufacturing industry expert, says "More customers will shop and pay for convenience, fit and personal relationship reasons." The company will be able to continually monitor the clothing's fit through its relationships with the parents of these children through both the online community and the style consultants.

Creating an Online Community for Parents: No other clothing company provides this kind of community to meet the needs of its customers. This enables us to be more than just a clothing company but a company that exists to meet the physical and emotional health needs of these children. The network will allow us to continually receive feedback which will allow us to maintain the best fit possible for the clothing line. This community not only will create a loyalty to the brand but will, in turn, provide opportunities to expand our product offerings in any number of directions. Additionally, it will provide opportunities to generate additional revenue through advertising and business development deals.

Jenny's Sizing System: Jennifer's Clothing Corner's proprietary sizing system will enable it to continue to provide more accurate fit through a system which is unique in two facets: it takes into account the different body shapes of girls aged 5–12 and it is more granular than current models in the marketplace.

Network Marketing Model: This direct sales model provides a true network effect of style consultants and customers spreading the message virally. This sales model provides a level of privacy and personal connection that is unmatched in a traditional retail setting. Additionally, direct sales models perform better in recessions, due to people looking for additional means of generating income or to start their own businesses. Currently, while there are a couple of network marketing children's clothing companies, none provides plus–sized options in their lines.

Because of these factors, Jennifer's Clothing Corner will build a brand that is recognized for its superior fit, quality and compassion. In addition to the appeal we will have to parents due to our exceptional fit, we will gain the loyalty and trust of our customers because of our high quality, fashionable clothing, the relationships our customers have with our style consultants, and the online parent support network. The brand loyalty, Jennifer's Clothing Corner, will enable it to resist losing market share to new entrants into this space.

Critical Success Factors

The critical success factors to help the company achieve this competitive advantage are the following:

- Creating a trendy, high–quality line of clothing that fits well.

- Building an online community, or social network, of parents and children who are struggling with this very emotionally sensitive and frustrating issue. This will increase traffic to the online store, loyalty in purchasers, and provide direct access to our target market which will increase our knowledge and ability to serve our customers.

- Instituting a top–notch return policy which will encourage initial purchases and repeat business.

- Developing a solid internet presence early by search engine optimization and other web marketing initiatives such as: affiliate marketing, pay–per–click advertising, business development deals, press releases, and blogs which increase traffic to the site and conversions (sales).

PROPRIETARY ELEMENTS

Given the low tech nature of our business there are few proprietary elements which can be protected. We will have a trademark for our name and branding but that is the extent of our protection. There has been movement in the fashion industry to patent or trademark designs. While that might be another element of protection down the road, at this point legally enforcing these IP rights has not been proven as a cost–effective method.

However, in the fashion industry trade secrets for fashion design reside in a designer's "blocks." A "block" is a basic or master pattern that reflects the styling of a manufacturer. The fit and sizing of a block is specific to each company. As Jennifer's Clothing Corner continues to solicit customer feedback and perform market research, our blocks will reflect our knowledge of our customer base with improved fit which will provide a source of competitive advantage.

Jenny's Sizing System is proprietary which will make it more difficult for followers to copy the sizing model we have created. This can be defended through common law trademark rules. As we grow, we will continue to evaluate the benefit of applying for trademark rights to this system.

GROWTH STRATEGY

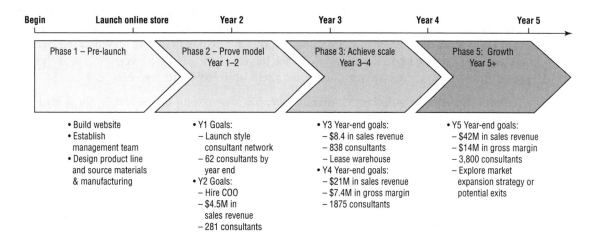

The test market line of clothing launched May 12, 2008. The first style consultants signed up in June, 2008. The Fall/Winter Line of clothing began selling in September, 2008. Updates to the product line will occur on a bi–annual cycle; one line will feature back–to–school and winter clothing, and the other update will feature spring and summer designs. The social network will launch in 2009.

By the end of the first full year of operations after the clothing launches, Jennifer's Clothing Corner will have 62 independent style consultants. The expectation is that the number of sales representatives will increase to over 3,700 by the end of year 5.

Market Expansion Opportunities

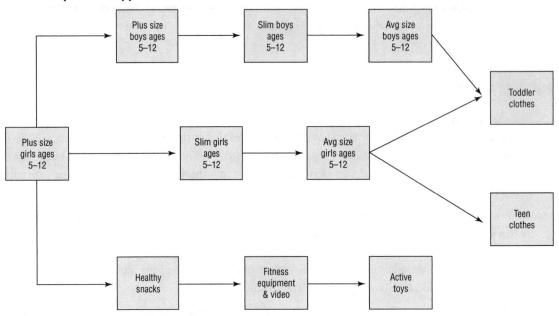

MANAGEMENT SUMMARY

Jennifer Whittaker, Founder and CEO, received her MBA from Ohio State University and her BA from Penn State University. She began her career managing operations at a small communications company and saw that company through a growth phase from a 19 person, one location enterprise to a company with 50+ employees at five locations in three states. Jennifer owned her own professional organizing service and founded the 17th chapter of the National Association of Professional Organizers. Jennifer also has nine years of experience as a network marketer. She most recently served as the web marketing manager for an online apparel retailer where she increased the online conversion rate at the site by 400 percent from .4 percent to 2 percent, bringing them up to the industry average.

Since launching Jennifer's Clothing Corner, Jennifer has managed the design and production of two lines of clothing and successfully brought them to market. This process includes patternmaking, grading, marker making, sourcing, and cut–and–sew production. She also directed the process for developing the proprietary Jenny' Sizing System which is utilized in the design of the clothing. She has been effective at generating positive and ongoing press. Jennifer's Clothing Corner has been featured in a year–long series of articles in the major newspapers and industry journals.

Anna Shambline, Director of Sales and Network Development, earned a BA in Social Work from University of Michigan in 1988. She shifted her focus to selling in 1995. Her sales experience includes retailing, insurance, medical devices and direct selling. She has extensive experience training others in consultative sales, networking techniques, business development, and sales presentations.

Wyatt Harric, Interim CFO, has over 25 years in small business management and commercial lending. Wyatt earned an MBA from Duke University and a BA Economics from the University of North Carolina. He serves as Director of Finance of Deeton Technological Services and is financial advisor to a number of early–stage companies.

Helena Martin, Director of Marketing, provides Jennifer's Clothing Corner with over twelve years of operational marketing experience. Her experience includes strategic planning and tactical execution across several marketing mediums. She has experience in both global and local grass–roots organizations developing key skills including market research, project management, public relations, graphic design and web development.

Board of Directors

Wyatt Harric is a consultant to early–stage companies in business strategy and capital structure and formation. Through his company, Deeton Technological Services, he has assisted in raising over $ 100 mil. Prior to founding Deeton in 2002, he spent seven years in the machine tool industry followed by 28 years in the securities industry. In 1999, he co–founded and was Chairman and CEO of Boyton Brothers, where he raised $11.0 million of initial capital. Wyatt began early–stage private investing in 1962, and has invested in 44 early–stage companies. Wyatt currently serves as a consultant to several companies in Maine.

Denise Zalinger is the co–founder of Stationary at Your Door, a network marketing company. After a successful career in marketing, she co–founded Stationary at Your Door with her sister–in–law. She took the company to 500 representatives and almost $2M in revenue, when the company was purchased for $48.5M.

Patrick Ritter spent twenty years as an attorney specializing in corporate law and mergers and acquisitions, representing private and public clients in a broad range of industries, including information technology, franchising and retail. He has since become involved in the entrepreneurial community as an investor and advisor.

Key Advisors

Olivia Deven, Consultant, has worked in the needle trades for over 25 years and is a master pattern maker. Olivia has consulted for numerous designer entrepreneur start–ups and continues to add to her profession through her various projects. One project in anthropometric ergonomic design for mature figures involves developing the application of the research she has conducted over a period of eight years with regards to designing clothing for older (55+) women.

Tetley USA, founded in 1998, is a Direct Selling Association, DSA, and Direct Selling Women's Association, DSWA, Supplier Member that specializes in Direct Selling. They are a full service consulting firm that provides the entire spectrum of support from Sales Management, Sales Training, Sales Development and Events Planning to Operations and IT. From the corporate side they work with the Direct Selling Company to assess needs, develop compensation plans, create training programs, manuals and materials to build strong recruiting cultures while they develop and oversee the installation of IT solutions to support these functions. From the Field side, Tetley USA conducts training seminars and coaching calls to help independent sales consultants raise their skill levels and develop into leaders.

Over that last ten years, Tetley USA has worked with a number of start–up companies and turn–around companies as well as established companies that want to improve their growth rates. Tetley USA also provides IT services to several firms across the country.

MILESTONES

Jennifer's Clothing Corner has achieved many significant milestones.

- August 2007: Website launched, ecommerce model validated, revenues generated and new consultant candidates identified.

- May 2008: Test market line of clothing launched; demand for products validated.

- June 2008 : First style consultants signed up; revenue from consultants validates model.

- June 2008: Featured prominently in an industry journal article on plus–size children's clothing; evidenced uniqueness of business model and confirmed strong demand for products.

- September 2008: Fall/Winter line launched.

- October 2008: Received trademark on Jenny's Social Network.

- November 2008: Closed $142,000 funding round.

To date, we have expanded to 8 style consultants, sold over 250 pieces of clothing, brought in revenue of over $4500, and realized zero percent customer returns. This was all achieved with bootstrapping and essentially no marketing budget. The recent funding enables the company to implement several strategic initiatives. The first project is developing the infrastructure and launch plan for the network of style consultants. The company has engaged a professional direct selling consulting firm with extensive experience in the direct selling industry. Second, the company will further develop its website and implement search engine optimization strategies, using experienced consultants in these fields. These funds will also finance the design and manufacture of the company's Spring/Summer 2009 line.

The company anticipates achieving a number of milestones in the near future.

- January 2009: Launch Pilot Program for Style Consultants' coordinated recruitment of consultants and testing and revision of direct selling program assumptions

- February 2009: Launch upgraded website and search engine optimization strategies; begin to see increased traffic and conversions for online store

- April 2009: Official launch of Jenny's Style Consultant Network, the Spring/Summer 2009 clothing line, and Jenny's Support Network

RISK FACTORS

One challenge the company faces is the possibility that the major retail players will decide to expand their product offerings for plus–sized children ages 5–12. As the *Packaged Facts Plus–Size and Big and Tall Clothing* report points out, specialty retailers for plus–sizes are "on the bubble." In other words, as long as the mass retailers seem to ignore this segment of the population they will do well. However, once plus–size people feel they are able to have their needs met at the same places as their slimmer friends, they will choose to shop there. As Jennifer's Clothing Corner fills out its proprietary sizing model, offering clothing to 5–12 year old girls of all sizes, it will become known as the brand that provides the best fit. Additionally, the loyalty to the company and brand generated by both the consultant marketing model and the online social network will enable the company to maintain its position in the market.

Another risk is the possibility that sales do not increase in line with our projections. This risk is mitigated by the amount of initial investment we are requesting. We are asking enough to make sure we can get through year 2 if need be without requesting additional funding. We can miss our projections by 20 percent and still be positioned for cash positive in year 2. Further we will manage our production runs to minimizethat risk by using manufacturers that allow for smaller minimum runs. Finally, we will be able to manage our costs by keeping our hiring in line with our revenue projections.

A final challenge Jennfier's Clothing Corner must prepare for is the potential that our growth exceeds our expectations. When there is such a severe pain in the market, the reaction to solving that pain might be more than one can reasonably anticipate in responsible financials and business model planning. The company anticipates that by constantly communicating with its customers and keeping them updated through the online network and the style consultants, it will be able to manage expectations and create a feeling of cooperation between the company and its customers.

CONCLUSION

Jennifer's Clothing Corner will be successful because it is addressing a clear, compelling customer pain in a large, growing, and underserved market. The company will see strong financial performance due to an effective combination and implementation of direct–to–consumer channels and an online social network for families. Jennifer's Clothing Corner has an advantage over most high growth start up opportunities due to its ability to generate revenue early on with minimal investment through clothing sales. The major growth opportunities reside in the consultant sales model and in the social network that the company will build to support families who are trying to raise healthy, confident children in this age of computer games, reduced funding for sports and abundant fast food drive–through restaurants.

Jennfier's Clothing Corner is an attractive and solid investment due to the unique combination of the apparel retail and online social networking models. This combination is currently unmatched in the industry. The exponential growth potential inherent in the consultant sales model will be supported due to the highly organized infrastructure it is developing.

APPENDIX

Exhibits
Exhibit 1: Trends in child and adolescent weight

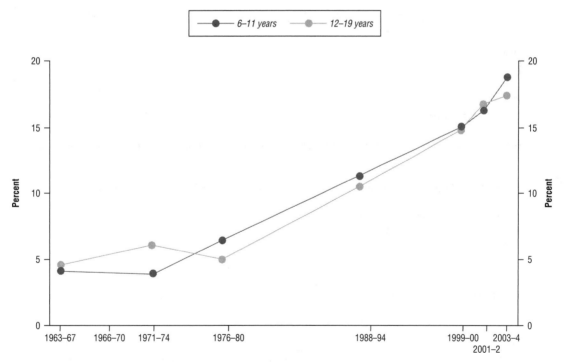

Note: Overweight is defined as BMI >= gender - and weight specific 95th percentage from the 2000 CDC Growth Chairs.

SOURCE: National Health Examination Surveys II (ages 6–11) and III (ages 12–17), National Health and Nutrition Examination Surveys I, II, III and 1999–2004, NCHS, CDC

The number of overweight children has tripled since the 1980's.

Exhibit 2: Percentage of parents making purchasing decision in each age group of female child

Age of female	% of parents making clothing purchasing decision with child	% of parents making clothing decision child's input
3 – 5	7.3%	92.7%
6 – 9	9.6%	90.4%
10 – 11	12.6%	87.4%
Average of 3 – 11	8.9%	91.1%

Parents are still heavily involved in the apparel purchasing decisions for girls ages 5–12.

Exhibit 3: Spending level on clothes, per year, per age group

Approximately half of parents between the ages of 25–44 spend $400 or more per year on children's clothing.

	All	18–24	25–34	35–44	45–54	55–64	65+
Under $50	13%	15%	8%	8%	19%	18%	24%
$50–99	11	10	7	7	16	15	24
$100–149	10	11	8	8	12	13	12
$150–199	7	7	6	7	8	10	8
$200–249	13	12	13	13	11	14	12
$250–399	26	27	31	29	23	23	17
$400+	38	38	51	49	27	23	12

Exhibit 4: Spending level on clothes, per year, by race ethnicity

	All	White	Black	Asian	Hispanic*
Under $50	13%	14%	10%	19%	7%
$50–99	11	13	4	10	7
$100–149	10	11	9	4	5
$150–199	7	7	6	3	7
$200–249	13	13	13	11	14
$250–399	26	26	24	39	32
$400+	38	35	53	39	51

*Hispanics can be of any race

Blacks and Hispanics are more likely than whites and Asians to spend in excess of $400 per year on kids' clothing.

Exhibit 5: Mean cost of items that go into the making and supply of apparel.

Cost of item	0–100,000	101K–200K	201,000+
Raw materials	$ 9.60	$ 8.32	$ 7.04
Labor	$ 1.80	$ 1.56	$ 1.32
Transport	$ 3.60	$ 3.12	$ 2.64
Total cost	$15.00	$13.00	$11.00

A majority of the cost associated with producing apparel is in sourcing of raw materials.

Exhibit 6: Similar Product Offerings by Company and Price

Competitor	Jeans	Pants	Tops	Sleepwear	Styling
JCPenny	$18.99–$39.99	$12.99–$28.99	$10.99–$24.99	N/A	Medium
Sears	$19.20–$36.00	$19.20–$26.99	N/A	N/A	Low
Lands End	$25.50–$26.00	$18.50–$34.50	$22.50–$24.50	N/A	Low
Gap	$19.99–$44.50	$19.50–$48.00	$ 4.99–$29.50	N/A	Medium
Old Navy	$16.50–$22.50	$ 7.99–$17.50	$ 2.99–$24.50	N/A	Low
Wal-Mart	$12.00–$18.88	$ 8.88–$19.23	$ 5.00–$13.23	$ 6.00–$13.44	Medium
www.jeenybeans.com	$23.00–$40.00	$25.00–$35.00	$12.00–$23.05	N/A	Low

Our pricing will be more similar to the upper ranges found at Lands End and Gap.

Exhibit 7: Compensation Structure

Leadership Benefits
- 25 % Personal Commission
- Up to 10% PSB
- 5% Override on entire Central Team
- Leadership Overrides
- Personal Sponsoring Account
- Promotion Bonues
- Training, Recognition, Travel

PS(B)=Personal Sales (Bonuses)
CT(S)=Central Team (Sales)

Style Consultant
- 25% Commission
- Up to 10% PSB
- Fest Seart Awards
- Founders Program
- Personal Sponsoring Account

Senior Consultant
$800 PS+ 2 Active Consultant
- 25% Commission
- Up to 10% PSB
- 25% Bonus on Personal Recruits
- Personal Sponsoring Account

Director
$800 PS+ 5 Active Consultant
- 25% Commission
- Up to 10% PSB
- 5% Overcode on Entire Central Team
- Personal Sponsoring Account
- Promotion Bouns

Senior Director
Qualified As Director+ One Direct Director
- 25% Commission
- Up to 10% PSB
- 5% Overcode on Entire Central Team
- 5% Override on Directors
- Personal Sponsoring Account
- Promotion Bouns

Executive Director
Qualified As Director+ Two Direct Directors
- 25% Commission
- Up to 10% PSB
- 5% Overcode on Entire Central Team
- 5% Override on Directors
- 1% Override on Indirect Directors
- Personal Sponsoring Account
- Promotion Bouns

Vice President
Qualified As Director+ Four Direct Directors
- 25% Commission
- Up to 10% PSB
- 5% Overcode on Entire Central Team
- 6% Override on Directors
- 1.5% Override on Indirect Directors
- 1% Override on 3rd Generation Directors
- Personal Sponsoring Account
- Promotion Bouns

Senior Vice President
Qualified As Director+ Six Direct Directors
- 25% Commission
- Up to 10% PSB
- 5% Overcode on Entire Central Team
- 5% Overcode on Directors
- 2% Override on Indirect Directors
- 1% Override on 3rd Generation Directors
- 0.5% Override on 4rd Generation Directors
- Personal Sponsoring Account
- Promotion Bouns

Executive Vice President
Qualified As Director+ Eight Direct Directors
- 25% Commission
- Up to 10% PSB
- 5% Overcode on Entire Central Team
- 5% Overcode on Directors
- 2.5% Override on Indirect Directors
- 2% Override on 3rd Generation Directors
- 1% Override on 4th Generation Directors
- Personal Sponsoring Account
- Promotion Bouns

VEB 1-2009

Exhibit 8: Revenue Projections

Consultant marketing	Year 1	Year 2	Year 3	Year 4	Year 5
Total # of style consultants	62	838	838	1,875	3,872
Sales base/consultant (# of kids)	55	180	180	200	200
Style consultant effectiveness	40%	40%	40%	45%	45%
Avg. sales/child/period	$ 110	$115	$ 115	$115	$ 115
Total network marketing	$ 862,243	$3,580,200	$ 6,938,640	$19,406,250	$ 40,075,200
Returns & allowances	8.0%	8.0%	7.5%	7.0%	6.0%
Net consultant marketing	**$ 793,264**	**$3,293,784**	**$ 6,418,242**	**$18,047,813**	**$37,670,688**
Internet retail					
Forecasted sales impressions	129,000	690,000	1,000,000	1,500,000	2,000,000
Organic portion (40%)	51,600	276,600	400,000	600,000	800,000
Organic conversion rate	2%	2%	3%	4%	4%
Paid conversion rate	2%	2%	2%	2%	2%
Organic sales transactions	961	5,520	12,000	24,000	32,000
Paid sales transactions	1,441	8,280	12,000	18,000	24,000
Average transaction value	$70	$94	$ 98	$98	$ 98
Total internet retail	$ 146,640	$1,476,000	$ 2,352,000	$4,116,000	$ 5,488,000
Returns & allowances	14.0%	14.0%	12.0%	10.5%	8.5%
Net internet retail	**$ 126,110**	**$1,269,360**	**$ 2,069,760**	**$3,683,820**	**$ 5,021,520**
Total revenue	**$1,008,883**	**$5,056,200**	**$ 9,290,640**	**$23,522,250**	**$45,563,200**
Net revenue	**$ 919,374**	**$4,563,144**	**$ 8,488,002**	**$21,731,633**	**$42,692,208**

Discussion of Revenue Projection Model Above:

To get the Total Network Marketing figure, the four inputs (#of style consultants, sales base, effectiveness, and average ticket price) are multiplied together. Because year one has been generated using monthly projections of growth in these figures and year two has been generate with quarterly figures, the TNM figure does not directly correspond. The input numbers listed are end of year figures, except for the number of consultants which is the average for the year.

The internet retail takes the number of forecasted impressions and divides it by whether they were derived from organic (or natural) search or whether they came in through a paid marketing effort such as Google Adwords. Then the impressions are multiplied by the conversion rates and the average transaction value.

Exhibit 9: Cost of Goods Sold

Schedule C- Cost of Sales

	Network marketing	Online retail	Blended average
Average retail price/unit	$ 30.00	$30.00	$30.00[a]
Per-unit cost elements			
Material cost	4.00	4.00	4.00[b]
Mfg. labor cost	5.00	5.00	5.00
Freight cost (Materials to mfr.)	0.50	0.50	0.50
Packaging cost	1.00	1.00	1.00
30% Wholesale discount	9.00	—	4.50
Total per-unit cost	$ 19.50	$10.50	$15.00[a]
Gross margin	35%	65%	50%

Memo:
[a]Average retail price/unit across entire line. Actual individual items may cost more or less than $30.
[b]Rates for per-unit cost elements and estimates. Actual cost will vary by item, and is not yet finalized.
[c]Per-Unit blended average rates are not volume-adjusted.

Real Estate Brokerage

Thomasson Real Estate

79 Cady St.
Los Angeles, California 90071

BizPlanDB.com

The purpose of this business plan is to secure the necessary funds, allowing us to open a real estate brokerage firm. The primary business of Thomasson Real Estate is to assist homebuyers and home owners with purchasing and selling property.

EXECUTIVE SUMMARY

The purpose of this business plan is to raise $100,000 for the development of a real estate brokerage while showcasing the expected financials and operations over the next three years. Thomasson Real Estate ("the Company") is a California–based corporation that will provide real estate brokering and property management services to customers in its targeted market. The Company was founded in 2007 by Roger Kramer.

The primary business of the Thomasson Real Estate is to assist homebuyers and homeowners with purchasing and selling property. The Company will receive commissions of up to 7 percent of the transaction value for each home sold by the business. As the current market conditions of the real estate market are lackluster, Mr. Kramer intends to use a number of marketing strategies to ensure that the business can generate a client list at the start of business.

The Company will also provide property management services to residential and commercial property owners.

Mission

Thomasson Real Estate's mission is to become the recognized leader in its targeted market for real estate brokering and property management services.

Management Summary

The Company was founded by Roger Kramer. Mr. Kramer has more than ten years of experience in the real estate brokerage and property management industry. Through his expertise, he will be able to bring the operations of the business to profitability within its first year of operations. Since beginning his career as a real estate agent, Mr. Kramer has acquired his real estate brokerage license, and he is now ready to launch his own brokerage. His skill set includes:

- The ability to oversee agents and employees; and

- A complete understanding of accounting licensure to operate as a real estate broker.

BUSINESS STRATEGY

Mr. Kramer is seeking to raise $100,000 from an investor. The terms, dividend payouts, and aspects of the deal are to be determined at negotiation. This business plan assumes that an investor will receive 50 percent of the Company's stock, a regular stream of dividends, and a seat on the board of directors. The financing will be used for the following:

- Development of the Company's office

- Financing for the first six months of operation

- Capital to purchase a company vehicle

Mr. Kramer will contribute an additional $10,000 to the venture.

Sales Forecasts

Mr. Kramer expects a strong rate of growth at the start of operations. Below are the expected financials over the next three years.

Sales, operating costs, and profit forecast

Proforma profit and loss (yearly)			
Year	2008	2009	2010
Sales	$806,778	$968,134	$1,132,716
Operating costs	$321,317	$349,003	$ 378,006
EBITDA	$404,783	$522,317	$ 641,439
Taxes, interest, and depreciation	$157,746	$202,409	$ 247,675
Net profit	$247,037	$323,837	$ 397,692

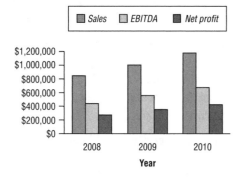

Below is a breakdown of how the start–up funds will be used:

Projected Start-up costs	
Business startup year	2008
Initial lease payments (3 months)	$ 10,000
Working capital	$ 25,000
FF&E	$ 23,000
Leasehold improvements	$ 5,000
Security deposits	$ 5,000
Insurance	$ 2,500
Opening supplies	$ 17,000
Marketing budget	$ 7,500
Miscellaneous and unforeseen costs	$ 5,000
Total startup costs	**$100,000**

Use of funds

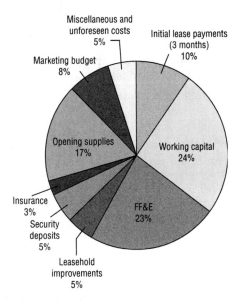

Miscellaneous and unforeseen costs 5%
Initial lease payments (3 months) 10%
Marketing budget 8%
Opening supplies 17%
Working capital 24%
Insurance 3%
Security deposits 5%
FF&E 23%
Leasehold improvements 5%

Investor Equity

Roger Kramer intends to sell 50 percent of the Company in exchange for the capital.

Management Equity

Roger Kramer will retain 50 percent of the business once the capital is raised.

Exit Strategy

If Thomasson Real Estate is very successful, Mr. Kramer may seek to sell the business to a third party for a significant earnings multiple. Most likely, the Company will hire a qualified business broker to sell the business on behalf of Thomasson Real Estate. Based on historical numbers, the business could fetch a sales premium of up to four times its earnings.

Investor Divestiture

This will be discussed during negotiations.

Expansion Plan

The Founder expects that the business will aggressively expand during the first three years of operation. As the real estate market returns to normal conditions, the Company will be an excellent position to capture a significant portion of its targeted market. In the future, the business may also develop mortgage brokering operations to assist homebuyers with financing their purchases.

Registered Name and Corporate Structure

Thomasson Real Estate is registered as a corporation in the State of California.

SERVICES

Below is a description of the real estate services offered by the Real Estate Brokerage.

1. *Real Estate Brokerage Services*: The Company's principal service consists of selling residential real estate its targeted market, and surrounding market area. The Real Estate Brokerage services provide clients with an international network of buyers and sellers through the multiple listing service

(MLS). Because of the Company's capabilities to network with other brokers, the brokerage will sell homes faster than our clients could if they tried to market their home without the assistance of a licensed real estate agent.

2. *Property Management*: In addition to providing real estate brokering services, the business will also manage residential and commercial properties for customers in the targeted market. This is an important part of the business as it will provide the Company with a recurring stream of revenue. This is especially important in today's real estate market as real estate sales have slowed.

Pricing

For each transaction, the Company will receive 7 percent of the aggregate value of the sale or purchase. In co–brokering transactions, the business may receive up to 3.5 percent of the face value.

In regards to property management, the Company will receive 10 percent of each month's rent.

MARKET ANALYSIS

Economic Outlook

Real estate brokerages have exploded with growth over the last ten years. As interest rates decreased, and the overall value of properties skyrocketed, the number of agents in this market has more than tripled.

Currently, the economic market condition in the United States is moderate. The meltdown of the sub prime mortgage market coupled with increasing gas prices has led many people to believe that the US is on the cusp of an economic recession. This slowdown in the economy has also greatly impacted real estate sales, which has halted to historical lows. As will be discussed later, the business will generate income from managing properties, which will offset the risks associated with the real estate brokering aspect of the business.

Industry Analysis

The real estate brokerage industry is one of the United States' biggest industries. It is estimated that there are over 221,000 establishments actively engaged in the business of acting as broker or agent for real estate transactions. Each year, these businesses aggregately generate more than $138 billion dollars of revenue and provide jobs for more than 1.1 million people. Gross average annual payrolls are now exceeding $30 billion dollars per year.

The growth rate of this industry has been tremendous, with gross receipts tripling over the last ten years. The extreme growth of the real estate market over the past five years has caused the number of establishments to increase significantly as the revenues generated by the industry have grown in step with increased value of real estate.

This trend is expected to continue, as smaller local and regional brokerages can now compete with large national franchised and non–franchised brokerages. As stated earlier, the advent of the Internet has allowed brokers of all sizes to actively engage the business of real estate brokering by maintaining a presence on the Internet.

CUSTOMERS

Many people require the services of real estate agents. People that sell their homes "for sale by owner" have had tremendous difficulty with selling their homes in the last year. As such, Mr. Kramer has developed an extensive demographic profile that the Company will use in regards to its target market. These demographics include:

- Currently owns a property as their primary residence or rental unit

- Annual Household income of $45,000+ per year

- Home value exceeds $250,000

COMPETITION

The field of real estate brokering is an extremely competitive industry. As such, Mr. Kramer will use the marketing strategies discussed in the next section to assist the business in reaching a large audience within the target market. Within the targeted market, there are approximately ninety businesses that will compete directly with Thomasson Real Estate.

Major Competitors

- ERA

- ReMax

- Century 21

- Prudential

MARKETING & SALES

Thomasson Real Estate intends to maintain an extensive marketing campaign that will ensure maximum visibility for the business in its targeted market. Below is an overview of the marketing strategies and objectives of the Company.

Marketing Objectives

- Develop an online presence by acquiring accounts for major online real estate portals.

- Implement a local campaign with the Company's targeted market via the use of flyers, local newspaper advertisements, and word of mouth.

- Establish relationships with other real estate brokers and agents within the targeted market.

Marketing Strategies

Property and home buyer marketing will be the most difficult portion of the marketing strategy. This is because one of the essential elements to reaching this audience is that the Company must build a brand affinity with the customer. This task will be accomplished through the business's broad marketing campaign throughout its targeted market.

Thomasson Real Estate will also use an internet–based strategy. This is very important, as many people seeking real estate for purchase or rent use the internet to conduct their preliminary searches. Mr. Kramer will register the Real Estate Brokerage and its agents with these online portals so that potential buyers/renters can easily reach Thomasson Real Estate. The Company will also develop its own online website.

The Company will maintain a sizable amount of print and traditional advertising methods within local markets to promote the homes and properties that the Company is selling.

OPERATIONS

Corporate Organization

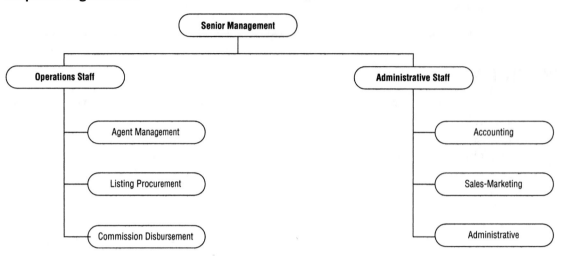

Organizational Budget

Personnel Plan-Yearly

Year	2008	2009	2010
Owners	$ 80,000	$ 82,400	$ 84,872
Real estate agent manager	$ 35,000	$ 36,050	$ 37,132
Marketing staff	$ 32,500	$ 33,475	$ 34,479
Non-commissioned agents	$ 37,500	$ 51,500	$ 66,306
Administrative staff	$ 44,000	$ 45,320	$ 46,680
Total	**$229,000**	**$248,745**	**$269,469**

Numbers of personnel

Year	2008	2009	2010
Owners	2	2	2
Real estate agent manager	1	1	1
Marketing staff	1	1	1
Non-commissioned agents	3	4	5
Administrative staff	2	2	2
Totals	**9**	**10**	**11**

Personnel expense breakdown

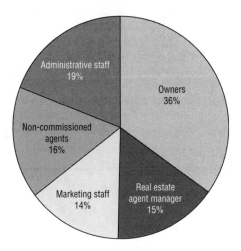

FINANCIAL ANALYSIS

Assumptions

The Company has based its proforma financial statements on the following:

- Thomasson Real Estate will have an annual revenue growth rate of 18 percent per year.

- The Owner will acquire $100,000 of investor funds to develop the business.

- Thomasson Real Estate will not seek debt financing in the first three years of operations.

Sensitivity Analysis

The Company's revenues can change depending on the general economic climate of the real estate industry. In times of economic recession, Thomasson Real Estate may have issues with its top line income as fewer sales will be made. However, Thomasson Real Estate will generate income from its property management business, which will reduce the risks associated with this business.

Source of Funds

Financing

Equity contributions	
Investor(s)	
Total equity financing	$100,000.00
Banks and lenders	**$100,000.00**
Total debt financing	
	$ 0.00
Total financing	
	$100,000.00

General Assumptions

General assumptions

Year	2008	2009	2010
Short term interest rate	9.5%	9.5%	9.5%
Long term interest rate	10.0%	10.0%	10.0%
Federal tax rate	33.0%	33.0%	33.0%
State tax rate	5.0%	5.0%	5.0%
Personnel taxes	15.0%	15.0%	15.0%

Profit and Loss Statements

	Proforma profit and loss (yearly)		
Year	2008	2009	2010
Sales	$806,778	$968,134	$1,132,716
Costs of goods Sold	$ 80,678	$ 96,813	$ 113,272
Gross margin	90.00%	90.00%	90.00%
Operating income	$726,100	$871,320	$1,019,445
Expenses			
Payroll	$229,000	$248,745	$ 269,469
General and administrative	$ 25,200	$ 26,208	$ 27,256
Marketing expenses	$ 4,034	$ 4,841	$ 5,664
Professional fees and licensure	$ 5,219	$ 5,376	$ 5,537
Insurance costs	$ 1,987	$ 2,086	$ 2,191
Travel and vehicle costs	$ 7,596	$ 8,356	$ 9,191
Rent and utilities	$ 4,250	$ 4,463	$ 4,686
Miscellaneous costs	$ 9,681	$ 11,618	$ 13,593
Payroll taxes	$ 34,350	$ 37,312	$ 40,420
Total operating costs	**$321,317**	**$349,003**	**$ 378,006**
EBITDA	$404,783	$522,317	$ 641,439
Federal income tax	$133,578	$172,365	$ 211,675
State income tax	$ 20,239	$ 26,116	$ 32,072
Interest expenses	$ 0	$ 0	$ 0
Depreciation expenses	$ 3,929	$ 3,929	$ 3,929
Net profits	**$247,037**	**$323,837**	**$ 397,692**
Profit margin	**30.62%**	**33.45%**	**35.11%**

Sales, operating costs, and profit forecast

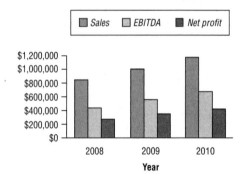

Cash Flow Analysis

Proforma cash flow analysis — yearly

Year	2008	2009	2010
Cash from operations	$250,965	$327,765	$401,621
Cash from receivables	$ 0	$ 0	$ 0
Operating cash inflow	$250,965	$327,765	$401,621
Other cash inflows			
Equity investment	$100,000	$ 0	$ 0
Increased borrowings	$ 0	$ 0	$ 0
Sales of business assets	$ 0	$ 0	$ 0
A/P increases	$ 37,902	$ 43,587	$ 50,125
Total other cash inflows	$137,902	$ 43,587	$ 50,125
Total cash inflow	**$388,867**	**$371,353**	**$451,746**
Cash outflows			
Repayment of principal	$ 0	$ 0	$ 0
A/P decreases	$ 24,897	$ 29,876	$ 35,852
A/R increases	$ 0	$ 0	$ 0
Asset purchases	$ 56,854	$ 81,941	$100,405
Dividends	$175,676	$229,436	$281,135
Total cash outflows	$257,427	$341,253	$417,391
Net cash flow	**$131,441**	**$ 30,099**	**$ 34,355**
Cash balance	**$131,441**	**$161,540**	**$195,895**

Proforma cash flow (yearly)

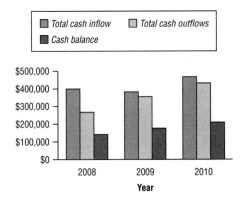

Balance Sheet

Proforma balance sheet — yearly			
Year	2008	2009	2010
Assets			
Cash	$131,441	$161,540	$195,895
Amortized expansion costs	$ 15,000	$ 23,194	$ 33,235
Inventory	$ 25,000	$ 86,456	$161,760
FF&E	$ 15,000	$ 27,291	$ 42,352
Miscellaneous assets	$ 13,000	$ 14,950	$ 17,193
Accumulated depreciation	($ 3,929)	($ 7,857)	($ 11,786)
Total assets	**$195,512**	**$305,574**	**$438,648**
Liabilities and equity			
Accounts payable	$ 13,005	$ 26,716	$ 40,990
Long term liabilities	$ 0	$ 0	$ 0
Other liabilities	$ 8,200	$ 8,528	$ 8,869
Total liabilities	**$ 21,205**	**$ 35,244**	**$ 49,859**
Net worth	$174,307	$270,330	$388,789
Total liabilities and equity	**$195,512**	**$305,574**	**$438,648**

Proforma balance sheet

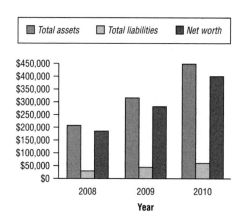

Breakeven Analysis

Monthly break even analysis

Year	2008	2009	2010
Monthly revenue	$ 29,752	$ 32,315	$ 35,001
Yearly revenue	$357,019	$387,781	$420,006

Break even analysis

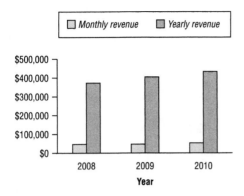

Business Ratios

Business ratios — yearly			
Year	2008	2009	2010
Sales			
Sales growth	0.0%	20.0%	17.0%
Gross margin	90.0%	90.0%	90.0%
Financials			
Profit margin	30.62%	33.45%	35.11%
Assets to liabilities	9.22	8.67	8.80
Equity to liabilities	8.22	7.67	7.80
Assets to equity	1.12	1.13	1.13
Liquidity			
Acid test	6.20	4.58	3.93
Cash to assets	0.67	0.53	0.45

Real Estate Renovation and Resale

HouseFlipperz

421 Wiltershare Dr.
Las Vegas, NV 89110

Gerald Rekve

We will set up our business up to help people with the home crisis they are facing and assist banks in liquidating homes inventory on their books.

EXECUTIVE SUMMARY

HouseFlipperz will be owned equally by two partners. As the company goes forward, other investors who want to get involved in the business will be allowed to invest for a return on their investment, but they will not own the company or any part of it. HouseFlipperz's main objective is to buy houses from homeowners, banks, and others who need to sell their home for fair market value. In determining fair market value, it must be said that with the housing crash of 2008, a lot of homes are listed, have been sold, and are going to be sold for 50 cents on the dollar. In most of these cases, the homeowner did not have any down payment, and only bought the home with sub prime loans.

Objectives

The objective of our business is to make money by helping these sectors achieve their goal of selling their home for fair market value.

We will not take advantage of any homeowner who is in the position that they need to sell their home. Instead, we will offer advice on how to apply for loans, government grants and other helpful tools to assist the home owner and help them stay in their home.

We will assist banks in liquidating homes that are vacant, with the caveat that the homeowner does not live in the home nor does a renter. The home must be vacant when we take the home into our listing service. We feel this method of offering a solution to the housing crisis will help us in the long run; we do not want to be looked on as a pariah of the home market, but a company that is helpful.

Mission

Our mission is simple. We will set up our business to help people with the home crisis they are facing and assist banks in liquidating homes inventory on their books due to the homes crisis of 2008.

BUSINESS OVERVIEW

HouseFlipperz is going to be set up as a limited liability company with focus on the Las Vegas market. The owners of the company are Donald Divens and Gladys Allen. The owners will each invest

$1,500,000 to the start up of the company, for a total of $3,000,000. We will retain an operating line of credit of $10,000,000. The cost of real estate being what it is and the system that HouseFlipperz has set up will ensure that this funding will be enough to operate this business.

Management Summary

HouseFlipperz will be owned equally by two partners. As the company goes forward, other investors who want to get involved in the business will be allowed to invest for a return on their investment, but they will not own the company or any part of it.

Start–up Summary

HouseFlipperz's start up summary is based on our ability to find quality homes that are in good locations and are in clean and resalable condition. This means that the homes can easily be resold. In simple terms, we will be buying homes at a discount and then reselling them for a profit. We also provide advisory services, where we will be providing advice to homeowners on staying in their homes.

The start–up of this company will take about $3,000,000 of which the two partners will invest. Added to this investment will be an operating line of credit from a large lending group. This investment amount will be $13,000,000.

Start-up requirements

Start-up expenses		
Legal	$	25,000
Office equipment	$	10,000
Accounting	$	50,000
Travel	$	50,000
Carring costs	$	150,000
Total start-up expenses	**$**	**285,000**
Start-up assets		
Cash required		$13,000,000
Start-up stock	$	0
Other current assets	$	5,000
Fixed assets	$	0
Total assets		**$13,005,000**
Total requirements		**$13,290,000**

PRODUCTS & SERVICES

The product we will be selling is single family homes in the Las Vegas housing market. We will also be selling advisory services to homeowners; these services will be for home owners to assist them in finding funding for their home mortgage and/or to renegotiate the mortgage for the homeowner.

Services Provided

- Home buying: We buy distressed assets from homeowners and banks

- Homeowner advisory assistance services

MARKET ANALYSIS

The United States has seen a 112 percent increase in the number of foreclosures in the past 12 months. This is an indicator that most of the American citizens are not in a position to pay their mortgages in time hence they are evicted out of their houses. There has also been an increase in the number of lawsuits that are related to foreclosures and since the complainants are the people who have been forced out of the houses, they are not in a position to hire a good attorney and this leads to a defeat in court.

There are expectations that if the economy in the United States does not improve, there will be an increase in the number of foreclosures and the percentage may hit 150 percent. This is because more people are becoming bankrupt each day. This is as a result of a survey that shows that over 1.1 million homeowners will face foreclosures at the rate that the economy of the United States is moving. The greatest issue is that if the 1.1 million lose homes, the lenders too will not be in a safe position since there are estimates that they will also lose over $112.5 million. The assumption is that this is a minor loss since the expected income in the real–estate industry could be close to $12 trillion.

The current statistics show that 286,000 out of 44 million mortgages result in foreclosures. This is a very large figure when it is translated to the total number of mortgages that people are taking up. The result could be a great number of people losing their hard–earned money on foreclosures and left homeless. With such alarming figures, the economy is likely to take a greater nosedive since research has shown that most of the people who take up mortgages are people who are financially unstable. This statistics shows that there is a high probability that such houses will be foreclosures.

However, if there will be such a great number of foreclosures for sale, the houses will become more affordable and people will get shelter. The housing agents too are likely to make profits in trillions and this will mean creation of more jobs in the real–estate industry. This statistics is regardless of the people who are new in the job market and they will also need housing, hence the figures will increase exponentially in the next few years.

Foreclosures are houses that are closed after the owner is unable to pay the mortgage in time. They are mainly houses that are owned by housing institutions and when the mortgage borrower is unable to pay, the house it taken away from them. Such houses are characterized by lower prices. This is because the money that the borrower had paid prior to the foreclosure reduces the amount that the housing institution requires to regain their money back. There has been alarming statistics on the increase in the number of foreclosure in the United States and other parts of the world.

In Nevada today there are over 50,000 homes that have been either foreclosed or are going to be foreclosed. It is predicted that these numbers will increase to over 5,000 homes per month in 2009. If this is true, these numbers will reflect a great number of potential clients.

Market Segmentation

Our market segmentation is based on the ability for us to secure enough good properties that we can then resell for a profit. The homeowner buy–and–resell market will be based on us buying quality real estate for fair prices. We will not take advantage of any home owner; this must be understood. We provide services that will focus on helping homeowners stay in their home and make their payments so they never go into default.

When the founder of this company was ten years old, his family was forced out of their home. This forced his family to live on the streets until they got their accounts together. HouseFlipperz's founder said that at a early age in life, he vowed that he would never do to anyone what was done to his family at such a young age.

The second part of our market segment will be for us to target the advisory services to homeowners. This is where we advise the client on government grants he can obtain to save his home. We make money from this in two ways. The first way is an up–front fee of $495. Then, when the homeowner secures the grants, is stable in the home, and the threat of foreclosure is lifted, we will get another fee of $995 and an additional fee of 0.25 basis points of the value of the loan payable by the lending bank for saving the loan.

Market analysis	Growth	2008	2009	2010	2011	2012	CAGR
Potential customers							
Buying and selling homes	0%	20,000	20,000	20,000	20,000	20,000	0.00%
Advice to home owners	10%	50,000	55,000	60,500	66,550	73,205	10.00%
Other	0%	0	0	0	0	0	0.00%
Total	**7.42%**	**70,000**	**75,000**	**80,500**	**86,550**	**93,205**	**7.42%**

Market Analysis

Target Market Segment Strategy

The main reason why we are focusing on these two segments is our ability to help the people in this market make it through these turbulent times. We realize that we will not be able to help everyone. However, we will help those who are willing to work with us to change the situation.

BUSINESS STRATEGY

Competition

Our competitive edge will be our ability to have feeling for our clients. Once word of mouth gets around, we will be in a position to win additional clients. Most of our competitors are in the business of getting people kicked out of their homes so they can buy and resell these homes. This is not what we are doing in our business model and we feel this will allow us to compete with our competitors and win.

Marketing & Sales

Our sales forecast is based on buying homes and selling them for 50 percent more. In some cases we may need to carry the home for a while in order to sell it, or we may need to do renovations to the home. We will attempt to buy homes with little renovations required.

Sales forecast	FY 2009	FY 2010	FY 2011
Sales			
Buying & selling homes	$3,600,000	$4,000,000	$ 6,000,000
Advisory services	$2,379,283	$4,000,000	$ 5,000,000
Total sales	**$5,979,283**	**$8,000,000**	**$11,000,000**
Direct cost of sales			
Homes we buy	$1,800,000	$2,500,000	$ 3,000,000
Advisory services we offer	$ 580,033	$ 600,000	$ 400,000
Subtotal direct cost of sales	$2,380,033	$3,100,000	$ 3,400,000

Sales by Month

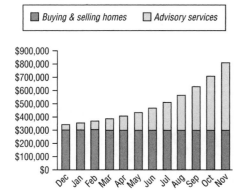

Sales by Year

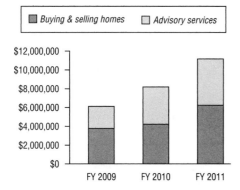

MANAGEMENT SUMMARY

The company will be owned equally by Donald Divens and Gladys Allen. Here is a breakdown of the management team:

- CEO: Donald Divens
- VP of Sales: Gladys Allen
- Comptroller: TBD
- Legal Advisor: TBD
- Office Manager: TBD
- Product Acquisition Manager: TBD
- Client Advisory Manager: TBD

Personnel Plan

Personnel plan	FY 2009	FY 2010	FY 2011
CEO	$ 97,536	$110,000	$120,000
VP—sales	$ 97,690	$100,000	$100,000
Product acquisition manager	$ 66,000	$ 80,000	$ 80,000
Advisory sales manager	$ 60,000	$ 70,000	$ 70,000
Office manager	$ 48,000	$ 55,000	$ 55,000
Comptroller	$ 54,000	$ 56,000	$ 56,000
Total people	**15**	**15**	**15**
Total payroll	**$423,226**	**$471,000**	**$481,000**

FINANCIAL PROJECTIONS

Start-up Funding

Start-up funding

Start-up expenses to fund	$ 285,000
Start-up assets to fund	$13,005,000
Total funding required	$13,290,000

Assets

Non-cash assets from start-up	$ 5,000
Cash requirements from start-up	$13,000,000
Additional cash raised	$ 610,000
Cash balance on starting date	$13,610,000
Total assets	**$13,615,000**

Liabilities and capital

Liabilities

Current borrowing	$13,900,000
Fixed liabilities	$ 0
Accounts payable (outstanding bills)	$ 0
Other current liabilities	$ 0
Total liabilities	**$13,900,000**

Capital

Planned investment

Owner	$ 0
Investor	$ 0
Additional investment requirement	$ 0
Total planned investment	**$ 0**
Loss at start-up (start-up expenses)	$ 285,000
Total capital	**$ 285,000**
Total capital and liabilities	**$13,615,000**
Total funding	**$13,900,000**

Break-even Analysis

Break-even analysis

Monthly revenue break-even	$ 62,692

Assumptions:

Average percent variable cost	40%
Estimated monthly fixed cost	$37,737.62

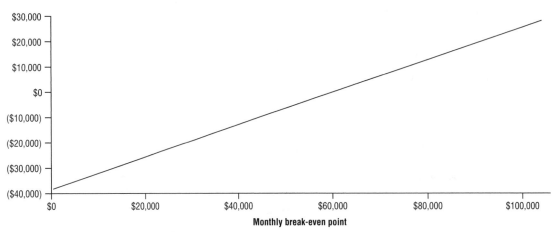

Break-even point = where line intersects with 0

Projected Profit and Loss

Pro forma profit and loss	FY 2009	FY 2010	FY 2011
Sales	$5,979,283	$8,000,000	$11,000,000
Direct costs of goods	$2,380,033	$3,100,000	$ 3,400,000
Other costs of goods	$ 0	$ 0	$0
Cost of goods sold	$2,380,033	$3,100,000	$ 3,400,000
Gross margin	$3,599,249	$4,900,000	$ 7,600,000
Gross margin %	60.20%	61.25%	69.09%
Expenses			
Payroll	$ 423,226	$ 471,000	$ 481,000
Marketing/promotion	$ 0	$ 0	$ 0
Depreciation	$ 0	$ 0	$ 0
Rent	$ 0	$ 0	$ 0
Utilities	$ 0	$ 0	$ 0
Insurance	$ 0	$ 0	$ 0
Payroll taxes	$ 29,626	$ 32,970	$ 33,670
Other	$ 0	$ 0	$ 0
Total operating expenses	**$ 452,851**	**$ 503,970**	**$ 514,670**
Profit before interest and taxes	$3,146,398	$4,396,030	$ 7,085,330
Interest expense	$1,387,707	$1,383,017	$ 1,377,017
Taxes incurred	$ 527,607	$ 903,904	$ 1,712,494
Net profit	$1,231,083	$2,109,109	$ 3,995,819
Net profit/sales	20.59%	26.36%	36.33%

Profit Monthly

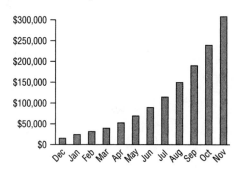

Profit Yearly

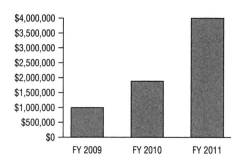

Projected Cash Flow

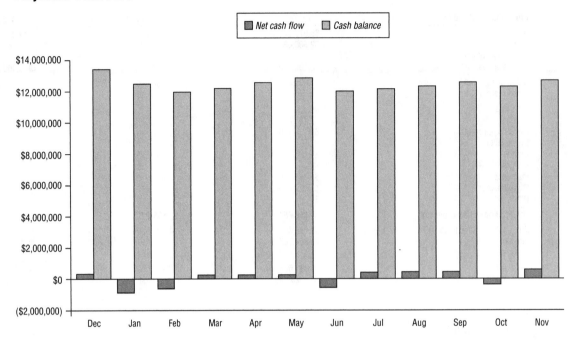

Pro forma cash flow	FY 2009	FY 2010	FY 2011
Cash received			
Cash from operations			
Cash sales	$ 5,979,283	$ 8,000,000	$11,000,000
Subtotal cash from operations	$ 5,979,283	$ 8,000,000	$11,000,000
Additional cash received			
GST/HST received (output Tax)	$ 0	$ 0	$ 0
GST/HST repayments	$ 0	$ 0	$ 0
New current borrowing	$ 0	$ 0	$ 0
New other liabilities (interest-free)	$ 0	$ 0	$ 0
New fixed liabilities	$ 0	$ 0	$ 0
Sales of other current assets	$ 0	$ 0	$ 0
Sales of fixed assets	$ 0	$ 0	$ 0
New investment received	$ 0	$ 0	$ 0
Subtotal cash received	**$ 5,979,283**	**$ 8,000,000**	**$11,000,000**
Expenditures			
Expenditures from operations			
Cash spending	$ 423,226	$ 471,000	$ 481,000
Bill payments	$ 5,900,658	$ 5,973,809	$ 6,721,389
Subtotal spent on operations	**$ 6,323,884**	**$ 6,444,809**	**$ 7,202,389**
Additional cash spent			
GST/HST paid out (input tax)	$ 0	$ 0	$ 0
GST/HST payments	$ 0	$ 0	$ 0
Principal repayment of current borrowing	$ 42,326	$ 55,000	$ 65,000
Other liabilities principal repayment	$ 0	$ 0	$ 0
Fixed liabilities principal repayment	$ 0	$ 0	$ 0
Purchase other current assets	$ 0	$ 0	$ 0
Purchase fixed assets	$ 0	$ 0	$ 0
Dividends	$ 100,000	$ 200,000	$ 300,000
Subtotal cash spent	$ 6,466,210	$ 6,699,809	$ 7,567,389
Net cash flow	$ 486,928	$ 1,300,191	$ 3,432,611
Cash balance	$13,123,072	$14,423,264	$17,855,875

Projected Balance Sheet

Pro forma balance sheet	FY 2009	FY 2010	FY 2011
Assets			
Current assets			
Cash	$13,123,072	$ 14,423,264	$ 17,855,875
Stock	$ 1,809,967	$ 2,357,487	$ 2,585,630
Other current assets	$ 5,000	$ 5,000	$ 5,000
Total current assets	**$14,938,039**	**$16,785,750**	**$20,446,505**
Fixed assets			
Fixed assets	$ 0	$ 0	$ 0
Accumulated depreciation	$ 0	$ 0	$ 0
Total fixed assets	**$ 0**	**$ 0**	**$ 0**
Total assets	**$14,938,039**	**$16,785,750**	**$20,446,505**
Liabilities and capital			
Current liabilities			
Accounts payable	$ 234,282	$ 227,884	$ 257,821
Current borrowing	$13,857,674	$13,802,674	$13,737,674
Other current liabilities	$ 0	$ 0	$ 0
Subtotal current liabilities	$14,091,956	$14,030,558	$13,995,494
Fixed liabilities	$ 0	$ 0	$ 0
Total liabilities	**$14,091,956**	**$14,030,558**	**$13,995,494**
Paid-in capital	$ 0	$ 0	$ 0
Retained earnings	$ 385,000	$ 646,083	$ 2,455,192
Earnings	$ 1,231,083	$ 2,109,109	$ 3,995,819
Total capital	**$ 846,083**	**$ 2,755,192**	**$ 6,451,011**
Total liabilities and capital	**$14,938,039**	**$16,785,750**	**$20,446,505**
Net worth	**$ 846,083**	**$ 2,755,192**	**$ 6,451,011**

Rental Defibrillator Service

HeartSong Defibrillator, LLC

10001 Red Bud St.
Framingham, Massachusetts, 01701

Jonathan Rekve

HeartSong Defibrillator, LLC will provide life saving machines on a leased basis across North America. The units will be rented to a variety of businesses, industries, sports teams, government departments, fire halls, police departments, and so on. The new units that are manufactured today are small, easy–to–carry and store in vehicles. With the new and easy–to–use equipment, governments are realizing that every service vehicle and public place should have one of these units on hand.

EXECUTIVE SUMMARY

HeartSong Defibrillator, LLC will provide life saving machines on a leased basis across North America. The units will be rented to a variety of businesses, industries, sports teams, government departments, fire halls, police departments, and so on. The new units that are manufactured today are small, easy–to–carry and store in vehicles. With the new and easy–to–use equipment, governments are realizing that every service vehicle and public place should have one of these units on hand. This is why this business will expand and we will be able to make a great deal for money leasing these units versus selling them. We will have ongoing revenue from a single client instead of a one time sale to this client.

Business Overview

It will be our goal in the first year of business to achieve sales of $6,000,000. Our mission will be to save lives while making a profit from a business that has a lot of good will attached to it. This goodwill will pay forward dividends on and on for our business and our partners.

HeartSong Defibrillator, LLC is owned by Scott Peru. Scott has been a fireman for over 25 years, and when the defibrillators came to the market, a lot of fire halls and ambulances could not afford to buy these and the lease options were just to expensive for their budgets. Scott figured out how he could get these units into as many hands as possible without breaking the bank.

After careful review of the market, Scott launched HeartSong Defibrillator. While the business is a for–profit business, the goal of Scott was to return the profit to the company in order to make business viable for the long term. The key to success is the fact that our lease rates are about 60 percent less than the nearest competitor; this means we have a large protection against any competitor trying to enter the market or an existing seller reducing their pricing based on their existing business model.

Therefore with $150,000 start–up capital Scott Peru has started this business and will secure operating loans of $500,000. Our net profit for 2010 is forecasted to be $3,555,160 on sales of $6,662,950.

Objectives

HeartSong Defibrillator LLC's objective is to provide life–saving machines on a leased basis across North America. The units will be rented to a variety of businesses, industries, sports teams, government departments, fire hall, police departments, and so on.

Mission

Our mission will be to save lives while making a profit from a business that has a lot of goodwill attached to it. This goodwill will pay forward dividends on and on for our business and our partners.

Keys of Success

- Our ability to sign up key lease clients like fire hall halls and police departments.

- The ability to get the exposure for our business, so we get free media coverage. This will greatly reduce our operating expenses for advertising and marketing.

- Our existing competitors do not follow our direction when marketing against us.

- We are able to secure a good line of defibrillator as our main product line.

BUSINESS OVERVIEW

HeartSong is owned by Scott Peru. Scott has been a fireman for over twenty-five years, and when the defibrillators came to the market, a lot of fire halls and ambulances could not afford to buy these and the lease options were just to expensive for budgets. Scott figured out how he could get these units into as many hands as possible, without breaking the bank. Therefore with $150,000 start–up capital, Scott has started this business.

Operations

HeartSong's company ownership is owned by Scott Peru. Scott will use this business plan to attract investors and help fund the business for the long term. The company will be set up as a limited liability company. No part of the business will be given to the investors; instead there will be a percentage of the profit shared with the owner of the business.

Start-up requirements

Start-up expenses

Legal	$ 2,500
Office supplies	$ 5,000
Insurance	$ 2,000
Rent	$ 4,000
Office equipment	$ 5,000
Shipping expense	$ 7,000
Training expense	$ 10,000
First 3 months inventory	$100,000
Travel expense	$ 10,000
Total start-up expenses	**$145,500**

Start-up assets

Cash required	$200,000
Start-up stock	$100,000
Other current assets	$ 25,000
Total assets	**$325,000**
Total requirements	**$470,500**

Products

We will lease as well sell defibrillator units to a variety of clients. Most of our target group of clients will be those who cannot afford to buy these units directly from the manufacturer or distributors.

We will subsidize the sale of these leased units to our clients. This will keep the costs of these units down within a margin so that more users can afford to have these units in their cars, businesses, or other places where these units can save as many lives as possible.

Product Types

- The type that is placed in a car

- The type that is placed in a business

- The type that is placed in buildings like banks, libraries, etc.

- The type that can be carried in a backpack

- The type that can be placed in buses and airplanes

MARKET ANALYSIS

Our market for our type of sales solution is quite large. When you look at the average city of 200,000 people, our product can be placed in several locations.

- 150 police vehicles

- 55 fire trucks

- 26 sporting facilities

- 90 taxi cabs

- 120 public buses

- 110 public businesses

- 15,000 private businesses

There are 15,551 total possible customers for our unit sales at an average of $30 per month per unit, or $466,530 total annual sales just for a city with 200,000 people. When you multiply this by the number of cities in USA and Canada it gives you the size of potential market for our product.

If we secure 10% of this market, our annual sales will be $46,653. If we sell to 100 comparable cities with 10% market share in each, our annual sales will jump to $4,665,300.

With the growth of this business, we feel there will be a larger share of the market that will lease these units versus buying them outright. With leasing the units the clients can upgrade their unit whenever they want. Knowing this allows us to secure a large percentage of the market before our competitors take a keen interest in this market.

We will use people like firemen, law enforcement, bus drivers, anyone that has a lot of access to the streets of our market on a daily basis; this will allow for people to quickly determine where these units are needed and can be sold to those units. The front line is always the best place to put your product if there are not any real competitors in the area.

Market Segmentation

A maturing hospital market, declining numbers of hospital beds, and an under–served public access sector have seen the tide turn in favor of automatic external defibrillators (AED) and away from manual external defibrillators. With penetration rates lower than 50 percent in the public access sector, AEDs are expected to make a splash in the home sector in the next five to ten years.

U.S. External Defibrillators Markets finds that the market earned revenues of $540.0 million in 2006 and estimates this to reach $911.3 million in 2013.

There is a trend by many cities to put these units in all public buildings and service vehicles like police cars, fire trucks, city utility trucks and so on. When this happens, there will be two results. The cities will look to buying the machines, and then when they realize the cost will be too expensive, they will look to other options. Our pricing model is such that we will charge a very low lease fee, knowing that we will get monthly payments over a long period of time. So far, the test markets have accepted this pricing model strategy; we feel this will be the trend going forward.

Market analysis	Growth	2008	2009	2010	2011	2012	CAGR
Potential customers	10%	15,000	16,500	18,150	19,965	21,962	10.00%
City # 1	10%	15,000	16,500	18,150	19,965	21,962	10.00%
City # 2	10%	15,000	16,500	18,150	19,965	21,962	10.00%
City # 3	10%	15,000	16,500	18,150	19,965	21,962	10.00%
Total	**10.00%**	**60,000**	**66,000**	**72,600**	**79,860**	**87,848**	**10.00%**

Competition

We will be the only provider of the defibrillator product to lease the units; every one of our competitors sells the units and does not lease them out. This allows us to ensure a large market share because of the cost of the units. Our clients can pay for the items over time. If they buy 10 units for example, their monthly lease payment will be around $300; this is reasonable, especially considering the cost if they were to buy them outright from the start.

We also will allow our clients to trade up as part of their lease, where if they buy one then they will need to buy another one once the new units are on the market. We will then have two pricing strategies: a lower price for the old units (as long as they still function normally) and a somewhat higher price for the new units. All of our competitors require clients to buy the new one when it comes out. This gives us a very distinctive advantage over our competitors.

This flexibility will allow us to be market leaders and not followers. We will pass any saving on to our clients for the new units. Over time when we get the old units back, we will look to sell these units outright so as to keep our inventory low.

MARKETING & SALES

Our marketing strategy will be to have our products placed in every city in North America. We will do this by attending trade shows, advertising and getting our message to city managers.

We will use our clients as our sales staff; by giving them a sample of the units for trail use, they can sell the use of our units to their various departments. We will offer sales incentives for these city managers to sell our products. These sales will cover the police, fire, as well as other departments within the city structure. We will also make use of free media coverage by donating units to various non profits throughout the country. We will also hire a consulting firm to offer research and advice as we grow our business.

This media coverage will be on TV, radio, and newspapers in each of the markets we are targeting.

Sales Strategy

Our sales strategy will be to focus our sales calls to the city administrator level and also the front line users like fire departments and police forces. These sales strategies will have a dual role; they will allow our potential end users to help sell our product for us, to the decision makers at all levels of the city managers.

There is a growing trend for media to cover stories when one of these units save a life; this coverage in itself gives us a sales tool. All we need to do then is make sure local managers for the cities departments have our contact information, so the customers will call us.

Sales Forecast

The sales forecast is based on the lease payment made to our company from various clients. We will be leasing each unit out and will not be selling them directly. This way we can keep the costs down for our end users, yet be able to make a decent profit.

Our sales forecast is based on an average market acceptance from our clients. If we are able to get a higher than average amount of clients leasing from us, the market share will increase and so will our profits.

Sales forecast	2008	2009	2010
Unit sales	22,976	24,500	35,700
Unit prices	$ 290.00	$ 290.00	$ 290.00
Sales	$6,662,950	$7,105,000	$10,353,000
Direct unit costs	$ 49.30	$ 49.30	$ 49.30
Direct cost of sales	$1,132,702	$1,207,850	$ 1,760,010

MANAGEMENT SUMMARY

HeartSong Defibrillator LLC will be owned by Scott Peru. Scott brings to this business about twenty years worth of experience in the medical sales market in addition to bring a volunteer fire fighter. Scott worked with a local distributor of medical supplies to hospitals in the region. Seeing the need for this product, Scott decided to take the leap and invested in this concept.

Personnel Plan

Personnel plan	2008	2009	2010
General manager	$ 61,094	$ 70,000	$ 75,000
CFO	$ 41,030	$ 45,000	$ 55,000
Sales manager	$ 58,829	$ 65,000	$ 65,000
Total people	**10**	**12**	**15**
Total payroll	**$160,954**	**$180,000**	**$195,000**

FINANCIAL ANALYSIS

Start–up Funding

With a loan of $500,000 and the cost for inventory of $350,000 gives us a great place to start. We will be getting an operating line from our supplier of the units.

Start-up funding

Start-up expenses to fund	$145,500
Start-up assets to fund	$325,000
Total funding required	**$470,500**

Assets

Non-cash assets from start-up	$125,000
Cash requirements from start-up	$200,000
Additional cash raised	$179,500
Cash balance on starting date	$379,500
Total assets	**$504,500**

Liabilities and capital

Liabilities

Current borrowing	$350,000
Fixed liabilities	$ 0
Accounts payable (outstanding bills)	$300,000
Other current liabilities	$ 0
Total liabilities	**$650,000**

Capital

Planned investment

Owner	$ 0
Investor	$ 0
Additional investment requirement	$ 0
Total planned investment	**$ 0**
Loss at start-up (start-up expenses)	$145,500
Total capital	**$145,500**
Total capital and liabilities	**$504,500**
Total funding	**$650,000**

Break–Even Analysis

Break-even analysis

Monthly units break-even	135.00
Monthly revenue break-even	$39,185.00

Assumptions:

Average per-unit revenue	$ 290.00
Average per-unit variable cost	$ 49.30
Estimated monthly fixed cost	$32,523.56

Projected Profit and Loss

Pro forma profit and loss	2008	2009	2010
Sales	$6,662,950	$7,105,000	$10,353,000
Direct costs of goods	$1,132,702	$1,207,850	$ 1,760,010
Other costs of goods	$ 289,971	$ 320,000	$ 450,000
Cost of goods sold	**$1,422,672**	**$1,527,850**	**$ 2,210,010**
Gross margin	$5,240,278	$5,577,150	$ 8,142,990
Gross margin %	78.65%	78.50%	78.65%
Expenses			
Payroll	$ 160,954	$ 180,000	$ 195,000
Marketing/promotion	$ 30,547	$ 35,000	$ 40,000
Depreciation	$ 0	$ 0	$ 0
Rent	$ 14,587	$ 17,000	$ 23,000
Utilities	$ 10,474	$ 12,000	$ 14,000
Insurance	$ 1,366	$ 1,500	$ 1,600
Payroll taxes	$ 11,267	$ 12,600	$ 13,650
Other	$ 161,088	$ 195,000	$ 205,000
Total operating expenses	**$ 390,283**	**$ 453,100**	**$ 492,250**
Profit before interest and taxes	$4,849,995	$5,124,050	$ 7,650,740
Interest expense	$ 33,991	$ 31,787	$ 28,787
Taxes incurred	$1,444,801	$1,527,679	$ 2,286,586
Net profit	$3,371,203	$3,564,584	$ 5,335,367
Net profit/sales	50.60%	50.17%	51.53%

Projected Cash Flow

Pro forma cash flow	2008	2009	2010
Cash received			
Cash from operations			
Cash sales	$4,997,213	$5,328,750	$ 7,764,750
Cash from receivables	$1,101,152	$1,738,793	$ 2,313,030
Subtotal cash from operations	$6,098,364	$7,067,543	$10,077,780
Additional cash received			
GST/HST received (output tax)	$ 0	$ 0	$ 0
GST/HST repayments	$ 0	$ 0	$ 0
New current borrowing	$ 15,062	$ 18,000	$ 23,000
New other liabilities (interest-free)	$ 9,192	$ 12,000	$ 14,000
New fixed liabilities	$ 0	$ 0	$ 0
Sales of other current sssets	$ 0	$ 0	$ 0
Sales of fixed assets	$ 0	$ 0	$ 0
New investment received	$ 0	$ 0	$ 0
Subtotal cash received	$6,122,619	$7,097,543	$10,114,780
Expenditures			
Expenditures from operations			
Cash spending	$ 160,954	$ 180,000	$ 195,000
Bill payments	$3,322,298	$3,449,595	$ 4,828,627
Subtotal spent on operations	$3,483,251	$3,629,595	$ 5,023,627
Additional cash spent			
GST/HST paid out (input tax)	$ 0	$ 0	$ 0
GST/HST payments	$ 0	$ 0	$ 0
Principal repayment of current borrowing	$ 33,696	$ 45,000	$ 56,000
Other liabilities principal repayment	$ 0	$ 0	$ 0
Fixed liabilities principal repayment	$ 0	$ 0	$ 0
Purchase other current assets	$ 0	$ 0	$ 0
Purchase fixed assets	$ 0	$ 0	$ 0
Dividends	$ 11,014	$ 19,000	$ 30,000
Subtotal cash spent	$3,527,961	$3,693,595	$ 5,109,627
Net cash flow	$2,594,658	$3,403,948	$ 5,005,153
Cash balance	$2,974,158	$6,378,106	$11,383,259

Projected Balance Sheet

Pro forma balance sheet	2008	2009	2010
Assets			
Current assets			
Cash	$2,974,158	$6,378,106	$11,383,259
Accounts receivable	$ 564,586	$ 602,043	$ 877,262
Stock	$ 637,895	$ 680,216	$ 991,171
Other current assets	$ 25,000	$ 25,000	$ 25,000
Total current assets	**$4,201,638**	**$7,685,364**	**$13,276,693**
Fixed assets			
Fixed assets	$ 0	$ 0	$ 0
Accumulated depreciation	$ 0	$ 0	$ 0
Total fixed assets	**$ 0**	**$ 0**	**$ 0**
Total assets	**$4,201,638**	**$7,685,364**	**$13,276,693**
Liabilities and capital			
Current liabilities			
Accounts payable	$ 501,391	$ 599,532	$ 904,493
Current borrowing	$ 331,366	$ 304,366	$ 271,366
Other current liabilities	$ 9,192	$ 21,192	$ 35,192
Subtotal current liabilities	$ 841,949	$ 925,091	$ 1,211,052
Fixed liabilities	$ 0	$ 0	$ 0
Total liabilities	**$ 841,949**	**$ 925,091**	**$ 1,211,052**
Paid-in capital	$ 0	$ 0	$ 0
Retained earnings	$ 156,514	$3,195,689	$ 6,730,274
Earnings	$3,371,203	$3,564,584	$ 5,335,367
Total capital	**$3,214,689**	**$6,760,274**	**$12,065,641**
Total liabilities and capital	**$4,056,638**	**$7,685,364**	**$13,276,693**
Net worth	$3,359,689	$6,760,274	$12,065,641

Windmill Distributor
Pierson Windmills

519 Black St.
Hurricane, Utah 84737

Gerald Rekve

Our mission is to provide homeowners with the ability to own their own electrical supply source, allowing them to actually sell energy back to utility companies. This will let the homeowner profit from owning our products.

BUSINESS OVERVIEW

Pierson Windmills was formed in early 2008 with the sole purpose to sell windmills to the home market in the Salt Lake City, Utah area. With the growth in the green area for energy over the past few years, we need to generate our own energy rather than using the oil or fossil fuels of yesterday.

With the wind volumes in North America, along with the wind in Utah, it was decided that we would focus our green business on windmill sales. The company started with an investment from the owner Mark Pierson and three other investors. It was decided to keep the investment pool to a total of $400,000.

The payback for the investors will be in year four and five when it is projected that all of the original investment will be repaid to the shareholders. All profits other than dividends will be placed back into the company and used for future growth opportunities. With net profit margins hovering around 38 percent it is projected that we will be able to roll out similar business models in other markets starting in year four and five.

OBJECTIVES

The main objective for Pierson Windmills is to provide a home use type of windmill product that can be plugged into the grid and allow for the home owner to decrease their electrical consumption and, therefore, their cost. Oil prices rose in 2008 reaching over $135 per barrel. This number has shown that in the future prices will average this high; it will not be a one-time spike.

Our main goal is to be able to sell these units at a price that is affordable for the home owner. Market share is critical for Pierson's ability to earn a decent return on investment for the shareholders and main owners.

Another objective is to take advantage of the market we operate in, with the large number of qualified employees in the market today. We are confidant that this will help us attract qualified production staff.

MISSION

Our mission is to provide homeowners with the ability to own their own electrical supply source, allowing them to actually sell energy back to utility companies. This will let the homeowner profit from owning our products.

This business, as well our product, will be revolutionary to the market on a number of fronts. Here are a few areas where Pierson Windmills will be different.

- Ability to sell energy back to the utility
- Allows homeowner to provide for their own method of heating or providing electricity to their home
- Allows homeowner to add to their windmills as long as they have enough land

BUSINESS STRATEGY

Keys for Success

- Low price point of our products
- Good quality manufacturing
- Reliable transportation firms
- Good work ethic for manufacturing staff and installation staff
- No other competitor enters the market within six months of our January, 2008 start date
- We are able to purchase materials required to build the windmills at a competitive price
- We will be able to secure global network of distribution points
- Our partners in selling these products will provide good service
- Installation of our windmills will be done correctly

Pierson Windmills will manufacture windmills used to provide energy to the home owner. Our products are simple in design, yet they are leading edge in terms of energy they provide to the home owner. The company will be started from the ground up, everything from hiring of staff to putting together the production facility to produce the products we sell.

Our company will also put together suppliers who will provide us with parts to the products we sell. For example, the turbine engines will be supplied to us, along with the fins for the propellers that are on the windmill.

Operations

Pierson Windmills will be owned by Mark Pierson and a combination of shareholders and other investors. Mark has been in the manufacturing business for over twenty years, working in all departments from shipping to VP of Sales.

Pierson Windmills's start up funding is only $280,000. This being said, it is a low dollar investment start-up considering the industry we are going into.

We will start up our products's roll–out in stages; first will be the smallest of the windmills and we will gradually proceed to the largest windmills. The product design has already taken place. All that is required will be the putting the production unit together and hiring and training staff.

There is about a thirty–day time period from hiring staff to first products being ready for the market. This is one of the shortest production cycles there is; normally it takes about three months for this process to take place.

Start-up Costs

Start-up Requirements

Start-up expenses	
Payroll	$ 20,000
Building	$ 25,000
Equipment	$ 50,000
Rent	$ 10,000
Supplies	$ 20,000
Manufacturing supplies	$ 30,000
Shipping supplies	$ 5,000
Tools	$ 40,000
Small machinery	$ 60,000
Vehicles	$ 10,000
Total start-up expenses	**$270,000**
Start-up assets	
Cash required	$ 5,000
Start-up stock	$ 1,000
Other current assets	$ 2,000
Fixed assets	$ 2,000
Total assets	**$ 10,000**
Total requirements	**$280,000**

PRODUCTS

Our products are windmills that are used for energy production for the home. We will produce the eight–foot windmill first, then the 12–foot, the 16–foot, and finally the 22–foot.

Our windmills are measured by the size of the tower.

Parts that will be manufactured either on–site or off–site include:

1. Rotor Blade
2. Nacelle
3. Hub
4. Tower
5. Transformer
6. High speed shaft
7. Gearbox
8. Low Speed shaft
9. Rotor Hub
10. Brake
11. Generator

MARKET ANALYSIS

The 2008 IEA WEO—Renewable Energy Report Highlights:

World energy demand is forecasted to grow from 11,730 Mtoe (million metric tons of oil equivalents) in 2006 to 17,010 Mtoe in 2030. Fossil fuels, with oil as the primary source, will account for 80 percent of energy used in 2030.

China and India will be responsible for over half of the increased energy demand between now and 2030. Global demand for oil (excluding biofuels) is forecast to rise from 85 million bpd in 2007 to 106 million bpd in 2030. This forecast was revised downward by 10 million bpd since last year's forecast.

World demand for electricity is forecasted to rise from 15,665 TWh in 2006 to 28,141 TWh in 2030. Renewable energy will displace gas to become the second largest producer of electrical energy by 2015, but will still lag far behind coal. For OECD countries, the increase in renewable electricity is greater than the increase in electricity from fossil fuels and nuclear. The share of nuclear power in the world energy mix falls from 6 percent in 2008 to 5 percent in 2030.

Electricity generation from PV and CSP in 2030 is forecasted to be 245 TWh and 107 TWh, respectively. Solar PV will continue to have the highest investment cost of all commercially deployed renewable energy sources.

Geothermal and wave technologies are forecast to produce 180 TWh and 14 TWh of electricity in 2030. Over 860 TWh of electricity from biomass is forecast to be produced in 2030. Present conversion of biomass to electricity is at 20 percent efficiency.

Global output of wind power is forecast to grow from 130 TWh in 2006 to more than 660 TWh in 2015 to 1,490 TWh in 2030. It will become the 2nd largest source of renewable electricity (after hydropower) by 2010. Potential for hydropower in non–OECD countries is still large. Most good sites in OECD countries have been utilized.

Energy storage is rarely the cheapest way of dealing with variability of wind and solar power, but several next generation storage technologies are under development. These include ultracapacitors, superconducting magnetic systems, and vanadium redox batteries. Electrolysis to produce hydrogen, later used in fuel cells on demand is an option, but the overall efficiency is only 40 percent.

Carbon dioxide emissions from coal combustion are forecasted to rise from 11.7 billion metric tons in 2006 to 18.6 billion metric tons in 2030. The ability of carbon sequestration to limit carbon dioxide emissions by 2030 is limited.

The reference scenario presumes that by 2030, the U.S. will only meet 40 percent of the biofuel mandate set in 2007. In Brazil, biofuels are projected to account for 28 percent of road–transport fuel demand by 2030. The present amount supplied is equivalent to 13 percent of road–transport fuel demand. Demand for biodiesel is expected to grow faster than demand for ethanol.

Biofuels in 2006 provided the equivalent of 0.6 million bpd, representing around 1.5 percent of global road transport fuel demand. The United States is the largest user of biofuels, and most of the recent growth has been in the U.S.

The share of biofuels in road transport fuels is forecasted to grow from 1.5 percent in 2006 to 5 percent (3.2 million bpd) in 2030. Second generation biofuels based on lignocellulosic biomass, converted via enzyme hydrolysis or biomass gasification (BTL) are expected to become commercially viable. However, the contribution will be minor, and not until after 2020. Capital costs for cellulosic ethanol are "significantly more" than sugarcane or grain–based facilities. As a result, full commercialization hinges on "major cost reductions."

The United States and Brazil both export soybean biodiesel to the EU. (The fact that the U.S. exports any biodiesel is very surprising to me, given the high demand/prices for diesel in the U.S.) Some countries are beginning to scale back their biofuel policies due to concerns about environmental sustainability. Shortages of water availability will be a potential constraint for further expansion of biofuels.

Most biomass will still come from agricultural and forestry residues in 2030, but a growing portion will come from biomass farmed for biofuels. A growing share of biomass is also projected to fuel combined heat and power (CHP) plants.

There is considerable room for growth of solar water heating (water heating consumes 20 percent of all residential energy consumption). China currently has 60 percent of the world's installed solar water heating capacity. Solar water and space heating is projected to grow from 7.6 Mtoe in 2006 to 45 Mtoe in 2030.

Hybrid vehicles are commercially viable today; electric vehicles have yet to gain traction. Electric vehicle technology is advancing rapidly, but further improvements in storage technology are needed for efficiency and cost improvements. Long term, electric hybrids, fully electric vehicles, and fuel cell vehicles have the most potential for minimizing the need for oil–based fuels. In the very long term—projecting out to 2050—fuel cell vehicles are forecasted to make up 33 percent to 50 percent of new vehicle sales in the OECD.

Cumulative investment in renewable energy between 2007 and 2030 is projected to be $5.5 trillion, with 60 percent of that for electricity generation.

Our Commentary on the Findings

The report reiterates the points I have argued on numerous occasions: Biofuels will not scale up to produce more than a small fraction of our fuel demand, and even then with potentially serious consequences. While the report spreads the blame for higher food prices on a combination of competition with biofuels, higher energy prices, poor harvests, and various agricultural policies, it correctly identifies water as a (highly underrated) issue in the future scaling of biofuels. On the other hand, the report identifies Latin America and Africa as regions with the potential for boosting biomass production by modernizing farming techniques.

I think the report correctly identifies renewable electricity and renewable heating (especially solar water heating) as areas poised for growth. However, it also predicts that carbon dioxide emissions will continue to rise.

By 2030, the cost for solar PV and CSP will still be higher than all other renewable technologies are today. And not just a little higher: solar PV is predicted to be twice as expensive in 2030 as hydro and onshore wind are today. So much for Moore's Law applying to solar PV.

However the nagging issue for me is the credibility of the predictions. How much stock can I put into the renewable energy predictions from an agency that thinks oil production won't peak until 2030, and that demand will exceed 100 million bpd (contrary to the opinions of two Big Oil executives?)

Conclusions

The renewable energy portion was a tale of two technologies: Renewable electricity and renewable biofuels. Renewable electricity is forecast to grow rapidly, and make up an increasing portion of electricity supplies. The share of nuclear power falls, but coal usage is projected to rise 60 percent by 2030 (with 90 percent of that increase in non–OECD countries). The expected increase in coal usage helps explain why greenhouse gas emissions are forecasted to continue rising.

Renewable biofuels, by contrast, are forecasted to still make a very small contribution to overall road transport fuel by 2030. Cellulosic ethanol will be slow to be commercialized, and the contribution to fuel supplies by 2030 is expected to be small. Concerns about negative externalities will grow, and the impact of biofuel production on water supplies will be hotly debated.

Target Market Segment Strategy

Pierson Windmills will target the home owner for our windmill products. We realize that we will not be able to convert all home owners for our products for a number of reasons. Some of which are economical and others are no need or desire to change to our new form of energy. Because this will be a slow transmission to our form of energy, we feel that the long term growth of our products will be great for our products.

To start, we feel our target market will be the home owner who lives either on an acreage or large lot or farm. The reason for this is the large land mass required in order to ensure the home owners has the ability to get enough wind through the blades of the windmill. In urban centers the wind can be blocked due to other homes, trees etc.

Windmills require a certain amount of unencumbered wind in order to insure they get the required wind volume through the blades. This will insure the wind turbine turns enough to create the required electrical current.

Our strategy will be to sell the small windmill units to home owners living in these areas. While this will limit our potential home owners, it will decrease our marketing cost in targeting to this group. We will get requests from home owners in all sectors of the market; however, with our target market to this group we will keeps costs down while knowing that we will be able to garner a large percentage of the potential market.

Utah has a large land mass. The roll out of our products will result in a slow but steady increase in market share, allowing us to build our systems as well suppliers to meet the needs of our production requirements.

Market Segmentation

Market analysis	Growth	2008	2009	2010	2011	2012	CAGR
Potential customers							
Home owners	15%	100,000	115,000	132,250	152,088	174,901	15.00%
Buidling owners	5%	20,000	21,000	22,050	23,153	24,311	5.00%
Other	0%	0	0	0	0	0	0.00%
Total	13.51%	120,000	136,000	154,300	175,241	199,212	13.51%

PRODUCTS & SERVICES

The global energy challenge requires urgent actions in tackling the threat of climate change and meeting the rising demand for energy. A renewable, safe, and clean resource, wind energy is emerging to be part of the solution to the global energy challenge. The US wind industry achieved the highest annual installed wind power capacity of 5,329 MW in 2007. In 1999–98 turbine size was 0.71 MW which is increased to 1.65 MW by 2007–2008. But, expiring of Production Tax Credit is a matter of concern since expiring of this will affect negatively the rate of wind turbines installations.

Our Research Findings

- US wind power accounted for nearly 30 percent of all new electricity–generating capacity added nationally in 2007, up from less than 1 percent in 2002.

- US wind power installations have fallen by 93 percent (2000), 73 percent (2002) and 77 percent (2004) when credit was not extended.

- In cumulative wind energy capacity, US has improved its position from no. 3 (2006) to no. 2 (2007) globally.

- Unlike most other electricity generation sources, wind turbines don't consume water. So 4 trillions gallons of water will be saved if 20 percent wind scenario is achieved by 2030.

- The wind power industry of US is expected to grow from 9,000 annual construction jobs in 2007 to 65,000 new annual construction jobs in 2021.

- US electricity from wind could reduce annual electric sector carbon dioxide (CO_2) emissions by 825 Million metric tons by 2030.

COMPETITION

Pierson Windmills's competitive advantage is our ability to be agile enough that we can change to market conditions within days and not months. Also our product design is such that all the parts for all models are interchangeable with each other. This design feature is critical to our long-term success. In five years we will be able to sell parts to aging windmills because of our inventory of unique windmill parts.

All of our windmills will be made the same, except for the shell that covers the windmills's working parts. This means we will run a more cost–effective backend business, while offering our clients quick replacement parts. All of this will be passed on to the customer as lower prices, therefore insuring our long-term success and customer loyalty.

Key Competition

- *Turbine Controls*: Turbine Controls manufactures small (50–kW) turbines, with special expertise in hybrid systems combining wind and diesel engines.

- *Millers Inc.*: Millers Inc. has manufactured almost 2,000 tubular towers for wind turbines for customers worldwide.

- *Unique Energy*: Unique Energy manufactures small wind turbines for electric generation and water pumping, with sales in all fifty states and 80 countries.

- *Worldwide Engineering*: The world's largest environmental engineering and project implementation company (gross annual revenue of $1.3 billion and over 7,000 employees) undertakes permitting, design, and construction of wind energy projects for developers, utilities, and institutions.

- *Waltz*: The generating subsidiary of an energy company with annual revenues of $6 billion, Waltz is the nation's largest provider of wind energy, with ownership interest in approximately 1,000 MW of windfarms in Texas, California, Iowa and Oregon.

- *Desom*: Desom provides structuring advice and financing for wind (and other alternative energy) and industrial projects. The firm provides equity, junior and senior construction and term loans, and bridge financing for alternative energy projects. Desom has $1.0 billion in annual interest income.

- *Kissners*: Wire and cable manufacturer Kissners is the largest cable specialist for wind turbine cables in the U.S., Canadian and international markets.

MARKETING & SALES

Marketing Strategy

Our marketing strategy is to place our products in front of our target market using print, electronic, and TV media, along with key selling points of our product of which are its ability to interchange parts. This was a similar design that was used by Henry Ford with the Model T and also during World War Two with tanks and airplane engines.

Another marketing strategy will be for us to offer green solutions to non–profit groups; this will give us free media exposure while assisting groups that will benefit from our wind technology.

Sales Strategy

Pierson's sales strategy will be to focus our sales efforts on sales channels; this will allow us to target key segments, while increasing our focus on sales channels that give us the greatest return on investment.

Some of the areas where we will target will be sales channels with major retailers like Home Depot, Target, Lowes, and so on. We are building a fairly new business segment; therefore we will be covering new ground. Knowing this allows us to be very flexible in our marketing and sales strategy, giving us this flexibility to change direction on a dime if we need to.

Our Sales Channels

- Major home improvement stores

- Distributor sales agents–small independent stores

- Online web–based sales

- Advertising–supported print & electronic media

- TV Infomercials

Sales Forecast

Our first three years in business are based on a very conservative approach to the market. The main reason we have done this is because we have to make certain that the changes in the opinion of the government in the past five years has flipped a number of times. In some cases there is a hyper need to act now by the government and then months later they are saying no action is required. In 2008 we seen oil prices rise from a nominal $80 a barrel to $140 a barrel. There is some predicting that oil will fall flat on its face later in 2008. Therefore we will be sure all our budgeting is very conservative.

If, for example, the worst case event happens and oil hits $200 a barrel we will be ready for it; however if oil hits $50 a barrel in late 2008, we will have not been tooled up for large production numbers.

Sales forecast	2008	2009	2010
Unit sales			
Small WIND MILLS	854	1,200	1,400
Large WIND MILLS	449	550	650
Total unit sales	**1,303**	**1,750**	**2,050**
Unit prices			
Small WIND MILLS	$ 2,500.00	$ 2,500.00	$ 2,500.00
Large WIND MILLS	$ 4,500.00	$ 4,500.00	$ 4,500.00
Sales			
Small WIND MILLS	$2,135,755	$3,000,000	$3,500,000
Large WIND MILLS	$2,020,815	$2,475,000	$2,925,000
Total sales	**$4,156,570**	**$5,475,000**	**$6,425,000**
Direct unit costs			
Small WIND MILLS	$ 675.00	$ 675.00	$ 675.00
Large WIND MILLS	$ 1,035.00	$ 1,035.00	$ 1,035.00
Direct cost of sales			
Small WIND MILLS	$ 576,654	$ 810,000	$ 945,000
Large WIND MILLS	$ 464,787	$ 569,250	$ 672,750
Subtotal direct cost of sales	$1,041,441	$ 1,379,250	$ 1,617,750

MANAGEMENT SUMMARY

Our management summary is going to focus on the key people in our organization.

- *CEO/General Manager—Mark Pierson*: Mr. Pierson is responsible for the overall direction of the company, dealing with investors, shareholders and the vision of the company. His major responsibility is to focus on ensuring all the goals set forth are achieved in the timelines set out.

- *CFO/Accountant*—TBD: Keep current the financials of the company, ensure the accounts payable and receivable are current, along with all the reporting of monthly financials.

- *Production Manager*—TBD: Buy the parts and supplies in order to produce the products in a timely fashion.

- *Distribution Manager*—TBD: Make sure all shipments of products are sent when they are certain to meet shipping deadlines; keep the sales manager and the production manager up to date if there is no product to ship to clients.

- *Sales Manager*—TBD: Achieve the sales numbers set forth by the CEO, and keep the production manager and the distribution manager in tune with large orders coming down the pipe.

- *HR Manager*—TBD: To maintain the productive operating environment of the business, so all staff have been vested with the ownership to work with each other.

- *Warehouse Inventory Manager*—TBD: To maintain the inventory on hand and ensure there is enough to meet the short and long term sales volume of orders in the pipeline.

Personnel Plan

Personnel plan	2008	2009	2010
CEO general manager	$ 54,144	$ 65,000	$ 75,000
CFO accountant	$ 43,248	$ 46,000	$ 48,000
Production manager	$ 32,256	$ 35,000	$ 38,000
Distribution manager	$ 28,992	$ 33,990	$ 35,990
Sales manager	$ 42,384	$ 47,000	$ 49,000
HR manager	$ 33,408	$ 35,000	$ 37,000
Warehouse inventory manager	$ 33,120	$ 36,000	$ 39,000
Total people	**23**	**29**	**35**
Total payroll	**$267,552**	**$297,990**	**$321,990**

FINANCIAL ANALYSIS

Start–up Funding

The start–up funding for Pierson Windmills will be as laid out here. Mark Pierson will invest $100,000, while three other investors will each invest $100,000 into the business for a total of 15 percent stake in the company. Mark Pierson will retain the majority share in the business at 55 percent ownership.

The funding will be used to get the business running, buy inventory, purchase assets and equipment, lease the building, and to hire a management consulting firm for ongoing support and advice.

Start-up funding

Start-up expenses to fund	$270,000
Start-up assets to fund	$ 10,000
Total funding required	**$280,000**

Assets

Non-cash assets from start-up	$ 5,000
Cash requirements from start-up	$ 5,000
Additional cash raised	$490,000
Cash balance on starting date	$495,000
Total assets	**$500,000**

Liabilities and capital

Liabilities	
Current borrowing	$100,000
Fixed liabilities	$ 20,000
Accounts payable (outstanding bills)	$ 50,000
Other current liabilities	$200,000
Total liabilities	**$370,000**
Capital	
Planned investment	
Owner	$100,000
Investor # 1	$100,000
Investor # 2	$100,000
Investor # 3	$100,000
Additional investment requirement	$ 0
Total planned investment	**$400,000**
Loss at start-up (start-up expenses)	$270,000
Total capital	**$130,000**
Total capital and liabilities	**$500,000**
Total funding	**$770,000**

Break-even Analysis

Break-even analysis

Monthly units break-even	24
Monthly revenue break-even	$ 75,931
Assumptions:	
Average per-unit revenue	$ 3,190.00
Average per-unit variable cost	$ 799.26
Estimated monthly fixed cost	$56,906.15

Projected Profit and Loss

- 2008: Sales of $4,156,570 with a net profit of $1,577,502 or 37.95 percent

- 2009: Sales of $5,475,000 with a net profit of $2,204,930 or 40.27 percent

- 2010: Sales of $6,425,000 with a net profit of $2,636,704 or 41.04 percent

Pro forma profit and loss	2008	2009	2010
Sales	$4,156,570	$5,475,000	$6,425,000
Direct costs of goods	$1,041,441	$1,379,250	$1,617,750
Other costs of goods	$ 166,680	$ 170,000	$ 180,000
Cost of goods sold	$1,208,121	$1,549,250	$1,797,750
Gross margin	$2,948,449	$3,925,750	$4,627,250
Gross margin %	70.93%	71.70%	72.02%
Expenses			
Payroll	$ 267,552	$ 297,990	$ 321,990
Marketing/promotion	$ 28,262	$ 35,000	$ 45,000
Depreciation	$ 16,682	$ 22,000	$ 26,000
Rent	$ 23,208	$ 27,000	$ 35,000
Utilities	$ 15,732	$ 20,000	$ 25,000
Production materials	$ 89,672	$ 100,000	$ 110,000
Payroll production	$ 18,729	$ 20,859	$ 22,539
Maintain repairs	$ 22,218	$ 25,000	$ 29,000
Sales & marketing	$ 87,478	$ 95,000	$ 100,000
Set up cost	$ 31,392	$ 35,000	$ 39,000
Shipping cost	$ 81,948	$ 86,000	$ 95,000
Total operating expenses	**$ 682,874**	**$ 763,849**	**$ 848,529**
Profit before interest and taxes	$2,265,575	$3,161,901	$3,778,721
Interest expense	$ 21,346	$ 53,134	$ 90,634
Taxes incurred	$ 673,269	$ 932,630	$1,106,426
Net profit	$1,570,961	$2,176,137	$2,581,661
Net profit/sales	37.79%	39.75%	40.18%

Projected Cash Flow

Pro forma cash flow	2008	2009	2010
Cash received			
Cash from operations			
Cash sales	$1,039,143	$1,368,750	$1,606,250
Cash from receivables	$2,335,982	$3,858,382	$4,640,148
Subtotal cash from operations	$3,375,124	$5,227,132	$6,246,398
Additional cash received			
GST/HST received (output tax)	$ 0	$ 0	$ 0
GST/HST repayments	$ 0	$ 0	$ 0
New current borrowing	$ 308,923	$ 410,000	$ 500,000
New other liabilities (interest-free)	$ 0	$ 0	$ 0
New fixed liabilities	$ 0	$ 0	$ 0
Sales of other current assets	$ 0	$ 0	$ 0
Sales of fixed assets	$ 0	$ 0	$ 0
New investment received	$ 0	$ 0	$ 0
Subtotal cash received	$3,684,047	$5,637,132	$6,746,398
Expenditures			
Expenditures from operations			
Cash spending	$ 267,552	$ 297,990	$ 321,990
Bill payments	$2,670,357	$3,109,327	$3,576,689
Subtotal spent on operations	$2,937,909	$3,407,317	$3,898,679
Additional cash spent			
GST/HST paid out (input tax)	$ 0	$ 0	$ 0
GST/HST payments	$ 0	$ 0	$ 0
Principal repayment of current borrowing	$ 65,088	$ 75,000	$ 85,000
Other liabilities principal repayment	$ 0	$ 0	$ 0
Fixed liabilities principal repayment	$ 0	$ 0	$ 0
Purchase other current assets	$ 0	$ 0	$ 0
Purchase fixed assets	$ 0	$ 0	$ 0
Dividends	$ 85,704	$ 145,000	$ 250,000
Subtotal cash spent	$3,088,701	$3,627,317	$4,233,679
Net cash fow	$ 595,347	$2,009,814	$2,512,719
Cash balance	$1,090,347	$3,100,161	$5,612,880

Projected Balance Sheet

Pro forma balance sheet	2008	2009	2010
Assets			
Current assets			
Cash	$1,090,347	$3,100,161	$5,612,880
Accounts receivable	$ 781,446	$1,029,314	$1,207,917
Stock	$ 459,559	$ 608,624	$ 713,867
Other current assets	$ 2,000	$ 2,000	$ 2,000
Total current assets	**$2,333,351**	**$4,740,099**	**$7,536,664**
Fixed assets			
Fixed assets	$ 2,000	$ 2,000	$ 2,000
Accumulated depreciation	$ 16,682	$ 38,682	$ 64,682
Total fixed assets	**$ 14,682**	**$ 36,682**	**$ 62,682**
Total assets	**$2,318,669**	**$4,703,417**	**$7,473,981**
Liabilities and capital			
Current liabilities			
Accounts payable	$ 343,756	$ 158,188	$ 182,092
Current borrowing	$ 343,835	$ 678,835	$1,093,835
Other current liabilities	$ 200,000	$ 200,000	$ 200,000
Subtotal current liabilities	$ 200,079	$1,037,023	$1,475,927
Fixed liabilities	$ 20,000	$ 20,000	$ 20,000
Total liabilities	**$ 220,079**	**$1,057,023**	**$1,495,927**
Paid-in capital	$ 400,000	$ 400,000	$ 400,000
Retained earnings	$ 355,704	$1,070,257	$2,996,394
Earnings	$1,570,961	$2,176,137	$2,581,661
Total capital	**$1,615,257**	**$3,646,394**	**$5,978,055**
Total liabilities and capital	**$1,835,336**	**$4,703,417**	**$7,473,981**
Net worth	$2,098,590	$3,646,394	$5,978,055

Yoga Studio

Namaste Family Yoga Studio

20 St NE
Grand Forks, North Dakota 58201

Lubnah Shomali

This business plan outlines the creation, operation and financial investment involved in the start-up and maintenance of a yoga facility for one year.

EXECUTIVE SUMMARY

Yoga is derived from a Sanskrit word which means "union." The union occurs between: the mind through meditation (dyana); the body through postures (asanas); and the breath (pranayama). According to the *Yoga Journal,* 7.5 percent of American adults practice yoga and one out of every seven intend to try it within 12 months.

To absorb this influx of future yoga practitioners, Namaste Family, a one-stop yoga facility, will be constructed on a two-acre lot in Grand Forks, North Dakota. It will be a street front property with ample parking on the side and rear of the building. It is accessible from Grand Forks main streets and highways, yet secluded enough to provide the tranquil atmosphere necessary for the practice of yoga.

Namaste Family will offer comprehensive and all inclusive yoga classes to attract all age groups, taught by qualified yoga instructors throughout the day. Namaste Family will be offering 17 classes a day, seven days a week, for a total of 102 classes a month. Classes will be varied in focus and purpose, allowing members to select the class or classes that suit them.

The key to Namaste Family's success is two-fold:

1. To encourage new members to experience the benefits of yoga;

2. Retaining those members through class variety AND encouraging members to make their practice a family inclusive experience by incorporating other family members and social relations.

Namaste Family's goal is to provide an alternative, healthy pastime for families and the whole community. Our philosophy is to promote a healthy, inclusive community that supports familial and social bonds.

The serene, beautiful and well-lit facility will be owned and operated by Shadra Newman. Not only a yoga master, Shadra has been a fitness instructor for 20 years. As a former employee of the YMCA in Grand Forks, Shadra acquired an excellent reputation as a yoga instructor and an instructor trainer. She also developed a loyal member following and the competencies to operate a health facility successfully.

Mission

Our mission at Namaste Family is:

- To provide a peaceful, calming, familial atmosphere for families to practice yoga together;

- To support and encourage all who wish to travel the yogic journey;

- To cultivate connectedness by providing a sense of belonging through listening, supported activities, and to establish and maintain kinship;

- To promote the integration of yoga into everyday family routine.

Vision

Our vision at Namaste Family is to enhance the relationship between family members by encouraging them to find peace, serenity, unity and patience through participatory yoga practice.

Objectives

The objectives of Namaste Family are:

- To acquire 300 registrations/month by the end of the first year of operation;

- Increase the customer base 20 percent by the second year of operation.

COMPANY SUMMARY

Namaste Family teaches the Hatha style of yoga. Yoga is derived from a Sanskrit word which means "union." The union occurs between: the mind through meditation (dyana); the body through postures (asanas); and the breath (pranayama). The company will feature well-trained, professional instructors who will facilitate and promote the complete system of Hatha yoga in combination with modern communication and coaching for peaceful and loving family living. Family members will be encouraged to register together in classes; in other words, multiple family members in each class. Namaste Family will also offer retreats, workshops and yoga-themed events. Namaste Family features fun, festive, well lit rooms that are child friendly.

Namaste Family's goal is to provide an alternative, healthy pastime for families and the whole community. Our philosophy is to promote a healthy, inclusive community that supports familial and social bonds.

This industry faces high competition and low barriers to entry. Additionally, most start-ups take one to two years to turn a profit. However, according to the *Yoga Journal*, 7.5 percent of American adults practice yoga and one out of every seven intend to try it within 12 months. Namaste Family will be poised to introduce yoga to these individuals, providing many beginners classes at various times during the day to suit all schedules. Namaste Family will also encourage the enrollment of members' children (those under 18) by promoting the benefits of yoga and providing child friendly specialty classes.

The facility is located near a suburban section of Grand Forks, North Dakota. Purchasing the two acre site costs $85,000; construction, including the blueprints, requires $325,000.

Namaste Family will operate as a sole proprietorship, owned and operated by Shadra Newman. Not only a yoga master, Shadra has been a fitness instructor for 20 years; she is competent in teaching all forms of group fitness. Shadra, a former employee of the YMCA in Grand Forks, acquired an excellent reputation as a yoga instructor and an instructor trainer. She also developed a loyal member following.

Start-up Summary

The start-up expenses for Namaste Family are focused chiefly in the purchase of a commercial piece of land and construction of an adequate yoga facility with the proper equipment. Shadra will invest $100,000 and Namaste Family will secure a $400,000 long-term loan.

Location and Facility

The two-acre lot is located near a suburban section of Grand Forks. Namaste Family will appeal to the neighboring communities by offering a wide variety of classes for all members of the family. The building plans call for 3 sizeable workshops, men's and women's changing facilities and restrooms, a reception area, and an additional unfinished workshop to be completed upon expansion. The property also has ample parking space.

SERVICES

Namaste Family will provide a wide variety of yoga classes by qualified yoga instructors throughout the day. Classes will be varied in focus and purpose, allowing members to select the class or classes that suit them. The classes will be taught by the owner, Shadra, and four other part-time employees. There will be two yoga rooms in the facility. Business hours will be 6:00am to 9:00pm, Monday-Saturday.

Class Descriptions

- *Rise & Shine Yoga*: a soothing yet invigorating practice that energizes the body and the mind; 1 hour 15 min.

- *Yoga I*: a beginner's yoga practice that introduces the basic poses, breathing and meditation; 1 hour 15 min.

- *Gentle Yoga*: a practice that focuses on alignment, posture and meditation specifically for the relief of back tension and pain or to relax; 1 hour.

- *Lunch Time Yoga*: a quick, refreshing yoga practice for working individuals designed to elevate tension and reduce stress; 45 minutes.

- *Yoga II/Vinyasa*: an advanced yoga practice that promotes cardiovascular health, flexibility and strength; 1hour 30 min.

- *Prenatal Yoga*: a practice that considers the needs and restrictions of expecting mothers; 1 hour.

- *Live, Laugh, Learn Yoga*: a yoga practice that includes laughter, inclusiveness, and health education geared toward multiple family members, friends and couples; 1 hour.

- *Sibling Yoga*: a practice designed to promote harmony between siblings, young and old; involves collaborative poses (poses requiring 2 or more individuals); 45 min.

- *(Grand) Mommy and Me/(Grand) Daddy and Me*: a yoga practice designed to enhance the relationship between grandparents and grandchildren and/or parents and their children; 45 min.

- *Couples Yoga*: an intense yoga experience geared to boost couple's awareness, trust and understanding of each other; 1 hour.

Namaste Family will also provide workshops and retreats on yoga and health-related issues in the third workshop of the facility. This room will also be leased to the community for various events. Pricing for retreats, workshops, and community events will be determined at the time of service as each occasion requires individual consideration.

MARKETING

According to the *Yoga Journal*, 7.5 percent of American adults practice yoga (approximately 15 million practitioners). Additionally, 1 in 7 intends to try within the next 12 months. Namaste Family will be poised to accept this influx of yoga initiates with a variety of beginner's classes with many approaches, with encouragement to enroll other family members and friends.

Area Demographics

The Grand Forks location was chosen due to the following factors:

- Grand Forks is on the list of Forbes.com "Best Small Places for Businesses and Careers";

- The town has a population of 53,000 with 89 percent of residents having high school diplomas and 64 percent having an education beyond high school;

- The unemployment is 3.9 percent under the national average;

- The median income for a family is $46,600 with 93 percent of the population in non-laborer positions.

Namaste Family believes the demographics of this market are conducive to growth and opportunity for our business. The initial marketing focus will be persons aged 25 and above who have healthy lifestyle priorities. Namaste Family will create an all-inclusive family atmosphere that appeals to all age groups. Once exposed to Namaste Family's professionalism, high quality trainers, beautiful facility and welcoming atmosphere, this group will progress to include family members, friends and significant others.

Industry Analysis

This industry faces high completion and a low barrier to entry. However, Namaste Family will appeal to all age groups providing a high quality varied yoga practice that will develop into a family/community pastime. The owner, Shadra, having been in the business of practicing and teaching yoga for 20 years, is investing a substantial amount into the business. That, combined with the fact that she will own and not rent, creates deeper financial and personal obligation to the success of Namaste Family.

According to Bizminer.com industry market reports average sales for a start-up health facility is $155,772 annually. The national failure rate for these start-ups is 22.54 percent due to the fact that owner's did not have enough capital on hand the first year to be able to make payment on expenses, specifically employee wages.

To account for this possibility, Namaste Family procured a $400,000 long-term loan to allow for a contingency fund of $64,800. This fund will be used to pay wages, unforeseen expenses, and as a cushion for an unexpected drop in sales and during the slow seasons of registration.

The key to Namaste Family's success is two-fold:

1. To encourage new member to experience the benefits of yoga;

2. Retaining those members through class variety AND encouraging members to make their practice a family inclusive experience by incorporating other family members and social relations.

Competition

There are three main competitors in the Grand Forks area:

1. Center for Healing and Wholeness

2. Yoga with Carol

3. YMCA

Competitors 1 and 2 do not pose a threat to Namaste Family as they offer limited classes and times—once a week and only in the evenings. Namaste Family provides classes during the whole day, appealing to diverse schedules.

The YMCA, former employer of Namaste Family's owner, offers a wide variety of traditional fitness classes and two yoga classes which are intermediate and advanced in character. These classes will not appeal to new practitioners, children, the elderly and expecting mothers. Namaste Family will offer comprehensive and all inclusive yoga classes to attract all age groups, encouraging a one-stop yoga facility. Additionally, members of the YMCA are familiar with Shadra and many are motivated to continue their practice with her. She is a well-respected and knowledgeable teacher that will infuse the business with enthusiasm, professionalism and superiority.

Niche

Hence, there seems to be a void in the particular niche that Namaste Family intends on satisfying by tapping into this underdeveloped market. A serene facility combined with knowledgeable instructors and an inclusive atmosphere will allow Namaste Family to provide a desirable service to customers.

Promotion

Since Shadra is part of the Grand Forks community, she has voiced her intentions of opening a studio and has received support from her current yoga practitioners to spread the word about Namaste Family. Shadra will use her network of friends and professionals to promote her business.

Additionally, she has designed a logo that will be used on letterheads, stationary, signage and brochures.

Namaste Family intends on distributing flyers to all the homes in the area, as well as posters in supermarkets, post offices, public parks and recreation areas, businesses, churches and other high traffic areas.

In addition, a radio advertisement will be purchased with the local radio station to air at prominent listening times during the day.

The start-up promotional budget is $1,100, with continual installments of $400 per month.

Pricing

The pricing structure is as follows:

Family Plans

- Unlimited Family Plan—$300

- Super Family Plan—$200

- Standard Family Plan—$150

Individual Plans

- Unlimited Individual Plan—$200

- Super Individual Plan—$150

- Standard Individual Plan—$100

Family Plans allow for a family of 4, children under 12 only. There is a drop-in fee of $15 per class.

Registration will occur through pre-payment in the form of cash or credit card. In addition customers will be able to set up automatic payments on their credit cards or through their checking accounts.

Proposed Location

Namaste Family will be constructed on a two-acre lot at the edge of a Grand Forks suburban area. It will be a street-front property with ample parking on the side and rear of the building. It is accessible from Grand Forks' main streets and highways, yet secluded enough to provide the serene atmosphere necessary for the practice of yoga.

OPERATIONS

The Facility

The facility will be 5,000 square feet in size with a reception area, 4 workshops (2 for yoga, one for events, and one unfinished for expansion in the future), and men's and women's changing and restroom facilities. The reception area will be 500 square feet and the men's and women's dressing rooms will be 1,500 square feet. The event room will be 1,000 square feet, leaving 125 square feet for a boiler room. Allotting 25 square feet for each practitioner and having space in each workshop for 20 practitioners, that makes each viable workshop 500 square feet. Additionally, the two viable workshops will have cabinets to hold yoga mats, blocks and straps. We will allot another 100 square feet for the cabinets. Yoga mats and straps will be purchased from a wholesale yoga equipment supplier. The straps will be donated by registering members in the form of men's old ties. The workshops will also have water fountains to supply drinking water to members and sound systems to play CDs. We will allot 25 square feet for the drinking fountains. Yoga music CDs will be supplied by the individual instructors. Therefore, three workshops will require 1,875 square feet of space. The facility will be handicapped accessible and have ample space for parking.

Daily Operations

Namaste Family will be offering 17 classes a day, seven days a week, for a total of 102 classes a month. The classes will be taught by Shadra and 4 other highly-qualified instructors.

Member management software, hardware and maintenance will be purchased and installed from a leading health facility member management supplier to organize and track member registration and to process payments and options.

During the first year, Shadra and the other instructors will also be equally responsible for manning the reception area. After the first year, once member registration increases, a full-time receptionist will be hired.

An outside contractor will be hired to clean the facility.

Yearly Personnel Plan

- Shadra Newman, owner—$40,800
- Four part-time instructors—$48,000
- Total People—5
- Total Payroll—$88,800

Personnel will be paid monthly by check. Shadra will be responsible for the selection and hiring of instructors. In order to hire and retain a high quality staff, Namaste Family will provide for the continuing education of employees that remain with the company for one year.

FINANCIAL INFORMATION

Break-even Analysis

Monthly Fixed Costs

Salaries (includes payroll taxes)—$7,400

Supplies—$250

Repairs & maintenance—$250

Advertising—$400

Accounting and legal—$200

Telephone—$90

Utilities—$450

Insurance—$200

Taxes (Real estate, etc.)—$284

Interest—$1,520

Depreciation—$789

Principal portion of debt payment—$3,334

Total Fixed Costs—$15,167

Total Variable Costs—$0.00

Breakeven Sales level—$15,167

The monthly break-even point is calculated to be $15,167, with 0% variable cost.

Start-up Summary

Sources of Capital

Owners' Investment—$100,000

Bank Loans—$400,000

Total Source of Funds—$500,000

Expenses

Buildings/Real Estate

Purchase—$85,000

Construction—$335,000

Total Buildings/Real Estate—$420,000

Capital Equipment

Furniture—$3,000

Equipment—$3,500

Fixtures—$2,600

Total Capital Equipment—$9,100

Location and Administration

Legal and accounting fees—$1,000

Prepaid insurance—$2,000

Total Location and Admin Expenses—$3,000

Advertising and Promotion

Advertising—$400

Printing—$700

Total Advertising/Promotional Expenses—$1,100

Other Expenses

Building permits/fees—$2,000

Contingency fund—$64,800

Total Expenses—$500,000

Business Plan Template

USING THIS TEMPLATE

A business plan carefully spells out a company's projected course of action over a period of time, usually the first two to three years after the start-up. In addition, banks, lenders, and other investors examine the information and financial documentation before deciding whether or not to finance a new business venture. Therefore, a business plan is an essential tool in obtaining financing and should describe the business itself in detail as well as all important factors influencing the company, including the market, industry, competition, operations and management policies, problem solving strategies, financial resources and needs, and other vital information. The plan enables the business owner to anticipate costs, plan for difficulties, and take advantage of opportunities, as well as design and implement strategies that keep the company running as smoothly as possible.

This template has been provided as a model to help you construct your own business plan. Please keep in mind that there is no single acceptable format for a business plan, and that this template is in no way comprehensive, but serves as an example.

The business plans provided in this section are fictional and have been used by small business agencies as models for clients to use in compiling their own business plans.

GENERIC BUSINESS PLAN

Main headings included below are topics that should be covered in a comprehensive business plan. They include:

Business Summary

Purpose
Provides a brief overview of your business, succinctly highlighting the main ideas of your plan.

Includes

- Name and Type of Business
- Description of Product/Service
- Business History and Development
- Location
- Market

- Competition
- Management
- Financial Information
- Business Strengths and Weaknesses
- Business Growth

Table of Contents

Purpose
Organized in an Outline Format, the Table of Contents illustrates the selection and arrangement of information contained in your plan.

Includes

- Topic Headings and Subheadings
- Page Number References

Business History and Industry Outlook

Purpose

Examines the conception and subsequent development of your business within an industry specific context.

Includes

- Start-up Information
- Owner/Key Personnel Experience
- Location
- Development Problems and Solutions
- Investment/Funding Information

- Future Plans and Goals
- Market Trends and Statistics
- Major Competitors
- Product/Service Advantages
- National, Regional, and Local Economic Impact

Product/Service

Purpose

Introduces, defines, and details the product and/or service that inspired the information of your business.

Includes

- Unique Features
- Niche Served
- Market Comparison
- Stage of Product/Service Development

- Production
- Facilities, Equipment, and Labor
- Financial Requirements
- Product/Service Life Cycle
- Future Growth

Market Examination

Purpose

Assessment of product/service applications in relation to consumer buying cycles.

Includes

- Target Market
- Consumer Buying Habits
- Product/Service Applications
- Consumer Reactions
- Market Factors and Trends

- Penetration of the Market
- Market Share
- Research and Studies
- Cost
- Sales Volume and Goals

Competition

Purpose

Analysis of Competitors in the Marketplace.

Includes

- Competitor Information
- Product/Service Comparison
- Market Niche

- Product/Service Strengths and Weaknesses
- Future Product/Service Development

Marketing

Purpose

Identifies promotion and sales strategies for your product/service.

Includes

- Product/Service Sales Appeal
- Special and Unique Features
- Identification of Customers
- Sales and Marketing Staff
- Sales Cycles
- Type of Advertising/ Promotion
- Pricing
- Competition
- Customer Services

Operations

Purpose

Traces product/service development from production/inception to the market environment.

Includes

- Cost Effective Production Methods
- Facility
- Location
- Equipment
- Labor
- Future Expansion

Administration and Management

Purpose

Offers a statement of your management philosophy with an in-depth focus on processes and procedures.

Includes

- Management Philosophy
- Structure of Organization
- Reporting System
- Methods of Communication
- Employee Skills and Training
- Employee Needs and Compensation
- Work Environment
- Management Policies and Procedures
- Roles and Responsibilities

Key Personnel

Purpose

Describes the unique backgrounds of principle employees involved in business.

Includes

- Owner(s)/Employee Education and Experience
- Positions and Roles
- Benefits and Salary
- Duties and Responsibilities
- Objectives and Goals

Potential Problems and Solutions

Purpose

Discussion of problem solving strategies that change issues into opportunities.

Includes

- Risks
- Litigation
- Future Competition
- Economic Impact
- Problem Solving Skills

Financial Information

Purpose

Secures needed funding and assistance through worksheets and projections detailing financial plans, methods of repayment, and future growth opportunities.

Includes

- Financial Statements
- Bank Loans
- Methods of Repayment
- Tax Returns
- Start-up Costs
- Projected Income (3 years)
- Projected Cash Flow (3 Years)
- Projected Balance Statements (3 years)

Appendices

Purpose

Supporting documents used to enhance your business proposal.

Includes

- Photographs of product, equipment, facilities, etc.
- Copyright/Trademark Documents
- Legal Agreements
- Marketing Materials
- Research and or Studies
- Operation Schedules
- Organizational Charts
- Job Descriptions
- Resumes
- Additional Financial Documentation

Fictional Food Distributor

Commercial Foods, Inc.

This plan demonstrates how a partnership can have a positive impact on a new business. It demonstrates how two individuals can carve a niche in the specialty foods market by offering gourmet foods to upscale restaurants and fine hotels. This plan is fictional and has not been used to gain funding from a bank or other lending institution.

3003 Avondale Ave.
Knoxville, TN 37920

STATEMENT OF PURPOSE

Commercial Foods, Inc. seeks a loan of $75,000 to establish a new business. This sum, together with $5,000 equity investment by the principals, will be used as follows:

- Merchandise inventory $25,000

- Office fixture/equipment $12,000

- Warehouse equipment $14,000

- One delivery truck $10,000

- Working capital $39,000

- Total $100,000

DESCRIPTION OF THE BUSINESS

Commercial Foods, Inc. will be a distributor of specialty food service products to hotels and upscale restaurants in the geographical area of a 50 mile radius of Knoxville. Richard Roberts will direct the sales effort and John Williams will manage the warehouse operation and the office. One delivery truck will be used initially with a second truck added in the third year. We expect to begin operation of the business within 30 days after securing the requested financing.

MANAGEMENT

A. Richard Roberts is a native of Memphis, Tennessee. He is a graduate of Memphis State University with a Bachelor's degree from the School of Business. After graduation, he worked for a major manufacturer of specialty food service products as a detail sales person for five years, and, for the past three years, he has served as a product sales manager for this firm.

213

B. John Williams is a native of Nashville, Tennessee. He holds a B.S. Degree in Food Technology from the University of Tennessee. His career includes five years as a product development chemist in gourmet food products and five years as operations manager for a food service distributor.

Both men are healthy and energetic. Their backgrounds complement each other, which will ensure the success of Commercial Foods, Inc. They will set policies together and personnel decisions will be made jointly. Initial salaries for the owners will be $1,000 per month for the first few years. The spouses of both principals are successful in the business world and earn enough to support the families.

They have engaged the services of Foster Jones, CPA, and William Hale, Attorney, to assist them in an advisory capacity.

PERSONNEL

The firm will employ one delivery truck driver at a wage of $8.00 per hour. One office worker will be employed at $7.50 per hour. One part-time employee will be used in the office at $5.00 per hour. The driver will load and unload his own trucks. Mr. Williams will assist in the warehouse operation as needed to assist one stock person at $7.00 per hour. An additional delivery truck and driver will be added the third year.

LOCATION

The firm will lease a 20,000 square foot building at 3003 Avondale Ave., in Knoxville, which contains warehouse and office areas equipped with two-door truck docks. The annual rental is $9,000. The building was previously used as a food service warehouse and very little modification to the building will be required.

PRODUCTS AND SERVICES

The firm will offer specialty food service products such as soup bases, dessert mixes, sauce bases, pastry mixes, spices, and flavors, normally used by upscale restaurants and nice hotels. We are going after a niche in the market with high quality gourmet products. There is much less competition in this market than in standard run of the mill food service products. Through their work experiences, the principals have contacts with supply sources and with local chefs.

THE MARKET

We know from our market survey that there are over 200 hotels and upscale restaurants in the area we plan to serve. Customers will be attracted by a direct sales approach. We will offer samples of our products and product application data on use of our products in the finished prepared foods. We will cultivate the chefs in these establishments. The technical background of John Williams will be especially useful here.

COMPETITION

We find that we will be only distributor in the area offering a full line of gourmet food service products. Other foodservice distributors offer only a few such items in conjunction with their standard product line. Our survey shows that many of the chefs are ordering products from Atlanta and Memphis because of a lack of adequate local supply.

SUMMARY

Commercial Foods, Inc. will be established as a foodservice distributor of specialty food in Knoxville. The principals, with excellent experience in the industry, are seeking a $75,000 loan to establish the business. The principals are investing $25,000 as equity capital.

The business will be set up as an S Corporation with each principal owning 50% of the common stock in the corporation.

Fictional Hardware Store

Oshkosh Hardware, Inc.

The following plan outlines how a small hardware store can survive competition from large discount chains by offering products and providing expert advice in the use of any product it sells. This plan is fictional and has not been used to gain funding from a bank or other lending institution.

123 Main St.
Oshkosh, WI 54901

EXECUTIVE SUMMARY

Oshkosh Hardware, Inc. is a new corporation that is going to establish a retail hardware store in a strip mall in Oshkosh, Wisconsin. The store will sell hardware of all kinds, quality tools, paint, and housewares. The business will make revenue and a profit by servicing its customers not only with needed hardware but also with expert advice in the use of any product it sells.

Oshkosh Hardware, Inc. will be operated by its sole shareholder, James Smith. The company will have a total of four employees. It will sell its products in the local market. Customers will buy our products because we will provide free advice on the use of all of our products and will also furnish a full refund warranty.

Oshkosh Hardware, Inc. will sell its products in the Oshkosh store staffed by three sales representatives. No additional employees will be needed to achieve its short and long range goals. The primary short range goal is to open the store by October 1, 1994. In order to achieve this goal a lease must be signed by July 1, 1994 and the complete inventory ordered by August 1, 1994.

Mr. James Smith will invest $30,000 in the business. In addition, the company will have to borrow $150,000 during the first year to cover the investment in inventory, accounts receivable, and furniture and equipment. The company will be profitable after six months of operation and should be able to start repayment of the loan in the second year.

THE BUSINESS

The business will sell hardware of all kinds, quality tools, paint, and housewares. We will purchase our products from three large wholesale buying groups.

In general our customers are homeowners who do their own repair and maintenance, hobbyists, and housewives. Our business is unique in that we will have a complete line of all hardware items and will be able to get special orders by overnight delivery. The business makes revenue and profits by servicing our customers not only with needed hardware but also with expert advice in the use of any product we sell. Our major costs for bringing our products to market are cost of merchandise of 36%, salaries of $45,000, and occupancy costs of $60,000.

Oshkosh Hardware, Inc.'s retail outlet will be located at 1524 Frontage Road, which is in a newly developed retail center of Oshkosh. Our location helps facilitate accessibility from all parts of town and reduces our delivery costs. The store will occupy 7500 square feet of space. The major equipment involved in our business is counters and shelving, a computer, a paint mixing machine, and a truck.

THE MARKET

Oshkosh Hardware, Inc. will operate in the local market. There are 15,000 potential customers in this market area. We have three competitors who control approximately 98% of the market at present. We feel we can capture 25% of the market within the next four years. Our major reason for believing this is that our staff is technically competent to advise our customers in the correct use of all products we sell.

After a careful market analysis, we have determined that approximately 60% of our customers are men and 40% are women. The percentage of customers that fall into the following age categories are:

Under 16: 0%
17-21: 5%
22-30: 30%
31-40: 30%
41-50: 20%
51-60: 10%
61-70: 5%
Over 70: 0%

The reasons our customers prefer our products is our complete knowledge of their use and our full refund warranty.

We get our information about what products our customers want by talking to existing customers. There seems to be an increasing demand for our product. The demand for our product is increasing in size based on the change in population characteristics.

SALES

At Oshkosh Hardware, Inc. we will employ three sales people and will not need any additional personnel to achieve our sales goals. These salespeople will need several years experience in home repair and power tool usage. We expect to attract 30% of our customers from newspaper ads, 5% of our customers from local directories, 5% of our customers from the yellow pages, 10% of our customers from family and friends, and 50% of our customers from current customers. The most cost effect source will be current customers. In general our industry is growing.

MANAGEMENT

We would evaluate the quality of our management staff as being excellent. Our manager is experienced and very motivated to achieve the various sales and quality assurance objectives we have set. We will use a management information system that produces key inventory, quality assurance, and sales data on a weekly basis. All data is compared to previously established goals for that week, and deviations are the primary focus of the management staff.

GOALS IMPLEMENTATION

The short term goals of our business are:

1.   Open the store by October 1, 1994
2.   Reach our breakeven point in two months
3.   Have sales of $100,000 in the first six months

In order to achieve our first short term goal we must:

1.   Sign the lease by July 1, 1994
2.   Order a complete inventory by August 1, 1994

In order to achieve our second short term goal we must:

1.   Advertise extensively in Sept. and Oct.
2.   Keep expenses to a minimum

In order to achieve our third short term goal we must:

1.   Promote power tool sales for the Christmas season
2.   Keep good customer traffic in Jan. and Feb.

The long term goals for our business are:

1.   Obtain sales volume of $600,000 in three years
2.   Become the largest hardware dealer in the city
3.   Open a second store in Fond du Lac

The most important thing we must do in order to achieve the long term goals for our business is to develop a highly profitable business with excellent cash flow.

FINANCE

Oshkosh Hardware, Inc. Faces some potential threats or risks to our business. They are discount house competition. We believe we can avoid or compensate for this by providing quality products complimented by quality advice on the use of every product we sell. The financial projections we have prepared are located at the end of this document.

JOB DESCRIPTION-GENERAL MANAGER

The General Manager of the business of the corporation will be the president of the corporation. He will be responsible for the complete operation of the retail hardware store which is owned by the corporation. A detailed description of his duties and responsibilities is as follows.

Sales

Train and supervise the three sales people. Develop programs to motivate and compensate these employees. Coordinate advertising and sales promotion effects to achieve sales totals as outlined in budget. Oversee purchasing function and inventory control procedures to insure adequate merchandise at all times at a reasonable cost.

Finance

Prepare monthly and annual budgets. Secure adequate line of credit from local banks. Supervise office personnel to insure timely preparation of records, statements, all government reports, control of receivables and payables, and monthly financial statements.

Administration

Perform duties as required in the areas of personnel, building leasing and maintenance, licenses and permits, and public relations.

Organizations, Agencies, & Consultants

A listing of Associations and Consultants of interest to entrepreneurs, followed by the ten Small Business Administration Regional Offices, Small Business Development Centers, Service Corps of Retired Executives offices, and Venture Capital and Finance Companies.

Organizations, Agencies, & Consultants

Associations

This section contains a listing of associations and other agencies of interest to the small business owner. Entries are listed alphabetically by organization name.

American Business Women's Association
9100 Ward Pkwy.
PO Box 8728
Kansas City, MO 64114-0728
(800)228-0007
E-mail: abwa@abwa.org
Website: http://www.abwa.org
Jeanne Banks, National President

American Franchisee Association
53 W Jackson Blvd., Ste. 1157
Chicago, IL 60604
(312)431-0545
E-mail: info@franchisee.org
Website: http://www.franchisee.org
Susan P. Kezios, President

American Independent Business Alliance
222 S Black Ave.
Bozeman, MT 59715
(406)582-1255
E-mail: info@amiba.net
Website: http://www.amiba.net
Jennifer Rockne, Director

American Small Businesses Association
206 E College St., Ste. 201
Grapevine, TX 76051
800-942-2722
E-mail: info@asbaonline.org
Website: http://www.asbaonline.org/

American Women's Economic Development Corporation
216 East 45th St., 10th Floor
New York, NY 10017
(917)368-6100

Fax: (212)986-7114
E-mail: info@awed.org
Website: http://www.awed.org
Roseanne Antonucci, Exec. Dir.

Association for Enterprise Opportunity
1601 N Kent St., Ste. 1101
Arlington, VA 22209
(703)841-7760
Fax: (703)841-7748
E-mail: aeo@assoceo.org
Website: http://www.micro enterpriseworks.org
Bill Edwards, Exec.Dir.

Association of Small Business Development Centers
c/o Don Wilson
8990 Burke Lake Rd.
Burke, VA 22015
(703)764-9850
Fax: (703)764-1234
E-mail: info@asbdc-us.org
Website: http://www.asbdc-us.org
Don Wilson, Pres./CEO

BEST Employers Association
2505 McCabe Way
Irvine, CA 92614
(949)253-4080
800-433-0088
Fax: (714)553-0883
E-mail: info@bestlife.com
Website: http://www.bestlife.com
Donald R. Lawrenz, CEO

Center for Family Business
PO Box 24219
Cleveland, OH 44124
(440)460-5409
E-mail: grummi@aol.com
Dr. Leon A. Danco, Chm.

Coalition for Government Procurement
1990 M St. NW, Ste. 400
Washington, DC 20036
(202)331-0975
E-mail: info@thecgp.org
Website: http://www.coalgovpro.org
Paul Caggiano, Pres.

Employers of America
PO Box 1874
Mason City, IA 50402-1874
(641)424-3187
800-728-3187
Fax: (641)424-1673
E-mail: employer@employerhelp.org
Website: http://www.employerhelp.org
Jim Collison, Pres.

Family Firm Institute
200 Lincoln St., Ste. 201
Boston, MA 02111
(617)482-3045
Fax: (617)482-3049
E-mail: ffi@ffi.org
Website: http://www.ffi.org
Judy L. Green, Ph.D., Exec.Dir.

Independent Visually Impaired Enterprisers
500 S 3rd St., Apt. H
Burbank, CA 91502
(818)238-9321
E-mail: abazyn@bazyn communications.com
http://www.acb.org/affiliates
Adris Bazyn, Pres.

International Association for Business Organizations
3 Woodthorn Ct., Ste. 12
Owings Mills, MD 21117
(410)581-1373
E-mail: nahbb@msn.com
Rudolph Lewis, Exec. Officer

International Council for Small Business

The George Washington University
School of Business and Public
Management
2115 G St. NW, Ste. 403
Washington, DC 20052
(202)994-0704
Fax: (202)994-4930
E-mail: icsb@gwu.edu
Website: http://www.icsb.org
Susan G. Duffy. Admin.

International Small Business Consortium

3309 Windjammer St.
Norman, OK 73072
E-mail: sb@isbc.com
Website: http://www.isbc.com

Kauffman Center for Entrepreneurial Leadership

4801 Rockhill Rd.
Kansas City, MO 64110-2046
(816)932-1000
E-mail: info@kauffman.org
Website: http://www.entreworld.org

National Alliance for Fair Competition

3 Bethesda Metro Center, Ste. 1100
Bethesda, MD 20814
(410)235-7116
Fax: (410)235-7116
E-mail: ampesq@aol.com
Tony Ponticelli, Exec.Dir.

National Association for the Self-Employed

PO Box 612067
DFW Airport
Dallas, TX 75261-2067
(800)232-6273
E-mail: mpetron@nase.org
Website: http://www.nase.org
Robert Hughes, Pres.

National Association of Business Leaders

4132 Shoreline Dr., Ste. J & H
Earth City, MO 63045
Fax: (314)298-9110
E-mail: nabl@nabl.com
Website: http://www.nabl.com/
Gene Blumenthal, Contact

National Association of Private Enterprise

PO Box 15550
Long Beach, CA 90815
888-224-0953

Fax: (714)844-4942
Website: http://www.napeonline.net
Laura Squiers, Exec.Dir.

National Association of Small Business Investment Companies

666 11th St. NW, Ste. 750
Washington, DC 20001
(202)628-5055
Fax: (202)628-5080
E-mail: nasbic@nasbic.org
Website: http://www.nasbic.org
Lee W. Mercer, Pres.

National Business Association

PO Box 700728
5151 Beltline Rd., Ste. 1150
Dallas, TX 75370
(972)458-0900
800-456-0440
Fax: (972)960-9149
E-mail: info@nationalbusiness.org
Website: http://www.national
business.org
Raj Nisankarao, Pres.

National Business Owners Association

PO Box 111
Stuart, VA 24171
(276)251-7500
(866)251-7505
Fax: (276)251-2217
E-mail: membershipservices@nboa.org
Website: http://www.rvmdb.com.nboa
Paul LaBarr, Pres.

National Center for Fair Competition

PO Box 220
Annandale, VA 22003
(703)280-4622
Fax: (703)280-0942
E-mail: kentonp1@aol.com
Kenton Pattie, Pres.

National Family Business Council

1640 W. Kennedy Rd.
Lake Forest, IL 60045
(847)295-1040
Fax: (847)295-1898
E-mail: lmsnfbc@email.msn.com
Jogn E. Messervey, Pres.

National Federation of Independent Business

53 Century Blvd., Ste. 250
Nashville, TN 37214
(615)872-5800
800-NFIBNOW
Fax: (615)872-5353
Website: http://www.nfib.org
Jack Faris, Pres. and CEO

National Small Business Association

1156 15th St. NW, Ste. 1100
Washington, DC 20005
(202)293-8830
800-345-6728
Fax: (202)872-8543
E-mail: press@nsba.biz
Website: http://www.nsba.biz
Rob Yunich, Dir. of Communications

PUSH Commercial Division

930 E 50th St.
Chicago, IL 60615-2702
(773)373-3366
Fax: (773)373-3571
E-mail: info@rainbowpush.org
Website: http://www.rainbowpush.org
Rev. Willie T. Barrow, Co-Chm.

Research Institute for Small and Emerging Business

722 12th St. NW
Washington, DC 20005
(202)628-8382
Fax: (202)628-8392
E-mail: info@riseb.org
Website: http://www.riseb.org
Allan Neece, Jr., Chm.

Sales Professionals USA

PO Box 149
Arvada, CO 80001
(303)534-4937
888-736-7767
E-mail: salespro@salesprofessionals-usa.com
Website: http://www.salesprofessionals-usa.com
Sharon Herbert, Natl. Pres.

Score Association - Service Corps of Retired Executives

409 3rd St. SW, 6th Fl.
Washington, DC 20024
(202)205-6762
800-634-0245
Fax: (202)205-7636
E-mail: media@score.org
Website: http://www.score.org
W. Kenneth Yancey, Jr., CEO

Small Business and Entrepreneurship Council

1920 L St. NW, Ste. 200
Washington, DC 20036
(202)785-0238
Fax: (202)822-8118
E-mail: membership@sbec.org
Website: http://www.sbcouncil.org
Karen Kerrigan, Pres./CEO

Small Business in Telecommunications
1331 H St. NW, Ste. 500
Washington, DC 20005
(202)347-4511
Fax: (202)347-8607
E-mail: sbt@sbthome.org
Website: http://www.sbthome.org
Lonnie Danchik, Chm.

Small Business Legislative Council
1010 Massachusetts Ave. NW, Ste. 540
Washington, DC 20005
(202)639-8500
Fax: (202)296-5333
E-mail: email@sblc.org
Website: http://www.sblc.org
John Satagaj, Pres.

Small Business Service Bureau
554 Main St.
PO Box 15014
Worcester, MA 01615-0014
(508)756-3513
800-343-0939
Fax: (508)770-0528
E-mail: membership@sbsb.com
Website: http://www.sbsb.com
Francis R. Carroll, Pres.

Small Publishers Association of North America
1618 W COlorado Ave.
Colorado Springs, CO 80904
(719)475-1726
Fax: (719)471-2182
E-mail: span@spannet.org
Website: http://www.spannet.org
Scott Flora, Exec. Dir.

SOHO America
PO Box 941
Hurst, TX 76053-0941
800-495-SOHO
E-mail: soho@1sas.com
Website: http://www.soho.org

Structured Employment Economic Development Corporation
915 Broadway, 17th Fl.
New York, NY 10010
(212)473-0255
Fax: (212)473-0357
E-mail: info@seedco.org
Website: http://www.seedco.org
William Grinker, CEO

Support Services Alliance
107 Prospect St.
Schoharie, NY 12157
800-836-4772

E-mail: info@ssamembers.com
Website: http://www.ssainfo.com
Steve COle, Pres.

United States Association for Small Business and Entrepreneurship
975 University Ave., No. 3260
Madison, WI 53706
(608)262-9982
Fax: (608)263-0818
E-mail: jgillman@wisc.edu
Website: http://www.ususbe.org
Joan Gillman, Exec. Dir.

Consultants

This section contains a listing of consultants specializing in small business development. It is arranged alphabetically by country, then by state or province, then by city, then by firm name.

Canada

Alberta

Common Sense Solutions
3405 16A Ave.
Edmonton, AB, Canada
(403)465-7330
Fax: (403)465-7380
E-mail: gcoulson@comsense solutions.com
Website: http://www.comsensesolutions. com

Varsity Consulting Group
School of Business
University of Alberta
Edmonton, AB, Canada T6G 2R6
(780)492-2994
Fax: (780)492-5400
Website: http://www.bus.ualberta.ca/vcg

Viro Hospital Consulting
42 Commonwealth Bldg., 9912 - 106 St. NW
Edmonton, AB, Canada T5K 1C5
(403)425-3871
Fax: (403)425-3871
E-mail: rpb@freenet.edmonton.ab.ca

British Columbia

SRI Strategic Resources Inc.
4330 Kingsway, Ste. 1600
Burnaby, BC, Canada V5H 4G7
(604)435-0627
Fax: (604)435-2782

E-mail: inquiry@sri.bc.ca
Website: http://www.sri.com

Andrew R. De Boda Consulting
1523 Milford Ave.
Coquitlam, BC, Canada V3J 2V9
(604)936-4527
Fax: (604)936-4527
E-mail: deboda@intergate.bc.ca
Website: http://www.ourworld. compuserve.com/homepages/deboda

The Sage Group Ltd.
980 - 355 Burrard St.
744 W Haistings, Ste. 410
Vancouver, BC, Canada V6C 1A5
(604)669-9269
Fax: (604)669-6622

Tikkanen-Bradley
1345 Nelson St., Ste. 202
Vancouver, BC, Canada V6E 1J8
(604)669-0583
E-mail: webmaster@tikkanen bradley.com
Website: http://www.tikkanenbradley.com

Ontario

The Cynton Co.
17 Massey St.
Brampton, ON, Canada L6S 2V6
(905)792-7769
Fax: (905)792-8116
E-mail: cynton@home.com
Website: http://www.cynton.com

Begley & Associates
RR 6
Cambridge, ON, Canada N1R 5S7
(519)740-3629
Fax: (519)740-3629
E-mail: begley@in.on.ca
Website: http://www.in.on.ca/~begley/ index.htm

CRO Engineering Ltd.
1895 William Hodgins Ln.
Carp, ON, Canada K0A 1L0
(613)839-1108
Fax: (613)839-1406
E-mail: J.Grefford@ieee.ca
Website: http://www.geocities.com/ WallStreet/District/7401/

Task Enterprises
Box 69, RR 2 Hamilton
Flamborough, ON, Canada L8N 2Z7
(905)659-0153
Fax: (905)659-0861

HST Group Ltd.
430 Gilmour St.
Ottawa, ON, Canada K2P 0R8
(613)236-7303
Fax: (613)236-9893

Harrison Associates
BCE Pl.
181 Bay St., Ste. 3740
PO Box 798
Toronto, ON, Canada M5J 2T3
(416)364-5441
Fax: (416)364-2875

TCI Convergence Ltd. Management Consultants
99 Crown's Ln.
Toronto, ON, Canada M5R 3P4
(416)515-4146
Fax: (416)515-2097
E-mail: tci@inforamp.net
Website: http://tciconverge.com/
index.1.html

Ken Wyman & Associates Inc.
64B Shuter St., Ste. 200
Toronto, ON, Canada M5B 1B1
(416)362-2926
Fax: (416)362-3039
E-mail: kenwyman@compuserve.com

JPL Business Consultants
82705 Metter Rd.
Wellandport, ON, Canada L0R 2J0
(905)386-7450
Fax: (905)386-7450
E-mail: plamarch@freenet.npiec.on.ca

Quebec

The Zimmar Consulting Partnership Inc.
Westmount
PO Box 98
Montreal, QC, Canada H3Z 2T1
(514)484-1459
Fax: (514)484-3063

Saskatchewan

Trimension Group
No. 104-110 Research Dr.
Innovation Place, SK, Canada S7N 3R3
(306)668-2560
Fax: (306)975-1156
E-mail: trimension@trimension.ca
Website: http://www.trimension.ca

Corporate Management Consultants
40 Government Road - PO Box 185
Prud Homme, SK, Canada, S0K 3K0
(306)654-4569

E-mail: gerald.rekve@corporate
managementconsultant.com
Website: http://www.Corporate
managementconsultants.com
Gerald Rekve

United states

Alabama

Business Planning Inc.
300 Office Park Dr.
Birmingham, AL 35223-2474
(205)870-7090
Fax: (205)870-7103

Tradebank of Eastern Alabama
546 Broad St., Ste. 3
Gadsden, AL 35901
(205)547-8700
Fax: (205)547-8718
E-mail: mansion@webex.com
Website: http://www.webex.com/~tea

Alaska

AK Business Development Center
3335 Arctic Blvd., Ste. 203
Anchorage, AK 99503
(907)562-0335
Free: 800-478-3474
Fax: (907)562-6988
E-mail: abdc@gci.net
Website: http://www.abdc.org

Business Matters
PO Box 287
Fairbanks, AK 99707
(907)452-5650

Arizona

Carefree Direct Marketing Corp.
8001 E Serene St.
PO Box 3737
Carefree, AZ 85377-3737
(480)488-4227
Fax: (480)488-2841

Trans Energy Corp.
1739 W 7th Ave.
Mesa, AZ 85202
(480)827-7915
Fax: (480)967-6601
E-mail: aha@clean-air.org
Website: http://www.clean-air.org

CMAS
5125 N 16th St.
Phoenix, AZ 85016

(602)395-1001
Fax: (602)604-8180

Comgate Telemanagement Ltd.
706 E Bell Rd., Ste. 105
Phoenix, AZ 85022
(602)485-5708
Fax: (602)485-5709
E-mail: comgate@netzone.com
Website: http://www.comgate.com

Moneysoft Inc.
1 E Camelback Rd. #550
Phoenix, AZ 85012
Free: 800-966-7797
E-mail: mbray@moneysoft.com

Harvey C. Skoog
PO Box 26439
Prescott Valley, AZ 86312
(520)772-1714
Fax: (520)772-2814

LMC Services
8711 E Pinnacle Peak Rd., No. 340
Scottsdale, AZ 85255-3555
(602)585-7177
Fax: (602)585-5880
E-mail: louws@earthlink.com

Sauerbrun Technology Group Ltd.
7979 E Princess Dr., Ste. 5
Scottsdale, AZ 85255-5878
(602)502-4950
Fax: (602)502-4292
E-mail: info@sauerbrun.com
Website: http://www.sauerbrun.com

Gary L. McLeod
PO Box 230
Sonoita, AZ 85637
Fax: (602)455-5661

Van Cleve Associates
6932 E 2nd St.
Tucson, AZ 85710
(520)296-2587
Fax: (520)296-3358

California

Acumen Group Inc.
(650)949-9349
Fax: (650)949-4845
E-mail: acumen-g@ix.netcom.com
Website: http://pw2.netcom.com/~janed/
acumen.html

On-line Career and Management Consulting
420 Central Ave., No. 314
Alameda, CA 94501

(510)864-0336
Fax: (510)864-0336
E-mail: career@dnai.com
Website: http://www.dnai.com/~career

Career Paths-Thomas E. Church & Associates Inc.
PO Box 2439
Aptos, CA 95001
(408)662-7950
Fax: (408)662-7955
E-mail: church@ix.netcom.com
Website: http://www.careerpaths-tom.com

Keck & Co. Business Consultants
410 Walsh Rd.
Atherton, CA 94027
(650)854-9588
Fax: (650)854-7240
E-mail: info@keckco.com
Website: http://www.keckco.com

Ben W. Laverty III, PhD, REA, CEI
4909 Stockdale Hwy., Ste. 132
Bakersfield, CA 93309
(661)283-8300
Free: 800-833-0373
Fax: (661)283-8313
E-mail: cstc@cstcsafety.com
Website: http://www.cstcsafety.com/cstc

Lindquist Consultants-Venture Planning
225 Arlington Ave.
Berkeley, CA 94707
(510)524-6685
Fax: (510)527-6604

Larson Associates
PO Box 9005
Brea, CA 92822
(714)529-4121
Fax: (714)572-3606
E-mail: ray@consultlarson.com
Website: http://www.consultlarson.com

Kremer Management Consulting
PO Box 500
Carmel, CA 93921
(408)626-8311
Fax: (408)624-2663
E-mail: ddkremer@aol.com

W and J PARTNERSHIP
PO Box 2499
18876 Edwin Markham Dr.
Castro Valley, CA 94546
(510)583-7751
Fax: (510)583-7645
E-mail: wamorgan@wjpartnership.com
Website: http://www.wjpartnership.com

JB Associates
21118 Gardena Dr.
Cupertino, CA 95014
(408)257-0214
Fax: (408)257-0216
E-mail: semarang@sirius.com

House Agricultural Consultants
PO Box 1615
Davis, CA 95617-1615
(916)753-3361
Fax: (916)753-0464
E-mail: infoag@houseag.com
Website: http://www.houseag.com/

3C Systems Co.
16161 Ventura Blvd., Ste. 815
Encino, CA 91436
(818)907-1302
Fax: (818)907-1357
E-mail: mark@3CSysCo.com
Website: http://www.3CSysCo.com

Technical Management Consultants
3624 Westfall Dr.
Encino, CA 91436-4154
(818)784-0626
Fax: (818)501-5575
E-mail: tmcrs@aol.com

RAINWATER-GISH & Associates, Business Finance & Development
317 3rd St., Ste. 3
Eureka, CA 95501
(707)443-0030
Fax: (707)443-5683

Global Tradelinks
451 Pebble Beach Pl.
Fullerton, CA 92835
(714)441-2280
Fax: (714)441-2281
E-mail: info@globaltradelinks.com
Website: http://www.globaltradelinks.com

Strategic Business Group
800 Cienaga Dr.
Fullerton, CA 92835-1248
(714)449-1040
Fax: (714)525-1631

Burnes Consulting
20537 Wolf Creek Rd.
Grass Valley, CA 95949
(530)346-8188
Free: 800-949-9021
Fax: (530)346-7704
E-mail: kent@burnesconsulting.com
Website: http://www.burnesconsulting.com

Pioneer Business Consultants
9042 Garfield Ave., Ste. 312
Huntington Beach, CA 92646
(714)964-7600

Beblie, Brandt & Jacobs Inc.
16 Technology, Ste. 164
Irvine, CA 92618
(714)450-8790
Fax: (714)450-8799
E-mail: darcy@bbjinc.com
Website: http://198.147.90.26

Fluor Daniel Inc.
3353 Michelson Dr.
Irvine, CA 92612-0650
(949)975-2000
Fax: (949)975-5271
E-mail: sales.consulting@fluordaniel.com
Website: http://www.fluordanielconsulting.com

MCS Associates
18300 Von Karman, Ste. 710
Irvine, CA 92612
(949)263-8700
Fax: (949)263-0770
E-mail: info@mcsassociates.com
Website: http://www.mcsassociates.com

Inspired Arts Inc.
4225 Executive Sq., Ste. 1160
La Jolla, CA 92037
(619)623-3525
Free: 800-851-4394
Fax: (619)623-3534
E-mail: info@inspiredarts.com
Website: http://www.inspiredarts.com

The Laresis Companies
PO Box 3284
La Jolla, CA 92038
(619)452-2720
Fax: (619)452-8744

RCL & Co.
PO Box 1143
737 Pearl St., Ste. 201
La Jolla, CA 92038
(619)454-8883
Fax: (619)454-8880

Comprehensive Business Services
3201 Lucas Cir.
Lafayette, CA 94549
(925)283-8272
Fax: (925)283-8272

The Ribble Group
27601 Forbes Rd., Ste. 52
Laguna Niguel, CA 92677

(714)582-1085
Fax: (714)582-6420
E-mail: ribble@deltanet.com

Norris Bernstein, CMC
9309 Marina Pacifica Dr. N
Long Beach, CA 90803
(562)493-5458
Fax: (562)493-5459
E-mail: norris@ctecomputer.com
Website: http://foodconsultants.com/
bernstein/

Horizon Consulting Services
1315 Garthwick Dr.
Los Altos, CA 94024
(415)967-0906
Fax: (415)967-0906

Brincko Associates Inc.
1801 Avenue of the Stars, Ste. 1054
Los Angeles, CA 90067
(310)553-4523
Fax: (310)553-6782

Rubenstein/Justman Management Consultants
2049 Century Park E, 24th Fl.
Los Angeles, CA 90067
(310)282-0800
Fax: (310)282-0400
E-mail: info@rjmc.net
Website: http://www.rjmc.net

F.J. Schroeder & Associates
1926 Westholme Ave.
Los Angeles, CA 90025
(310)470-2655
Fax: (310)470-6378
E-mail: fjsacons@aol.com
Website: http://www.mcninet.com/
GlobalLook/Fjschroe.html

Western Management Associates
5959 W Century Blvd., Ste. 565
Los Angeles, CA 90045-6506
(310)645-1091
Free: (888)788-6534
Fax: (310)645-1092
E-mail: gene@cfoforrent.com
Website: http://www.cfoforrent.com

Darrell Sell and Associates
Los Gatos, CA 95030
(408)354-7794
E-mail: darrell@netcom.com

Leslie J. Zambo
3355 Michael Dr.
Marina, CA 93933
(408)384-7086

Fax: (408)647-4199
E-mail: 104776.1552@compuserve.com

Marketing Services Management
PO Box 1377
Martinez, CA 94553
(510)370-8527
Fax: (510)370-8527
E-mail: markserve@biotechnet.com

William M. Shine Consulting Service
PO Box 127
Moraga, CA 94556-0127
(510)376-6516

Palo Alto Management Group Inc.
2672 Bayshore Pky., Ste. 701
Mountain View, CA 94043
(415)968-4374
Fax: (415)968-4245
E-mail: mburwen@pamg.com

BizplanSource
1048 Irvine Ave., Ste. 621
Newport Beach, CA 92660
Free: 888-253-0974
Fax: 800-859-8254
E-mail: info@bizplansource.com
Website: http://www.bizplansource.com
Adam Greengrass, President

The Market Connection
4020 Birch St., Ste. 203
Newport Beach, CA 92660
(714)731-6273
Fax: (714)833-0253

Muller Associates
PO Box 7264
Newport Beach, CA 92658
(714)646-1169
Fax: (714)646-1169

International Health Resources
PO Box 329
North San Juan, CA 95960-0329
(530)292-1266
Fax: (530)292-1243
Website: http://www.futureof
healthcare.com

NEXUS - Consultants to Management
PO Box 1531
Novato, CA 94948
(415)897-4400
Fax: (415)898-2252
E-mail: jimnexus@aol.com

Aerospcace.Org
PO Box 28831
Oakland, CA 94604-8831

(510)530-9169
Fax: (510)530-3411
Website: http://www.aerospace.org

Intelequest Corp.
722 Gailen Ave.
Palo Alto, CA 94303
(415)968-3443
Fax: (415)493-6954
E-mail: frits@iqix.com

McLaughlin & Associates
66 San Marino Cir.
Rancho Mirage, CA 92270
(760)321-2932
Fax: (760)328-2474
E-mail: jackmcla@msn.com

Carrera Consulting Group, a division of Maximus
2110 21st St., Ste. 400
Sacramento, CA 95818
(916)456-3300
Fax: (916)456-3306
E-mail: central@carreraconsulting.com
Website: http://www.carreraconsulting.com

Bay Area Tax Consultants and Bayhill Financial Consultants
1150 Bayhill Dr., Ste. 1150
San Bruno, CA 94066-3004
(415)952-8786
Fax: (415)588-4524
E-mail: baytax@compuserve.com
Website: http://www.baytax.com/

AdCon Services, LLC
8871 Hillery Dr.
Dan Diego, CA 92126
(858)433-1411
E-mail: adam@adconservices.com
Website: http://www.adconservices.com
Adam Greengrass

California Business Incubation Network
101 W Broadway, No. 480
San Diego, CA 92101
(619)237-0559
Fax: (619)237-0521

G.R. Gordetsky Consultants Inc.
11414 Windy Summit Pl.
San Diego, CA 92127
(619)487-4939
Fax: (619)487-5587
E-mail: gordet@pacbell.net

Freeman, Sullivan & Co.
131 Steuart St., Ste. 500
San Francisco, CA 94105
(415)777-0707

Free: 800-777-0737
Fax: (415)777-2420
Website: http://www.fsc-research.com

Ideas Unlimited
2151 California St., Ste. 7
San Francisco, CA 94115
(415)931-0641
Fax: (415)931-0880

Russell Miller Inc.
300 Montgomery St., Ste. 900
San Francisco, CA 94104
(415)956-7474
Fax: (415)398-0620
E-mail: rmi@pacbell.net
Website: http://www.rmisf.com

PKF Consulting
425 California St., Ste. 1650
San Francisco, CA 94104
(415)421-5378
Fax: (415)956-7708
E-mail: callahan@pkfc.com
Website: http://www.pkfonline.com

Welling & Woodard Inc.
1067 Broadway
San Francisco, CA 94133
(415)776-4500
Fax: (415)776-5067

Highland Associates
16174 Highland Dr.
San Jose, CA 95127
(408)272-7008
Fax: (408)272-4040

ORDIS Inc.
6815 Trinidad Dr.
San Jose, CA 95120-2056
(408)268-3321
Free: 800-446-7347
Fax: (408)268-3582
E-mail: ordis@ordis.com
Website: http://www.ordis.com

Stanford Resources Inc.
20 Great Oaks Blvd., Ste. 200
San Jose, CA 95119
(408)360-8400
Fax: (408)360-8410
E-mail: sales@stanfordsources.com
Website: http://www.stanfordresources.com

Technology Properties Ltd. Inc.
PO Box 20250
San Jose, CA 95160
(408)243-9898
Fax: (408)296-6637
E-mail: sanjose@tplnet.com

Helfert Associates
1777 Borel Pl., Ste. 508
San Mateo, CA 94402-3514
(650)377-0540
Fax: (650)377-0472

Mykytyn Consulting Group Inc.
185 N Redwood Dr., Ste. 200
San Rafael, CA 94903
(415)491-1770
Fax: (415)491-1251
E-mail: info@mcgi.com
Website: http://www.mcgi.com

Omega Management Systems Inc.
3 Mount Darwin Ct.
San Rafael, CA 94903-1109
(415)499-1300
Fax: (415)492-9490
E-mail: omegamgt@ix.netcom.com

The Information Group Inc.
4675 Stevens Creek Blvd., Ste. 100
Santa Clara, CA 95051
(408)985-7877
Fax: (408)985-2945
E-mail: dvincent@tig-usa.com
Website: http://www.tig-usa.com

Cast Management Consultants
1620 26th St., Ste. 2040N
Santa Monica, CA 90404
(310)828-7511
Fax: (310)453-6831

Cuma Consulting Management
Box 724
Santa Rosa, CA 95402
(707)785-2477
Fax: (707)785-2478

The E-Myth Academy
131B Stony Cir., Ste. 2000
Santa Rosa, CA 95401
(707)569-5600
Free: 800-221-0266
Fax: (707)569-5700
E-mail: info@e-myth.com
Website: http://www.e-myth.com

Reilly, Connors & Ray
1743 Canyon Rd.
Spring Valley, CA 91977
(619)698-4808
Fax: (619)460-3892
E-mail: davidray@adnc.com

Management Consultants
Sunnyvale, CA 94087-4700
(408)773-0321

RJR Associates
1639 Lewiston Dr.
Sunnyvale, CA 94087
(408)737-7720
E-mail: bobroy@rjrassoc.com
Website: http://www.rjrassoc.com

Schwafel Associates
333 Cobalt Way, Ste. 21
Sunnyvale, CA 94085
(408)720-0649
Fax: (408)720-1796
E-mail: schwafel@ricochet.net
Website: http://www.patca.org

Staubs Business Services
23320 S Vermont Ave.
Torrance, CA 90502-2940
(310)830-9128
Fax: (310)830-9128
E-mail: Harry_L_Staubs@Lamg.com

Out of Your Mind . . . and Into the Marketplace
13381 White Sands Dr.
Tustin, CA 92780-4565
(714)544-0248
Free: 800-419-1513
Fax: (714)730-1414
E-mail: lpinson@aol.com
Website: http://www.business-plan.com

Independent Research Services
PO Box 2426
Van Nuys, CA 91404-2426
(818)993-3622

Ingman Company Inc.
7949 Woodley Ave., Ste. 120
Van Nuys, CA 91406-1232
(818)375-5027
Fax: (818)894-5001

Innovative Technology Associates
3639 E Harbor Blvd., Ste. 203E
Ventura, CA 93001
(805)650-9353

Grid Technology Associates
20404 Tufts Cir.
Walnut, CA 91789
(909)444-0922
Fax: (909)444-0922
E-mail: grid_technology@msn.com

Ridge Consultants Inc.
100 Pringle Ave., Ste. 580
Walnut Creek, CA 94596
(925)274-1990
Fax: (510)274-1956
E-mail: info@ridgecon.com
Website: http://www.ridgecon.com

Bell Springs Publishing
PO Box 1240
Willits, CA 95490
(707)459-6372
E-mail: bellsprings@sabernet
Website: http://www.bellsprings.com

Hutchinson Consulting and Appraisal
23245 Sylvan St., Ste. 103
Woodland Hills, CA 91367
(818)888-8175
Free: 800-977-7548
Fax: (818)888-8220
E-mail: r.f.hutchinson-cpa@worldnet.
att.net

Colorado

Sam Boyer & Associates
4255 S Buckley Rd., No. 136
Aurora, CO 80013
Free: 800-785-0485
Fax: (303)766-8740
E-mail: samboyer@samboyer.com
Website: http://www.samboyer.com/

Ameriwest Business Consultants Inc.
PO Box 26266
Colorado Springs, CO 80936
(719)380-7096
Fax: (719)380-7096
E-mail: email@abchelp.com
Website: http://www.abchelp.com

GVNW Consulting Inc.
2270 La Montana Way
Colorado Springs, CO 80936
(719)594-5800
Fax: (719)594-5803
Website: http://www.gvnw.com

M-Squared Inc.
755 San Gabriel Pl.
Colorado Springs, CO 80906
(719)576-2554
Fax: (719)576-2554

Thornton Financial FNIC
1024 Centre Ave., Bldg. E
Fort Collins, CO 80526-1849
(970)221-2089
Fax: (970)484-5206

TenEyck Associates
1760 Cherryville Rd.
Greenwood Village, CO 80121-1503
(303)758-6129
Fax: (303)761-8286

Associated Enterprises Ltd.
13050 W Ceder Dr., Unit 11
Lakewood, CO 80228

(303)988-6695
Fax: (303)988-6739
E-mail: ael1@classic.msn.com

The Vincent Company Inc.
200 Union Blvd., Ste. 210
Lakewood, CO 80228
(303)989-7271
Free: 800-274-0733
Fax: (303)989-7570
E-mail: vincent@vincentco.com
Website: http://www.vincentco.com

Johnson & West Management Consultants Inc.
7612 S Logan Dr.
Littleton, CO 80122
(303)730-2810
Fax: (303)730-3219

Western Capital Holdings Inc.
10050 E Applwood Dr.
Parker, CO 80138
(303)841-1022
Fax: (303)770-1945

Connecticut

Stratman Group Inc.
40 Tower Ln.
Avon, CT 06001-4222
(860)677-2898
Free: 800-551-0499
Fax: (860)677-8210

Cowherd Consulting Group Inc.
106 Stephen Mather Rd.
Darien, CT 06820
(203)655-2150
Fax: (203)655-6427

Greenwich Associates
8 Greenwich Office Park
Greenwich, CT 06831-5149
(203)629-1200
Fax: (203)629-1229
E-mail: lisa@greenwich.com
Website: http://www.greenwich.com

Follow-up News
185 Pine St., Ste. 818
Manchester, CT 06040
(860)647-7542
Free: 800-708-0696
Fax: (860)646-6544
E-mail: Followupnews@aol.com

Lovins & Associates Consulting
309 Edwards St.
New Haven, CT 06511
(203)787-3367

Fax: (203)624-7599
E-mail: Alovinsphd@aol.com
Website: http://www.lovinsgroup.com

JC Ventures Inc.
4 Arnold St.
Old Greenwich, CT 06870-1203
(203)698-1990
Free: 800-698-1997
Fax: (203)698-2638

Charles L. Hornung Associates
52 Ned's Mountain Rd.
Ridgefield, CT 06877
(203)431-0297

Manus
100 Prospect St., S Tower
Stamford, CT 06901
(203)326-3880
Free: 800-445-0942
Fax: (203)326-3890
E-mail: manus1@aol.com
Website: http://www.RightManus.com

RealBusinessPlans.com
156 Westport Rd.
Wilton, CT 06897
(914)837-2886
E-mail: ct@realbusinessplans.com
Website: http://www.RealBusinessPlans.com
Tony Tecce

Delaware

Focus Marketing
61-7 Habor Dr.
Claymont, DE 19703
(302)793-3064

Daedalus Ventures Ltd.
PO Box 1474
Hockessin, DE 19707
(302)239-6758
Fax: (302)239-9991
E-mail: daedalus@mail.del.net

The Formula Group
PO Box 866
Hockessin, DE 19707
(302)456-0952
Fax: (302)456-1354
E-mail: formula@netaxs.com

Selden Enterprises Inc.
2502 Silverside Rd., Ste. 1
Wilmington, DE 19810-3740
(302)529-7113
Fax: (302)529-7442
E-mail: selden2@bellatlantic.net
Website: http://www.seldenenterprises.com

District of Columbia

Bruce W. McGee and Associates
7826 Eastern Ave. NW, Ste. 30
Washington, DC 20012
(202)726-7272
Fax: (202)726-2946

McManis Associates Inc.
1900 K St. NW, Ste. 700
Washington, DC 20006
(202)466-7680
Fax: (202)872-1898
Website: http://www.mcmanis-mmi.com

Smith, Dawson & Andrews Inc.
1000 Connecticut Ave., Ste. 302
Washington, DC 20036
(202)835-0740
Fax: (202)775-8526
E-mail: webmaster@sda-inc.com
Website: http://www.sda-inc.com

Florida

BackBone, Inc.
20404 Hacienda Court
Boca Raton, FL 33498
(561)470-0965
Fax: 516-908-4038
E-mail: BPlans@backboneinc.com
Website: http://www.backboneinc.com
Charles Epstein, President

Whalen & Associates Inc.
4255 Northwest 26 Ct.
Boca Raton, FL 33434
(561)241-5950
Fax: (561)241-7414
E-mail: drwhalen@ix.netcom.com

E.N. Rysso & Associates
180 Bermuda Petrel Ct.
Daytona Beach, FL 32119
(386)760-3028
E-mail: erysso@aol.com

Virtual Technocrats LLC
560 Lavers Circle, #146
Delray Beach, FL 33444
(561)265-3509
E-mail: josh@virtualtechnocrats.com;
info@virtualtechnocrats.com
Website: http://www.virtualtechnocrats.
com
Josh Eikov, Managing Director

Eric Sands Consulting Services
6193 Rock Island Rd., Ste. 412
Fort Lauderdale, FL 33319
(954)721-4767

Fax: (954)720-2815
E-mail: easands@aol.com
Website: http://www.ericsandsconsultig.com

Professional Planning Associates, Inc.
1975 E. Sunrise Blvd. Suite 607
Fort Lauderdale, FL 33304
(954)764-5204
Fax: 954-463-4172
E-mail: Mgoldstein@proplana.com
Website: http://proplana.com
Michael Goldstein, President

Host Media Corp.
3948 S 3rd St., Ste. 191
Jacksonville Beach, FL 32250
(904)285-3239
Fax: (904)285-5618
E-mail: msconsulting@compuserve.com
Website: http://www.media
servicesgroup.com

William V. Hall
1925 Brickell, Ste. D-701
Miami, FL 33129
(305)856-9622
Fax: (305)856-4113
E-mail: williamvhall@compuserve.com

F.A. McGee Inc.
800 Claughton Island Dr., Ste. 401
Miami, FL 33131
(305)377-9123

Taxplan Inc.
Mirasol International Ctr.
2699 Collins Ave.
Miami Beach, FL 33140
(305)538-3303

T.C. Brown & Associates
8415 Excalibur Cir., Apt. B1
Naples, FL 34108
(941)594-1949
Fax: (941)594-0611
E-mail: tcater@naples.net.com

RLA International Consulting
713 Lagoon Dr.
North Palm Beach, FL 33408
(407)626-4258
Fax: (407)626-5772

Comprehensive Franchising Inc.
2465 Ridgecrest Ave.
Orange Park, FL 32065
(904)272-6567
Free: 800-321-6567
Fax: (904)272-6750
E-mail: theimp@cris.com
Website: http://www.franchise411.com

Hunter G. Jackson Jr. - Consulting Environmental Physicist
PO Box 618272
Orlando, FL 32861-8272
(407)295-4188
E-mail: hunterjackson@juno.com

F. Newton Parks
210 El Brillo Way
Palm Beach, FL 33480
(561)833-1727
Fax: (561)833-4541

Avery Business Development Services
2506 St. Michel Ct.
Ponte Vedra Beach, FL 32082
(904)285-6033
Fax: (904)285-6033

Strategic Business Planning Co.
PO Box 821006
South Florida, FL 33082-1006
(954)704-9100
Fax: (954)438-7333
E-mail: info@bizplan.com
Website: http://www.bizplan.com

Dufresne Consulting Group Inc.
10014 N Dale Mabry, Ste. 101
Tampa, FL 33618-4426
(813)264-4775
Fax: (813)264-9300
Website: http://www.dcgconsult.com

Agrippa Enterprises Inc.
PO Box 175
Venice, FL 34284-0175
(941)355-7876
E-mail: webservices@agrippa.com
Website: http://www.agrippa.com

Center for Simplified Strategic Planning Inc.
PO Box 3324
Vero Beach, FL 32964-3324
(561)231-3636
Fax: (561)231-1099
Website: http://www.cssp.com

Georgia

Marketing Spectrum Inc.
115 Perimeter Pl., Ste. 440
Atlanta, GA 30346
(770)395-7244
Fax: (770)393-4071

Business Ventures Corp.
1650 Oakbrook Dr., Ste. 405
Norcross, GA 30093
(770)729-8000
Fax: (770)729-8028

Informed Decisions Inc.
100 Falling Cheek
Sautee Nacoochee, GA 30571
(706)878-1905
Fax: (706)878-1802
E-mail: skylake@compuserve.com

Tom C. Davis & Associates, P.C.
3189 Perimeter Rd.
Valdosta, GA 31602
(912)247-9801
Fax: (912)244-7704
E-mail: mail@tcdcpa.com
Website: http://www.tcdcpa.com/

Illinois

TWD and Associates
431 S Patton
Arlington Heights, IL 60005
(847)398-6410
Fax: (847)255-5095
E-mail: tdoo@aol.com

Management Planning Associates Inc.
2275 Half Day Rd., Ste. 350
Bannockburn, IL 60015-1277
(847)945-2421
Fax: (847)945-2425

Phil Faris Associates
86 Old Mill Ct.
Barrington, IL 60010
(847)382-4888
Fax: (847)382-4890
E-mail: pfaris@meginsnet.net

Seven Continents Technology
787 Stonebridge
Buffalo Grove, IL 60089
(708)577-9653
Fax: (708)870-1220

Grubb & Blue Inc.
2404 Windsor Pl.
Champaign, IL 61820
(217)366-0052
Fax: (217)356-0117

ACE Accounting Service Inc.
3128 N Bernard St.
Chicago, IL 60618
(773)463-7854
Fax: (773)463-7854

AON Consulting Worldwide
200 E Randolph St., 10th Fl.
Chicago, IL 60601
(312)381-4800
Free: 800-438-6487
Fax: (312)381-0240
Website: http://www.aon.com

FMS Consultants
5801 N Sheridan Rd., Ste. 3D
Chicago, IL 60660
(773)561-7362
Fax: (773)561-6274

Grant Thornton
800 1 Prudential Plz.
130 E Randolph St.
Chicago, IL 60601
(312)856-0001
Fax: (312)861-1340
E-mail: gtinfo@gt.com
Website: http://www.grantthornton.com

Kingsbury International Ltd.
5341 N Glenwood Ave.
Chicago, IL 60640
(773)271-3030
Fax: (773)728-7080
E-mail: jetlag@mcs.com
Website: http://www.kingbiz.com

MacDougall & Blake Inc.
1414 N Wells St., Ste. 311
Chicago, IL 60610-1306
(312)587-3330
Fax: (312)587-3699
E-mail: jblake@compuserve.com

James C. Osburn Ltd.
6445 N. Western Ave., Ste. 304
Chicago, IL 60645
(773)262-4428
Fax: (773)262-6755
E-mail: osburnltd@aol.com

Tarifero & Tazewell Inc.
211 S Clark
Chicago, IL 60690
(312)665-9714
Fax: (312)665-9716

Human Energy Design Systems
620 Roosevelt Dr.
Edwardsville, IL 62025
(618)692-0258
Fax: (618)692-0819

China Business Consultants Group
931 Dakota Cir.
Naperville, IL 60563
(630)778-7992
Fax: (630)778-7915
E-mail: cbcq@aol.com

Center for Workforce Effectiveness
500 Skokie Blvd., Ste. 222
Northbrook, IL 60062
(847)559-8777
Fax: (847)559-8778

E-mail: office@cwelink.com
Website: http://www.cwelink.com

Smith Associates
1320 White Mountain Dr.
Northbrook, IL 60062
(847)480-7200
Fax: (847)480-9828

Francorp Inc.
20200 Governors Dr.
Olympia Fields, IL 60461
(708)481-2900
Free: 800-372-6244
Fax: (708)481-5885
E-mail: francorp@aol.com
Website: http://www.francorpinc.com

Camber Business Strategy Consultants
1010 S Plum Tree Ct
Palatine, IL 60078-0986
(847)202-0101
Fax: (847)705-7510
E-mail: camber@ameritech.net

Partec Enterprise Group
5202 Keith Dr.
Richton Park, IL 60471
(708)503-4047
Fax: (708)503-9468

Rockford Consulting Group Ltd.
Century Plz., Ste. 206
7210 E State St.
Rockford, IL 61108
(815)229-2900
Free: 800-667-7495
Fax: (815)229-2612
E-mail: rligus@RockfordConsulting.com
Website: http://www.Rockford
Consulting.com

RSM McGladrey Inc.
1699 E Woodfield Rd., Ste. 300
Schaumburg, IL 60173-4969
(847)413-6900
Fax: (847)517-7067
Website: http://www.rsmmcgladrey.com

A.D. Star Consulting
320 Euclid
Winnetka, IL 60093
(847)446-7827
Fax: (847)446-7827
E-mail: startwo@worldnet.att.net

Indiana

Modular Consultants Inc.
3109 Crabtree Ln.
Elkhart, IN 46514

(219)264-5761
Fax: (219)264-5761
E-mail: sasabo5313@aol.com

Midwest Marketing Research
PO Box 1077
Goshen, IN 46527
(219)533-0548
Fax: (219)533-0540
E-mail: 103365.654@compuserve

Ketchum Consulting Group
8021 Knue Rd., Ste. 112
Indianapolis, IN 46250
(317)845-5411
Fax: (317)842-9941

**MDI Management
Consulting**
1519 Park Dr.
Munster, IN 46321
(219)838-7909
Fax: (219)838-7909

Iowa

McCord Consulting Group Inc.
4533 Pine View Dr. NE
PO Box 11024
Cedar Rapids, IA 52410
(319)378-0077
Fax: (319)378-1577
E-mail: smmccord@hom.com
Website: http://www.mccordgroup.com

Management Solutions L.C.
3815 Lincoln Pl. Dr.
Des Moines, IA 50312
(515)277-6408
Fax: (515)277-3506
E-mail: wasunimers@uswest.net

Grandview Marketing
15 Red Bridge Dr.
Sioux City, IA 51104
(712)239-3122
Fax: (712)258-7578
E-mail: eandrews@pionet.net

Kansas

Assessments in Action
513A N Mur-Len
Olathe, KS 66062
(913)764-6270
Free: (888)548-1504
Fax: (913)764-6495
E-mail: lowdene@qni.com
Website: http://www.assessments-
in-action.com

Maine

Edgemont Enterprises
PO Box 8354
Portland, ME 04104
(207)871-8964
Fax: (207)871-8964

Pan Atlantic Consultants
5 Milk St.
Portland, ME 04101
(207)871-8622
Fax: (207)772-4842
E-mail: pmurphy@maine.rr.com
Website: http://www.panatlantic.net

Maryland

Clemons & Associates Inc.
5024-R Campbell Blvd.
Baltimore, MD 21236
(410)931-8100
Fax: (410)931-8111
E-mail: info@clemonsmgmt.com
Website: http://www.clemonsmgmt.com

Imperial Group Ltd.
305 Washington Ave., Ste. 204
Baltimore, MD 21204-6009
(410)337-8500
Fax: (410)337-7641

Leadership Institute
3831 Yolando Rd.
Baltimore, MD 21218
(410)366-9111
Fax: (410)243-8478
E-mail: behconsult@aol.com

Burdeshaw Associates Ltd.
4701 Sangamore Rd.
Bethesda, MD 20816-2508
(301)229-5800
Fax: (301)229-5045
E-mail: jstacy@burdeshaw.com
Website: http://www.burdeshaw.com

Michael E. Cohen
5225 Pooks Hill Rd., Ste. 1119 S
Bethesda, MD 20814
(301)530-5738
Fax: (301)530-2988
E-mail: mecohen@crosslink.net

World Development Group Inc.
5272 River Rd., Ste. 650
Bethesda, MD 20816-1405
(301)652-1818
Fax: (301)652-1250
E-mail: wdg@has.com
Website: http://www.worlddg.com

Swartz Consulting
PO Box 4301
Crofton, MD 21114-4301
(301)262-6728

Software Solutions International Inc.
9633 Duffer Way
Gaithersburg, MD 20886
(301)330-4136
Fax: (301)330-4136

Strategies Inc.
8 Park Center Ct., Ste. 200
Owings Mills, MD 21117
(410)363-6669
Fax: (410)363-1231
E-mail: strategies@strat1.com
Website: http://www.strat1.com

Hammer Marketing Resources
179 Inverness Rd.
Severna Park, MD 21146
(410)544-9191
Fax: (305)675-3277
E-mail: info@gohammer.com
Website: http://www.gohammer.com

Andrew Sussman & Associates
13731 Kretsinger
Smithsburg, MD 21783
(301)824-2943
Fax: (301)824-2943

Massachusetts

Geibel Marketing and Public Relations
PO Box 611
Belmont, MA 02478-0005
(617)484-8285
Fax: (617)489-3567
E-mail: jgeibel@geibelpr.com
Website: http://www.geibelpr.com

Bain & Co.
2 Copley Pl.
Boston, MA 02116
(617)572-2000
Fax: (617)572-2427
E-mail: corporate.inquiries@bain.com
Website: http://www.bain.com

Mehr & Co.
62 Kinnaird St.
Cambridge, MA 02139
(617)876-3311
Fax: (617)876-3023
E-mail: mehrco@aol.com

Monitor Company Inc.
2 Canal Park
Cambridge, MA 02141

(617)252-2000
Fax: (617)252-2100
Website: http://www.monitor.com

Information & Research Associates
PO Box 3121
Framingham, MA 01701
(508)788-0784

Walden Consultants Ltd.
252 Pond St.
Hopkinton, MA 01748
(508)435-4882
Fax: (508)435-3971
Website: http://www.waldencon
sultants.com

Jeffrey D. Marshall
102 Mitchell Rd.
Ipswich, MA 01938-1219
(508)356-1113
Fax: (508)356-2989

Consulting Resources Corp.
6 Northbrook Park
Lexington, MA 02420
(781)863-1222
Fax: (781)863-1441
E-mail: res@consultingresources.net
Website: http://www.consulting
resources.net

Planning Technologies Group L.L.C.
92 Hayden Ave.
Lexington, MA 02421
(781)778-4678
Fax: (781)861-1099
E-mail: ptg@plantech.com
Website: http://www.plantech.com

Kalba International Inc.
23 Sandy Pond Rd.
Lincoln, MA 01773
(781)259-9589
Fax: (781)259-1460
E-mail: info@kalbainternational.com
Website: http://www.kalbainter
national.com

VMB Associates Inc.
115 Ashland St.
Melrose, MA 02176
(781)665-0623
Fax: (425)732-7142
E-mail: vmbinc@aol.com

The Company Doctor
14 Pudding Stone Ln.
Mendon, MA 01756
(508)478-1747
Fax: (508)478-0520

Data and Strategies Group Inc.
190 N Main St.
Natick, MA 01760
(508)653-9990
Fax: (508)653-7799
E-mail: dsginc@dsggroup.com
Website: http://www.dsggroup.com

The Enterprise Group
73 Parker Rd.
Needham, MA 02494
(617)444-6631
Fax: (617)433-9991
E-mail: lsacco@world.std.com
Website: http://www.enterprise-group.com

PSMJ Resources Inc.
10 Midland Ave.
Newton, MA 02458
(617)965-0055
Free: 800-537-7765
Fax: (617)965-5152
E-mail: psmj@tiac.net
Website: http://www.psmj.com

Scheur Management Group Inc.
255 Washington St., Ste. 100
Newton, MA 02458-1611
(617)969-7500
Fax: (617)969-7508
E-mail: smgnow@scheur.com
Website: http://www.scheur.com

I.E.E.E., Boston Section
240 Bear Hill Rd., 202B
Waltham, MA 02451-1017
(781)890-5294
Fax: (781)890-5290

Business Planning and Consulting Services
20 Beechwood Ter.
Wellesley, MA 02482
(617)237-9151
Fax: (617)237-9151

Michigan

Walter Frederick Consulting
1719 South Blvd.
Ann Arbor, MI 48104
(313)662-4336
Fax: (313)769-7505

Fox Enterprises
6220 W Freeland Rd.
Freeland, MI 48623
(517)695-9170
Fax: (517)695-9174
E-mail: foxjw@concentric.net
Website: http://www.cris.com/~foxjw

G.G.W. and Associates
1213 Hampton
Jackson, MI 49203
(517)782-2255
Fax: (517)782-2255

Altamar Group Ltd.
6810 S Cedar, Ste. 2-B
Lansing, MI 48911
(517)694-0910
Free: 800-443-2627
Fax: (517)694-1377

Sheffieck Consultants Inc.
23610 Greening Dr.
Novi, MI 48375-3130
(248)347-3545
Fax: (248)347-3530
E-mail: cfsheff@concentric.net

Rehmann, Robson PC
5800 Gratiot
Saginaw, MI 48605
(517)799-9580
Fax: (517)799-0227
Website: http://www.rrpc.com

Francis & Co.
17200 W 10 Mile Rd., Ste. 207
Southfield, MI 48075
(248)559-7600
Fax: (248)559-5249

Private Ventures Inc.
16000 W 9 Mile Rd., Ste. 504
Southfield, MI 48075
(248)569-1977
Free: 800-448-7614
Fax: (248)569-1838
E-mail: pventuresi@aol.com

JGK Associates
14464 Kerner Dr.
Sterling Heights, MI 48313
(810)247-9055
Fax: (248)822-4977
E-mail: kozlowski@home.com

Minnesota

Health Fitness Corp.
3500 W 80th St., Ste. 130
Bloomington, MN 55431
(612)831-6830
Fax: (612)831-7264

Consatech Inc.
PO Box 1047
Burnsville, MN 55337
(612)953-1088
Fax: (612)435-2966

Robert F. Knotek
14960 Ironwood Ct.
Eden Prairie, MN 55346
(612)949-2875

DRI Consulting
7715 Stonewood Ct.
Edina, MN 55439
(612)941-9656
Fax: (612)941-2693
E-mail: dric@dric.com
Website: http://www.dric.com

Markin Consulting
12072 87th Pl. N
Maple Grove, MN 55369
(612)493-3568
Fax: (612)493-5744
E-mail: markin@markinconsulting.com
Website: http://www.markin
consulting.com

**Minnesota Cooperation Office for
Small Business & Job Creation Inc.**
5001 W 80th St., Ste. 825
Minneapolis, MN 55437
(612)830-1230
Fax: (612)830-1232
E-mail: mncoop@msn.com
Website: http://www.mnco.org

Enterprise Consulting Inc.
PO Box 1111
Minnetonka, MN 55345
(612)949-5909
Fax: (612)906-3965

Amdahl International
724 1st Ave. SW
Rochester, MN 55902
(507)252-0402
Fax: (507)252-0402
E-mail: amdahl@best-service.com
Website: http://www.wp.com/amdahl_int

Power Systems Research
1365 Corporate Center Curve, 2nd Fl.
St. Paul, MN 55121
(612)905-8400
Free: (888)625-8612
Fax: (612)454-0760
E-mail: Barb@Powersys.com
Website: http://www.powersys.com

Missouri

**Business Planning and Development
Corp.**
4030 Charlotte St.
Kansas City, MO 64110
(816)753-0495

E-mail: humph@bpdev.demon.co.uk
Website: http://www.bpdev.demon.co.uk

CFO Service
10336 Donoho
St. Louis, MO 63131
(314)750-2940
E-mail: jskae@cfoservice.com
Website: http://www.cfoservice.com

Nebraska

**International Management Consulting
Group Inc.**
1309 Harlan Dr., Ste. 205
Bellevue, NE 68005
(402)291-4545
Free: 800-665-IMCG
Fax: (402)291-4343
E-mail: imcg@neonramp.com
Website: http://www.mgtcon
sulting.com

**Heartland Management Consulting
Group**
1904 Barrington Pky.
Papillion, NE 68046
(402)339-2387
Fax: (402)339-1319

Nevada

The DuBois Group
865 Tahoe Blvd., Ste. 108
Incline Village, NV 89451
(775)832-0550
Free: 800-375-2935
Fax: (775)832-0556
E-mail: DuBoisGrp@aol.com

New Hampshire

Wolff Consultants
10 Buck Rd.
Hanover, NH 03755
(603)643-6015

BPT Consulting Associates Ltd.
12 Parmenter Rd., Ste. B-6
Londonderry, NH 03053
(603)437-8484
Free: (888)278-0030
Fax: (603)434-5388
E-mail: bptcons@tiac.net
Website: http://www.bptconsulting.com

New Jersey

Bedminster Group Inc.
1170 Rte. 22 E
Bridgewater, NJ 08807

(908)500-4155
Fax: (908)766-0780
E-mail: info@bedminstergroup.com
Website: http://www.bedminster
group.com
Fax: (202)806-1777
Terry Strong, Acting Regional Dir.

Delta Planning Inc.
PO Box 425
Denville, NJ 07834
(913)625-1742
Free: 800-672-0762
Fax: (973)625-3531
E-mail: DeltaP@worldnet.att.net
Website: http://deltaplanning.com

Kumar Associates Inc.
1004 Cumbermeade Rd.
Fort Lee, NJ 07024
(201)224-9480
Fax: (201)585-2343
E-mail: mail@kumarassociates.com
Website: http://kumarassociates.com

John Hall & Company Inc.
PO Box 187
Glen Ridge, NJ 07028
(973)680-4449
Fax: (973)680-4581
E-mail: jhcompany@aol.com

Market Focus
PO Box 402
Maplewood, NJ 07040
(973)378-2470
Fax: (973)378-2470
E-mail: mcss66@marketfocus.com

Vanguard Communications Corp.
100 American Rd.
Morris Plains, NJ 07950
(973)605-8000
Fax: (973)605-8329
Website: http://www.vanguard.net/

ConMar International Ltd.
1901 US Hwy. 130
North Brunswick, NJ 08902
(732)940-8347
Fax: (732)274-1199

KLW New Products
156 Cedar Dr.
Old Tappan, NJ 07675
(201)358-1300
Fax: (201)664-2594
E-mail: lrlarsen@usa.net
Website: http://www.klwnew
products.com

PA Consulting Group
315A Enterprise Dr.
Plainsboro, NJ 08536
(609)936-8300
Fax: (609)936-8811
E-mail: info@paconsulting.com
Website: http://www.pa-consulting.com

Aurora Marketing Management Inc.
66 Witherspoon St., Ste. 600
Princeton, NJ 08542
(908)904-1125
Fax: (908)359-1108
E-mail: aurora2@voicenet.com
Website: http://www.auroramarketing.net

Smart Business Supersite
88 Orchard Rd., CN-5219
Princeton, NJ 08543
(908)321-1924
Fax: (908)321-5156
E-mail: irv@smartbiz.com
Website: http://www.smartbiz.com

Tracelin Associates
1171 Main St., Ste. 6K
Rahway, NJ 07065
(732)381-3288

Schkeeper Inc.
130-6 Bodman Pl.
Red Bank, NJ 07701
(732)219-1965
Fax: (732)530-3703

Henry Branch Associates
2502 Harmon Cove Twr.
Secaucus, NJ 07094
(201)866-2008
Fax: (201)601-0101
E-mail: hbranch161@home.com

Robert Gibbons & Company Inc.
46 Knoll Rd.
Tenafly, NJ 07670-1050
(201)871-3933
Fax: (201)871-2173
E-mail: crisisbob@aol.com

PMC Management Consultants Inc.
6 Thistle Ln.
Three Bridges, NJ 08887-0332
(908)788-1014
Free: 800-PMC-0250
Fax: (908)806-7287
E-mail: int@pmc-management.com
Website: http://www.pmc-management.com

R.W. Bankart & Associates
20 Valley Ave., Ste. D-2

Westwood, NJ 07675-3607
(201)664-7672

New Mexico

Vondle & Associates Inc.
4926 Calle de Tierra, NE
Albuquerque, NM 87111
(505)292-8961
Fax: (505)296-2790
E-mail: vondle@aol.com

InfoNewMexico
2207 Black Hills Rd., NE
Rio Rancho, NM 87124
(505)891-2462
Fax: (505)896-8971

New York

Powers Research and Training Institute
PO Box 78
Bayville, NY 11709
(516)628-2250
Fax: (516)628-2252
E-mail: powercocch@compuserve.com
Website: http://www.nancypowers.com

Consortium House
296 Wittenberg Rd.
Bearsville, NY 12409
(845)679-8867
Fax: (845)679-9248
E-mail: eugenegs@aol.com
Website: http://www.chpub.com

Progressive Finance Corp.
3549 Tiemann Ave.
Bronx, NY 10469
(718)405-9029
Free: 800-225-8381
Fax: (718)405-1170

Wave Hill Associates Inc.
2621 Palisade Ave., Ste. 15-C
Bronx, NY 10463
(718)549-7368
Fax: (718)601-9670
E-mail: pepper@compuserve.com

Management Insight
96 Arlington Rd.
Buffalo, NY 14221
(716)631-3319
Fax: (716)631-0203
E-mail: michalski@foodservice insight.com
Website: http://www.foodservice insight.com

Samani International Enterprises, Marions Panyaught Consultancy
2028 Parsons
Flushing, NY 11357-3436
(917)287-8087
Fax: 800-873-8939
E-mail: vjp2@biostrategist.com
Website: http://www.biostrategist.com

Marketing Resources Group
71-58 Austin St.
Forest Hills, NY 11375
(718)261-8882

Mangabay Business Plans & Development Subsidiary of Innis Asset Allocation
125-10 Queens Blvd., Ste. 2202
Kew Gardens, NY 11415
(905)527-1947
Fax: 509-472-1935
E-mail: mangabay@mangabay.com
Website: http://www.mangabay.com
Lee Toh, Managing Partner

ComputerEase Co.
1301 Monmouth Ave.
Lakewood, NY 08701
(212)406-9464
Fax: (914)277-5317
E-mail: crawfordc@juno.com

Boice Dunham Group
30 W 13th St.
New York, NY 10011
(212)924-2200
Fax: (212)924-1108

Elizabeth Capen
27 E 95th St.
New York, NY 10128
(212)427-7654
Fax: (212)876-3190

Haver Analytics
60 E 42nd St., Ste. 2424
New York, NY 10017
(212)986-9300
Fax: (212)986-5857
E-mail: data@haver.com
Website: http://www.haver.com

The Jordan, Edmiston Group Inc.
150 E 52nd Ave., 18th Fl.
New York, NY 10022
(212)754-0710
Fax: (212)754-0337

KPMG International
345 Park Ave.
New York, NY 10154-0102
(212)758-9700

Fax: (212)758-9819
Website: http://www.kpmg.com

Mahoney Cohen Consulting Corp.
111 W 40th St., 12th Fl.
New York, NY 10018
(212)490-8000
Fax: (212)790-5913

Management Practice Inc.
342 Madison Ave.
New York, NY 10173-1230
(212)867-7948
Fax: (212)972-5188
Website: http://www.mpiweb.com

Moseley Associates Inc.
342 Madison Ave., Ste. 1414
New York, NY 10016
(212)213-6673
Fax: (212)687-1520

Practice Development Counsel
60 Sutton Pl. S
New York, NY 10022
(212)593-1549
Fax: (212)980-7940
E-mail: pwhaserot@pdcounsel.com
Website: http://www.pdcounsel.com

Unique Value International Inc.
575 Madison Ave., 10th Fl.
New York, NY 10022-1304
(212)605-0590
Fax: (212)605-0589

The Van Tulleken Co.
126 E 56th St.
New York, NY 10022
(212)355-1390
Fax: (212)755-3061
E-mail: newyork@vantulleken.com

Vencon Management Inc.
301 W 53rd St.
New York, NY 10019
(212)581-8787
Fax: (212)397-4126
Website: http://www.venconinc.com

Werner International Inc.
55 E 52nd, 29th Fl.
New York, NY 10055
(212)909-1260
Fax: (212)909-1273
E-mail: richard.downing@rgh.com
Website: http://www.wernertex.com

Zimmerman Business Consulting Inc.
44 E 92nd St., Ste. 5-B
New York, NY 10128

(212)860-3107
Fax: (212)860-7730
E-mail: ljzzbci@aol.com
Website: http://www.zbcinc.com

Overton Financial
7 Allen Rd.
Peekskill, NY 10566
(914)737-4649
Fax: (914)737-4696

Stromberg Consulting
2500 Westchester Ave.
Purchase, NY 10577
(914)251-1515
Fax: (914)251-1562
E-mail: strategy@stromberg_consul
ting.com
Website: http://www.stromberg_
consulting.com

Innovation Management Consulting Inc.
209 Dewitt Rd.
Syracuse, NY 13214-2006
(315)425-5144
Fax: (315)445-8989
E-mail: missonneb@axess.net

M. Clifford Agress
891 Fulton St.
Valley Stream, NY 11580
(516)825-8955
Fax: (516)825-8955

Destiny Kinal Marketing Consultancy
105 Chemung St.
Waverly, NY 14892
(607)565-8317
Fax: (607)565-4083

Valutis Consulting Inc.
5350 Main St., Ste. 7
Williamsville, NY 14221-5338
(716)634-2553
Fax: (716)634-2554
E-mail: valutis@localnet.com
Website: http://www.valutisconsulting.com

North Carolina

Best Practices L.L.C.
6320 Quadrangle Dr., Ste. 200
Chapel Hill, NC 27514
(919)403-0251
Fax: (919)403-0144
E-mail: best@best:in/class
Website: http://www.best-in-class.com

Norelli & Co.
Bank of America Corporate Ctr.
100 N Tyron St., Ste. 5160

Charlotte, NC 28202-4000
(704)376-5484
Fax: (704)376-5485
E-mail: consult@norelli.com
Website: http://www.norelli.com

North Dakota

Center for Innovation
4300 Dartmouth Dr.
PO Box 8372
Grand Forks, ND 58202
(701)777-3132
Fax: (701)777-2339
E-mail: bruce@innovators.net
Website: http://www.innovators.net

Ohio

Transportation Technology Services
208 Harmon Rd.
Aurora, OH 44202
(330)562-3596

Empro Systems Inc.
4777 Red Bank Expy., Ste. 1
Cincinnati, OH 45227-1542
(513)271-2042
Fax: (513)271-2042

Alliance Management International Ltd.
1440 Windrow Ln.
Cleveland, OH 44147-3200
(440)838-1922
Fax: (440)838-0979
E-mail: bgruss@amiltd.com
Website: http://www.amiltd.com

Bozell Kamstra Public Relations
1301 E 9th St., Ste. 3400
Cleveland, OH 44114
(216)623-1511
Fax: (216)623-1501
E-mail: jfeniger@cleveland.bozellk
amstra.com
Website: http://www.bozellk
amstra.com

Cory Dillon Associates
111 Schreyer Pl. E
Columbus, OH 43214
(614)262-8211
Fax: (614)262-3806

Holcomb Gallagher Adams
300 Marconi, Ste. 303
Columbus, OH 43215
(614)221-3343
Fax: (614)221-3367
E-mail: riadams@acme.freenet.oh.us

Young & Associates
PO Box 711
Kent, OH 44240
(330)678-0524
Free: 800-525-9775
Fax: (330)678-6219
E-mail: online@younginc.com
Website: http://www.younginc.com

Robert A. Westman & Associates
8981 Inversary Dr. SE
Warren, OH 44484-2551
(330)856-4149
Fax: (330)856-2564

Oklahoma

Innovative Partners L.L.C.
4900 Richmond Sq., Ste. 100
Oklahoma City, OK 73118
(405)840-0033
Fax: (405)843-8359
E-mail: ipartners@juno.com

Oregon

INTERCON - The International Converting Institute
5200 Badger Rd.
Crooked River Ranch, OR 97760
(541)548-1447
Fax: (541)548-1618
E-mail: johnbowler@
crookedriverranch.com

Talbott ARM
HC 60, Box 5620
Lakeview, OR 97630
(541)635-8587
Fax: (503)947-3482

Management Technology Associates Ltd.
2768 SW Sherwood Dr, Ste. 105
Portland, OR 97201-2251
(503)224-5220
Fax: (503)224-5334
E-mail: lcuster@mta-ltd.com
Website: http://www.mgmt-tech.com

Pennsylvania

Healthscope Inc.
400 Lancaster Ave.
Devon, PA 19333
(610)687-6199
Fax: (610)687-6376
E-mail: health@voicenet.com
Website: http://www.healthscope.net/

Elayne Howard & Associates Inc.
3501 Masons Mill Rd., Ste. 501

Huntingdon Valley, PA 19006-3509
(215)657-9550

GRA Inc.
115 West Ave., Ste. 201
Jenkintown, PA 19046
(215)884-7500
Fax: (215)884-1385
E-mail: gramail@gra-inc.com
Website: http://www.gra-inc.com

Mifflin County Industrial Development Corp.
Mifflin County Industrial Plz.
6395 SR 103 N
Bldg. 50
Lewistown, PA 17044
(717)242-0393
Fax: (717)242-1842
E-mail: mcide@acsworld.net

Autech Products
1289 Revere Rd.
Morrisville, PA 19067
(215)493-3759
Fax: (215)493-9791
E-mail: autech4@yahoo.com

Advantage Associates
434 Avon Dr.
Pittsburgh, PA 15228
(412)343-1558
Fax: (412)362-1684
E-mail: ecocba1@aol.com

Regis J. Sheehan & Associates
Pittsburgh, PA 15220
(412)279-1207

James W. Davidson Company Inc.
23 Forest View Rd.
Wallingford, PA 19086
(610)566-1462

Puerto Rico

Diego Chevere & Co.
Metro Parque 7, Ste. 204
Metro Office
Caparra Heights, PR 00920
(787)774-9595
Fax: (787)774-9566
E-mail: dcco@coqui.net

Manuel L. Porrata and Associates
898 Munoz Rivera Ave., Ste. 201
San Juan, PR 00927
(787)765-2140
Fax: (787)754-3285
E-mail: m_porrata@manuelporrata.com
Website: http://manualporrata.com

South Carolina

Aquafood Business Associates
PO Box 13267
Charleston, SC 29422
(843)795-9506
Fax: (843)795-9477
E-mail: rraba@aol.com

Profit Associates Inc.
PO Box 38026
Charleston, SC 29414
(803)763-5718
Fax: (803)763-5719
E-mail: bobrog@awod.com
Website: http://www.awod.com/gallery/
business/proasc

Strategic Innovations International
12 Executive Ct.
Lake Wylie, SC 29710
(803)831-1225
Fax: (803)831-1177
E-mail: stratinnov@aol.com
Website: http://www.
strategicinnovations.com

Minus Stage
Box 4436
Rock Hill, SC 29731
(803)328-0705
Fax: (803)329-9948

Tennessee

Daniel Petchers & Associates
8820 Fernwood CV
Germantown, TN 38138
(901)755-9896

Business Choices
1114 Forest Harbor, Ste. 300
Hendersonville, TN 37075-9646
(615)822-8692
Free: 800-737-8382
Fax: (615)822-8692
E-mail: bz-ch@juno.com

RCFA Healthcare Management Services L.L.C.
9648 Kingston Pke., Ste. 8
Knoxville, TN 37922
(865)531-0176
Free: 800-635-4040
Fax: (865)531-0722
E-mail: info@rcfa.com
Website: http://www.rcfa.com

Growth Consultants of America
3917 Trimble Rd.
Nashville, TN 37215

(615)383-0550
Fax: (615)269-8940
E-mail: 70244.451@compuserve.com

Texas

**Integrated Cost Management
Systems Inc.**
2261 Brookhollow Plz. Dr., Ste. 104
Arlington, TX 76006
(817)633-2873
Fax: (817)633-3781
E-mail: abm@icms.net
Website: http://www.icms.net

Lori Williams
1000 Leslie Ct.
Arlington, TX 76012
(817)459-3934
Fax: (817)459-3934

Business Resource Software Inc.
2013 Wells Branch Pky., Ste. 305
Austin, TX 78728
Free: 800-423-1228
Fax: (512)251-4401
E-mail: info@brs-inc.com
Website: http://www.brs-inc.com

Erisa Adminstrative Services Inc.
12325 Hymeadow Dr., Bldg. 4
Austin, TX 78750-1847
(512)250-9020
Fax: (512)250-9487
Website: http://www.cserisa.com

R. Miller Hicks & Co.
1011 W 11th St.
Austin, TX 78703
(512)477-7000
Fax: (512)477-9697
E-mail: millerhicks@rmhicks.com
Website: http://www.rmhicks.com

Pragmatic Tactics Inc.
3303 Westchester Ave.
College Station, TX 77845
(409)696-5294
Free: 800-570-5294
Fax: (409)696-4994
E-mail: ptactics@aol.com
Website: http://www.ptatics.com

Perot Systems
12404 Park Central Dr.
Dallas, TX 75251
(972)340-5000
Free: 800-688-4333
Fax: (972)455-4100
E-mail: corp.comm@ps.net
Website: http://www.perotsystems.com

ReGENERATION Partners
3838 Oak Lawn Ave.
Dallas, TX 75219
(214)559-3999
Free: 800-406-1112
E-mail: info@regeneration-partner.com
Website: http://www.regeneration-partners.com

**High Technology Associates - Division
of Global Technologies Inc.**
1775 St. James Pl., Ste. 105
Houston, TX 77056
(713)963-9300
Fax: (713)963-8341
E-mail: hta@infohwy.com

MasterCOM
103 Thunder Rd.
Kerrville, TX 78028
(830)895-7990
Fax: (830)443-3428
E-mail: jmstubblefield@master
training.com
Website: http://www.mastertraining.com

PROTEC
4607 Linden Pl.
Pearland, TX 77584
(281)997-9872
Fax: (281)997-9895
E-mail: p.oman@ix.netcom.com

Alpha Quadrant Inc.
10618 Auldine
San Antonio, TX 78230
(210)344-3330
Fax: (210)344-8151
E-mail: mbussone@sbcglobal.net
Website:http://www.a-quadrant.com
Michele Bussone

Bastian Public Relations
614 San Dizier
San Antonio, TX 78232
(210)404-1839
E-mail: lisa@bastianpr.com
Website: http://www.bastianpr.com
Lisa Bastian CBC

**Business Strategy Development
Consultants**
PO Box 690365
San Antonio, TX 78269
(210)696-8000
Free: 800-927-BSDC
Fax: (210)696-8000

Tom Welch, CPC
6900 San Pedro Ave., Ste. 147
San Antonio, TX 78216-6207

(210)737-7022
Fax: (210)737-7022
E-mail: bplan@iamerica.net
Website: http://www.moneywords.com

Utah

Business Management Resource
PO Box 521125
Salt Lake City, UT 84152-1125
(801)272-4668
Fax: (801)277-3290
E-mail: pingfong@worldnet.att.net

Virginia

Tindell Associates
209 Oxford Ave.
Alexandria, VA 22301
(703)683-0109
Fax: 703-783-0219
E-mail: scott@tindell.net
Website: http://www.tindell.net
Scott Lockett, President

Elliott B. Jaffa
2530-B S Walter Reed Dr.
Arlington, VA 22206
(703)931-0040
E-mail: thetrainingdoctor@excite.com
Website: http://www.tregistry.com/jaffa.htm

Koach Enterprises - USA
5529 N 18th St.
Arlington, VA 22205
(703)241-8361
Fax: (703)241-8623

Federal Market Development
5650 Chapel Run Ct.
Centreville, VA 20120-3601
(703)502-8930
Free: 800-821-5003
Fax: (703)502-8929

Huff, Stuart & Carlton
2107 Graves Mills Rd., Ste. C
Forest, VA 24551
(804)316-9356
Free: (888)316-9356
Fax: (804)316-9357
Website: http://www.wealthmgt.net

AMX International Inc.
1420 Spring Hill Rd. , Ste. 600
McLean, VA 22102-3006
(703)690-4100
Fax: (703)643-1279
E-mail: amxmail@amxi.com
Website: http://www.amxi.com

Charles Scott Pugh (Investor)
4101 Pittaway Dr.
Richmond, VA 23235-1022
(804)560-0979
Fax: (804)560-4670

John C. Randall and Associates Inc.
PO Box 15127
Richmond, VA 23227
(804)746-4450
Fax: (804)730-8933
E-mail: randalljcx@aol.com
Website: http://www.johncrandall.com

McLeod & Co.
410 1st St.
Roanoke, VA 24011
(540)342-6911
Fax: (540)344-6367
Website: http://www.mcleodco.com/

Salzinger & Company Inc.
8000 Towers Crescent Dr., Ste. 1350
Vienna, VA 22182
(703)442-5200
Fax: (703)442-5205
E-mail: info@salzinger.com
Website: http://www.salzinger.com

The Small Business Counselor
12423 Hedges Run Dr., Ste. 153
Woodbridge, VA 22192
(703)490-6755
Fax: (703)490-1356

Washington

Burlington Consultants
10900 NE 8th St., Ste. 900
Bellevue, WA 98004
(425)688-3060
Fax: (425)454-4383
E-mail: partners@burlingt
onconsultants.com
Website: http://www.burlington
consultants.com

Perry L. Smith Consulting
800 Bellevue Way NE, Ste. 400
Bellevue, WA 98004-4208
(425)462-2072
Fax: (425)462-5638

St. Charles Consulting Group
1420 NW Gilman Blvd.
Issaquah, WA 98027
(425)557-8708
Fax: (425)557-8731
E-mail: info@stcharlesconsulting.com
Website: http://www.stcharlescon
sulting.com

Independent Automotive Training Services
PO Box 334
Kirkland, WA 98083
(425)822-5715
E-mail: ltunney@autosvccon.com
Website: http://www.autosvccon.com

Kahle Associate Inc.
6203 204th Dr. NE
Redmond, WA 98053
(425)836-8763
Fax: (425)868-3770
E-mail: randykahle@kahleassociates.com
Website: http://www.kahleassociates.com

Dan Collin
3419 Wallingord Ave N, No. 2
Seattle, WA 98103
(206)634-9469
E-mail: dc@dancollin.com
Website: http://members.home.net/
dcollin/

ECG Management Consultants Inc.
1111 3rd Ave., Ste. 2700
Seattle, WA 98101-3201
(206)689-2200
Fax: (206)689-2209
E-mail: ecg@ecgmc.com
Website: http://www.ecgmc.com

Northwest Trade Adjustment Assistance Center
900 4th Ave., Ste. 2430
Seattle, WA 98164-1001
(206)622-2730
Free: 800-667-8087
Fax: (206)622-1105
E-mail: matchingfunds@nwtaac.org
Website: http://www.taacenters.org

Business Planning Consultants
S 3510 Ridgeview Dr.
Spokane, WA 99206
(509)928-0332
Fax: (509)921-0842
E-mail: bpci@nextdim.com

West Virginia

**Stanley & Associates Inc./
BusinessandMarketingPlans.com**
1687 Robert C. Byrd Dr.
Beckley, WV 25801
(304)252-0324
Free: 888-752-6720
Fax: (304)252-0470
E-mail: cclay@charterinternet.com

Website: http://www.Businessand-
MarketingPlans.com
Christopher Clay

Wisconsin

White & Associates Inc.
5349 Somerset Ln. S
Greenfield, WI 53221
(414)281-7373
Fax: (414)281-7006
E-mail: wnaconsult@aol.com

Small business administration regional offices

This section contains a listing of Small Business Administration offices arranged numerically by region. Service areas are provided. Contact the appropriate office for a referral to the nearest field office, or visit the Small Business Administration online at www.sba.gov.

Region 1

U.S. Small Business Administration
Region I Office
10 Causeway St., Ste. 812
Boston, MA 02222-1093
Phone: (617)565-8415
Fax: (617)565-8420
Serves Connecticut, Maine, Massachusetts, New Hampshire, Rhode Island, and Vermont.

Region 2

U.S. Small Business Administration
Region II Office
26 Federal Plaza, Ste. 3108
New York, NY 10278
Phone: (212)264-1450
Fax: (212)264-0038
Serves New Jersey, New York, Puerto Rico, and the Virgin Islands.

Region 3

U.S. Small Business Administration
Region III Office
Robert N C Nix Sr. Federal Building
900 Market St., 5th Fl.
Philadelphia, PA 19107
(215)580-2807
Serves Delaware, the District of Columbia, Maryland, Pennsylvania, Virginia, and West Virginia.

Region 4

U.S. Small Business Administration
Region IV Office
233 Peachtree St. NE
Harris Tower 1800
Atlanta, GA 30303
Phone: (404)331-4999
Fax: (404)331-2354
Serves Alabama, Florida, Georgia, Kentucky, Mississippi, North Carolina, South Carolina, and Tennessee.

Region 5

U.S. Small Business Administration
Region V Office
500 W. Madison St.
Citicorp Center, Ste. 1240
Chicago, IL 60661-2511
Phone: (312)353-0357
Fax: (312)353-3426
Serves Illinois, Indiana, Michigan, Minnesota, Ohio, and Wisconsin.

Region 6

U.S. Small Business Administration
Region VI Office
4300 Amon Carter Blvd., Ste. 108
Fort Worth, TX 76155
Phone: (817)684-5581
Fax: (817)684-5588
Serves Arkansas, Louisiana, New Mexico, Oklahoma, and Texas.

Region 7

U.S. Small Business Administration
Region VII Office
323 W. 8th St., Ste. 307
Kansas City, MO 64105-1500
Phone: (816)374-6380
Fax: (816)374-6339
Serves Iowa, Kansas, Missouri, and Nebraska.

Region 8

U.S. Small Business Administration
Region VIII Office
721 19th St., Ste. 400
Denver, CO 80202
Phone: (303)844-0500
Fax: (303)844-0506
Serves Colorado, Montana, North Dakota, South Dakota, Utah, and Wyoming.

Region 9

U.S. Small Business Administration
Region IX Office
330 N Brand Blvd., Ste. 1270
Glendale, CA 91203-2304
Phone: (818)552-3434
Fax: (818)552-3440
Serves American Samoa, Arizona, California, Guam, Hawaii, Nevada, and the Trust Territory of the Pacific Islands.

Region 10

U.S. Small Business Administration
Region X Office
2401 Fourth Ave., Ste. 400
Seattle, WA 98121
Phone: (206)553-5676
Fax: (206)553-4155
Serves Alaska, Idaho, Oregon, and Washington.

Small business development centers

This section contains a listing of all Small Business Development Centers, organized alphabetically by state/U.S. territory, then by city, then by agency name.

Alabama

Alabama SBDC
UNIVERSITY OF ALABAMA
2800 Milan Court Suite 124
Birmingham, AL 35211-6908
Phone: 205-943-6750
Fax: 205-943-6752
E-Mail: wcampbell@provost.uab.edu
Website: http://www.asbdc.org
Mr. William Campbell Jr, State Director

Alaska

Alaska SBDC
UNIVERSITY OF ALASKA - ANCHORAGE
430 West Seventh Avenue, Suite 110
Anchorage, AK 99501
Phone: 907-274 -7232
Fax: 907-274-9524
E-Mail: anerw@uaa.alaska.edu
Website: http://www.aksbdc.org
Ms. Jean R. Wall, State Director

American Samoa

American Samoa SBDC
AMERICAN SAMOA COMMUNITY COLLEGE
P.O. Box 2609
Pago Pago, American Samoa 96799
Phone: 011-684-699-4830
Fax: 011-684-699-6132
E-Mail: htalex@att.net
Mr. Herbert Thweatt, Director

Arizona

Arizona SBDC
MARICOPA COUNTY COMMUNITY COLLEGE
2411 West 14th Street, Suite 132
Tempe, AZ 85281
Phone: 480-731-8720
Fax: 480-731-8729
E-Mail: mike.york@domail.maricopa.edu
Website: http://www.dist.maricopa.edu.sbdc
Mr. Michael York, State Director

Arkansas

Arkansas SBDC
UNIVERSITY OF ARKANSAS
2801 South University Avenue
Little Rock, AR 72204
Phone: 501-324-9043
Fax: 501-324-9049
E-Mail: jmroderick@ualr.edu
Website: http://asbdc.ualr.edu
Ms. Janet M. Roderick, State Director

California

California - San Francisco SBDC
Northern California SBDC Lead Center
HUMBOLDT STATE UNIVERSITY
Office of Economic Development
1 Harpst Street 2006A, Siemens Hall
Arcata, CA, 95521
Phone: 707-826-3922
Fax: 707-826-3206
E-Mail: gainer@humboldt.edu
Ms. Margaret A. Gainer, Regional Director

California - Sacramento SBDC
CALIFORNIA STATE UNIVERSITY - CHICO
Chico, CA 95929-0765
Phone: 530-898-4598
Fax: 530-898-4734

E-Mail: dripke@csuchico.edu
Website: http://gsbdc.csuchico.edu
Mr. Dan Ripke, Interim Regional Director

California - San Diego SBDC
SOUTHWESTERN COMMUNITY
COLLEGE DISTRICT
900 Otey Lakes Road
Chula Vista, CA 91910
Phone: 619-482-6388
Fax: 619-482-6402
E-Mail: dtrujillo@swc.cc.ca.us
Website: http://www.sbditc.org
Ms. Debbie P. Trujillo, Regional Director

California - Fresno SBDC
UC Merced Lead Center
UNIVERSITY OF CALIFORNIA -
MERCED
550 East Shaw, Suite 105A
Fresno, CA 93710
Phone: 559-241-6590
Fax: 559-241-7422
E-Mail: crosander@ucmerced.edu
Website: http://sbdc.ucmerced.edu
Mr. Chris Rosander, State Director

California - Santa Ana SBDC
Tri-County Lead SBDC
CALIFORNIA STATE UNIVERSITY -
FULLERTON
800 North State College Boulevard, LH640
Fullerton, CA 92834
Phone: 714-278-2719
Fax: 714-278-7858
E-Mail: vpham@fullerton.edu
Website: http://www.leadsbdc.org
Ms. Vi Pham, Lead Center Director

California - Los Angeles Region SBDC
LONG BEACH COMMUNITY
COLLEGE DISTRICT
3950 Paramount Boulevard, Ste 101
Lakewood, CA 90712
Phone: 562-938-5004
Fax: 562-938-5030
E-Mail: ssloan@lbcc.edu
Ms. Sheneui Sloan, Interim Lead Center
Director

Colorado

Colorado SBDC
OFFICE OF ECONOMIC
DEVELOPMENT
1625 Broadway, Suite 170
Denver, CO 80202
Phone: 303-892-3864
Fax: 303-892-3848
E-Mail: Kelly.Manning@state.co.us

Website: http://www.state.co.us/oed/sbdc
Ms. Kelly Manning, State Director

Connecticut

Connecticut SBDC
UNIVERSITY OF CONNECTICUT
1376 Storrs Road, Unit 4094
Storrs, CT 06269-1094
Phone: 860-870-6370
Fax: 860-870-6374
E-Mail: richard.cheney@uconn.edu
Website: http://www.sbdc.uconn.edu
Mr. Richard Cheney, Interim State Director

Delaware

Delaware SBDC
DELAWARE TECHNOLOGY PARK
1 Innovation Way, Suite 301
Newark, DE 19711
Phone: 302-831-2747
Fax: 302-831-1423
E-Mail: Clinton.tymes@mvs.udel.edu
Website: http://www.delawaresbdc.org
Mr. Clinton Tymes, State Director

District of Columbia

District of Columbia SBDC
HOWARD UNIVERSITY
2600 6th Street, NW Room 128
Washington, DC 20059
Phone: 202-806-1550
Fax: 202-806-1777
E-Mail: hturner@howard.edu
Website: http://www.dcsbdc.com/
Mr. Henry Turner, Executive Director

Florida

Florida SBDC
UNIVERSITY OF WEST FLORIDA
401 East Chase Street, Suite 100
Pensacola, FL 32502
Phone: 850-473-7800
Fax: 850-473-7813
E-Mail: jcartwri@uwf.edu
Website: http://www.floridasbdc.com
Mr. Jerry Cartwright, State Director

Georgia

Georgia SBDC
UNIVERSITY OF GEORGIA
1180 East Broad Street
Athens, GA 30602
Phone: 706-542-6762
Fax: 706-542-6776
E-mail: aadams@sbdc.uga.edu

Website: http://www.sbdc.uga.edu
Mr. Allan Adams, Interim State Director

Guam

Guam Small Business Development
Center
UNIVERSITY OF GUAM
Pacific Islands SBDC
P.O. Box 5014 - U.O.G. Station
Mangilao, GU 96923
Phone: 671-735-2590
Fax: 671-734-2002
E-mail: casey@pacificsbdc.com
Website: http://www.uog.edu/sbdc
Mr. Casey Jeszenka, Director

Hawaii

Hawaii SBDC
UNIVERSITY OF HAWAII - HILO
308 Kamehameha Avenue, Suite 201
Hilo, HI 96720
Phone: 808-974-7515
Fax: 808-974-7683
E-Mail: darrylm@interpac.net
Website: http://www.hawaii-sbdc.org
Mr. Darryl Mleynek, State Director

Idaho

Idaho SBDC
BOISE STATE UNIVERSITY
1910 University Drive
Boise, ID 83725
Phone: 208-426-3799
Fax: 208-426-3877
E-mail: jhogge@boisestate.edu
Website: http://www.idahosbdc.org
Mr. Jim Hogge, State Director

Illinois

Illinois SBDC
DEPARTMENT OF COMMERCE
AND ECONOMIC OPPORTUNITY
620 E. Adams, S-4
Springfield, IL 62701
Phone: 217-524-5700
Fax: 217-524-0171
E-mail: mpatrilli@ildceo.net
Website: http://www.ilsbdc.biz
Mr. Mark Petrilli, State Director

Indiana

Indiana SBDC
INDIANA ECONOMIC
DEVELOPMENT CORPORATION
One North Capitol, Suite 900
Indianapolis, IN 46204

Phone: 317-234-8872
Fax: 317-232-8874
E-mail: dtrocha@isbdc.org
Website: http://www.isbdc.org
Ms. Debbie Bishop Trocha, State Director

Iowa

Iowa SBDC
IOWA STATE UNIVERSITY
340 Gerdin Business Bldg.
Ames, IA 50011-1350
Phone: 515-294-2037
Fax: 515-294-6522
E-mail: jonryan@iastate.edu
Website: http://www.iabusnet.org
Mr. Jon Ryan, State Director

Kansas

Kansas SBDC
FORT HAYS STATE UNIVERSITY
214 SW Sixth Street, Suite 301
Topeka, KS 66603
Phone: 785-296-6514
Fax: 785-291-3261
E-mail: ksbdc.wkearns@fhsu.edu
Website: http://www.fhsu.edu/ksbdc
Mr. Wally Kearns, State Director

Kentucky

Kentucky SBDC
UNIVERSITY OF KENTUCKY
225 Gatton College of Business Economics Building
Lexington, KY 40506-0034
Phone: 859-257-7668
Fax: 859-323-1907
E-mail: lrnaug0@pop.uky.edu
Website: http://www.ksbdc.org
Ms. Becky Naugle, State Director

Louisiana

Louisiana SBDC
UNIVERSITY OF LOUISIANA - MONROE
College of Business Administration
700 University Avenue
Monroe, LA 71209
Phone: 318-342-5506
Fax: 318-342-5510
E-mail: wilkerson@ulm.edu
Website: http://www.lsbdc.org
Ms. Mary Lynn Wilkerson, State Director

Maine

Maine SBDC
UNIVERSITY OF SOUTHERN MAINE
96 Falmouth Street P.O. Box 9300
Portland, ME 04103
Phone: 207-780-4420
Fax: 207-780-4810
E-mail: jrmassaua@maine.edu
Website: http://www.mainesbdc.org
Mr. John Massaua, State Director

Maryland

Maryland SBDC
UNIVERSITY OF MARYLAND
7100 Baltimore Avenue, Suite 401
College Park, MD 20742
Phone: 301-403-8300
Fax: 301-403-8303
E-mail: rsprow@mdsbdc.umd.edu
Website: http://www.mdsbdc.umd.edu
Ms. Renee Sprow, State Director

Massachusetts

Massachusetts SBDC
UNIVERSITY OF MASSACHUSETTS
School of Management, Room 205
Amherst, MA 01003-4935
Phone: 413-545-6301
Fax: 413-545-1273
E-mail: gep@msbdc.umass.edu
Website: http://msbdc.som.umass.edu
Ms. Georgianna Parkin, State Director

Michigan

Michigan SBTDC
GRAND VALLEY STATE UNIVERSITY
510 West Fulton Avenue
Grand Rapids, MI 49504
Phone: 616-331-7485
Fax: 616-331-7389
E-mail: lopuckic@gvsu.edu
Website: http://www.misbtdc.org
Ms. Carol Lopucki, State Director

Minnesota

Minnesota SBDC
MINNESOTA SMALL BUSINESS DEVELOPMENT CENTER
1st National Bank Building
332 Minnesota Street, Suite E200
St. Paul, MN 55101-1351
Phone: 651-297-5773
Fax: 651-296-5287

E-mail: michael.myhre@state.mn.us
Website: http://www.mnsbdc.com
Mr. Michael Myhre, State Director

Mississippi

Mississippi SBDC
UNIVERSITY OF MISSISSIPPI
B-19 Jeanette Phillips Drive
P.O. Box 1848
University, MS 38677
Phone: 662-915-5001
Fax: 662-915-5650
E-mail: wgurley@olemiss.edu
Website: http://www.olemiss.edu/depts/mssbdc
Mr. Doug Gurley, Jr., State Director

Missouri

Missouri SBDC
UNIVERSITY OF MISSOURI
1205 University Avenue, Suite 300
Columbia, MO 65211
Phone: 573-882-1348
Fax: 573-884-4297
E-mail: summersm@missouri.edu
Website: http://www.mo-sbdc.org/index.shtml
Mr. Max Summers, State Director

Montana

Montana SBDC
DEPARTMENT OF COMMERCE
301 South Park Avenue, Room 114 / P.O. Box 200505
Helena, MT 59620
Phone: 406-841-2746
Fax: 406-444-1872
E-mail: adesch@state.mt.us
Website: http://commerce.state.mt.us/brd/BRD_SBDC.html
Ms. Ann Desch, State Director

Nebraska

Nebraska SBDC
UNIVERSITY OF NEBRASKA - OMAHA
60th & Dodge Street, CBA Room 407
Omaha, NE 68182
Phone: 402-554-2521
Fax: 402-554-3473
E-mail: rbernier@unomaha.edu
Website: http://nbdc.unomaha.edu
Mr. Robert Bernier, State Director

Nevada

Nevada SBDC
UNIVERSITY OF NEVADA - RENO
Reno College of Business
Administration, Room 411
Reno, NV 89557-0100
Phone: 775-784-1717
Fax: 775-784-4337
E-mail: males@unr.edu
Website: http://www.nsbdc.org
Mr. Sam Males, State Director

New Hampshire

New Hampshire SBDC
UNIVERSITY OF NEW HAMPSHIRE
108 McConnell Hall
Durham, NH 03824-3593
Phone: 603-862-4879
Fax: 603-862-4876
E-mail: Mary.Collins@unh.edu
Website: http://www.nhsbdc.org
Ms. Mary Collins, State Director

New Jersey

New Jersey SBDC
RUTGERS UNIVERSITY
49 Bleeker Street
Newark, NJ 07102-1993
Phone: 973-353-5950
Fax: 973-353-1110
E-mail: bhopper@njsbdc.com
Website: http://www.njsbdc.com/home
Ms. Brenda Hopper, State Director

New Mexico

New Mexico SBDC
SANTA FE COMMUNITY COLLEGE
6401 Richards Avenue
Santa Fe, NM 87505
Phone: 505-428-1362
Fax: 505-471-9469
E-mail: rmiller@santa-fe.cc.nm.us
Website: http://www.nmsbdc.org
Mr. Roy Miller, State Director

New York

New York SBDC
STATE UNIVERSITY OF NEW YORK
SUNY Plaza, S-523
Albany, NY 12246
Phone: 518-443-5398
Fax: 518-443-5275
E-mail: j.king@nyssbdc.org
Website: http://www.nyssbdc.org
Mr. Jim King, State Director

North Carolina

North Carolina SBDTC
UNIVERSITY OF NORTH CAROLINA
5 West Hargett Street, Suite 600
Raleigh, NC 27601
Phone: 919-715-7272
Fax: 919-715-7777
E-mail: sdaugherty@sbtdc.org
Website: http://www.sbtdc.org
Mr. Scott Daugherty, State Director

North Dakota

North Dakota SBDC
UNIVERSITY OF NORTH DAKOTA
1600 E. Century Avenue, Suite 2
Bismarck, ND 58503
Phone: 701-328-5375
Fax: 701-328-5320
E-mail: christine.martin@und.nodak.edu
Website: http://www.ndsbdc.org
Ms. Christine Martin-Goldman, State
Director

Ohio

Ohio SBDC
**OHIO DEPARTMENT
OF DEVELOPMENT**
77 South High Street
Columbus, OH 43216
Phone: 614-466-5102
Fax: 614-466-0829
E-mail: mabraham@odod.state.oh.us
Website: http://www.ohiosbdc.org
Ms. Michele Abraham, State Director

Oklahoma

Oklahoma SBDC
**SOUTHEAST OKLAHOMA STATE
UNIVERSITY**
517 University, Box 2584, Station A
Durant, OK 74701
Phone: 580-745-7577
Fax: 580-745-7471
E-mail: gpennington@sosu.edu
Website: http://www.osbdc.org
Mr. Grady Pennington, State Director

Oregon

Oregon SBDC
LANE COMMUNITY COLLEGE
99 West Tenth Avenue, Suite 390
Eugene, OR 97401-3021
Phone: 541-463-5250
Fax: 541-345-6006
E-mail: carterb@lanecc.edu

Website: http://www.bizcenter.org
Mr. William Carter, State Director

Pennsylvania

Pennsylvania SBDC
UNIVERSITY OF PENNSYLVANIA
The Wharton School
3733 Spruce Street
Philadelphia, PA 19104-6374
Phone: 215-898-1219
Fax: 215-573-2135
E-mail: ghiggins@wharton.upenn.edu
Website: http://pasbdc.org
Mr. Gregory Higgins, State Director

Puerto Rico

Puerto Rico SBDC
**INTER-AMERICAN UNIVERSITY
OF PUERTO RICO**
416 Ponce de Leon Avenue, Union Plaza,
Seventh Floor
Hato Rey, PR 00918
Phone: 787-763-6811
Fax: 787-763-4629
E-mail: cmarti@prsbdc.org
Website: http://www.prsbdc.org
Ms. Carmen Marti, Executive Director

Rhode Island

Rhode Island SBDC
BRYANT UNIVERSITY
1150 Douglas Pike
Smithfield, RI 02917
Phone: 401-232-6923
Fax: 401-232-6933
E-mail: adawson@bryant.edu
Website: http://www.risbdc.org
Ms. Diane Fournaris, Interim State Director

South Carolina

South Carolina SBDC
UNIVERSITY OF SOUTH CAROLINA
College of Business Administration
1710 College Street
Columbia, SC 29208
Phone: 803-777-4907
Fax: 803-777-4403
E-mail: lenti@moore.sc.edu
Website: http://scsbdc.moore.sc.edu
Mr. John Lenti, State Director

South Dakota

South Dakota SBDC
UNIVERSITY OF SOUTH DAKOTA
414 East Clark Street, Patterson Hall
Vermillion, SD 57069

Phone: 605-677-6256
Fax: 605-677-5427
E-mail: jshemmin@usd.edu
Website: http://www.sdsbdc.org
Mr. John S. Hemmingstad, State Director

Tennessee

Tennessee SBDC
TENNESSEE BOARD OF REGENTS
1415 Murfressboro Road, Suite 540
Nashville, TN 37217-2833
Phone: 615-898-2745
Fax: 615-893-7089
E-mail: pgeho@mail.tsbdc.org
Website: http://www.tsbdc.org
Mr. Patrick Geho, State Director

Texas

Texas-North SBDC
DALLAS COUNTY COMMUNITY COLLEGE
1402 Corinth Street
Dallas, TX 75215
Phone: 214-860-5835
Fax: 214-860-5813
E-mail: emk9402@dcccd.edu
Website: http://www.ntsbdc.org
Ms. Liz Klimback, Region Director

Texas-Houston SBDC
UNIVERSITY OF HOUSTON
2302 Fannin, Suite 200
Houston, TX 77002
Phone: 713-752-8425
Fax: 713-756-1500
E-mail: fyoung@uh.edu
Website: http://sbdcnetwork.uh.edu
Mr. Mike Young, Executive Director

Texas-NW SBDC
TEXAS TECH UNIVERSITY
2579 South Loop 289, Suite 114
Lubbock, TX 79423
Phone: 806-745-3973
Fax: 806-745-6207
E-mail: c.bean@nwtsbdc.org
Website: http://www.nwtsbdc.org
Mr. Craig Bean, Executive Director

Texas-South-West Texas Border Region SBDC
UNIVERSITY OF TEXAS - SAN ANTONIO
501 West Durango Boulevard
San Antonio, TX 78207-4415
Phone: 210-458-2742
Fax: 210-458-2464

E-mail: albert.salgado@utsa.edu
Website: http://www.iedtexas.org
Mr. Alberto Salgado, Region Director

Utah

Utah SBDC
SALT LAKE COMMUNITY COLLEGE
9750 South 300 West
Sandy, UT 84070
Phone: 801-957-3493
Fax: 801-957-3488
E-mail: Greg.Panichello@slcc.edu
Website:http://www.slcc.edu/sbdc
Mr. Greg Panichello, State Director

Vermont

Vermont SBDC
VERMONT TECHNICAL COLLEGE
PO Box 188, 1 Main Street
Randolph Center, VT 05061-0188
Phone: 802-728-9101
Fax: 802-728-3026
E-mail: lquillen@vtc.edu
Website: http://www.vtsbdc.org
Ms. Lenae Quillen-Blume, State Director

Virgin Islands

Virgin Islands SBDC
UNIVERSITY OF THE VIRGIN ISLANDS
8000 Nisky Center, Suite 720
St. Thomas, VI 00802-5804
Phone: 340-776-3206
Fax: 340-775-3756
E-mail: wbush@webmail.uvi.edu
Website: http://rps.uvi.edu/SBDC
Mr. Warren Bush, State Director

Virginia

Virginia SBDC
GEORGE MASON UNIVERSITY
4031 University Drive, Suite 200
Fairfax, VA 22030-3409
Phone: 703-277-7727
Fax: 703-352-8515
E-mail: jkeenan@gmu.edu
Website: http://www.virginiasbdc.org
Ms. Jody Keenan, Director

Washington

Washington SBDC
WASHINGTON STATE UNIVERSITY
534 E. Trent Avenue
P.O. Box 1495
Spokane, WA 99210-1495

Phone: 509-358-7765
Fax: 509-358-7764
E-mail: barogers@wsu.edu
Website: http://www.wsbdc.org
Mr. Brett Rogers, State Director

West Virginia

West Virginia SBDC
WEST VIRGINIA DEVELOPMENT OFFICE
Capital Complex, Building 6, Room 652
Charleston, WV 25301
Phone: 304-558-2960
Fax: 304-558-0127
E-mail: csalyer@wvsbdc.org
Website: http://www.wvsbdc.org
Mr. Conley Salyor, State Director

Wisconsin

Wisconsin SBDC
UNIVERSITY OF WISCONSIN
432 North Lake Street, Room 423
Madison, WI 53706
Phone: 608-263-7794
Fax: 608-263-7830
E-mail: erica.kauten@uwex.edu
Website: http://www.wisconsinsbdc.org
Ms. Erica Kauten, State Director

Wyoming

Wyoming SBDC
UNIVERSITY OF WYOMING
P.O. Box 3922
Laramie, WY 82071-3922
Phone: 307-766-3505
Fax: 307-766-3406
E-mail: DDW@uwyo.edu
Website: http://www.uwyo.edu/sbdc
Ms. Debbie Popp, Acting State Director

Service corps of retired executives (score) offices

This section contains a listing of all SCORE offices organized alphabetically by state/U.S. territory, then by city, then by agency name.

Alabama

SCORE Office (Northeast Alabama)
1330 Quintard Ave.
Anniston, AL 36202
(256)237-3536

SCORE Office (North Alabama)
901 South 15th St, Rm. 201
Birmingham, AL 35294-2060
(205)934-6868
Fax: (205)934-0538

SCORE Office (Baldwin County)
29750 Larry Dee Cawyer Dr.
Daphne, AL 36526
(334)928-5838

SCORE Office (Shoals)
612 S. COurt
Florence, AL 35630
(256)764-4661
Fax: (256)766-9017
E-mail: shoals@shoalschamber.com

SCORE Office (Mobile)
600 S Court St.
Mobile, AL 36104
(334)240-6868
Fax: (334)240-6869

SCORE Office (Alabama Capitol City)
600 S. Court St.
Montgomery, AL 36104
(334)240-6868
Fax: (334)240-6869

SCORE Office (East Alabama)
601 Ave. A
Opelika, AL 36801
(334)745-4861
E-mail: score636@hotmail.com
Website: http://www.angelfire.com/sc/
score636/

SCORE Office (Tuscaloosa)
2200 University Blvd.
Tuscaloosa, AL 35402
(205)758-7588

Alaska

SCORE Office (Anchorage)
510 L St., Ste. 310
Anchorage, AK 99501
(907)271-4022
Fax: (907)271-4545

Arizona

SCORE Office (Lake Havasu)
10 S. Acoma Blvd.
Lake Havasu City, AZ 86403
(520)453-5951
E-mail: SCORE@ctaz.com
Website: http://www.scorearizona.org/
lake_havasu/

SCORE Office (East Valley)
Federal Bldg., Rm. 104
26 N. MacDonald St.
Mesa, AZ 85201
(602)379-3100
Fax: (602)379-3143
E-mail: 402@aol.com
Website: http://www.scorearizona.
org/mesa/

SCORE Office (Phoenix)
2828 N. Central Ave., Ste. 800
Central & One Thomas
Phoenix, AZ 85004
(602)640-2329
Fax: (602)640-2360
E-mail: e-mail@SCORE-phoenix.org
Website: http://www.score-phoenix.org/

SCORE Office (Prescott Arizona)
1228 Willow Creek Rd., Ste. 2
Prescott, AZ 86301
(520)778-7438
Fax: (520)778-0812
E-mail: score@northlink.com
Website: http://www.scorearizona.org/
prescott/

SCORE Office (Tucson)
110 E. Pennington St.
Tucson, AZ 85702
(520)670-5008
Fax: (520)670-5011
E-mail: score@azstarnet.com
Website: http://www.scorearizona.org/
tucson/

SCORE Office (Yuma)
281 W. 24th St., Ste. 116
Yuma, AZ 85364
(520)314-0480
E-mail: score@C2i2.com
Website: http://www.scorearizona.
org/yuma

Arkansas

SCORE Office (South Central)
201 N. Jackson Ave.
El Dorado, AR 71730-5803
(870)863-6113
Fax: (870)863-6115

SCORE Office (Ozark)
Fayetteville, AR 72701
(501)442-7619

SCORE Office (Northwest Arkansas)
Glenn Haven Dr., No. 4
Ft. Smith, AR 72901
(501)783-3556

SCORE Office (Garland County)
Grand & Ouachita
PO Box 6012
Hot Springs Village, AR 71902
(501)321-1700

SCORE Office (Little Rock)
2120 Riverfront Dr., Rm. 100
Little Rock, AR 72202-1747
(501)324-5893
Fax: (501)324-5199

SCORE Office (Southeast Arkansas)
121 W. 6th
Pine Bluff, AR 71601
(870)535-7189
Fax: (870)535-1643

California

SCORE Office (Golden Empire)
1706 Chester Ave., No. 200
Bakersfield, CA 93301
(805)322-5881
Fax: (805)322-5663

SCORE Office (Greater Chico Area)
1324 Mangrove St., Ste. 114
Chico, CA 95926
(916)342-8932
Fax: (916)342-8932

SCORE Office (Concord)
2151-A Salvio St., Ste. B
Concord, CA 94520
(510)685-1181
Fax: (510)685-5623

SCORE Office (Covina)
935 W. Badillo St.
Covina, CA 91723
(818)967-4191
Fax: (818)966-9660

SCORE Office (Rancho Cucamonga)
8280 Utica, Ste. 160
Cucamonga, CA 91730
(909)987-1012
Fax: (909)987-5917

SCORE Office (Culver City)
PO Box 707
Culver City, CA 90232-0707
(310)287-3850
Fax: (310)287-1350

SCORE Office (Danville)
380 Diablo Rd., Ste. 103
Danville, CA 94526
(510)837-4400

SCORE Office (Downey)
11131 Brookshire Ave.
Downey, CA 90241
(310)923-2191
Fax: (310)864-0461

SCORE Office (El Cajon)
109 Rea Ave.
El Cajon, CA 92020
(619)444-1327
Fax: (619)440-6164

SCORE Office (El Centro)
1100 Main St.
El Centro, CA 92243
(619)352-3681
Fax: (619)352-3246

SCORE Office (Escondido)
720 N. Broadway
Escondido, CA 92025
(619)745-2125
Fax: (619)745-1183

SCORE Office (Fairfield)
1111 Webster St.
Fairfield, CA 94533
(707)425-4625
Fax: (707)425-0826

SCORE Office (Fontana)
17009 Valley Blvd., Ste. B
Fontana, CA 92335
(909)822-4433
Fax: (909)822-6238

SCORE Office (Foster City)
1125 E. Hillsdale Blvd.
Foster City, CA 94404
(415)573-7600
Fax: (415)573-5201

SCORE Office (Fremont)
2201 Walnut Ave., Ste. 110
Fremont, CA 94538
(510)795-2244
Fax: (510)795-2240

SCORE Office (Central California)
2719 N. Air Fresno Dr., Ste. 200
Fresno, CA 93727-1547
(559)487-5605
Fax: (559)487-5636

SCORE Office (Gardena)
1204 W. Gardena Blvd.
Gardena, CA 90247
(310)532-9905
Fax: (310)515-4893

SCORE Office (Lompoc)
330 N. Brand Blvd., Ste. 190
Glendale, CA 91203-2304

(818)552-3206
Fax: (818)552-3323

SCORE Office (Los Angeles)
330 N. Brand Blvd., Ste. 190
Glendale, CA 91203-2304
(818)552-3206
Fax: (818)552-3323

SCORE Office (Glendora)
131 E. Foothill Blvd.
Glendora, CA 91740
(818)963-4128
Fax: (818)914-4822

SCORE Office (Grover Beach)
177 S. 8th St.
Grover Beach, CA 93433
(805)489-9091
Fax: (805)489-9091

SCORE Office (Hawthorne)
12477 Hawthorne Blvd.
Hawthorne, CA 90250
(310)676-1163
Fax: (310)676-7661

SCORE Office (Hayward)
22300 Foothill Blvd., Ste. 303
Hayward, CA 94541
(510)537-2424

SCORE Office (Hemet)
1700 E. Florida Ave.
Hemet, CA 92544-4679
(909)652-4390
Fax: (909)929-8543

SCORE Office (Hesperia)
16367 Main St.
PO Box 403656
Hesperia, CA 92340
(619)244-2135

SCORE Office (Holloster)
321 San Felipe Rd., No. 11
Hollister, CA 95023

SCORE Office (Hollywood)
7018 Hollywood Blvd.
Hollywood, CA 90028
(213)469-8311
Fax: (213)469-2805

SCORE Office (Indio)
82503 Hwy. 111
PO Drawer TTT
Indio, CA 92202
(619)347-0676

SCORE Office (Inglewood)
330 Queen St.

Inglewood, CA 90301
(818)552-3206

SCORE Office (La Puente)
218 N. Grendanda St. D.
La Puente, CA 91744
(818)330-3216
Fax: (818)330-9524

SCORE Office (La Verne)
2078 Bonita Ave.
La Verne, CA 91750
(909)593-5265
Fax: (714)929-8475

SCORE Office (Lake Elsinore)
132 W. Graham Ave.
Lake Elsinore, CA 92530
(909)674-2577

SCORE Office (Lakeport)
PO Box 295
Lakeport, CA 95453
(707)263-5092

SCORE Office (Lakewood)
5445 E. Del Amo Blvd., Ste. 2
Lakewood, CA 90714
(213)920-7737

SCORE Office (Long Beach)
1 World Trade Center
Long Beach, CA 90831

SCORE Office (Los Alamitos)
901 W. Civic Center Dr., Ste. 160
Los Alamitos, CA 90720

SCORE Office (Los Altos)
321 University Ave.
Los Altos, CA 94022
(415)948-1455

SCORE Office (Manhattan Beach)
PO Box 3007
Manhattan Beach, CA 90266
(310)545-5313
Fax: (310)545-7203

SCORE Office (Merced)
1632 N. St.
Merced, CA 95340
(209)725-3800
Fax: (209)383-4959

SCORE Office (Milpitas)
75 S. Milpitas Blvd., Ste. 205
Milpitas, CA 95035
(408)262-2613
Fax: (408)262-2823

SCORE Office (Yosemite)
1012 11th St., Ste. 300
Modesto, CA 95354
(209)521-9333

SCORE Office (Montclair)
5220 Benito Ave.
Montclair, CA 91763

SCORE Office (Monterey Bay)
380 Alvarado St.
PO Box 1770
Monterey, CA 93940-1770
(408)649-1770

SCORE Office (Moreno Valley)
25480 Alessandro
Moreno Valley, CA 92553

SCORE Office (Morgan Hill)
25 W. 1st St.
PO Box 786
Morgan Hill, CA 95038
(408)779-9444
Fax: (408)778-1786

SCORE Office (Morro Bay)
880 Main St.
Morro Bay, CA 93442
(805)772-4467

SCORE Office (Mountain View)
580 Castro St.
Mountain View, CA 94041
(415)968-8378
Fax: (415)968-5668

SCORE Office (Napa)
1556 1st St.
Napa, CA 94559
(707)226-7455
Fax: (707)226-1171

SCORE Office (North Hollywood)
5019 Lankershim Blvd.
North Hollywood, CA 91601
(818)552-3206

SCORE Office (Northridge)
8801 Reseda Blvd.
Northridge, CA 91324
(818)349-5676

SCORE Office (Novato)
807 De Long Ave.
Novato, CA 94945
(415)897-1164
Fax: (415)898-9097

SCORE Office (East Bay)
519 17th St.
Oakland, CA 94612

(510)273-6611
Fax: (510)273-6015
E-mail: webmaster@eastbayscore.org
Website: http://www.eastbayscore.org

SCORE Office (Oceanside)
928 N. Coast Hwy.
Oceanside, CA 92054
(619)722-1534

SCORE Office (Ontario)
121 West B. St.
Ontario, CA 91762
Fax: (714)984-6439

SCORE Office (Oxnard)
PO Box 867
Oxnard, CA 93032
(805)385-8860
Fax: (805)487-1763

SCORE Office (Pacifica)
450 Dundee Way, Ste. 2
Pacifica, CA 94044
(415)355-4122

SCORE Office (Palm Desert)
72990 Hwy. 111
Palm Desert, CA 92260
(619)346-6111
Fax: (619)346-3463

SCORE Office (Palm Springs)
650 E. Tahquitz Canyon Way Ste. D
Palm Springs, CA 92262-6706
(760)320-6682
Fax: (760)323-9426

SCORE Office (Lakeside)
2150 Low Tree
Palmdale, CA 93551
(805)948-4518
Fax: (805)949-1212

SCORE Office (Palo Alto)
325 Forest Ave.
Palo Alto, CA 94301
(415)324-3121
Fax: (415)324-1215

SCORE Office (Pasadena)
117 E. Colorado Blvd., Ste. 100
Pasadena, CA 91105
(818)795-3355
Fax: (818)795-5663

SCORE Office (Paso Robles)
1225 Park St.
Paso Robles, CA 93446-2234
(805)238-0506
Fax: (805)238-0527

SCORE Office (Petaluma)
799 Baywood Dr., Ste. 3
Petaluma, CA 94954
(707)762-2785
Fax: (707)762-4721

SCORE Office (Pico Rivera)
9122 E. Washington Blvd.
Pico Rivera, CA 90660

SCORE Office (Pittsburg)
2700 E. Leland Rd.
Pittsburg, CA 94565
(510)439-2181
Fax: (510)427-1599

SCORE Office (Pleasanton)
777 Peters Ave.
Pleasanton, CA 94566
(510)846-9697

SCORE Office (Monterey Park)
485 N. Garey
Pomona, CA 91769

SCORE Office (Pomona)
485 N. Garey Ave.
Pomona, CA 91766
(909)622-1256

SCORE Office (Antelope Valley)
4511 West Ave. M-4
Quartz Hill, CA 93536
(805)272-0087
E-mail: avscore@ptw.com
Website: http://www.score.av.org/

SCORE Office (Shasta)
737 Auditorium Dr.
Redding, CA 96099
(916)225-2770

SCORE Office (Redwood City)
1675 Broadway
Redwood City, CA 94063
(415)364-1722
Fax: (415)364-1729

SCORE Office (Richmond)
3925 MacDonald Ave.
Richmond, CA 94805

SCORE Office (Ridgecrest)
PO Box 771
Ridgecrest, CA 93555
(619)375-8331
Fax: (619)375-0365

SCORE Office (Riverside)
3685 Main St., Ste. 350
Riverside, CA 92501
(909)683-7100

SCORE Office (Sacramento)
9845 Horn Rd., 260-B
Sacramento, CA 95827
(916)361-2322
Fax: (916)361-2164
E-mail: sacchapter@directcon.net

SCORE Office (Salinas)
PO Box 1170
Salinas, CA 93902
(408)424-7611
Fax: (408)424-8639

SCORE Office (Inland Empire)
777 E. Rialto Ave.
Purchasing
San Bernardino, CA 92415-0760
(909)386-8278

SCORE Office (San Carlos)
San Carlos Chamber of Commerce
PO Box 1086
San Carlos, CA 94070
(415)593-1068
Fax: (415)593-9108

SCORE Office (Encinitas)
550 W. C St., Ste. 550
San Diego, CA 92101-3540
(619)557-7272
Fax: (619)557-5894

SCORE Office (San Diego)
550 West C. St., Ste. 550
San Diego, CA 92101-3540
(619)557-7272
Fax: (619)557-5894
Website: http://www.score-sandiego.org

SCORE Office (Menlo Park)
1100 Merrill St.
San Francisco, CA 94105
(415)325-2818
Fax: (415)325-0920

SCORE Office (San Francisco)
455 Market St., 6th Fl.
San Francisco, CA 94105
(415)744-6827
Fax: (415)744-6750
E-mail: sfscore@sfscore.
Website: http://www.sfscore.com

SCORE Office (San Gabriel)
401 W. Las Tunas Dr.
San Gabriel, CA 91776
(818)576-2525
Fax: (818)289-2901

SCORE Office (San Jose)
Deanza College
208 S. 1st. St., Ste. 137
San Jose, CA 95113
(408)288-8479
Fax: (408)535-5541

SCORE Office (Silicon Valley)
84 W. Santa Clara St., Ste. 100
San Jose, CA 95113
(408)288-8479
Fax: (408)535-5541
E-mail: info@svscore.org
Website: http://www.svscore.org

SCORE Office (San Luis Obispo)
3566 S. Hiquera, No. 104
San Luis Obispo, CA 93401
(805)547-0779

SCORE Office (San Mateo)
1021 S. El Camino, 2nd Fl.
San Mateo, CA 94402
(415)341-5679

SCORE Office (San Pedro)
390 W. 7th St.
San Pedro, CA 90731
(310)832-7272

SCORE Office (Orange County)
200 W. Santa Anna Blvd., Ste. 700
Santa Ana, CA 92701
(714)550-7369
Fax: (714)550-0191
Website: http://www.score114.org

SCORE Office (Santa Barbara)
3227 State St.
Santa Barbara, CA 93130
(805)563-0084

SCORE Office (Central Coast)
509 W. Morrison Ave.
Santa Maria, CA 93454
(805)347-7755

SCORE Office (Santa Maria)
614 S. Broadway
Santa Maria, CA 93454-5111
(805)925-2403
Fax: (805)928-7559

SCORE Office (Santa Monica)
501 Colorado, Ste. 150
Santa Monica, CA 90401
(310)393-9825
Fax: (310)394-1868

SCORE Office (Santa Rosa)
777 Sonoma Ave., Rm. 115E
Santa Rosa, CA 95404

(707)571-8342
Fax: (707)541-0331
Website: http://www.pressdemo.com/community/score/score.html

SCORE Office (Scotts Valley)
4 Camp Evers Ln.
Scotts Valley, CA 95066
(408)438-1010
Fax: (408)438-6544

SCORE Office (Simi Valley)
40 W. Cochran St., Ste. 100
Simi Valley, CA 93065
(805)526-3900
Fax: (805)526-6234

SCORE Office (Sonoma)
453 1st St. E
Sonoma, CA 95476
(707)996-1033

SCORE Office (Los Banos)
222 S. Shepard St.
Sonora, CA 95370
(209)532-4212

SCORE Office (Tuolumne County)
39 North Washington St.
Sonora, CA 95370
(209)588-0128
E-mail: score@mlode.com

SCORE Office (South San Francisco)
445 Market St., Ste. 6th Fl.
South San Francisco, CA 94105
(415)744-6827
Fax: (415)744-6812

SCORE Office (Stockton)
401 N. San Joaquin St., Rm. 215
Stockton, CA 95202
(209)946-6293

SCORE Office (Taft)
314 4th St.
Taft, CA 93268
(805)765-2165
Fax: (805)765-6639

SCORE Office (Conejo Valley)
625 W. Hillcrest Dr.
Thousand Oaks, CA 91360
(805)499-1993
Fax: (805)498-7264

SCORE Office (Torrance)
3400 Torrance Blvd., Ste. 100
Torrance, CA 90503
(310)540-5858
Fax: (310)540-7662

SCORE Office (Truckee)
PO Box 2757
Truckee, CA 96160
(916)587-2757
Fax: (916)587-2439

SCORE Office (Visalia)
113 S. M St,
Tulare, CA 93274
(209)627-0766
Fax: (209)627-8149

SCORE Office (Upland)
433 N. 2nd Ave.
Upland, CA 91786
(909)931-4108

SCORE Office (Vallejo)
2 Florida St.
Vallejo, CA 94590
(707)644-5551
Fax: (707)644-5590

SCORE Office (Van Nuys)
14540 Victory Blvd.
Van Nuys, CA 91411
(818)989-0300
Fax: (818)989-3836

SCORE Office (Ventura)
5700 Ralston St., Ste. 310
Ventura, CA 93001
(805)658-2688
Fax: (805)658-2252
E-mail: scoreven@jps.net
Website: http://www.jps.net/scoreven

SCORE Office (Vista)
201 E. Washington St.
Vista, CA 92084
(619)726-1122
Fax: (619)226-8654

SCORE Office (Watsonville)
PO Box 1748
Watsonville, CA 95077
(408)724-3849
Fax: (408)728-5300

SCORE Office (West Covina)
811 S. Sunset Ave.
West Covina, CA 91790
(818)338-8496
Fax: (818)960-0511

SCORE Office (Westlake)
30893 Thousand Oaks Blvd.
Westlake Village, CA 91362
(805)496-5630
Fax: (818)991-1754

Colorado

SCORE Office (Colorado Springs)
2 N. Cascade Ave., Ste. 110
Colorado Springs, CO 80903
(719)636-3074
Website: http://www.cscc.org/score02/
index.html

SCORE Office (Denver)
US Custom's House, 4th Fl.
721 19th St.
Denver, CO 80201-0660
(303)844-3985
Fax: (303)844-6490
E-mail: score62@csn.net
Website: http://www.sni.net/score62

SCORE Office (Tri-River)
1102 Grand Ave.
Glenwood Springs, CO 81601
(970)945-6589

SCORE Office (Grand Junction)
2591 B & 3/4 Rd.
Grand Junction, CO 81503
(970)243-5242

SCORE Office (Gunnison)
608 N. 11th
Gunnison, CO 81230
(303)641-4422

SCORE Office (Montrose)
1214 Peppertree Dr.
Montrose, CO 81401
(970)249-6080

SCORE Office (Pagosa Springs)
PO Box 4381
Pagosa Springs, CO 81157
(970)731-4890

SCORE Office (Rifle)
0854 W. Battlement Pky., Apt. C106
Parachute, CO 81635
(970)285-9390

SCORE Office (Pueblo)
302 N. Santa Fe
Pueblo, CO 81003
(719)542-1704
Fax: (719)542-1624
E-mail: mackey@iex.net
Website: http://www.pueblo.org/score

SCORE Office (Ridgway)
143 Poplar Pl.
Ridgway, CO 81432

SCORE Office (Silverton)
PO Box 480

Silverton, CO 81433
(303)387-5430

SCORE Office (Minturn)
PO Box 2066
Vail, CO 81658
(970)476-1224

Connecticut

SCORE Office (Greater Bridgeport)
230 Park Ave.
Bridgeport, CT 06601-0999
(203)576-4369
Fax: (203)576-4388

SCORE Office (Bristol)
10 Main St. 1st. Fl.
Bristol, CT 06010
(203)584-4718
Fax: (203)584-4722

SCORE office (Greater Danbury)
246 Federal Rd.
Unit LL2, Ste. 7
Brookfield, CT 06804
(203)775-1151

SCORE Office (Greater Danbury)
246 Federal Rd., Unit LL2, Ste. 7
Brookfield, CT 06804
(203)775-1151

SCORE Office (Eastern Connecticut)
Administration Bldg., Rm. 313
PO 625
61 Main St. (Chapter 579)
Groton, CT 06475
(203)388-9508

SCORE Office (Greater Hartford County)
330 Main St.
Hartford, CT 06106
(860)548-1749
Fax: (860)240-4659
Website: http://www.score56.org

SCORE Office (Manchester)
20 Hartford Rd.
Manchester, CT 06040
(203)646-2223
Fax: (203)646-5871

SCORE Office (New Britain)
185 Main St., Ste. 431
New Britain, CT 06051
(203)827-4492
Fax: (203)827-4480

SCORE Office (New Haven)
25 Science Pk., Bldg. 25, Rm. 366

New Haven, CT 06511
(203)865-7645

SCORE Office (Fairfield County)
24 Beldon Ave., 5th Fl.
Norwalk, CT 06850
(203)847-7348
Fax: (203)849-9308

SCORE Office (Old Saybrook)
146 Main St.
Old Saybrook, CT 06475
(860)388-9508

SCORE Office (Simsbury)
Box 244
Simsbury, CT 06070
(203)651-7307
Fax: (203)651-1933

SCORE Office (Torrington)
23 North Rd.
Torrington, CT 06791
(203)482-6586

Delaware

SCORE Office (Dover)
Treadway Towers
PO Box 576
Dover, DE 19903
(302)678-0892
Fax: (302)678-0189

SCORE Office (Lewes)
PO Box 1
Lewes, DE 19958
(302)645-8073
Fax: (302)645-8412

SCORE Office (Milford)
204 NE Front St.
Milford, DE 19963
(302)422-3301

SCORE Office (Wilmington)
824 Market St., Ste. 610
Wilmington, DE 19801
(302)573-6652
Fax: (302)573-6092
Website: http://www.scoredelaware.com

District of Columbia

SCORE Office (George Mason University)
409 3rd St. SW, 4th Fl.
Washington, DC 20024
800-634-0245

SCORE Office (Washington DC)
1110 Vermont Ave. NW, 9th Fl.

Washington, DC 20043
(202)606-4000
Fax: (202)606-4225
E-mail: dcscore@hotmail.com
Website: http://www.scoredc.org/

Florida

SCORE Office (Desota County Chamber of Commerce)
16 South Velucia Ave.
Arcadia, FL 34266
(941)494-4033

SCORE Office (Suncoast/Pinellas)
Airport Business Ctr.
4707 - 140th Ave. N, No. 311
Clearwater, FL 33755
(813)532-6800
Fax: (813)532-6800

SCORE Office (DeLand)
336 N. Woodland Blvd.
DeLand, FL 32720
(904)734-4331
Fax: (904)734-4333

SCORE Office (South Palm Beach)
1050 S. Federal Hwy., Ste. 132
Delray Beach, FL 33483
(561)278-7752
Fax: (561)278-0288

SCORE Office (Ft. Lauderdale)
Federal Bldg., Ste. 123
299 E. Broward Blvd.
Ft. Lauderdale, FL 33301
(954)356-7263
Fax: (954)356-7145

SCORE Office (Southwest Florida)
The Renaissance
8695 College Pky., Ste. 345 & 346
Ft. Myers, FL 33919
(941)489-2935
Fax: (941)489-1170

SCORE Office (Treasure Coast)
Professional Center, Ste. 2
3220 S. US, No. 1
Ft. Pierce, FL 34982
(561)489-0548

SCORE Office (Gainesville)
101 SE 2nd Pl., Ste. 104
Gainesville, FL 32601
(904)375-8278

SCORE Office (Hialeah Dade Chamber)
59 W. 5th St.
Hialeah, FL 33010

(305)887-1515
Fax: (305)887-2453

SCORE Office (Daytona Beach)
921 Nova Rd., Ste. A
Holly Hills, FL 32117
(904)255-6889
Fax: (904)255-0229
E-mail: score87@dbeach.com

SCORE Office (South Broward)
3475 Sheridian St., Ste. 203
Hollywood, FL 33021
(305)966-8415

SCORE Office (Citrus County)
5 Poplar Ct.
Homosassa, FL 34446
(352)382-1037

SCORE Office (Jacksonville)
7825 Baymeadows Way, Ste. 100-B
Jacksonville, FL 32256
(904)443-1911
Fax: (904)443-1980
E-mail: scorejax@juno.com
Website: http://www.scorejax.org/

SCORE Office (Jacksonville Satellite)
3 Independent Dr.
Jacksonville, FL 32256
(904)366-6600
Fax: (904)632-0617

SCORE Office (Central Florida)
5410 S. Florida Ave., No. 3
Lakeland, FL 33801
(941)687-5783
Fax: (941)687-6225

SCORE Office (Lakeland)
100 Lake Morton Dr.
Lakeland, FL 33801
(941)686-2168

SCORE Office (St. Petersburg)
800 W. Bay Dr., Ste. 505
Largo, FL 33712
(813)585-4571

SCORE Office (Leesburg)
9501 US Hwy. 441
Leesburg, FL 34788-8751
(352)365-3556
Fax: (352)365-3501

SCORE Office (Cocoa)
1600 Farno Rd., Unit 205
Melbourne, FL 32935
(407)254-2288

SCORE Office (Melbourne)
Melbourne Professional Complex
1600 Sarno, Ste. 205
Melbourne, FL 32935
(407)254-2288
Fax: (407)245-2288

SCORE Office (Merritt Island)
1600 Sarno Rd., Ste. 205
Melbourne, FL 32935
(407)254-2288
Fax: (407)254-2288

SCORE Office (Space Coast)
Melbourn Professional Complex
1600 Sarno, Ste. 205
Melbourne, FL 32935
(407)254-2288
Fax: (407)254-2288

SCORE Office (Dade)
49 NW 5th St.
Miami, FL 33128
(305)371-6889
Fax: (305)374-1882
E-mail: score@netrox.net
Website: http://www.netrox.net/~score/

SCORE Office (Naples of Collier)
International College
2654 Tamiami Trl. E
Naples, FL 34112
(941)417-1280
Fax: (941)417-1281
E-mail: score@naples.net
Website: http://www.naples.net/clubs/score/index.htm

SCORE Office (Pasco County)
6014 US Hwy. 19, Ste. 302
New Port Richey, FL 34652
(813)842-4638

SCORE Office (Southeast Volusia)
115 Canal St.
New Smyrna Beach, FL 32168
(904)428-2449
Fax: (904)423-3512

SCORE Office (Ocala)
110 E. Silver Springs Blvd.
Ocala, FL 34470
(352)629-5959

Clay County SCORE Office
Clay County Chamber of Commerce
1734 Kingsdey Ave.
PO Box 1441
Orange Park, FL 32073
(904)264-2651
Fax: (904)269-0363

SCORE Office (Orlando)
80 N. Hughey Ave.
Rm. 445 Federal Bldg.
Orlando, FL 32801
(407)648-6476
Fax: (407)648-6425

SCORE Office (Emerald Coast)
19 W. Garden St., No. 325
Pensacola, FL 32501
(904)444-2060
Fax: (904)444-2070

SCORE Office (Charlotte County)
201 W. Marion Ave., Ste. 211
Punta Gorda, FL 33950
(941)575-1818
E-mail: score@gls3c.com
Website: http://www.charlotte-florida.com/business/scorepg01.htm

SCORE Office (St. Augustine)
1 Riberia St.
St. Augustine, FL 32084
(904)829-5681
Fax: (904)829-6477

SCORE Office (Bradenton)
2801 Fruitville, Ste. 280
Sarasota, FL 34237
(813)955-1029

SCORE Office (Manasota)
2801 Fruitville Rd., Ste. 280
Sarasota, FL 34237
(941)955-1029
Fax: (941)955-5581
E-mail: score116@gte.net
Website: http://www.score-suncoast.org/

SCORE Office (Tallahassee)
200 W. Park Ave.
Tallahassee, FL 32302
(850)487-2665

SCORE Office (Hillsborough)
4732 Dale Mabry Hwy. N, Ste. 400
Tampa, FL 33614-6509
(813)870-0125

SCORE Office (Lake Sumter)
122 E. Main St.
Tavares, FL 32778-3810
(352)365-3556

SCORE Office (Titusville)
2000 S. Washington Ave.
Titusville, FL 32780
(407)267-3036
Fax: (407)264-0127

SCORE Office (Venice)
257 N. Tamiami Trl.
Venice, FL 34285
(941)488-2236
Fax: (941)484-5903

SCORE Office (Palm Beach)
500 Australian Ave. S, Ste. 100
West Palm Beach, FL 33401
(561)833-1672
Fax: (561)833-1712

SCORE Office (Wildwood)
103 N. Webster St.
Wildwood, FL 34785

Georgia

SCORE Office (Atlanta)
Harris Tower, Suite 1900
233 Peachtree Rd., NE
Atlanta, GA 30309
(404)347-2442
Fax: (404)347-1227

SCORE Office (Augusta)
3126 Oxford Rd.
Augusta, GA 30909
(706)869-9100

SCORE Office (Columbus)
School Bldg.
PO Box 40
Columbus, GA 31901
(706)327-3654

SCORE Office (Dalton-Whitfield)
305 S. Thorton Ave.
Dalton, GA 30720
(706)279-3383

SCORE Office (Gainesville)
PO Box 374
Gainesville, GA 30503
(770)532-6206
Fax: (770)535-8419

SCORE Office (Macon)
711 Grand Bldg.
Macon, GA 31201
(912)751-6160

SCORE Office (Brunswick)
4 Glen Ave.
St. Simons Island, GA 31520
(912)265-0620
Fax: (912)265-0629

SCORE Office (Savannah)
111 E. Liberty St., Ste. 103
Savannah, GA 31401
(912)652-4335

Fax: (912)652-4184
E-mail: info@scoresav.org
Website: http://www.coastalempire.com/
score/index.htm

Guam

SCORE Office (Guam)
Pacific News Bldg., Rm. 103
238 Archbishop Flores St.
Agana, GU 96910-5100
(671)472-7308

Hawaii

SCORE Office (Hawaii, Inc.)
1111 Bishop St., Ste. 204
PO Box 50207
Honolulu, HI 96813
(808)522-8132
Fax: (808)522-8135
E-mail: hnlscore@juno.com

SCORE Office (Kahului)
250 Alamaha, Unit N16A
Kahului, HI 96732
(808)871-7711

SCORE Office (Maui, Inc.)
590 E. Lipoa Pkwy., Ste. 227
Kihei, HI 96753
(808)875-2380

Idaho

SCORE Office (Treasure Valley)
1020 Main St., No. 290
Boise, ID 83702
(208)334-1696
Fax: (208)334-9353

SCORE Office (Eastern Idaho)
2300 N. Yellowstone, Ste. 119
Idaho Falls, ID 83401
(208)523-1022
Fax: (208)528-7127

Illinois

SCORE Office (Fox Valley)
40 W. Downer Pl.
PO Box 277
Aurora, IL 60506
(630)897-9214
Fax: (630)897-7002

SCORE Office (Greater Belvidere)
419 S. State St.
Belvidere, IL 61008
(815)544-4357
Fax: (815)547-7654

SCORE Office (Bensenville)
1050 Busse Hwy. Suite 100
Bensenville, IL 60106
(708)350-2944
Fax: (708)350-2979

SCORE Office (Central Illinois)
402 N. Hershey Rd.
Bloomington, IL 61704
(309)644-0549
Fax: (309)663-8270
E-mail: webmaster@central-illinois-score.org
Website: http://www.central-illinois-score.org/

SCORE Office (Southern Illinois)
150 E. Pleasant Hill Rd.
Box 1
Carbondale, IL 62901
(618)453-6654
Fax: (618)453-5040

SCORE Office (Chicago)
Northwest Atrium Ctr.
500 W. Madison St., No. 1250
Chicago, IL 60661
(312)353-7724
Fax: (312)886-5688
Website: http://www.mcs.net/~bic/

SCORE Office (Chicago–Oliver Harvey College)
Pullman Bldg.
1000 E. 11th St., 7th Fl.
Chicago, IL 60628
Fax: (312)468-8086

SCORE Office (Danville)
28 W. N. Street
Danville, IL 61832
(217)442-7232
Fax: (217)442-6228

SCORE Office (Decatur)
Milliken University
1184 W. Main St.
Decatur, IL 62522
(217)424-6297
Fax: (217)424-3993
E-mail: charding@mail.millikin.edu
Website: http://www.millikin.edu/
academics/Tabor/score.html

SCORE Office (Downers Grove)
925 Curtis
Downers Grove, IL 60515
(708)968-4050
Fax: (708)968-8368

SCORE Office (Elgin)
24 E. Chicago, 3rd Fl.
PO Box 648
Elgin, IL 60120
(847)741-5660
Fax: (847)741-5677

SCORE Office (Freeport Area)
26 S. Galena Ave.
Freeport, IL 61032
(815)233-1350
Fax: (815)235-4038

SCORE Office (Galesburg)
292 E. Simmons St.
PO Box 749
Galesburg, IL 61401
(309)343-1194
Fax: (309)343-1195

SCORE Office (Glen Ellyn)
500 Pennsylvania
Glen Ellyn, IL 60137
(708)469-0907
Fax: (708)469-0426

SCORE Office (Greater Alton)
Alden Hall
5800 Godfrey Rd.
Godfrey, IL 62035-2466
(618)467-2280
Fax: (618)466-8289
Website: http://www.altonweb.com/
score/

SCORE Office (Grayslake)
19351 W. Washington St.
Grayslake, IL 60030
(708)223-3633
Fax: (708)223-9371

SCORE Office (Harrisburg)
303 S. Commercial
Harrisburg, IL 62946-1528
(618)252-8528
Fax: (618)252-0210

SCORE Office (Joliet)
100 N. Chicago
Joliet, IL 60432
(815)727-5371
Fax: (815)727-5374

SCORE Office (Kankakee)
101 S. Schuyler Ave.
Kankakee, IL 60901
(815)933-0376
Fax: (815)933-0380

SCORE Office (Macomb)
216 Seal Hall, Rm. 214

Macomb, IL 61455
(309)298-1128
Fax: (309)298-2520

SCORE Office (Matteson)
210 Lincoln Mall
Matteson, IL 60443
(708)709-3750
Fax: (708)503-9322

SCORE Office (Mattoon)
1701 Wabash Ave.
Mattoon, IL 61938
(217)235-5661
Fax: (217)234-6544

SCORE Office (Quad Cities)
622 19th St.
Moline, IL 61265
(309)797-0082
Fax: (309)757-5435
E-mail: score@qconline.com
Website: http://www.qconline.com/
business/score/

SCORE Office (Naperville)
131 W. Jefferson Ave.
Naperville, IL 60540
(708)355-4141
Fax: (708)355-8355

SCORE Office (Northbrook)
2002 Walters Ave.
Northbrook, IL 60062
(847)498-5555
Fax: (847)498-5510

SCORE Office (Palos Hills)
10900 S. 88th Ave.
Palos Hills, IL 60465
(847)974-5468
Fax: (847)974-0078

SCORE Office (Peoria)
124 SW Adams, Ste. 300
Peoria, IL 61602
(309)676-0755
Fax: (309)676-7534

SCORE Office (Prospect Heights)
1375 Wolf Rd.
Prospect Heights, IL 60070
(847)537-8660
Fax: (847)537-7138

SCORE Office (Quincy Tri-State)
300 Civic Center Plz., Ste. 245
Quincy, IL 62301
(217)222-8093
Fax: (217)222-3033

SCORE Office (River Grove)
2000 5th Ave.
River Grove, IL 60171
(708)456-0300
Fax: (708)583-3121

SCORE Office (Northern Illinois)
515 N. Court St.
Rockford, IL 61103
(815)962-0122
Fax: (815)962-0122

SCORE Office (St. Charles)
103 N. 1st Ave.
St. Charles, IL 60174-1982
(847)584-8384
Fax: (847)584-6065

SCORE Office (Springfield)
511 W. Capitol Ave., Ste. 302
Springfield, IL 62704
(217)492-4416
Fax: (217)492-4867

SCORE Office (Sycamore)
112 Somunak St.
Sycamore, IL 60178
(815)895-3456
Fax: (815)895-0125

SCORE Office (University)
Hwy. 50 & Stuenkel Rd. Ste. C3305
University Park, IL 60466
(708)534-5000
Fax: (708)534-8457

Indiana

SCORE Office (Anderson)
205 W. 11th St.
Anderson, IN 46015
(317)642-0264

SCORE Office (Bloomington)
Star Center
216 W. Allen
Bloomington, IN 47403
(812)335-7334
E-mail: wtfische@indiana.edu
Website: http://www.brainfreezemedia.
com/score527/

SCORE Office (South East Indiana)
500 Franklin St.
Box 29
Columbus, IN 47201
(812)379-4457

SCORE Office (Corydon)
310 N. Elm St.
Corydon, IN 47112

(812)738-2137
Fax: (812)738-6438

SCORE Office (Crown Point)
Old Courthouse Sq. Ste. 206
PO Box 43
Crown Point, IN 46307
(219)663-1800

SCORE Office (Elkhart)
418 S. Main St.
Elkhart, IN 46515
(219)293-1531
Fax: (219)294-1859

SCORE Office (Evansville)
1100 W. Lloyd Expy., Ste. 105
Evansville, IN 47708
(812)426-6144

SCORE Office (Fort Wayne)
1300 S. Harrison St.
Ft. Wayne, IN 46802
(219)422-2601
Fax: (219)422-2601

SCORE Office (Gary)
973 W. 6th Ave., Rm. 326
Gary, IN 46402
(219)882-3918

SCORE Office (Hammond)
7034 Indianapolis Blvd.
Hammond, IN 46324
(219)931-1000
Fax: (219)845-9548

SCORE Office (Indianapolis)
429 N. Pennsylvania St., Ste. 100
Indianapolis, IN 46204-1873
(317)226-7264
Fax: (317)226-7259
E-mail: inscore@indy.net
Website: http://www.score-
indianapolis.org/

SCORE Office (Jasper)
PO Box 307
Jasper, IN 47547-0307
(812)482-6866

SCORE Office (Kokomo/Howard Counties)
106 N. Washington St.
Kokomo, IN 46901
(765)457-5301
Fax: (765)452-4564

SCORE Office (Logansport)
300 E. Broadway, Ste. 103
Logansport, IN 46947
(219)753-6388

SCORE Office (Madison)
301 E. Main St.
Madison, IN 47250
(812)265-3135
Fax: (812)265-2923

SCORE Office (Marengo)
Rt. 1 Box 224D
Marengo, IN 47140
Fax: (812)365-2793

SCORE Office (Marion/Grant Counties)
215 S. Adams
Marion, IN 46952
(765)664-5107

SCORE Office (Merrillville)
255 W. 80th Pl.
Merrillville, IN 46410
(219)769-8180
Fax: (219)736-6223

SCORE Office (Michigan City)
200 E. Michigan Blvd.
Michigan City, IN 46360
(219)874-6221
Fax: (219)873-1204

SCORE Office (South Central Indiana)
4100 Charleston Rd.
New Albany, IN 47150-9538
(812)945-0066

SCORE Office (Rensselaer)
104 W. Washington
Rensselaer, IN 47978

SCORE Office (Salem)
210 N. Main St.
Salem, IN 47167
(812)883-4303
Fax: (812)883-1467

SCORE Office (South Bend)
300 N. Michigan St.
South Bend, IN 46601
(219)282-4350
E-mail: chair@southbend-score.org
Website: http://www.southbend-score.org/

SCORE Office (Valparaiso)
150 Lincolnway
Valparaiso, IN 46383
(219)462-1105
Fax: (219)469-5710

SCORE Office (Vincennes)
27 N. 3rd
PO Box 553
Vincennes, IN 47591
(812)882-6440
Fax: (812)882-6441

SCORE Office (Wabash)
PO Box 371
Wabash, IN 46992
(219)563-1168
Fax: (219)563-6920

Iowa

SCORE Office (Burlington)
Federal Bldg.
300 N. Main St.
Burlington, IA 52601
(319)752-2967

SCORE Office (Cedar Rapids)
2750 1st Ave. NE, Ste 350
Cedar Rapids, IA 52401-1806
(319)362-6405
Fax: (319)362-7861
E:mail: score@scorecr.org
Website: http://www.scorecr.org

SCORE Office (Illowa)
333 4th Ave. S
Clinton, IA 52732
(319)242-5702

SCORE Office (Council Bluffs)
7 N. 6th St.
Council Bluffs, IA 51502
(712)325-1000

SCORE Office (Northeast Iowa)
3404 285th St.
Cresco, IA 52136
(319)547-3377

SCORE Office (Des Moines)
Federal Bldg., Rm. 749
210 Walnut St.
Des Moines, IA 50309-2186
(515)284-4760

SCORE Office (Ft. Dodge)
Federal Bldg., Rm. 436
205 S. 8th St.
Ft. Dodge, IA 50501
(515)955-2622

SCORE Office (Independence)
110 1st. St. east
Independence, IA 50644
(319)334-7178
Fax: (319)334-7179

SCORE Office (Iowa City)
210 Federal Bldg.
PO Box 1853
Iowa City, IA 52240-1853
(319)338-1662

SCORE Office (Keokuk)
401 Main St.
Pierce Bldg., No. 1
Keokuk, IA 52632
(319)524-5055

SCORE Office (Central Iowa)
Fisher Community College
709 S. Center
Marshalltown, IA 50158
(515)753-6645

SCORE Office (River City)
15 West State St.
Mason City, IA 50401
(515)423-5724

SCORE Office (South Central)
SBDC, Indian Hills Community College
525 Grandview Ave.
Ottumwa, IA 52501
(515)683-5127
Fax: (515)683-5263

SCORE Office (Dubuque)
10250 Sundown Rd.
Peosta, IA 52068
(319)556-5110

SCORE Office (Southwest Iowa)
614 W. Sheridan
Shenandoah, IA 51601
(712)246-3260

SCORE Office (Sioux City)
Federal Bldg.
320 6th St.
Sioux City, IA 51101
(712)277-2324
Fax: (712)277-2325

SCORE Office (Iowa Lakes)
122 W. 5th St.
Spencer, IA 51301
(712)262-3059

SCORE Office (Vista)
119 W. 6th St.
Storm Lake, IA 50588
(712)732-3780

SCORE Office (Waterloo)
215 E. 4th
Waterloo, IA 50703
(319)233-8431

Kansas

SCORE Office (Southwest Kansas)
501 W. Spruce
Dodge City, KS 67801
(316)227-3119

SCORE Office (Emporia)
811 Homewood
Emporia, KS 66801
(316)342-1600

SCORE Office (Golden Belt)
1307 Williams
Great Bend, KS 67530
(316)792-2401

SCORE Office (Hays)
PO Box 400
Hays, KS 67601
(913)625-6595

SCORE Office (Hutchinson)
1 E. 9th St.
Hutchinson, KS 67501
(316)665-8468
Fax: (316)665-7619

SCORE Office (Southeast Kansas)
404 Westminster Pl.
PO Box 886
Independence, KS 67301
(316)331-4741

SCORE Office (McPherson)
306 N. Main
PO Box 616
McPherson, KS 67460
(316)241-3303

SCORE Office (Salina)
120 Ash St.
Salina, KS 67401
(785)243-4290
Fax: (785)243-1833

SCORE Office (Topeka)
1700 College
Topeka, KS 66621
(785)231-1010

SCORE Office (Wichita)
100 E. English, Ste. 510
Wichita, KS 67202
(316)269-6273
Fax: (316)269-6499

SCORE Office (Ark Valley)
205 E. 9th St.
Winfield, KS 67156
(316)221-1617

Kentucky

SCORE Office (Ashland)
PO Box 830
Ashland, KY 41105
(606)329-8011
Fax: (606)325-4607

SCORE Office (Bowling Green)
812 State St.
PO Box 51
Bowling Green, KY 42101
(502)781-3200
Fax: (502)843-0458

SCORE Office (Tri-Lakes)
508 Barbee Way
Danville, KY 40422-1548
(606)231-9902

SCORE Office (Glasgow)
301 W. Main St.
Glasgow, KY 42141
(502)651-3161
Fax: (502)651-3122

SCORE Office (Hazard)
B & I Technical Center
100 Airport Gardens Rd.
Hazard, KY 41701
(606)439-5856
Fax: (606)439-1808

SCORE Office (Lexington)
410 W. Vine St., Ste. 290, Civic C
Lexington, KY 40507
(606)231-9902
Fax: (606)253-3190
E-mail: scorelex@uky.campus.mci.net

SCORE Office (Louisville)
188 Federal Office Bldg.
600 Dr. Martin L. King Jr. Pl.
Louisville, KY 40202
(502)582-5976

SCORE Office (Madisonville)
257 N. Main
Madisonville, KY 42431
(502)825-1399
Fax: (502)825-1396

SCORE Office (Paducah)
Federal Office Bldg.
501 Broadway, Rm. B-36
Paducah, KY 42001
(502)442-5685

Louisiana

SCORE Office (Central Louisiana)
802 3rd St.
Alexandria, LA 71309
(318)442-6671

SCORE Office (Baton Rouge)
564 Laurel St.
PO Box 3217
Baton Rouge, LA 70801

(504)381-7130
Fax: (504)336-4306

SCORE Office (North Shore)
2 W. Thomas
Hammond, LA 70401
(504)345-4457
Fax: (504)345-4749

SCORE Office (Lafayette)
804 St. Mary Blvd.
Lafayette, LA 70505-1307
(318)233-2705
Fax: (318)234-8671
E-mail: score302@aol.com

SCORE Office (Lake Charles)
120 W. Pujo St.
Lake Charles, LA 70601
(318)433-3632

SCORE Office (New Orleans)
365 Canal St., Ste. 3100
New Orleans, LA 70130
(504)589-2356
Fax: (504)589-2339

SCORE Office (Shreveport)
400 Edwards St.
Shreveport, LA 71101
(318)677-2536
Fax: (318)677-2541

Maine

SCORE Office (Augusta)
40 Western Ave.
Augusta, ME 04330
(207)622-8509

SCORE Office (Bangor)
Peabody Hall, Rm. 229
One College Cir.
Bangor, ME 04401
(207)941-9707

SCORE Office (Central & Northern Arroostock)
111 High St.
Caribou, ME 04736
(207)492-8010
Fax: (207)492-8010

SCORE Office (Penquis)
South St.
Dover Foxcroft, ME 04426
(207)564-7021

SCORE Office (Maine Coastal)
Mill Mall
Box 1105
Ellsworth, ME 04605-1105

(207)667-5800
E-mail: score@arcadia.net

SCORE Office (Lewiston-Auburn)
BIC of Maine-Bates Mill Complex
35 Canal St.
Lewiston, ME 04240-7764
(207)782-3708
Fax: (207)783-7745

SCORE Office (Portland)
66 Pearl St., Rm. 210
Portland, ME 04101
(207)772-1147
Fax: (207)772-5581
E-mail: Score53@score.maine.org
Website: http://www.score.maine.org/
chapter53/

SCORE Office (Western Mountains)
255 River St.
PO Box 252
Rumford, ME 04257-0252
(207)369-9976

SCORE Office (Oxford Hills)
166 Main St.
South Paris, ME 04281
(207)743-0499

Maryland

SCORE Office (Southern Maryland)
2525 Riva Rd., Ste. 110
Annapolis, MD 21401
(410)266-9553
Fax: (410)573-0981
E-mail: score390@aol.com
Website: http://members.aol.com/
score390/index.htm

SCORE Office (Baltimore)
The City Crescent Bldg., 6th Fl.
10 S. Howard St.
Baltimore, MD 21201
(410)962-2233
Fax: (410)962-1805

SCORE Office (Bel Air)
108 S. Bond St.
Bel Air, MD 21014
(410)838-2020
Fax: (410)893-4715

SCORE Office (Bethesda)
7910 Woodmont Ave., Ste. 1204
Bethesda, MD 20814
(301)652-4900
Fax: (301)657-1973

SCORE Office (Bowie)
6670 Race Track Rd.
Bowie, MD 20715
(301)262-0920
Fax: (301)262-0921

SCORE Office (Dorchester County)
203 Sunburst Hwy.
Cambridge, MD 21613
(410)228-3575

SCORE Office (Upper Shore)
210 Marlboro Ave.
Easton, MD 21601
(410)822-4606
Fax: (410)822-7922

SCORE Office (Frederick County)
43A S. Market St.
Frederick, MD 21701
(301)662-8723
Fax: (301)846-4427

SCORE Office (Gaithersburg)
9 Park Ave.
Gaithersburg, MD 20877
(301)840-1400
Fax: (301)963-3918

SCORE Office (Glen Burnie)
103 Crain Hwy. SE
Glen Burnie, MD 21061
(410)766-8282
Fax: (410)766-9722

SCORE Office (Hagerstown)
111 W. Washington St.
Hagerstown, MD 21740
(301)739-2015
Fax: (301)739-1278

SCORE Office (Laurel)
7901 Sandy Spring Rd. Ste. 501
Laurel, MD 20707
(301)725-4000
Fax: (301)725-0776

SCORE Office (Salisbury)
300 E. Main St.
Salisbury, MD 21801
(410)749-0185
Fax: (410)860-9925

Massachusetts

SCORE Office (NE Massachusetts)
100 Cummings Ctr., Ste. 101 K
Beverly, MA 01923
(978)922-9441
Website: http://www1.shore.net/~score/

SCORE Office (Boston)
10 Causeway St., Rm. 265
Boston, MA 02222-1093
(617)565-5591
Fax: (617)565-5598
E-mail: boston-score-20@worldnet.att.net
Website: http://www.scoreboston.org/

SCORE office (Bristol/Plymouth County)
53 N. 6th St., Federal Bldg.
Bristol, MA 02740
(508)994-5093

SCORE Office (SE Massachusetts)
60 School St.
Brockton, MA 02401
(508)587-2673
Fax: (508)587-1340
Website: http://www.metrosouth
chamber.com/score.html

SCORE Office (North Adams)
820 N. State Rd.
Cheshire, MA 01225
(413)743-5100

SCORE Office (Clinton Satellite)
1 Green St.
Clinton, MA 01510
Fax: (508)368-7689

SCORE Office (Greenfield)
PO Box 898
Greenfield, MA 01302
(413)773-5463
Fax: (413)773-7008

SCORE Office (Haverhill)
87 Winter St.
Haverhill, MA 01830
(508)373-5663
Fax: (508)373-8060

SCORE Office (Hudson Satellite)
PO Box 578
Hudson, MA 01749
(508)568-0360
Fax: (508)568-0360

SCORE Office (Cape Cod)
Independence Pk., Ste. 5B
270 Communications Way
Hyannis, MA 02601
(508)775-4884
Fax: (508)790-2540

SCORE Office (Lawrence)
264 Essex St.
Lawrence, MA 01840
(508)686-0900
Fax: (508)794-9953

SCORE Office (Leominster Satellite)
110 Erdman Way
Leominster, MA 01453
(508)840-4300
Fax: (508)840-4896

SCORE Office (Bristol/Plymouth Counties)
53 N. 6th St., Federal Bldg.
New Bedford, MA 02740
(508)994-5093

SCORE Office (Newburyport)
29 State St.
Newburyport, MA 01950
(617)462-6680

SCORE Office (Pittsfield)
66 West St.
Pittsfield, MA 01201
(413)499-2485

SCORE Office (Haverhill-Salem)
32 Derby Sq.
Salem, MA 01970
(508)745-0330
Fax: (508)745-3855

SCORE Office (Springfield)
1350 Main St.
Federal Bldg.
Springfield, MA 01103
(413)785-0314

SCORE Office (Carver)
12 Taunton Green, Ste. 201
Taunton, MA 02780
(508)824-4068
Fax: (508)824-4069

SCORE Office (Worcester)
33 Waldo St.
Worcester, MA 01608
(508)753-2929
Fax: (508)754-8560

Michigan

SCORE Office (Allegan)
PO Box 338
Allegan, MI 49010
(616)673-2479

SCORE Office (Ann Arbor)
425 S. Main St., Ste. 103
Ann Arbor, MI 48104
(313)665-4433

SCORE Office (Battle Creek)
34 W. Jackson Ste. 4A
Battle Creek, MI 49017-3505

(616)962-4076
Fax: (616)962-6309

SCORE Office (Cadillac)
222 Lake St.
Cadillac, MI 49601
(616)775-9776
Fax: (616)768-4255

SCORE Office (Detroit)
477 Michigan Ave., Rm. 515
Detroit, MI 48226
(313)226-7947
Fax: (313)226-3448

SCORE Office (Flint)
708 Root Rd., Rm. 308
Flint, MI 48503
(810)233-6846

SCORE Office (Grand Rapids)
111 Pearl St. NW
Grand Rapids, MI 49503-2831
(616)771-0305
Fax: (616)771-0328
E-mail: scoreone@iserv.net
Website: http://www.iserv.net/~scoreone/

SCORE Office (Holland)
480 State St.
Holland, MI 49423
(616)396-9472

SCORE Office (Jackson)
209 East Washington
PO Box 80
Jackson, MI 49204
(517)782-8221
Fax: (517)782-0061

SCORE Office (Kalamazoo)
345 W. Michigan Ave.
Kalamazoo, MI 49007
(616)381-5382
Fax: (616)384-0096
E-mail: score@nucleus.net

SCORE Office (Lansing)
117 E. Allegan
PO Box 14030
Lansing, MI 48901
(517)487-6340
Fax: (517)484-6910

SCORE Office (Livonia)
15401 Farmington Rd.
Livonia, MI 48154
(313)427-2122
Fax: (313)427-6055

SCORE Office (Madison Heights)
26345 John R
Madison Heights, MI 48071
(810)542-5010
Fax: (810)542-6821

SCORE Office (Monroe)
111 E. 1st
Monroe, MI 48161
(313)242-3366
Fax: (313)242-7253

SCORE Office (Mt. Clemens)
58 S/B Gratiot
Mt. Clemens, MI 48043
(810)463-1528
Fax: (810)463-6541

SCORE Office (Muskegon)
PO Box 1087
230 Terrace Plz.
Muskegon, MI 49443
(616)722-3751
Fax: (616)728-7251

SCORE Office (Petoskey)
401 E. Mitchell St.
Petoskey, MI 49770
(616)347-4150

SCORE Office (Pontiac)
Executive Office Bldg.
1200 N. Telegraph Rd.
Pontiac, MI 48341
(810)975-9555

SCORE Office (Pontiac)
PO Box 430025
Pontiac, MI 48343
(810)335-9600

SCORE Office (Port Huron)
920 Pinegrove Ave.
Port Huron, MI 48060
(810)985-7101

SCORE Office (Rochester)
71 Walnut Ste. 110
Rochester, MI 48307
(810)651-6700
Fax: (810)651-5270

SCORE Office (Saginaw)
901 S. Washington Ave.
Saginaw, MI 48601
(517)752-7161
Fax: (517)752-9055

SCORE Office (Upper Peninsula)
2581 I-75 Business Spur
Sault Ste. Marie, MI 49783
(906)632-3301

SCORE Office (Southfield)
21000 W. 10 Mile Rd.
Southfield, MI 48075
(810)204-3050
Fax: (810)204-3099

SCORE Office (Traverse City)
202 E. Grandview Pkwy.
PO Box 387
Traverse City, MI 49685
(616)947-5075
Fax: (616)946-2565

SCORE Office (Warren)
30500 Van Dyke, Ste. 118
Warren, MI 48093
(810)751-3939

Minnesota

SCORE Office (Aitkin)
Aitkin, MN 56431
(218)741-3906

SCORE Office (Albert Lea)
202 N. Broadway Ave.
Albert Lea, MN 56007
(507)373-7487

SCORE Office (Austin)
PO Box 864
Austin, MN 55912
(507)437-4561
Fax: (507)437-4869

SCORE Office (South Metro)
Ames Business Ctr.
2500 W. County Rd., No. 42
Burnsville, MN 55337
(612)898-5645
Fax: (612)435-6972
E-mail: southmetro@scoreminn.org
Website: http://www.scoreminn.org/
southmetro/

SCORE Office (Duluth)
1717 Minnesota Ave.
Duluth, MN 55802
(218)727-8286
Fax: (218)727-3113
E-mail: duluth@scoreminn.org
Website: http://www.scoreminn.org

SCORE Office (Fairmont)
PO Box 826
Fairmont, MN 56031
(507)235-5547
Fax: (507)235-8411

SCORE Office (Southwest Minnesota)
112 Riverfront St.

Box 999
Mankato, MN 56001
(507)345-4519
Fax: (507)345-4451
Website: http://www.scoreminn.org/

SCORE Office (Minneapolis)
North Plaza Bldg., Ste. 51
5217 Wayzata Blvd.
Minneapolis, MN 55416
(612)591-0539
Fax: (612)544-0436
Website: http://www.scoreminn.org/

SCORE Office (Owatonna)
PO Box 331
Owatonna, MN 55060
(507)451-7970
Fax: (507)451-7972

SCORE Office (Red Wing)
2000 W. Main St., Ste. 324
Red Wing, MN 55066
(612)388-4079

SCORE Office (Southeastern Minnesota)
220 S. Broadway, Ste. 100
Rochester, MN 55901
(507)288-1122
Fax: (507)282-8960
Website: http://www.scoreminn.org/

SCORE Office (Brainerd)
St. Cloud, MN 56301

SCORE Office (Central Area)
1527 Northway Dr.
St. Cloud, MN 56301
(320)240-1332
Fax: (320)255-9050
Website: http://www.scoreminn.org/

SCORE Office (St. Paul)
350 St. Peter St., No. 295
Lowry Professional Bldg.
St. Paul, MN 55102
(651)223-5010
Fax: (651)223-5048
Website: http://www.scoreminn.org/

SCORE Office (Winona)
Box 870
Winona, MN 55987
(507)452-2272
Fax: (507)454-8814

SCORE Office (Worthington)
1121 3rd Ave.
Worthington, MN 56187
(507)372-2919
Fax: (507)372-2827

Mississippi

SCORE Office (Delta)
915 Washington Ave.
PO Box 933
Greenville, MS 38701
(601)378-3141

SCORE Office (Gulfcoast)
1 Government Plaza
2909 13th St., Ste. 203
Gulfport, MS 39501
(228)863-0054

SCORE Office (Jackson)
1st Jackson Center, Ste. 400
101 W. Capitol St.
Jackson, MS 39201
(601)965-5533

SCORE Office (Meridian)
5220 16th Ave.
Meridian, MS 39305
(601)482-4412

Missouri

SCORE Office (Lake of the Ozark)
University Extension
113 Kansas St.
PO Box 1405
Camdenton, MO 65020
(573)346-2644
Fax: (573)346-2694
E-mail: score@cdoc.net
Website: http://sites.cdoc.net/score/

Chamber of Commerce (Cape Girardeau)
PO Box 98
Cape Girardeau, MO 63702-0098
(314)335-3312

SCORE Office (Mid-Missouri)
1705 Halstead Ct.
Columbia, MO 65203
(573)874-1132

SCORE Office (Ozark-Gateway)
1486 Glassy Rd.
Cuba, MO 65453-1640
(573)885-4954

SCORE Office (Kansas City)
323 W. 8th St., Ste. 104
Kansas City, MO 64105
(816)374-6675
Fax: (816)374-6692
E-mail: SCOREBIC@AOL.COM
Website: http://www.crn.org/score/

SCORE Office (Sedalia)
Lucas Place
323 W. 8th St., Ste.104
Kansas City, MO 64105
(816)374-6675

SCORE office (Tri-Lakes)
PO Box 1148
Kimberling, MO 65686
(417)739-3041

SCORE Office (Tri-Lakes)
HCRI Box 85
Lampe, MO 65681
(417)858-6798

SCORE Office (Mexico)
111 N. Washington St.
Mexico, MO 65265
(314)581-2765

SCORE Office (Southeast Missouri)
Rte. 1, Box 280
Neelyville, MO 63954
(573)989-3577

SCORE office (Poplar Bluff Area)
806 Emma St.
Poplar Bluff, MO 63901
(573)686-8892

SCORE Office (St. Joseph)
3003 Frederick Ave.
St. Joseph, MO 64506
(816)232-4461

SCORE Office (St. Louis)
815 Olive St., Rm. 242
St. Louis, MO 63101-1569
(314)539-6970
Fax: (314)539-3785
E-mail: info@stlscore.org
Website: http://www.stlscore.org/

SCORE Office (Lewis & Clark)
425 Spencer Rd.
St. Peters, MO 63376
(314)928-2900
Fax: (314)928-2900
E-mail: score01@mail.win.org

SCORE Office (Springfield)
620 S. Glenstone, Ste. 110
Springfield, MO 65802-3200
(417)864-7670
Fax: (417)864-4108

SCORE office (Southeast Kansas)
1206 W. First St.
Webb City, MO 64870
(417)673-3984

Montana

SCORE Office (Billings)
815 S. 27th St.
Billings, MT 59101
(406)245-4111

SCORE Office (Bozeman)
1205 E. Main St.
Bozeman, MT 59715
(406)586-5421

SCORE Office (Butte)
1000 George St.
Butte, MT 59701
(406)723-3177

SCORE Office (Great Falls)
710 First Ave. N
Great Falls, MT 59401
(406)761-4434
E-mail: scoregtf@in.tch.com

SCORE Office (Havre, Montana)
518 First St.
Havre, MT 59501
(406)265-4383

SCORE Office (Helena)
Federal Bldg.
301 S. Park
Helena, MT 59626-0054
(406)441-1081

SCORE Office (Kalispell)
2 Main St.
Kalispell, MT 59901
(406)756-5271
Fax: (406)752-6665

SCORE Office (Missoula)
723 Ronan
Missoula, MT 59806
(406)327-8806
E-mail: score@safeshop.com
Website: http://missoula.bigsky.net/
score/

Nebraska

SCORE Office (Columbus)
Columbus, NE 68601
(402)564-2769

SCORE Office (Fremont)
92 W. 5th St.
Fremont, NE 68025
(402)721-2641

SCORE Office (Hastings)
Hastings, NE 68901
(402)463-3447

SCORE Office (Lincoln)
8800 O St.
Lincoln, NE 68520
(402)437-2409

SCORE Office (Panhandle)
150549 CR 30
Minatare, NE 69356
(308)632-2133
Website: http://www.tandt.com/
SCORE

SCORE Office (Norfolk)
3209 S. 48th Ave.
Norfolk, NE 68106
(402)564-2769

SCORE Office (North Platte)
3301 W. 2nd St.
North Platte, NE 69101
(308)532-4466

SCORE Office (Omaha)
11145 Mill Valley Rd.
Omaha, NE 68154
(402)221-3606
Fax: (402)221-3680
E-mail: infoctr@ne.uswest.net
Website: http://www.tandt.com/score/

Nevada

SCORE Office (Incline Village)
969 Tahoe Blvd.
Incline Village, NV 89451
(702)831-7327
Fax: (702)832-1605

SCORE Office (Carson City)
301 E. Stewart
PO Box 7527
Las Vegas, NV 89125
(702)388-6104

SCORE Office (Las Vegas)
300 Las Vegas Blvd. S, Ste. 1100
Las Vegas, NV 89101
(702)388-6104

SCORE Office (Northern Nevada)
SBDC, College of Business
Administration
Univ. of Nevada
Reno, NV 89557-0100
(702)784-4436
Fax: (702)784-4337

New Hampshire

SCORE Office (North Country)
PO Box 34

Berlin, NH 03570
(603)752-1090

SCORE Office (Concord)
143 N. Main St., Rm. 202A
PO Box 1258
Concord, NH 03301
(603)225-1400
Fax: (603)225-1409

SCORE Office (Dover)
299 Central Ave.
Dover, NH 03820
(603)742-2218
Fax: (603)749-6317

SCORE Office (Monadnock)
34 Mechanic St.
Keene, NH 03431-3421
(603)352-0320

SCORE Office (Lakes Region)
67 Water St., Ste. 105
Laconia, NH 03246
(603)524-9168

SCORE Office (Upper Valley)
Citizens Bank Bldg., Rm. 310
20 W. Park St.
Lebanon, NH 03766
(603)448-3491
Fax: (603)448-1908
E-mail: billt@valley.net
Website: http://www.valley.net/~score/

SCORE Office (Merrimack Valley)
275 Chestnut St., Rm. 618
Manchester, NH 03103
(603)666-7561
Fax: (603)666-7925

SCORE Office (Mt. Washington Valley)
PO Box 1066
North Conway, NH 03818
(603)383-0800

SCORE Office (Seacoast)
195 Commerce Way, Unit-A
Portsmouth, NH 03801-3251
(603)433-0575

New Jersey

SCORE Office (Somerset)
Paritan Valley Community College,
Rte. 28
Branchburg, NJ 08807
(908)218-8874
E-mail: nj-score@grizbiz.com.
Website: http://www.nj-score.org/

SCORE Office (Chester)
5 Old Mill Rd.
Chester, NJ 07930
(908)879-7080

**SCORE Office
(Greater Princeton)**
4 A George Washington Dr.
Cranbury, NJ 08512
(609)520-1776

SCORE Office (Freehold)
36 W. Main St.
Freehold, NJ 07728
(908)462-3030
Fax: (908)462-2123

SCORE Office (North West)
Picantinny Innovation Ctr.
3159 Schrader Rd.
Hamburg, NJ 07419
(973)209-8525
Fax: (973)209-7252
E-mail: nj-score@grizbiz.com
Website: http://www.nj-score.org/

SCORE Office (Monmouth)
765 Newman Springs Rd.
Lincroft, NJ 07738
(908)224-2573
E-mail: nj-score@grizbiz.com
Website: http://www.nj-score.org/

SCORE Office (Manalapan)
125 Symmes Dr.
Manalapan, NJ 07726
(908)431-7220

SCORE Office (Jersey City)
2 Gateway Ctr., 4th Fl.
Newark, NJ 07102
(973)645-3982
Fax: (973)645-2375

SCORE Office (Newark)
2 Gateway Center, 15th Fl.
Newark, NJ 07102-5553
(973)645-3982
Fax: (973)645-2375
E-mail: nj-score@grizbiz.com
Website: http://www.nj-score.org

SCORE Office (Bergen County)
327 E. Ridgewood Ave.
Paramus, NJ 07652
(201)599-6090
E-mail: nj-score@grizbiz.com
Website: http://www.nj-score.org/

SCORE Office (Pennsauken)
4900 Rte. 70

Pennsauken, NJ 08109
(609)486-3421

SCORE Office (Southern New Jersey)
4900 Rte. 70
Pennsauken, NJ 08109
(609)486-3421
E-mail: nj-score@grizbiz.com
Website: http://www.nj-score.org/

SCORE Office (Greater Princeton)
216 Rockingham Row
Princeton Forrestal Village
Princeton, NJ 08540
(609)520-1776
Fax: (609)520-9107
E-mail: nj-score@grizbiz.com
Website: http://www.nj-score.org/

SCORE Office (Shrewsbury)
Hwy. 35
Shrewsbury, NJ 07702
(908)842-5995
Fax: (908)219-6140

SCORE Office (Ocean County)
33 Washington St.
Toms River, NJ 08754
(732)505-6033
E-mail: nj-score@grizbiz.com
Website: http://www.nj-score.org/

SCORE Office (Wall)
2700 Allaire Rd.
Wall, NJ 07719
(908)449-8877

SCORE Office (Wayne)
2055 Hamburg Tpke.
Wayne, NJ 07470
(201)831-7788
Fax: (201)831-9112

New Mexico

SCORE Office (Albuquerque)
525 Buena Vista, SE
Albuquerque, NM 87106
(505)272-7999
Fax: (505)272-7963

SCORE Office (Las Cruces)
Loretto Towne Center
505 S. Main St., Ste. 125
Las Cruces, NM 88001
(505)523-5627
Fax: (505)524-2101
E-mail: score.397@zianet.com

SCORE Office (Roswell)
Federal Bldg., Rm. 237

Roswell, NM 88201
(505)625-2112
Fax: (505)623-2545

SCORE Office (Santa Fe)
Montoya Federal Bldg.
120 Federal Place, Rm. 307
Santa Fe, NM 87501
(505)988-6302
Fax: (505)988-6300

New York

SCORE Office (Northeast)
1 Computer Dr. S
Albany, NY 12205
(518)446-1118
Fax: (518)446-1228

SCORE Office (Auburn)
30 South St.
PO Box 675
Auburn, NY 13021
(315)252-7291

SCORE Office (South Tier Binghamton)
Metro Center, 2nd Fl.
49 Court St.
PO Box 995
Binghamton, NY 13902
(607)772-8860

SCORE Office (Queens County City)
12055 Queens Blvd., Rm. 333
Borough Hall, NY 11424
(718)263-8961

SCORE Office (Buffalo)
Federal Bldg., Rm. 1311
111 W. Huron St.
Buffalo, NY 14202
(716)551-4301
Website: http://www2.pcom.net/score/
buf45.html

SCORE Office (Canandaigua)
Chamber of Commerce Bldg.
113 S. Main St.
Canandaigua, NY 14424
(716)394-4400
Fax: (716)394-4546

SCORE Office (Chemung)
333 E. Water St., 4th Fl.
Elmira, NY 14901
(607)734-3358

SCORE Office (Geneva)
Chamber of Commerce Bldg.
PO Box 587

Geneva, NY 14456
(315)789-1776
Fax: (315)789-3993

SCORE Office (Glens Falls)
84 Broad St.
Glens Falls, NY 12801
(518)798-8463
Fax: (518)745-1433

SCORE Office (Orange County)
40 Matthews St.
Goshen, NY 10924
(914)294-8080
Fax: (914)294-6121

SCORE Office (Huntington Area)
151 W. Carver St.
Huntington, NY 11743
(516)423-6100

SCORE Office (Tompkins County)
904 E. Shore Dr.
Ithaca, NY 14850
(607)273-7080

SCORE Office (Long Island City)
120-55 Queens Blvd.
Jamaica, NY 11424
(718)263-8961
Fax: (718)263-9032

SCORE Office (Chatauqua)
101 W. 5th St.
Jamestown, NY 14701
(716)484-1103

SCORE Office (Westchester)
2 Caradon Ln.
Katonah, NY 10536
(914)948-3907
Fax: (914)948-4645
E-mail: score@w-w-w.com
Website: http://w-w-w.com/score/

SCORE Office (Queens County)
Queens Borough Hall
120-55 Queens Blvd. Rm. 333
Kew Gardens, NY 11424
(718)263-8961
Fax: (718)263-9032

SCORE Office (Brookhaven)
3233 Rte. 112
Medford, NY 11763
(516)451-6563
Fax: (516)451-6925

SCORE Office (Melville)
35 Pinelawn Rd., Rm. 207-W
Melville, NY 11747
(516)454-0771

SCORE Office (Nassau County)
400 County Seat Dr., No. 140
Mineola, NY 11501
(516)571-3303
E-mail: Counse1998@aol.com
Website: http://members.aol.com/
Counse1998/Default.htm

SCORE Office (Mt. Vernon)
4 N. 7th Ave.
Mt. Vernon, NY 10550
(914)667-7500

SCORE Office (New York)
26 Federal Plz., Rm. 3100
New York, NY 10278
(212)264-4507
Fax: (212)264-4963
E-mail: score1000@erols.com
Website: http://users.erols.com/
score-nyc/

SCORE Office (Newburgh)
47 Grand St.
Newburgh, NY 12550
(914)562-5100

SCORE Office (Owego)
188 Front St.
Owego, NY 13827
(607)687-2020

SCORE Office (Peekskill)
1 S. Division St.
Peekskill, NY 10566
(914)737-3600
Fax: (914)737-0541

SCORE Office (Penn Yan)
2375 Rte. 14A
Penn Yan, NY 14527
(315)536-3111

SCORE Office (Dutchess)
110 Main St.
Poughkeepsie, NY 12601
(914)454-1700

SCORE Office (Rochester)
601 Keating Federal Bldg., Rm. 410
100 State St.
Rochester, NY 14614
(716)263-6473
Fax: (716)263-3146
Website: http://www.ggw.org/score/

SCORE Office (Saranac Lake)
30 Main St.
Saranac Lake, NY 12983
(315)448-0415

SCORE Office (Suffolk)
286 Main St.
Setauket, NY 11733
(516)751-3886

SCORE Office (Staten Island)
130 Bay St.
Staten Island, NY 10301
(718)727-1221

SCORE Office (Ulster)
Clinton Bldg., Rm. 107
Stone Ridge, NY 12484
(914)687-5035
Fax: (914)687-5015
Website: http://www.scoreulster.org/

SCORE Office (Syracuse)
401 S. Salina, 5th Fl.
Syracuse, NY 13202
(315)471-9393

SCORE Office (Utica)
SUNY Institute of Technology, Route 12
Utica, NY 13504-3050
(315)792-7553

SCORE Office (Watertown)
518 Davidson St.
Watertown, NY 13601
(315)788-1200
Fax: (315)788-8251

North Carolina

SCORE office (Asheboro)
317 E. Dixie Dr.
Asheboro, NC 27203
(336)626-2626
Fax: (336)626-7077

SCORE Office (Asheville)
Federal Bldg., Rm. 259
151 Patton
Asheville, NC 28801-5770
(828)271-4786
Fax: (828)271-4009

SCORE Office (Chapel Hill)
104 S. Estes Dr.
PO Box 2897
Chapel Hill, NC 27514
(919)967-7075

SCORE Office (Coastal Plains)
PO Box 2897
Chapel Hill, NC 27515
(919)967-7075
Fax: (919)968-6874

SCORE Office (Charlotte)
200 N. College St., Ste. A-2015

Charlotte, NC 28202
(704)344-6576
Fax: (704)344-6769
E-mail: CharlotteSCORE47@AOL.com
Website: http://www.charweb.org/
business/score/

SCORE Office (Durham)
411 W. Chapel Hill St.
Durham, NC 27707
(919)541-2171

SCORE Office (Gastonia)
PO Box 2168
Gastonia, NC 28053
(704)864-2621
Fax: (704)854-8723

SCORE Office (Greensboro)
400 W. Market St., Ste. 103
Greensboro, NC 27401-2241
(910)333-5399

SCORE Office (Henderson)
PO Box 917
Henderson, NC 27536
(919)492-2061
Fax: (919)430-0460

SCORE Office (Hendersonville)
Federal Bldg., Rm. 108
W. 4th Ave. & Church St.
Hendersonville, NC 28792
(828)693-8702
E-mail: score@circle.net
Website: http://www.wncguide.com/
score/Welcome.html

SCORE Office (Unifour)
PO Box 1828
Hickory, NC 28603
(704)328-6111

SCORE Office (High Point)
1101 N. Main St.
High Point, NC 27262
(336)882-8625
Fax: (336)889-9499

SCORE Office (Outer Banks)
Collington Rd. and Mustain
Kill Devil Hills, NC 27948
(252)441-8144

SCORE Office (Down East)
312 S. Front St., Ste. 6
New Bern, NC 28560
(252)633-6688
Fax: (252)633-9608

SCORE Office (Kinston)
PO Box 95

New Bern, NC 28561
(919)633-6688

SCORE Office (Raleigh)
Century Post Office Bldg., Ste. 306
300 Federal St. Mall
Raleigh, NC 27601
(919)856-4739
E-mail: jendres@ibm.net
Website: http://www.intrex.net/score96/
score96.htm

SCORE Office (Sanford)
1801 Nash St.
Sanford, NC 27330
(919)774-6442
Fax: (919)776-8739

SCORE Office (Sandhills Area)
1480 Hwy. 15-501
PO Box 458
Southern Pines, NC 28387
(910)692-3926

SCORE Office (Wilmington)
Corps of Engineers Bldg.
96 Darlington Ave., Ste. 207
Wilmington, NC 28403
(910)815-4576
Fax: (910)815-4658

North Dakota

**SCORE Office
(Bismarck-Mandan)**
700 E. Main Ave., 2nd Fl.
PO Box 5509
Bismarck, ND 58506-5509
(701)250-4303

SCORE Office (Fargo)
657 2nd Ave., Rm. 225
Fargo, ND 58108-3083
(701)239-5677

SCORE Office (Upper Red River)
4275 Technology Dr., Rm. 156
Grand Forks, ND 58202-8372
(701)777-3051

SCORE Office (Minot)
100 1st St. SW
Minot, ND 58701-3846
(701)852-6883
Fax: (701)852-6905

Ohio

SCORE Office (Akron)
1 Cascade Plz., 7th Fl.
Akron, OH 44308

(330)379-3163
Fax: (330)379-3164

SCORE Office (Ashland)
Gill Center
47 W. Main St.
Ashland, OH 44805
(419)281-4584

SCORE Office (Canton)
116 Cleveland Ave. NW, Ste. 601
Canton, OH 44702-1720
(330)453-6047

SCORE Office (Chillicothe)
165 S. Paint St.
Chillicothe, OH 45601
(614)772-4530

SCORE Office (Cincinnati)
Ameritrust Bldg., Rm. 850
525 Vine St.
Cincinnati, OH 45202
(513)684-2812
Fax: (513)684-3251
Website: http://www.score.
chapter34.org/

SCORE Office (Cleveland)
Eaton Center, Ste. 620
1100 Superior Ave.
Cleveland, OH 44114-2507
(216)522-4194
Fax: (216)522-4844

SCORE Office (Columbus)
2 Nationwide Plz., Ste. 1400
Columbus, OH 43215-2542
(614)469-2357
Fax: (614)469-2391
E-mail: info@scorecolumbus.org
Website: http://www.scorecolumbus.org/

SCORE Office (Dayton)
Dayton Federal Bldg., Rm. 505
200 W. Second St.
Dayton, OH 45402-1430
(513)225-2887
Fax: (513)225-7667

SCORE Office (Defiance)
615 W. 3rd St.
PO Box 130
Defiance, OH 43512
(419)782-7946

SCORE Office (Findlay)
123 E. Main Cross St.
PO Box 923
Findlay, OH 45840
(419)422-3314

SCORE Office (Lima)
147 N. Main St.
Lima, OH 45801
(419)222-6045
Fax: (419)229-0266

SCORE Office (Mansfield)
55 N. Mulberry St.
Mansfield, OH 44902
(419)522-3211

SCORE Office (Marietta)
Thomas Hall
Marietta, OH 45750
(614)373-0268

SCORE Office (Medina)
County Administrative Bldg.
144 N. Broadway
Medina, OH 44256
(216)764-8650

SCORE Office (Licking County)
50 W. Locust St.
Newark, OH 43055
(614)345-7458

SCORE Office (Salem)
2491 State Rte. 45 S
Salem, OH 44460
(216)332-0361

SCORE Office (Tiffin)
62 S. Washington St.
Tiffin, OH 44883
(419)447-4141
Fax: (419)447-5141

SCORE Office (Toledo)
608 Madison Ave, Ste. 910
Toledo, OH 43624
(419)259-7598
Fax: (419)259-6460

SCORE Office (Heart of Ohio)
377 W. Liberty St.
Wooster, OH 44691
(330)262-5735
Fax: (330)262-5745

SCORE Office (Youngstown)
306 Williamson Hall
Youngstown, OH 44555
(330)746-2687

Oklahoma

SCORE Office (Anadarko)
PO Box 366
Anadarko, OK 73005
(405)247-6651

SCORE Office (Ardmore)
410 W. Main
Ardmore, OK 73401
(580)226-2620

SCORE Office (Northeast Oklahoma)
210 S. Main
Grove, OK 74344
(918)787-2796
Fax: (918)787-2796
E-mail: Score595@greencis.net

SCORE Office (Lawton)
4500 W. Lee Blvd., Bldg. 100, Ste. 107
Lawton, OK 73505
(580)353-8727
Fax: (580)250-5677

SCORE Office (Oklahoma City)
210 Park Ave., No. 1300
Oklahoma City, OK 73102
(405)231-5163
Fax: (405)231-4876
E-mail: score212@usa.net

SCORE Office (Stillwater)
439 S. Main
Stillwater, OK 74074
(405)372-5573
Fax: (405)372-4316

SCORE Office (Tulsa)
616 S. Boston, Ste. 406
Tulsa, OK 74119
(918)581-7462
Fax: (918)581-6908
Website: http://www.ionet.net/~tulscore/

Oregon

SCORE Office (Bend)
63085 N. Hwy. 97
Bend, OR 97701
(541)923-2849
Fax: (541)330-6900

SCORE Office (Willamette)
1401 Willamette St.
PO Box 1107
Eugene, OR 97401-4003
(541)465-6600
Fax: (541)484-4942

SCORE Office (Florence)
3149 Oak St.
Florence, OR 97439
(503)997-8444
Fax: (503)997-8448

SCORE Office (Southern Oregon)
33 N. Central Ave., Ste. 216

Medford, OR 97501
(541)776-4220
E-mail: pgr134f@prodigy.com

SCORE Office (Portland)
1515 SW 5th Ave., Ste. 1050
Portland, OR 97201
(503)326-3441
Fax: (503)326-2808
E-mail: gr134@prodigy.com

SCORE Office (Salem)
416 State St. (corner of Liberty)
Salem, OR 97301
(503)370-2896

Pennsylvania

SCORE Office (Altoona-Blair)
1212 12th Ave.
Altoona, PA 16601-3493
(814)943-8151

SCORE Office (Lehigh Valley)
Rauch Bldg. 37
Lehigh University
621 Taylor St.
Bethlehem, PA 18015
(610)758-4496
Fax: (610)758-5205

SCORE Office (Butler County)
100 N. Main St.
PO Box 1082
Butler, PA 16003
(412)283-2222
Fax: (412)283-0224

SCORE Office (Harrisburg)
4211 Trindle Rd.
Camp Hill, PA 17011
(717)761-4304
Fax: (717)761-4315

SCORE Office (Cumberland Valley)
75 S. 2nd St.
Chambersburg, PA 17201
(717)264-2935

SCORE Office (Monroe County-Stroudsburg)
556 Main St.
East Stroudsburg, PA 18301
(717)421-4433

SCORE Office (Erie)
120 W. 9th St.
Erie, PA 16501
(814)871-5650
Fax: (814)871-7530

SCORE Office (Bucks County)
409 Hood Blvd.
Fairless Hills, PA 19030
(215)943-8850
Fax: (215)943-7404

SCORE Office (Hanover)
146 Broadway
Hanover, PA 17331
(717)637-6130
Fax: (717)637-9127

SCORE Office (Harrisburg)
100 Chestnut, Ste. 309
Harrisburg, PA 17101
(717)782-3874

SCORE Office (East Montgomery County)
Baederwood Shopping Center
1653 The Fairways, Ste. 204
Jenkintown, PA 19046
(215)885-3027

SCORE Office (Kittanning)
2 Butler Rd.
Kittanning, PA 16201
(412)543-1305
Fax: (412)543-6206

SCORE Office (Lancaster)
118 W. Chestnut St.
Lancaster, PA 17603
(717)397-3092

SCORE Office (Westmoreland County)
300 Fraser Purchase Rd.
Latrobe, PA 15650-2690
(412)539-7505
Fax: (412)539-1850

SCORE Office (Lebanon)
252 N. 8th St.
PO Box 899
Lebanon, PA 17042-0899
(717)273-3727
Fax: (717)273-7940

SCORE Office (Lewistown)
3 W. Monument Sq., Ste. 204
Lewistown, PA 17044
(717)248-6713
Fax: (717)248-6714

SCORE Office (Delaware County)
602 E. Baltimore Pike
Media, PA 19063
(610)565-3677
Fax: (610)565-1606

SCORE Office (Milton Area)
112 S. Front St.
Milton, PA 17847

(717)742-7341
Fax: (717)792-2008

SCORE Office (Mon-Valley)
435 Donner Ave.
Monessen, PA 15062
(412)684-4277
Fax: (412)684-7688

SCORE Office (Monroeville)
William Penn Plaza
2790 Mosside Blvd., Ste. 295
Monroeville, PA 15146
(412)856-0622
Fax: (412)856-1030

SCORE Office (Airport Area)
986 Brodhead Rd.
Moon Township, PA 15108-2398
(412)264-6270
Fax: (412)264-1575

SCORE Office (Northeast)
8601 E. Roosevelt Blvd.
Philadelphia, PA 19152
(215)332-3400
Fax: (215)332-6050

SCORE Office (Philadelphia)
1315 Walnut St., Ste. 500
Philadelphia, PA 19107
(215)790-5050
Fax: (215)790-5057
E-mail: score46@bellatlantic.net
Website: http://www.pgweb.net/score46/

SCORE Office (Pittsburgh)
1000 Liberty Ave., Rm. 1122
Pittsburgh, PA 15222
(412)395-6560
Fax: (412)395-6562

SCORE Office (Tri-County)
801 N. Charlotte St.
Pottstown, PA 19464
(610)327-2673

SCORE Office (Reading)
601 Penn St.
Reading, PA 19601
(610)376-3497

SCORE Office (Scranton)
Oppenheim Bldg.
116 N. Washington Ave., Ste. 650
Scranton, PA 18503
(717)347-4611
Fax: (717)347-4611

SCORE Office (Central Pennsylvania)
200 Innovation Blvd., Ste. 242-B
State College, PA 16803

(814)234-9415
Fax: (814)238-9686
Website: http://countrystore.org/
business/score.htm

SCORE Office (Monroe-Stroudsburg)
556 Main St.
Stroudsburg, PA 18360
(717)421-4433

SCORE Office (Uniontown)
Federal Bldg.
Pittsburg St.
PO Box 2065 DTS
Uniontown, PA 15401
(412)437-4222
E-mail: uniontownscore@lcsys.net

SCORE Office (Warren County)
315 2nd Ave.
Warren, PA 16365
(814)723-9017

SCORE Office (Waynesboro)
323 E. Main St.
Waynesboro, PA 17268
(717)762-7123
Fax: (717)962-7124

SCORE Office (Chester County)
Government Service Center, Ste. 281
601 Westtown Rd.
West Chester, PA 19382-4538
(610)344-6910
Fax: (610)344-6919
E-mail: score@locke.ccil.org

SCORE Office (Wilkes-Barre)
7 N. Wilkes-Barre Blvd.
Wilkes Barre, PA 18702-5241
(717)826-6502
Fax: (717)826-6287

SCORE Office (North Central Pennsylvania)
240 W. 3rd St., Rm. 227
PO Box 725
Williamsport, PA 17703
(717)322-3720
Fax: (717)322-1607
E-mail: score234@mail.csrlink.net
Website: http://www.lycoming.org/
score/

SCORE Office (York)
Cyber Center
2101 Pennsylvania Ave.
York, PA 17404
(717)845-8830
Fax: (717)854-9333

Puerto Rico

SCORE Office (Puerto Rico & Virgin Islands)
PO Box 12383-96
San Juan, PR 00914-0383
(787)726-8040
Fax: (787)726-8135

Rhode Island

SCORE Office (Barrington)
281 County Rd.
Barrington, RI 02806
(401)247-1920
Fax: (401)247-3763

SCORE Office (Woonsocket)
640 Washington Hwy.
Lincoln, RI 02865
(401)334-1000
Fax: (401)334-1009

SCORE Office (Wickford)
8045 Post Rd.
North Kingstown, RI 02852
(401)295-5566
Fax: (401)295-8987

SCORE Office (J.G.E. Knight)
380 Westminster St.
Providence, RI 02903
(401)528-4571
Fax: (401)528-4539
Website: http://www.riscore.org

SCORE Office (Warwick)
3288 Post Rd.
Warwick, RI 02886
(401)732-1100
Fax: (401)732-1101

SCORE Office (Westerly)
74 Post Rd.
Westerly, RI 02891
(401)596-7761
800-732-7636
Fax: (401)596-2190

South Carolina

SCORE Office (Aiken)
PO Box 892
Aiken, SC 29802
(803)641-1111
800-542-4536
Fax: (803)641-4174

SCORE Office (Anderson)
Anderson Mall
3130 N. Main St.

Anderson, SC 29621
(864)224-0453

SCORE Office (Coastal)
284 King St.
Charleston, SC 29401
(803)727-4778
Fax: (803)853-2529

SCORE Office (Midlands)
Strom Thurmond Bldg., Rm. 358
1835 Assembly St., Rm 358
Columbia, SC 29201
(803)765-5131
Fax: (803)765-5962
Website: http://www.scoremid
lands.org/

SCORE Office (Piedmont)
Federal Bldg., Rm. B-02
300 E. Washington St.
Greenville, SC 29601
(864)271-3638

SCORE Office (Greenwood)
PO Drawer 1467
Greenwood, SC 29648
(864)223-8357

SCORE Office (Hilton Head Island)
52 Savannah Trail
Hilton Head, SC 29926
(803)785-7107
Fax: (803)785-7110

SCORE Office (Grand Strand)
937 Broadway
Myrtle Beach, SC 29577
(803)918-1079
Fax: (803)918-1083
E-mail: score381@aol.com

SCORE Office (Spartanburg)
PO Box 1636
Spartanburg, SC 29304
(864)594-5000
Fax: (864)594-5055

South Dakota

SCORE Office (West River)
Rushmore Plz. Civic Ctr.
444 Mount Rushmore Rd., No. 209
Rapid City, SD 57701
(605)394-5311
E-mail: score@gwtc.net

SCORE Office (Sioux Falls)
First Financial Center
110 S. Phillips Ave., Ste. 200
Sioux Falls, SD 57104-6727

(605)330-4231
Fax: (605)330-4231

Tennessee

SCORE Office (Chattanooga)
Federal Bldg., Rm. 26
900 Georgia Ave.
Chattanooga, TN 37402
(423)752-5190
Fax: (423)752-5335

SCORE Office (Cleveland)
PO Box 2275
Cleveland, TN 37320
(423)472-6587
Fax: (423)472-2019

SCORE Office (Upper Cumberland Center)
1225 S. Willow Ave.
Cookeville, TN 38501
(615)432-4111
Fax: (615)432-6010

SCORE Office (Unicoi County)
PO Box 713
Erwin, TN 37650
(423)743-3000
Fax: (423)743-0942

SCORE Office (Greeneville)
115 Academy St.
Greeneville, TN 37743
(423)638-4111
Fax: (423)638-5345

SCORE Office (Jackson)
194 Auditorium St.
Jackson, TN 38301
(901)423-2200

SCORE Office (Northeast Tennessee)
1st Tennessee Bank Bldg.
2710 S. Roan St., Ste. 584
Johnson City, TN 37601
(423)929-7686
Fax: (423)461-8052

SCORE Office (Kingsport)
151 E. Main St.
Kingsport, TN 37662
(423)392-8805

SCORE Office (Greater Knoxville)
Farragot Bldg., Ste. 224
530 S. Gay St.
Knoxville, TN 37902
(423)545-4203
E-mail: scoreknox@ntown.com
Website: http://www.scoreknox.org/

SCORE Office (Maryville)
201 S. Washington St.
Maryville, TN 37804-5728
(423)983-2241
800-525-6834
Fax: (423)984-1386

SCORE Office (Memphis)
Federal Bldg., Ste. 390
167 N. Main St.
Memphis, TN 38103
(901)544-3588

SCORE Office (Nashville)
50 Vantage Way, Ste. 201
Nashville, TN 37228-1500
(615)736-7621

Texas

SCORE Office (Abilene)
2106 Federal Post Office and Court Bldg.
Abilene, TX 79601
(915)677-1857

SCORE Office (Austin)
2501 S. Congress
Austin, TX 78701
(512)442-7235
Fax: (512)442-7528

SCORE Office (Golden Triangle)
450 Boyd St.
Beaumont, TX 77704
(409)838-6581
Fax: (409)833-6718

SCORE Office (Brownsville)
3505 Boca Chica Blvd., Ste. 305
Brownsville, TX 78521
(210)541-4508

SCORE Office (Brazos Valley)
3000 Briarcrest, Ste. 302
Bryan, TX 77802
(409)776-8876
E-mail: 102633.2612@compuserve.com

SCORE Office (Cleburne)
Watergarden Pl., 9th Fl., Ste. 400
Cleburne, TX 76031
(817)871-6002

SCORE Office (Corpus Christi)
651 Upper North Broadway, Ste. 654
Corpus Christi, TX 78477
(512)888-4322
Fax: (512)888-3418

SCORE Office (Dallas)
6260 E. Mockingbird
Dallas, TX 75214-2619

(214)828-2471
Fax: (214)821-8033

SCORE Office (El Paso)
10 Civic Center Plaza
El Paso, TX 79901
(915)534-0541
Fax: (915)534-0513

SCORE Office (Bedford)
100 E. 15th St., Ste. 400
Ft. Worth, TX 76102
(817)871-6002

SCORE Office (Ft. Worth)
100 E. 15th St., No. 24
Ft. Worth, TX 76102
(817)871-6002
Fax: (817)871-6031
E-mail: fwbac@onramp.net

SCORE Office (Garland)
2734 W. Kingsley Rd.
Garland, TX 75041
(214)271-9224

SCORE Office (Granbury Chamber of Commerce)
416 S. Morgan
Granbury, TX 76048
(817)573-1622
Fax: (817)573-0805

SCORE Office (Lower Rio Grande Valley)
222 E. Van Buren, Ste. 500
Harlingen, TX 78550
(956)427-8533
Fax: (956)427-8537

SCORE Office (Houston)
9301 Southwest Fwy., Ste. 550
Houston, TX 77074
(713)773-6565
Fax: (713)773-6550

SCORE Office (Irving)
3333 N. MacArthur Blvd., Ste. 100
Irving, TX 75062
(214)252-8484
Fax: (214)252-6710

SCORE Office (Lubbock)
1205 Texas Ave., Rm. 411D
Lubbock, TX 79401
(806)472-7462
Fax: (806)472-7487

SCORE Office (Midland)
Post Office Annex
200 E. Wall St., Rm. P121
Midland, TX 79701
(915)687-2649

SCORE Office (Orange)
1012 Green Ave.
Orange, TX 77630-5620
(409)883-3536
800-528-4906
Fax: (409)886-3247

SCORE Office (Plano)
1200 E. 15th St.
PO Drawer 940287
Plano, TX 75094-0287
(214)424-7547
Fax: (214)422-5182

SCORE Office (Port Arthur)
4749 Twin City Hwy., Ste. 300
Port Arthur, TX 77642
(409)963-1107
Fax: (409)963-3322

SCORE Office (Richardson)
411 Belle Grove
Richardson, TX 75080
(214)234-4141
800-777-8001
Fax: (214)680-9103

SCORE Office (San Antonio)
Federal Bldg., Rm. A527
727 E. Durango
San Antonio, TX 78206
(210)472-5931
Fax: (210)472-5935

SCORE Office (Texarkana State College)
819 State Line Ave.
Texarkana, TX 75501
(903)792-7191
Fax: (903)793-4304

SCORE Office (East Texas)
RTDC
1530 SSW Loop 323, Ste. 100
Tyler, TX 75701
(903)510-2975
Fax: (903)510-2978

SCORE Office (Waco)
401 Franklin Ave.
Waco, TX 76701
(817)754-8898
Fax: (817)756-0776
Website: http://www.brc-waco.com/

SCORE Office (Wichita Falls)
Hamilton Bldg.
900 8th St.
Wichita Falls, TX 76307
(940)723-2741
Fax: (940)723-8773

Utah

SCORE Office (Northern Utah)
160 N. Main
Logan, UT 84321
(435)746-2269

SCORE Office (Ogden)
1701 E. Windsor Dr.
Ogden, UT 84604
(801)629-8613
E-mail: score158@netscape.net

SCORE Office (Central Utah)
1071 E. Windsor Dr.
Provo, UT 84604
(801)373-8660

SCORE Office (Southern Utah)
225 South 700 East
St. George, UT 84770
(435)652-7751

SCORE Office (Salt Lake)
310 S Main St.
Salt Lake City, UT 84101
(801)746-2269
Fax: (801)746-2273

Vermont

SCORE Office (Champlain Valley)
Winston Prouty Federal Bldg.
11 Lincoln St., Rm. 106
Essex Junction, VT 05452
(802)951-6762

SCORE Office (Montpelier)
87 State St., Rm. 205
PO Box 605
Montpelier, VT 05601
(802)828-4422
Fax: (802)828-4485

SCORE Office (Marble Valley)
256 N. Main St.
Rutland, VT 05701-2413
(802)773-9147

SCORE Office (Northeast Kingdom)
20 Main St.
PO Box 904
St. Johnsbury, VT 05819
(802)748-5101

Virgin Islands

SCORE Office (St. Croix)
United Plaza Shopping Center
PO Box 4010, Christiansted
St. Croix, VI 00822
(809)778-5380

SCORE Office (St. Thomas-St. John)
Federal Bldg., Rm. 21
Veterans Dr.
St. Thomas, VI 00801
(809)774-8530

Virginia

SCORE Office (Arlington)
2009 N. 14th St., Ste. 111
Arlington, VA 22201
(703)525-2400

SCORE Office (Blacksburg)
141 Jackson St.
Blacksburg, VA 24060
(540)552-4061

SCORE Office (Bristol)
20 Volunteer Pkwy.
Bristol, VA 24203
(540)989-4850

SCORE Office (Central Virginia)
1001 E. Market St., Ste. 101
Charlottesville, VA 22902
(804)295-6712
Fax: (804)295-7066

SCORE Office (Alleghany Satellite)
241 W. Main St.
Covington, VA 24426
(540)962-2178
Fax: (540)962-2179

SCORE Office (Central Fairfax)
3975 University Dr., Ste. 350
Fairfax, VA 22030
(703)591-2450

SCORE Office (Falls Church)
PO Box 491
Falls Church, VA 22040
(703)532-1050
Fax: (703)237-7904

SCORE Office (Glenns)
Glenns Campus
Box 287
Glenns, VA 23149
(804)693-9650

SCORE Office (Peninsula)
6 Manhattan Sq.
PO Box 7269
Hampton, VA 23666
(757)766-2000
Fax: (757)865-0339
E-mail: score100@seva.net

SCORE Office (Tri-Cities)
108 N. Main St.

Hopewell, VA 23860
(804)458-5536

SCORE Office (Lynchburg)
Federal Bldg.
1100 Main St.
Lynchburg, VA 24504-1714
(804)846-3235

SCORE Office (Greater Prince William)
8963 Center St
Manassas, VA 20110
(703)368-4813
Fax: (703)368-4733

SCORE Office (Martinsvile)
115 Broad St.
Martinsville, VA 24112-0709
(540)632-6401
Fax: (540)632-5059

SCORE Office (Hampton Roads)
Federal Bldg., Rm. 737
200 Grandby St.
Norfolk, VA 23510
(757)441-3733
Fax: (757)441-3733
E-mail: scorehr60@juno.com

SCORE Office (Norfolk)
Federal Bldg., Rm. 737
200 Granby St.
Norfolk, VA 23510
(757)441-3733
Fax: (757)441-3733

SCORE Office (Virginia Beach)
Chamber of Commerce
200 Grandby St., Rm 737
Norfolk, VA 23510
(804)441-3733

SCORE Office (Radford)
1126 Norwood St.
Radford, VA 24141
(540)639-2202

SCORE Office (Richmond)
Federal Bldg.
400 N. 8th St., Ste. 1150
PO Box 10126
Richmond, VA 23240-0126
(804)771-2400
Fax: (804)771-8018
E-mail: scorechapter12@yahoo.com
Website: http://www.cvco.org/score/

SCORE Office (Roanoke)
Federal Bldg., Rm. 716
250 Franklin Rd.
Roanoke, VA 24011

(540)857-2834
Fax: (540)857-2043
E-mail: scorerva@juno.com
Website: http://hometown.aol.com/
scorerv/Index.html

SCORE Office (Fairfax)
8391 Old Courthouse Rd., Ste. 300
Vienna, VA 22182
(703)749-0400

SCORE Office (Greater Vienna)
513 Maple Ave. West
Vienna, VA 22180
(703)281-1333
Fax: (703)242-1482

SCORE Office (Shenandoah Valley)
301 W. Main St.
Waynesboro, VA 22980
(540)949-8203
Fax: (540)949-7740
E-mail: score427@intelos.net

SCORE Office (Williamsburg)
201 Penniman Rd.
Williamsburg, VA 23185
(757)229-6511
E-mail: wacc@williamsburgcc.com

SCORE Office (Northern Virginia)
1360 S. Pleasant Valley Rd.
Winchester, VA 22601
(540)662-4118

Washington

SCORE Office (Gray's Harbor)
506 Duffy St.
Aberdeen, WA 98520
(360)532-1924
Fax: (360)533-7945

SCORE Office (Bellingham)
101 E. Holly St.
Bellingham, WA 98225
(360)676-3307

SCORE Office (Everett)
2702 Hoyt Ave.
Everett, WA 98201-3556
(206)259-8000

SCORE Office (Gig Harbor)
3125 Judson St.
Gig Harbor, WA 98335
(206)851-6865

SCORE Office (Kennewick)
PO Box 6986
Kennewick, WA 99336
(509)736-0510

SCORE Office (Puyallup)
322 2nd St. SW
PO Box 1298
Puyallup, WA 98371
(206)845-6755
Fax: (206)848-6164

SCORE Office (Seattle)
1200 6th Ave., Ste. 1700
Seattle, WA 98101
(206)553-7320
Fax: (206)553-7044
E-mail: score55@aol.com
Website: http://www.scn.org/civic/score-
online/index55.html

SCORE Office (Spokane)
801 W. Riverside Ave., No. 240
Spokane, WA 99201
(509)353-2820
Fax: (509)353-2600
E-mail: score@dmi.net
Website: http://www.dmi.net/score/

SCORE Office (Clover Park)
PO Box 1933
Tacoma, WA 98401-1933
(206)627-2175

SCORE Office (Tacoma)
1101 Pacific Ave.
Tacoma, WA 98402
(253)274-1288
Fax: (253)274-1289

SCORE Office (Fort Vancouver)
1701 Broadway, S-1
Vancouver, WA 98663
(360)699-1079

SCORE Office (Walla Walla)
500 Tausick Way
Walla Walla, WA 99362
(509)527-4681

SCORE Office (Mid-Columbia)
1113 S. 14th Ave.
Yakima, WA 98907
(509)574-4944
Fax: (509)574-2943
Website: http://www.ellensburg.com/~
score/

West Virginia

SCORE Office (Charleston)
1116 Smith St.
Charleston, WV 25301
(304)347-5463
E-mail: score256@juno.com

SCORE Office (Virginia Street)
1116 Smith St., Ste. 302
Charleston, WV 25301
(304)347-5463

SCORE Office (Marion County)
PO Box 208
Fairmont, WV 26555-0208
(304)363-0486

SCORE Office (Upper Monongahela Valley)
1000 Technology Dr., Ste. 1111
Fairmont, WV 26555
(304)363-0486
E-mail: score537@hotmail.com

SCORE Office (Huntington)
1101 6th Ave., Ste. 220
Huntington, WV 25701-2309
(304)523-4092

SCORE Office (Wheeling)
1310 Market St.
Wheeling, WV 26003
(304)233-2575
Fax: (304)233-1320

Wisconsin

SCORE Office (Fox Cities)
227 S. Walnut St.
Appleton, WI 54913
(920)734-7101
Fax: (920)734-7161

SCORE Office (Beloit)
136 W. Grand Ave., Ste. 100
PO Box 717
Beloit, WI 53511
(608)365-8835
Fax: (608)365-9170

SCORE Office (Eau Claire)
Federal Bldg., Rm. B11
510 S. Barstow St.
Eau Claire, WI 54701
(715)834-1573
E-mail: score@ecol.net
Website: http://www.ecol.net/~score/

SCORE Office (Fond du Lac)
207 N. Main St.
Fond du Lac, WI 54935
(414)921-9500
Fax: (414)921-9559

SCORE Office (Green Bay)
835 Potts Ave.
Green Bay, WI 54304
(414)496-8930
Fax: (414)496-6009

SCORE Office (Janesville)
20 S. Main St., Ste. 11
PO Box 8008
Janesville, WI 53547
(608)757-3160
Fax: (608)757-3170

SCORE Office (La Crosse)
712 Main St.
La Crosse, WI 54602-0219
(608)784-4880

SCORE Office (Madison)
505 S. Rosa Rd.
Madison, WI 53719
(608)441-2820

SCORE Office (Manitowoc)
1515 Memorial Dr.
PO Box 903
Manitowoc, WI 54221-0903
(414)684-5575
Fax: (414)684-1915

SCORE Office (Milwaukee)
310 W. Wisconsin Ave., Ste. 425
Milwaukee, WI 53203
(414)297-3942
Fax: (414)297-1377

SCORE Office (Central Wisconsin)
1224 Lindbergh Ave.
Stevens Point, WI 54481
(715)344-7729

SCORE Office (Superior)
Superior Business Center Inc.
1423 N. 8th St.
Superior, WI 54880
(715)394-7388
Fax: (715)393-7414

SCORE Office (Waukesha)
223 Wisconsin Ave.
Waukesha, WI 53186-4926
(414)542-4249

SCORE Office (Wausau)
300 3rd St., Ste. 200
Wausau, WI 54402-6190
(715)845-6231

SCORE Office (Wisconsin Rapids)
2240 Kingston Rd.
Wisconsin Rapids, WI 54494
(715)423-1830

Wyoming

SCORE Office (Casper)
Federal Bldg., No. 2215
100 East B St.

Casper, WY 82602
(307)261-6529
Fax: (307)261-6530

Venture capital & financing companies

This section contains a listing of financing and loan companies in the United States and Canada. These listing are arranged alphabetically by country, then by state or province, then by city, then by organization name.

Canada

Alberta

Launchworks Inc.
1902J 11th St., S.E.
Calgary, AB, Canada T2G 3G2
(403)269-1119
Fax: (403)269-1141
Website: http://www.launchworks.com

Native Venture Capital Company, Inc.
21 Artist View Point, Box 7
Site 25, RR 12
Calgary, AB, Canada T3E 6W3
(903)208-5380

Miralta Capital Inc.
4445 Calgary Trail South
888 Terrace Plaza Alberta
Edmonton, AB, Canada T6H 5R7
(780)438-3535
Fax: (780)438-3129

Vencap Equities Alberta Ltd.
10180-101st St., Ste. 1980
Edmonton, AB, Canada T5J 3S4
(403)420-1171
Fax: (403)429-2541

British Columbia

Discovery Capital
5th Fl., 1199 West Hastings
Vancouver, BC, Canada V6E 3T5
(604)683-3000
Fax: (604)662-3457
E-mail: info@discoverycapital.com
Website: http://www.discoverycapital.com

Greenstone Venture Partners
1177 West Hastings St.
Ste. 400
Vancouver, BC, Canada V6E 2K3
(604)717-1977
Fax: (604)717-1976
Website: http://www.greenstonevc.com

Growthworks Capital
2600-1055 West Georgia St.
Box 11170 Royal Centre
Vancouver, BC, Canada V6E 3R5
(604)895-7259
Fax: (604)669-7605
Website: http://www.wofund.com

MDS Discovery Venture Management, Inc.
555 W. Eighth Ave., Ste. 305
Vancouver, BC, Canada V5Z 1C6
(604)872-8464
Fax: (604)872-2977
E-mail: info@mds-ventures.com

Ventures West Management Inc.
1285 W. Pender St., Ste. 280
Vancouver, BC, Canada V6E 4B1
(604)688-9495
Fax: (604)687-2145
Website: http://www.ventureswest.com

Nova Scotia

ACF Equity Atlantic Inc.
Purdy's Wharf Tower II
Ste. 2106
Halifax, NS, Canada B3J 3R7
(902)421-1965
Fax: (902)421-1808

Montgomerie, Huck & Co.
146 Bluenose Dr.
PO Box 538
Lunenburg, NS, Canada B0J 2C0
(902)634-7125
Fax: (902)634-7130

Ontario

IPS Industrial Promotion Services Ltd.
60 Columbia Way, Ste. 720
Markham, ON, Canada L3R 0C9
(905)475-9400
Fax: (905)475-5003

Betwin Investments Inc.
Box 23110
Sault Ste. Marie, ON, Canada P6A 6W6
(705)253-0744
Fax: (705)253-0744

Bailey & Company, Inc.
594 Spadina Ave.
Toronto, ON, Canada M5S 2H4
(416)921-6930
Fax: (416)925-4670

BCE Capital
200 Bay St.

South Tower, Ste. 3120
Toronto, ON, Canada M5J 2J2
(416)815-0078
Fax: (416)941-1073
Website: http://www.bcecapital.com

Castlehill Ventures
55 University Ave., Ste. 500
Toronto, ON, Canada M5J 2H7
(416)862-8574
Fax: (416)862-8875

CCFL Mezzanine Partners of Canada
70 University Ave.
Ste. 1450
Toronto, ON, Canada M5J 2M4
(416)977-1450
Fax: (416)977-6764
E-mail: info@ccfl.com
Website: http://www.ccfl.com

Celtic House International
100 Simcoe St., Ste. 100
Toronto, ON, Canada M5H 3G2
(416)542-2436
Fax: (416)542-2435
Website: http://www.celtic-house.com

Clairvest Group Inc.
22 St. Clair Ave. East
Ste. 1700
Toronto, ON, Canada M4T 2S3
(416)925-9270
Fax: (416)925-5753

Crosbie & Co., Inc.
One First Canadian Place
9th Fl.
PO Box 116
Toronto, ON, Canada M5X 1A4
(416)362-7726
Fax: (416)362-3447
E-mail: info@crosbieco.com
Website: http://www.crosbieco.com

Drug Royalty Corp.
Eight King St. East
Ste. 202
Toronto, ON, Canada M5C 1B5
(416)863-1865
Fax: (416)863-5161

Grieve, Horner, Brown & Asculai
8 King St. E, Ste. 1704
Toronto, ON, Canada M5C 1B5
(416)362-7668
Fax: (416)362-7660

Jefferson Partners
77 King St. West
Ste. 4010

PO Box 136
Toronto, ON, Canada M5K 1H1
(416)367-1533
Fax: (416)367-5827
Website: http://www.jefferson.com

J.L. Albright Venture Partners
Canada Trust Tower, 161 Bay St.
Ste. 4440
PO Box 215
Toronto, ON, Canada M5J 2S1
(416)367-2440
Fax: (416)367-4604
Website: http://www.jlaventures.com

McLean Watson Capital Inc.
One First Canadian Place
Ste. 1410
PO Box 129
Toronto, ON, Canada M5X 1A4
(416)363-2000
Fax: (416)363-2010
Website: http://www.mcleanwatson.com

Middlefield Capital Fund
One First Canadian Place
85th Fl.
PO Box 192
Toronto, ON, Canada M5X 1A6
(416)362-0714
Fax: (416)362-7925
Website: http://www.middlefield.com

Mosaic Venture Partners
24 Duncan St.
Ste. 300
Toronto, ON, Canada M5V 3M6
(416)597-8889
Fax: (416)597-2345

Onex Corp.
161 Bay St.
PO Box 700
Toronto, ON, Canada M5J 2S1
(416)362-7711
Fax: (416)362-5765

Penfund Partners Inc.
145 King St. West
Ste. 1920
Toronto, ON, Canada M5H 1J8
(416)865-0300
Fax: (416)364-6912
Website: http://www.penfund.com

Primaxis Technology Ventures Inc.
1 Richmond St. West, 8th Fl.
Toronto, ON, Canada M5H 3W4
(416)313-5210
Fax: (416)313-5218
Website: http://www.primaxis.com

Priveq Capital Funds
240 Duncan Mill Rd., Ste. 602
Toronto, ON, Canada M3B 3P1
(416)447-3330
Fax: (416)447-3331
E-mail: priveq@sympatico.ca

Roynat Ventures
40 King St. West, 26th Fl.
Toronto, ON, Canada M5H 1H1
(416)933-2667
Fax: (416)933-2783
Website: http://www.roynatcapital.com

Tera Capital Corp.
366 Adelaide St. East, Ste. 337
Toronto, ON, Canada M5A 3X9
(416)368-1024
Fax: (416)368-1427

Working Ventures Canadian Fund Inc.
250 Bloor St. East, Ste. 1600
Toronto, ON, Canada M4W 1E6
(416)934-7718
Fax: (416)929-0901
Website: http://www.workingventures.ca

Quebec

Altamira Capital Corp.
202 University
Niveau de Maisoneuve, Bur. 201
Montreal, QC, Canada H3A 2A5
(514)499-1656
Fax: (514)499-9570

Federal Business Development Bank
Venture Capital Division
Five Place Ville Marie, Ste. 600
Montreal, QC, Canada H3B 5E7
(514)283-1896
Fax: (514)283-5455

Hydro-Quebec Capitech Inc.
75 Boul, Rene Levesque Quest
Montreal, QC, Canada H2Z 1A4
(514)289-4783
Fax: (514)289-5420
Website: http://www.hqcapitech.com

Investissement Desjardins
2 complexe Desjardins
C.P. 760
Montreal, QC, Canada H5B 1B8
(514)281-7131
Fax: (514)281-7808
Website: http://www.desjardins.com/id

Marleau Lemire Inc.
One Place Ville-Marie, Ste. 3601
Montreal, QC, Canada H3B 3P2

(514)877-3800
Fax: (514)875-6415

Speirs Consultants Inc.
365 Stanstead
Montreal, QC, Canada H3R 1X5
(514)342-3858
Fax: (514)342-1977

Tecnocap Inc.
4028 Marlowe
Montreal, QC, Canada H4A 3M2
(514)483-6009
Fax: (514)483-6045
Website: http://www.technocap.com

Telsoft Ventures
1000, Rue de la Gauchetiere
Quest, 25eme Etage
Montreal, QC, Canada H3B 4W5
(514)397-8450
Fax: (514)397-8451

Saskatchewan

Saskatchewan Government Growth Fund
1801 Hamilton St., Ste. 1210
Canada Trust Tower
Regina, SK, Canada S4P 4B4
(306)787-2994
Fax: (306)787-2086

United states

Alabama

FHL Capital Corp.
600 20th Street North
Suite 350
Birmingham, AL 35203
(205)328-3098
Fax: (205)323-0001

Harbert Management Corp.
One Riverchase Pkwy. South
Birmingham, AL 35244
(205)987-5500
Fax: (205)987-5707
Website: http://www.harbert.net

Jefferson Capital Fund
PO Box 13129
Birmingham, AL 35213
(205)324-7709

Private Capital Corp.
100 Brookwood Pl., 4th Fl.
Birmingham, AL 35209
(205)879-2722
Fax: (205)879-5121

21st Century Health Ventures
One Health South Pkwy.
Birmingham, AL 35243
(256)268-6250
Fax: (256)970-8928

FJC Growth Capital Corp.
200 W. Side Sq., Ste. 340
Huntsville, AL 35801
(256)922-2918
Fax: (256)922-2909

Hickory Venture Capital Corp.
301 Washington St. NW
Suite 301
Huntsville, AL 35801
(256)539-1931
Fax: (256)539-5130
E-mail: hvcc@hvcc.com
Website: http://www.hvcc.com

Southeastern Technology Fund
7910 South Memorial Pkwy., Ste. F
Huntsville, AL 35802
(256)883-8711
Fax: (256)883-8558

Cordova Ventures
4121 Carmichael Rd., Ste. 301
Montgomery, AL 36106
(334)271-6011
Fax: (334)260-0120
Website: http://www.cordova
ventures.com

Small Business Clinic of Alabama/AG Bartholomew & Associates
PO Box 231074
Montgomery, AL 36123-1074
(334)284-3640

Arizona

Miller Capital Corp.
4909 E. McDowell Rd.
Phoenix, AZ 85008
(602)225-0504
Fax: (602)225-9024
Website: http://www.themiller
group.com

The Columbine Venture Funds
9449 North 90th St., Ste. 200
Scottsdale, AZ 85258
(602)661-9222
Fax: (602)661-6262

Koch Ventures
17767 N. Perimeter Dr., Ste. 101
Scottsdale, AZ 85255
(480)419-3600

Fax: (480)419-3606
Website: http://www.kochventures.com

McKee & Co.
7702 E. Doubletree Ranch Rd.
Suite 230
Scottsdale, AZ 85258
(480)368-0333
Fax: (480)607-7446

Merita Capital Ltd.
7350 E. Stetson Dr., Ste. 108-A
Scottsdale, AZ 85251
(480)947-8700
Fax: (480)947-8766

Valley Ventures / Arizona Growth Partners L.P.
6720 N. Scottsdale Rd., Ste. 208
Scottsdale, AZ 85253
(480)661-6600
Fax: (480)661-6262

Estreetcapital.com
660 South Mill Ave., Ste. 315
Tempe, AZ 85281
(480)968-8400
Fax: (480)968-8480
Website: http://www.estreetcapital.com

Coronado Venture Fund
PO Box 65420
Tucson, AZ 85728-5420
(520)577-3764
Fax: (520)299-8491

Arkansas

Arkansas Capital Corp.
225 South Pulaski St.
Little Rock, AR 72201
(501)374-9247
Fax: (501)374-9425
Website: http://www.arcapital.com

California

Sundance Venture Partners, L.P.
100 Clocktower Place, Ste. 130
Carmel, CA 93923
(831)625-6500
Fax: (831)625-6590

Westar Capital (Costa Mesa)
949 South Coast Dr., Ste. 650
Costa Mesa, CA 92626
(714)481-5160
Fax: (714)481-5166
E-mail: mailbox@westarcapital.com
Website: http://www.westarcapital.com

Alpine Technology Ventures
20300 Stevens Creek Boulevard, Ste. 495
Cupertino, CA 95014
(408)725-1810
Fax: (408)725-1207
Website: http://www.alpineventures.com

Bay Partners
10600 N. De Anza Blvd.
Cupertino, CA 95014-2031
(408)725-2444
Fax: (408)446-4502
Website: http://www.baypartners.com

Novus Ventures
20111 Stevens Creek Blvd., Ste. 130
Cupertino, CA 95014
(408)252-3900
Fax: (408)252-1713
Website: http://www.novusventures.com

Triune Capital
19925 Stevens Creek Blvd., Ste. 200
Cupertino, CA 95014
(310)284-6800
Fax: (310)284-3290

Acorn Ventures
268 Bush St., Ste. 2829
Daly City, CA 94014
(650)994-7801
Fax: (650)994-3305
Website: http://www.acornventures.com

Digital Media Campus
2221 Park Place
El Segundo, CA 90245
(310)426-8000
Fax: (310)426-8010
E-mail: info@thecampus.com
Website: http://www.digital
mediacampus.com

BankAmerica Ventures / BA Venture Partners
950 Tower Ln., Ste. 700
Foster City, CA 94404
(650)378-6000
Fax: (650)378-6040
Website: http://
www.baventurepartners.com

Starting Point Partners
666 Portofino Lane
Foster City, CA 94404
(650)722-1035
Website: http://www.startingpoint
partners.com

Opportunity Capital Partners
2201 Walnut Ave., Ste. 210

Fremont, CA 94538
(510)795-7000
Fax: (510)494-5439
Website: http://www.ocpcapital.com

Imperial Ventures Inc.
9920 S. La Cienega Boulevar, 14th Fl.
Inglewood, CA 90301
(310)417-5409
Fax: (310)338-6115

Ventana Global (Irvine)
18881 Von Karman Ave., Ste. 1150
Irvine, CA 92612
(949)476-2204
Fax: (949)752-0223
Website: http://www.ventanaglobal.com

Integrated Consortium Inc.
50 Ridgecrest Rd.
Kentfield, CA 94904
(415)925-0386
Fax: (415)461-2726

Enterprise Partners
979 Ivanhoe Ave., Ste. 550
La Jolla, CA 92037
(858)454-8833
Fax: (858)454-2489
Website: http://www.epvc.com

Domain Associates
28202 Cabot Rd., Ste. 200
Laguna Niguel, CA 92677
(949)347-2446
Fax: (949)347-9720
Website: http://www.domainvc.com

Cascade Communications Ventures
60 E. Sir Francis Drake Blvd., Ste. 300
Larkspur, CA 94939
(415)925-6500
Fax: (415)925-6501

Allegis Capital
One First St., Ste. Two
Los Altos, CA 94022
(650)917-5900
Fax: (650)917-5901
Website: http://www.allegiscapital.com

Aspen Ventures
1000 Fremont Ave., Ste. 200
Los Altos, CA 94024
(650)917-5670
Fax: (650)917-5677
Website: http://www.aspenventures.com

AVI Capital L.P.
1 First St., Ste. 2
Los Altos, CA 94022

(650)949-9862
Fax: (650)949-8510
Website: http://www.avicapital.com

Bastion Capital Corp.
1999 Avenue of the Stars, Ste. 2960
Los Angeles, CA 90067
(310)788-5700
Fax: (310)277-7582
E-mail: ga@bastioncapital.com
Website: http://www.bastioncapital.com

Davis Group
PO Box 69953
Los Angeles, CA 90069-0953
(310)659-6327
Fax: (310)659-6337

Developers Equity Corp.
1880 Century Park East, Ste. 211
Los Angeles, CA 90067
(213)277-0300

Far East Capital Corp.
350 S. Grand Ave., Ste. 4100
Los Angeles, CA 90071
(213)687-1361
Fax: (213)617-7939
E-mail: free@fareastnationalbank.com

Kline Hawkes & Co.
11726 San Vicente Blvd., Ste. 300
Los Angeles, CA 90049
(310)442-4700
Fax: (310)442-4707
Website: http://www.klinehawkes.com

Lawrence Financial Group
701 Teakwood
PO Box 491773
Los Angeles, CA 90049
(310)471-4060
Fax: (310)472-3155

Riordan Lewis & Haden
300 S. Grand Ave., 29th Fl.
Los Angeles, CA 90071
(213)229-8500
Fax: (213)229-8597

Union Venture Corp.
445 S. Figueroa St., 9th Fl.
Los Angeles, CA 90071
(213)236-4092
Fax: (213)236-6329

Wedbush Capital Partners
1000 Wilshire Blvd.
Los Angeles, CA 90017
(213)688-4545
Fax: (213)688-6642
Website: http://www.wedbush.com

Advent International Corp.
2180 Sand Hill Rd., Ste. 420
Menlo Park, CA 94025
(650)233-7500
Fax: (650)233-7515
Website: http://www.adventinter
national.com

Altos Ventures
2882 Sand Hill Rd., Ste. 100
Menlo Park, CA 94025
(650)234-9771
Fax: (650)233-9821
Website: http://www.altosvc.com

Applied Technology
1010 El Camino Real, Ste. 300
Menlo Park, CA 94025
(415)326-8622
Fax: (415)326-8163

APV Technology Partners
535 Middlefield, Ste. 150
Menlo Park, CA 94025
(650)327-7871
Fax: (650)327-7631
Website: http://www.apvtp.com

August Capital Management
2480 Sand Hill Rd., Ste. 101
Menlo Park, CA 94025
(650)234-9900
Fax: (650)234-9910
Website: http://www.augustcap.com

Baccharis Capital Inc.
2420 Sand Hill Rd., Ste. 100
Menlo Park, CA 94025
(650)324-6844
Fax: (650)854-3025

Benchmark Capital
2480 Sand Hill Rd., Ste. 200
Menlo Park, CA 94025
(650)854-8180
Fax: (650)854-8183
E-mail: info@benchmark.com
Website: http://www.benchmark.com

Bessemer Venture Partners (Menlo Park)
535 Middlefield Rd., Ste. 245
Menlo Park, CA 94025
(650)853-7000
Fax: (650)853-7001
Website: http://www.bvp.com

The Cambria Group
1600 El Camino Real Rd., Ste. 155
Menlo Park, CA 94025
(650)329-8600

Fax: (650)329-8601
Website: http://www.cambriagroup.com

Canaan Partners
2884 Sand Hill Rd., Ste. 115
Menlo Park, CA 94025
(650)854-8092
Fax: (650)854-8127
Website: http://www.canaan.com

Capstone Ventures
3000 Sand Hill Rd., Bldg. One, Ste. 290
Menlo Park, CA 94025
(650)854-2523
Fax: (650)854-9010
Website: http://www.capstonevc.com

Comdisco Venture Group (Silicon Valley)
3000 Sand Hill Rd., Bldg. 1, Ste. 155
Menlo Park, CA 94025
(650)854-9484
Fax: (650)854-4026

Commtech International
535 Middlefield Rd., Ste. 200
Menlo Park, CA 94025
(650)328-0190
Fax: (650)328-6442

Compass Technology Partners
1550 El Camino Real, Ste. 275
Menlo Park, CA 94025-4111
(650)322-7595
Fax: (650)322-0588
Website: http://www.compass
techpartners.com

Convergence Partners
3000 Sand Hill Rd., Ste. 235
Menlo Park, CA 94025
(650)854-3010
Fax: (650)854-3015
Website: http://www.conver
gencepartners.com

The Dakota Group
PO Box 1025
Menlo Park, CA 94025
(650)853-0600
Fax: (650)851-4899
E-mail: info@dakota.com

Delphi Ventures
3000 Sand Hill Rd.
Bldg. One, Ste. 135
Menlo Park, CA 94025
(650)854-9650
Fax: (650)854-2961
Website: http://www.delphiventures.com

El Dorado Ventures
2884 Sand Hill Rd., Ste. 121
Menlo Park, CA 94025
(650)854-1200
Fax: (650)854-1202
Website: http://www.eldorado
ventures.com

Glynn Ventures
3000 Sand Hill Rd., Bldg. 4, Ste. 235
Menlo Park, CA 94025
(650)854-2215

Indosuez Ventures
2180 Sand Hill Rd., Ste. 450
Menlo Park, CA 94025
(650)854-0587
Fax: (650)323-5561
Website: http://www.indosuez
ventures.com

Institutional Venture Partners
3000 Sand Hill Rd., Bldg. 2, Ste. 290
Menlo Park, CA 94025
(650)854-0132
Fax: (650)854-5762
Website: http://www.ivp.com

Interwest Partners (Menlo Park)
3000 Sand Hill Rd., Bldg. 3, Ste. 255
Menlo Park, CA 94025-7112
(650)854-8585
Fax: (650)854-4706
Website: http://www.interwest.com

**Kleiner Perkins Caufield & Byers
(Menlo Park)**
2750 Sand Hill Rd.
Menlo Park, CA 94025
(650)233-2750
Fax: (650)233-0300
Website: http://www.kpcb.com

Magic Venture Capital LLC
1010 El Camino Real, Ste. 300
Menlo Park, CA 94025
(650)325-4149

Matrix Partners
2500 Sand Hill Rd., Ste. 113
Menlo Park, CA 94025
(650)854-3131
Fax: (650)854-3296
Website: http://www.matrixpartners.com

Mayfield Fund
2800 Sand Hill Rd.
Menlo Park, CA 94025
(650)854-5560
Fax: (650)854-5712
Website: http://www.mayfield.com

**McCown De Leeuw and Co. (Menlo
Park)**
3000 Sand Hill Rd., Bldg. 3, Ste. 290
Menlo Park, CA 94025-7111
(650)854-6000
Fax: (650)854-0853
Website: http://www.mdcpartners.com

Menlo Ventures
3000 Sand Hill Rd., Bldg. 4, Ste. 100
Menlo Park, CA 94025
(650)854-8540
Fax: (650)854-7059
Website: http://www.menloventures.com

Merrill Pickard Anderson & Eyre
2480 Sand Hill Rd., Ste. 200
Menlo Park, CA 94025
(650)854-8600
Fax: (650)854-0345

**New Enterprise Associates (Menlo
Park)**
2490 Sand Hill Rd.
Menlo Park, CA 94025
(650)854-9499
Fax: (650)854-9397
Website: http://www.nea.com

Onset Ventures
2400 Sand Hill Rd., Ste. 150
Menlo Park, CA 94025
(650)529-0700
Fax: (650)529-0777
Website: http://www.onset.com

Paragon Venture Partners
3000 Sand Hill Rd., Bldg. 1, Ste. 275
Menlo Park, CA 94025
(650)854-8000
Fax: (650)854-7260

**Pathfinder Venture Capital Funds
(Menlo Park)**
3000 Sand Hill Rd., Bldg. 3, Ste. 255
Menlo Park, CA 94025
(650)854-0650
Fax: (650)854-4706

Rocket Ventures
3000 Sandhill Rd., Bldg. 1, Ste. 170
Menlo Park, CA 94025
(650)561-9100
Fax: (650)561-9183
Website: http://www.rocketventures.com

Sequoia Capital
3000 Sand Hill Rd., Bldg. 4, Ste. 280
Menlo Park, CA 94025
(650)854-3927
Fax: (650)854-2977

E-mail: sequoia@sequoiacap.com
Website: http://www.sequoiacap.com

Sierra Ventures
3000 Sand Hill Rd., Bldg. 4, Ste. 210
Menlo Park, CA 94025
(650)854-1000
Fax: (650)854-5593
Website: http://www.sierraventures.com

Sigma Partners
2884 Sand Hill Rd., Ste. 121
Menlo Park, CA 94025-7022
(650)853-1700
Fax: (650)853-1717
E-mail: info@sigmapartners.com
Website: http://www.sigmapartners.com

Sprout Group (Menlo Park)
3000 Sand Hill Rd.
Bldg. 3, Ste. 170
Menlo Park, CA 94025
(650)234-2700
Fax: (650)234-2779
Website: http://www.sproutgroup.com

TA Associates (Menlo Park)
70 Willow Rd., Ste. 100
Menlo Park, CA 94025
(650)328-1210
Fax: (650)326-4933
Website: http://www.ta.com

Thompson Clive & Partners Ltd.
3000 Sand Hill Rd., Bldg. 1, Ste. 185
Menlo Park, CA 94025-7102
(650)854-0314
Fax: (650)854-0670
E-mail: mail@tcvc.com
Website: http://www.tcvc.com

Trinity Ventures Ltd.
3000 Sand Hill Rd., Bldg. 1, Ste. 240
Menlo Park, CA 94025
(650)854-9500
Fax: (650)854-9501
Website: http://www.trinityventures.com

U.S. Venture Partners
2180 Sand Hill Rd., Ste. 300
Menlo Park, CA 94025
(650)854-9080
Fax: (650)854-3018
Website: http://www.usvp.com

USVP-Schlein Marketing Fund
2180 Sand Hill Rd., Ste. 300
Menlo Park, CA 94025
(415)854-9080
Fax: (415)854-3018
Website: http://www.usvp.com

Venrock Associates
2494 Sand Hill Rd., Ste. 200
Menlo Park, CA 94025
(650)561-9580
Fax: (650)561-9180
Website: http://www.venrock.com

Brad Peery Capital Inc.
145 Chapel Pkwy.
Mill Valley, CA 94941
(415)389-0625
Fax: (415)389-1336

Dot Edu Ventures
650 Castro St., Ste. 270
Mountain View, CA 94041
(650)575-5638
Fax: (650)325-5247
Website: http://www.dotedu
ventures.com

Forrest, Binkley & Brown
840 Newport Ctr. Dr., Ste. 480
Newport Beach, CA 92660
(949)729-3222
Fax: (949)729-3226
Website: http://www.fbbvc.com

Marwit Capital LLC
180 Newport Center Dr., Ste. 200
Newport Beach, CA 92660
(949)640-6234
Fax: (949)720-8077
Website: http://www.marwit.com

Kaiser Permanente / National Venture Development
1800 Harrison St., 22nd Fl.
Oakland, CA 94612
(510)267-4010
Fax: (510)267-4036
Website: http://www.kpventures.com

Nu Capital Access Group, Ltd.
7677 Oakport St., Ste. 105
Oakland, CA 94621
(510)635-7345
Fax: (510)635-7068

Inman and Bowman
4 Orinda Way, Bldg. D, Ste. 150
Orinda, CA 94563
(510)253-1611
Fax: (510)253-9037

Accel Partners (San Francisco)
428 University Ave.
Palo Alto, CA 94301
(650)614-4800
Fax: (650)614-4880
Website: http://www.accel.com

Advanced Technology Ventures
485 Ramona St., Ste. 200
Palo Alto, CA 94301
(650)321-8601
Fax: (650)321-0934
Website: http://www.atvcapital.com

Anila Fund
400 Channing Ave.
Palo Alto, CA 94301
(650)833-5790
Fax: (650)833-0590
Website: http://www.anila.com

Asset Management Company Venture Capital
2275 E. Bayshore, Ste. 150
Palo Alto, CA 94303
(650)494-7400
Fax: (650)856-1826
E-mail: postmaster@assetman.com
Website: http://www.assetman.com

BancBoston Capital / BancBoston Ventures
435 Tasso St., Ste. 250
Palo Alto, CA 94305
(650)470-4100
Fax: (650)853-1425
Website: http://www.bancboston
capital.com

Charter Ventures
525 University Ave., Ste. 1400
Palo Alto, CA 94301
(650)325-6953
Fax: (650)325-4762
Website: http://www.charterventures.com

Communications Ventures
505 Hamilton Avenue, Ste. 305
Palo Alto, CA 94301
(650)325-9600
Fax: (650)325-9608
Website: http://www.comven.com

HMS Group
2468 Embarcadero Way
Palo Alto, CA 94303-3313
(650)856-9862
Fax: (650)856-9864

Jafco America Ventures, Inc.
505 Hamilton Ste. 310
Palto Alto, CA 94301
(650)463-8800
Fax: (650)463-8801
Website: http://www.jafco.com

New Vista Capital
540 Cowper St., Ste. 200

Palo Alto, CA 94301
(650)329-9333
Fax: (650)328-9434
E-mail: fgreene@nvcap.com
Website: http://www.nvcap.com

Norwest Equity Partners (Palo Alto)
245 Lytton Ave., Ste. 250
Palo Alto, CA 94301-1426
(650)321-8000
Fax: (650)321-8010
Website: http://www.norwestvp.com

Oak Investment Partners
525 University Ave., Ste. 1300
Palo Alto, CA 94301
(650)614-3700
Fax: (650)328-6345
Website: http://www.oakinv.com

Patricof & Co. Ventures, Inc. (Palo Alto)
2100 Geng Rd., Ste. 150
Palo Alto, CA 94303
(650)494-9944
Fax: (650)494-6751
Website: http://www.patricof.com

RWI Group
835 Page Mill Rd.
Palo Alto, CA 94304
(650)251-1800
Fax: (650)213-8660
Website: http://www.rwigroup.com

Summit Partners (Palo Alto)
499 Hamilton Ave., Ste. 200
Palo Alto, CA 94301
(650)321-1166
Fax: (650)321-1188
Website: http://www.summit
partners.com

Sutter Hill Ventures
755 Page Mill Rd., Ste. A-200
Palo Alto, CA 94304
(650)493-5600
Fax: (650)858-1854
E-mail: shv@shv.com

Vanguard Venture Partners
525 University Ave., Ste. 600
Palo Alto, CA 94301
(650)321-2900
Fax: (650)321-2902
Website: http://www.vanguard
ventures.com

Venture Growth Associates
2479 East Bayshore St., Ste. 710
Palo Alto, CA 94303

(650)855-9100
Fax: (650)855-9104

Worldview Technology Partners
435 Tasso St., Ste. 120
Palo Alto, CA 94301
(650)322-3800
Fax: (650)322-3880
Website: http://www.worldview.com

Draper, Fisher, Jurvetson / Draper Associates
400 Seaport Ct., Ste.250
Redwood City, CA 94063
(415)599-9000
Fax: (415)599-9726
Website: http://www.dfj.com

Gabriel Venture Partners
350 Marine Pkwy., Ste. 200
Redwood Shores, CA 94065
(650)551-5000
Fax: (650)551-5001
Website: http://www.gabrielvp.com

Hallador Venture Partners, L.L.C.
740 University Ave., Ste. 110
Sacramento, CA 95825-6710
(916)920-0191
Fax: (916)920-5188
E-mail: chris@hallador.com

Emerald Venture Group
12396 World Trade Dr., Ste. 116
San Diego, CA 92128
(858)451-1001
Fax: (858)451-1003
Website: http://www.emerald
venture.com

Forward Ventures
9255 Towne Centre Dr.
San Diego, CA 92121
(858)677-6077
Fax: (858)452-8799
E-mail: info@forwardventure.com
Website: http://www.forward
venture.com

Idanta Partners Ltd.
4660 La Jolla Village Dr., Ste. 850
San Diego, CA 92122
(619)452-9690
Fax: (619)452-2013
Website: http://www.idanta.com

Kingsbury Associates
3655 Nobel Dr., Ste. 490
San Diego, CA 92122
(858)677-0600
Fax: (858)677-0800

Kyocera International Inc.
Corporate Development
8611 Balboa Ave.
San Diego, CA 92123
(858)576-2600
Fax: (858)492-1456

Sorrento Associates, Inc.
4370 LaJolla Village Dr., Ste. 1040
San Diego, CA 92122
(619)452-3100
Fax: (619)452-7607
Website: http://www.sorrento
ventures.com

Western States Investment Group
9191 Towne Ctr. Dr., Ste. 310
San Diego, CA 92122
(619)678-0800
Fax: (619)678-0900

Aberdare Ventures
One Embarcadero Center, Ste. 4000
San Francisco, CA 94111
(415)392-7442
Fax: (415)392-4264
Website: http://www.aberdare.com

Acacia Venture Partners
101 California St., Ste. 3160
San Francisco, CA 94111
(415)433-4200
Fax: (415)433-4250
Website: http://www.acaciavp.com

Access Venture Partners
319 Laidley St.
San Francisco, CA 94131
(415)586-0132
Fax: (415)392-6310
Website: http://www.access
venturepartners.com

Alta Partners
One Embarcadero Center, Ste. 4050
San Francisco, CA 94111
(415)362-4022
Fax: (415)362-6178
E-mail: alta@altapartners.com
Website: http://www.altapartners.com

Bangert Dawes Reade Davis & Thom
220 Montgomery St., Ste. 424
San Francisco, CA 94104
(415)954-9900
Fax: (415)954-9901
E-mail: bdrdt@pacbell.net

Berkeley International Capital Corp.
650 California St., Ste. 2800
San Francisco, CA 94108-2609

(415)249-0450
Fax: (415)392-3929
Website: http://www.berkeleyvc.com

Blueprint Ventures LLC
456 Montgomery St., 22nd Fl.
San Francisco, CA 94104
(415)901-4000
Fax: (415)901-4035
Website: http://www.blue
printventures.com

Blumberg Capital Ventures
580 Howard St., Ste. 401
San Francisco, CA 94105
(415)905-5007
Fax: (415)357-5027
Website: http://www.blumberg-
capital.com

Burr, Egan, Deleage, and Co. (San Francisco)
1 Embarcadero Center, Ste. 4050
San Francisco, CA 94111
(415)362-4022
Fax: (415)362-6178

Burrill & Company
120 Montgomery St., Ste. 1370
San Francisco, CA 94104
(415)743-3160
Fax: (415)743-3161
Website: http://www.burrillandco.com

CMEA Ventures
235 Montgomery St., Ste. 920
San Francisco, CA 94401
(415)352-1520
Fax: (415)352-1524
Website: http://www.cmeaventures.com

Crocker Capital
1 Post St., Ste. 2500
San Francisco, CA 94101
(415)956-5250
Fax: (415)959-5710

Dominion Ventures, Inc.
44 Montgomery St., Ste. 4200
San Francisco, CA 94104
(415)362-4890
Fax: (415)394-9245

Dorset Capital
Pier 1
Bay 2
San Francisco, CA 94111
(415)398-7101
Fax: (415)398-7141
Website: http://www.dorsetcapital.com

Gatx Capital
Four Embarcadero Center, Ste. 2200
San Francisco, CA 94904
(415)955-3200
Fax: (415)955-3449

IMinds
135 Main St., Ste. 1350
San Francisco, CA 94105
(415)547-0000
Fax: (415)227-0300
Website: http://www.iminds.com

LF International Inc.
360 Post St., Ste. 705
San Francisco, CA 94108
(415)399-0110
Fax: (415)399-9222
Website: http://www.lfvc.com

Newbury Ventures
535 Pacific Ave., 2nd Fl.
San Francisco, CA 94133
(415)296-7408
Fax: (415)296-7416
Website: http://www.newburyven.com

Quest Ventures (San Francisco)
333 Bush St., Ste. 1750
San Francisco, CA 94104
(415)782-1414
Fax: (415)782-1415

Robertson-Stephens Co.
555 California St., Ste. 2600
San Francisco, CA 94104
(415)781-9700
Fax: (415)781-2556
Website: http://www.omegaad
ventures.com

Rosewood Capital, L.P.
One Maritime Plaza, Ste. 1330
San Francisco, CA 94111-3503
(415)362-5526
Fax: (415)362-1192
Website: http://www.rosewoodvc.com

Ticonderoga Capital Inc.
555 California St., No. 4950
San Francisco, CA 94104
(415)296-7900
Fax: (415)296-8956

21st Century Internet Venture Partners
Two South Park
2nd Floor
San Francisco, CA 94107
(415)512-1221
Fax: (415)512-2650
Website: http://www.21vc.com

VK Ventures
600 California St., Ste.1700
San Francisco, CA 94111
(415)391-5600
Fax: (415)397-2744

Walden Group of Venture Capital Funds
750 Battery St., Seventh Floor
San Francisco, CA 94111
(415)391-7225
Fax: (415)391-7262

Acer Technology Ventures
2641 Orchard Pkwy.
San Jose, CA 95134
(408)433-4945
Fax: (408)433-5230

Authosis
226 Airport Pkwy., Ste. 405
San Jose, CA 95110
(650)814-3603
Website: http://www.authosis.com

Western Technology Investment
2010 N. First St., Ste. 310
San Jose, CA 95131
(408)436-8577
Fax: (408)436-8625
E-mail: mktg@westerntech.com

Drysdale Enterprises
177 Bovet Rd., Ste. 600
San Mateo, CA 94402
(650)341-6336
Fax: (650)341-1329
E-mail: drysdale@aol.com

Greylock
2929 Campus Dr., Ste. 400
San Mateo, CA 94401
(650)493-5525
Fax: (650)493-5575
Website: http://www.greylock.com

Technology Funding
2000 Alameda de las Pulgas, Ste. 250
San Mateo, CA 94403
(415)345-2200
Fax: (415)345-1797

2M Invest Inc.
1875 S. Grant St.
Suite 750
San Mateo, CA 94402
(650)655-3765
Fax: (650)372-9107
E-mail: 2minfo@2minvest.com
Website: http://www.2minvest.com

Phoenix Growth Capital Corp.
2401 Kerner Blvd.
San Rafael, CA 94901
(415)485-4569
Fax: (415)485-4663

NextGen Partners LLC
1705 East Valley Rd.
Santa Barbara, CA 93108
(805)969-8540
Fax: (805)969-8542
Website: http://www.nextgen
partners.com

Denali Venture Capital
1925 Woodland Ave.
Santa Clara, CA 95050
(408)690-4838
Fax: (408)247-6979
E-mail: wael@denaliventurecapital.com
Website: http://www.denali
venturecapital.com

Dotcom Ventures LP
3945 Freedom Circle, Ste. 740
Santa Clara, CA 95045
(408)919-9855
Fax: (408)919-9857
Website: http://www.dotcom
venturesatl.com

Silicon Valley Bank
3003 Tasman
Santa Clara, CA 95054
(408)654-7400
Fax: (408)727-8728

Al Shugart International
920 41st Ave.
Santa Cruz, CA 95062
(831)479-7852
Fax: (831)479-7852
Website: http://www.alshugart.com

Leonard Mautner Associates
1434 Sixth St.
Santa Monica, CA 90401
(213)393-9788
Fax: (310)459-9918

Palomar Ventures
100 Wilshire Blvd., Ste. 450
Santa Monica, CA 90401
(310)260-6050
Fax: (310)656-4150
Website: http://www.palomar
ventures.com

Medicus Venture Partners
12930 Saratoga Ave., Ste. D8
Saratoga, CA 95070

(408)447-8600
Fax: (408)447-8599
Website: http://www.medicusvc.com

Redleaf Venture Management
14395 Saratoga Ave., Ste. 130
Saratoga, CA 95070
(408)868-0800
Fax: (408)868-0810
E-mail: nancy@redleaf.com
Website: http://www.redleaf.com

Artemis Ventures
207 Second St., Ste. E
3rd Fl.
Sausalito, CA 94965
(415)289-2500
Fax: (415)289-1789
Website: http://www.artemisventures.com

Deucalion Venture Partners
19501 Brooklime
Sonoma, CA 95476
(707)938-4974
Fax: (707)938-8921

Windward Ventures
PO Box 7688
Thousand Oaks, CA 91359-7688
(805)497-3332
Fax: (805)497-9331

National Investment Management, Inc.
2601 Airport Dr., Ste.210
Torrance, CA 90505
(310)784-7600
Fax: (310)784-7605

Southern California Ventures
406 Amapola Ave. Ste. 125
Torrance, CA 90501
(310)787-4381
Fax: (310)787-4382

Sandton Financial Group
21550 Oxnard St., Ste. 300
Woodland Hills, CA 91367
(818)702-9283

Woodside Fund
850 Woodside Dr.
Woodside, CA 94062
(650)368-5545
Fax: (650)368-2416
Website: http://www.woodsidefund.com

Colorado

Colorado Venture Management
Ste. 300
Boulder, CO 80301

(303)440-4055
Fax: (303)440-4636

Dean & Associates
4362 Apple Way
Boulder, CO 80301
Fax: (303)473-9900

Roser Ventures LLC
1105 Spruce St.
Boulder, CO 80302
(303)443-6436
Fax: (303)443-1885
Website: http://www.roserventures.com

Sequel Venture Partners
4430 Arapahoe Ave., Ste. 220
Boulder, CO 80303
(303)546-0400
Fax: (303)546-9728
E-mail: tom@sequelvc.com
Website: http://www.sequelvc.com

New Venture Resources
445C E. Cheyenne Mtn. Blvd.
Colorado Springs, CO 80906-4570
(719)598-9272
Fax: (719)598-9272

The Centennial Funds
1428 15th St.
Denver, CO 80202-1318
(303)405-7500
Fax: (303)405-7575
Website: http://www.centennial.com

Rocky Mountain Capital Partners
1125 17th St., Ste. 2260
Denver, CO 80202
(303)291-5200
Fax: (303)291-5327

Sandlot Capital LLC
600 South Cherry St., Ste. 525
Denver, CO 80246
(303)893-3400
Fax: (303)893-3403
Website: http://www.sandlotcapital.com

Wolf Ventures
50 South Steele St., Ste. 777
Denver, CO 80209
(303)321-4800
Fax: (303)321-4848
E-mail: businessplan@wolf
ventures.com
Website: http://www.wolfventures.com

The Columbine Venture Funds
5460 S. Quebec St., Ste. 270
Englewood, CO 80111

(303)694-3222
Fax: (303)694-9007

Investment Securities of Colorado, Inc.
4605 Denice Dr.
Englewood, CO 80111
(303)796-9192

Kinship Partners
6300 S. Syracuse Way, Ste. 484
Englewood, CO 80111
(303)694-0268
Fax: (303)694-1707
E-mail: block@vailsys.com

Boranco Management, L.L.C.
1528 Hillside Dr.
Fort Collins, CO 80524-1969
(970)221-2297
Fax: (970)221-4787

Aweida Ventures
890 West Cherry St., Ste. 220
Louisville, CO 80027
(303)664-9520
Fax: (303)664-9530
Website: http://www.aweida.com

Access Venture Partners
8787 Turnpike Dr., Ste. 260
Westminster, CO 80030
(303)426-8899
Fax: (303)426-8828

Medmax Ventures LP
1 Northwestern Dr., Ste. 203
Bloomfield, CT 06002
(860)286-2960
Fax: (860)286-9960

James B. Kobak & Co.
Four Mansfield Place
Darien, CT 06820
(203)656-3471
Fax: (203)655-2905

Orien Ventures
1 Post Rd.
Fairfield, CT 06430
(203)259-9933
Fax: (203)259-5288

ABP Acquisition Corporation
115 Maple Ave.
Greenwich, CT 06830
(203)625-8287
Fax: (203)447-6187

Catterton Partners
9 Greenwich Office Park
Greenwich, CT 06830
(203)629-4901

Fax: (203)629-4903
Website: http://www.cpequity.com

Consumer Venture Partners
3 Pickwick Plz.
Greenwich, CT 06830
(203)629-8800
Fax: (203)629-2019

Insurance Venture Partners
31 Brookside Dr., Ste. 211
Greenwich, CT 06830
(203)861-0030
Fax: (203)861-2745

The NTC Group
Three Pickwick Plaza
Ste. 200
Greenwich, CT 06830
(203)862-2800
Fax: (203)622-6538

Regulus International Capital Co., Inc.
140 Greenwich Ave.
Greenwich, CT 06830
(203)625-9700
Fax: (203)625-9706

Axiom Venture Partners
City Place II
185 Asylum St., 17th Fl.
Hartford, CT 06103
(860)548-7799
Fax: (860)548-7797
Website: http://www.axiomventures.com

Conning Capital Partners
City Place II
185 Asylum St.
Hartford, CT 06103-4105
(860)520-1289
Fax: (860)520-1299
E-mail: pe@conning.com
Website: http://www.conning.com

First New England Capital L.P.
100 Pearl St.
Hartford, CT 06103
(860)293-3333
Fax: (860)293-3338
E-mail: info@firstnewenglandcapital.com
Website: http://www.firstnewengland
capital.com

Northeast Ventures
One State St., Ste. 1720
Hartford, CT 06103
(860)547-1414
Fax: (860)246-8755

Windward Holdings
38 Sylvan Rd.
Madison, CT 06443
(203)245-6870
Fax: (203)245-6865

Advanced Materials Partners, Inc.
45 Pine St.
PO Box 1022
New Canaan, CT 06840
(203)966-6415
Fax: (203)966-8448
E-mail: wkb@amplink.com

RFE Investment Partners
36 Grove St.
New Canaan, CT 06840
(203)966-2800
Fax: (203)966-3109
Website: http://www.rfeip.com

Connecticut Innovations, Inc.
999 West St.
Rocky Hill, CT 06067
(860)563-5851
Fax: (860)563-4877
E-mail: pamela.hartley@ctin
novations.com
Website: http://www.ctinnovations.com

Canaan Partners
105 Rowayton Ave.
Rowayton, CT 06853
(203)855-0400
Fax: (203)854-9117
Website: http://www.canaan.com

Landmark Partners, Inc.
10 Mill Pond Ln.
Simsbury, CT 06070
(860)651-9760
Fax: (860)651-8890
Website: http://
www.landmarkpartners.com

Sweeney & Company
PO Box 567
Southport, CT 06490
(203)255-0220
Fax: (203)255-0220
E-mail: sweeney@connix.com

Baxter Associates, Inc.
PO Box 1333
Stamford, CT 06904
(203)323-3143
Fax: (203)348-0622

Beacon Partners Inc.
6 Landmark Sq., 4th Fl.
Stamford, CT 06901-2792

(203)359-5776
Fax: (203)359-5876

Collinson, Howe, and Lennox, LLC
1055 Washington Blvd., 5th Fl.
Stamford, CT 06901
(203)324-7700
Fax: (203)324-3636
E-mail: info@chlmedical.com
Website: http://www.chlmedical.com

Prime Capital Management Co.
550 West Ave.
Stamford, CT 06902
(203)964-0642
Fax: (203)964-0862

Saugatuck Capital Co.
1 Canterbury Green
Stamford, CT 06901
(203)348-6669
Fax: (203)324-6995
Website: http://www.sauga
tuckcapital.com

Soundview Financial Group Inc.
22 Gatehouse Rd.
Stamford, CT 06902
(203)462-7200
Fax: (203)462-7350
Website: http://www.sndv.com

TSG Ventures, L.L.C.
177 Broad St., 12th Fl.
Stamford, CT 06901
(203)406-1500
Fax: (203)406-1590

Whitney & Company
177 Broad St.
Stamford, CT 06901
(203)973-1400
Fax: (203)973-1422
Website: http://www.jhwhitney.com

Cullinane & Donnelly Venture Partners L.P.
970 Farmington Ave.
West Hartford, CT 06107
(860)521-7811

The Crestview Investment and Financial Group
431 Post Rd. E, Ste. 1
Westport, CT 06880-4403
(203)222-0333
Fax: (203)222-0000

Marketcorp Venture Associates, L.P. (MCV)
274 Riverside Ave.
Westport, CT 06880

(203)222-3030
Fax: (203)222-3033

Oak Investment Partners (Westport)
1 Gorham Island
Westport, CT 06880
(203)226-8346
Fax: (203)227-0372
Website: http://www.oakinv.com

Oxford Bioscience Partners
315 Post Rd. W
Westport, CT 06880-5200
(203)341-3300
Fax: (203)341-3309
Website: http://www.oxbio.com

Prince Ventures (Westport)
25 Ford Rd.
Westport, CT 06880
(203)227-8332
Fax: (203)226-5302

LTI Venture Leasing Corp.
221 Danbury Rd.
Wilton, CT 06897
(203)563-1100
Fax: (203)563-1111
Website: http://www.ltileasing.com

Delaware

Blue Rock Capital
5803 Kennett Pike, Ste. A
Wilmington, DE 19807
(302)426-0981
Fax: (302)426-0982
Website: http://www.bluerockcapital.com

District of Columbia

Allied Capital Corp.
1919 Pennsylvania Ave. NW
Washington, DC 20006-3434
(202)331-2444
Fax: (202)659-2053
Website: http://www.alliedcapital.com

Atlantic Coastal Ventures, L.P.
3101 South St. NW
Washington, DC 20007
(202)293-1166
Fax: (202)293-1181
Website: http://www.atlanticcv.com

Columbia Capital Group, Inc.
1660 L St. NW, Ste. 308
Washington, DC 20036
(202)775-8815
Fax: (202)223-0544

Core Capital Partners
901 15th St., NW
9th Fl.
Washington, DC 20005
(202)589-0090
Fax: (202)589-0091
Website: http://www.core-capital.com

Next Point Partners
701 Pennsylvania Ave. NW, Ste. 900
Washington, DC 20004
(202)661-8703
Fax: (202)434-7400
E-mail: mf@nextpoint.vc
Website: http://www.nextpointvc.com

Telecommunications Development Fund
2020 K. St. NW
Ste. 375
Washington, DC 20006
(202)293-8840
Fax: (202)293-8850
Website: http://www.tdfund.com

Wachtel & Co., Inc.
1101 4th St. NW
Washington, DC 20005-5680
(202)898-1144

Winslow Partners LLC
1300 Connecticut Ave. NW
Washington, DC 20036-1703
(202)530-5000
Fax: (202)530-5010
E-mail: winslow@winslowpartners.com

Women's Growth Capital Fund
1054 31st St., NW
Ste. 110
Washington, DC 20007
(202)342-1431
Fax: (202)341-1203
Website: http://www.wgcf.com

Sigma Capital Corp.
22668 Caravelle Circle
Boca Raton, FL 33433
(561)368-9783

North American Business Development Co., L.L.C.
111 East Las Olas Blvd.
Ft. Lauderdale, FL 33301
(305)463-0681
Fax: (305)527-0904
Website: http://
www.northamericanfund.com

Chartwell Capital Management Co. Inc.
1 Independent Dr., Ste. 3120

Jacksonville, FL 32202
(904)355-3519
Fax: (904)353-5833
E-mail: info@chartwellcap.com

CEO Advisors
1061 Maitland Center Commons
Ste. 209
Maitland, FL 32751
(407)660-9327
Fax: (407)660-2109

Henry & Co.
8201 Peters Rd., Ste. 1000
Plantation, FL 33324
(954)797-7400

Avery Business Development Services
2506 St. Michel Ct.
Ponte Vedra, FL 32082
(904)285-6033

New South Ventures
5053 Ocean Blvd.
Sarasota, FL 34242
(941)358-6000
Fax: (941)358-6078
Website: http://www.newsouth
ventures.com

Venture Capital Management Corp.
PO Box 2626
Satellite Beach, FL 32937
(407)777-1969

Florida Capital Venture Ltd.
325 Florida Bank Plaza
100 W. Kennedy Blvd.
Tampa, FL 33602
(813)229-2294
Fax: (813)229-2028

Quantum Capital Partners
339 South Plant Ave.
Tampa, FL 33606
(813)250-1999
Fax: (813)250-1998
Website: http://www.quantum
capitalpartners.com

South Atlantic Venture Fund
614 W. Bay St.
Tampa, FL 33606-2704
(813)253-2500
Fax: (813)253-2360
E-mail: venture@southatlantic.com
Website: http://www.southatlantic.com

LM Capital Corp.
120 S. Olive, Ste. 400
West Palm Beach, FL 33401

(561)833-9700
Fax: (561)655-6587
Website: http://www.lmcapital
securities.com

Georgia

Venture First Associates
4811 Thornwood Dr.
Acworth, GA 30102
(770)928-3733
Fax: (770)928-6455

Alliance Technology Ventures
8995 Westside Pkwy., Ste. 200
Alpharetta, GA 30004
(678)336-2000
Fax: (678)336-2001
E-mail: info@atv.com
Website: http://www.atv.com

Cordova Ventures
2500 North Winds Pkwy., Ste. 475
Alpharetta, GA 30004
(678)942-0300
Fax: (678)942-0301
Website: http://www.cordovaventures.
com

Advanced Technology Development Fund
1000 Abernathy, Ste. 1420
Atlanta, GA 30328-5614
(404)668-2333
Fax: (404)668-2333

CGW Southeast Partners
12 Piedmont Center, Ste. 210
Atlanta, GA 30305
(404)816-3255
Fax: (404)816-3258
Website: http://www.cgwlp.com

Cyberstarts
1900 Emery St., NW
3rd Fl.
Atlanta, GA 30318
(404)267-5000
Fax: (404)267-5200
Website: http://www.cyberstarts.com

EGL Holdings, Inc.
10 Piedmont Center, Ste. 412
Atlanta, GA 30305
(404)949-8300
Fax: (404)949-8311

Equity South
1790 The Lenox Bldg.
3399 Peachtree Rd. NE
Atlanta, GA 30326

(404)237-6222
Fax: (404)261-1578

Five Paces
3400 Peachtree Rd., Ste. 200
Atlanta, GA 30326
(404)439-8300
Fax: (404)439-8301
Website: http://www.fivepaces.com

Frontline Capital, Inc.
3475 Lenox Rd., Ste. 400
Atlanta, GA 30326
(404)240-7280
Fax: (404)240-7281

Fuqua Ventures LLC
1201 W. Peachtree St. NW, Ste. 5000
Atlanta, GA 30309
(404)815-4500
Fax: (404)815-4528
Website: http://www.fuquaventures.com

Noro-Moseley Partners
4200 Northside Pkwy., Bldg. 9
Atlanta, GA 30327
(404)233-1966
Fax: (404)239-9280
Website: http://www.noro-moseley.com

Renaissance Capital Corp.
34 Peachtree St. NW, Ste. 2230
Atlanta, GA 30303
(404)658-9061
Fax: (404)658-9064

River Capital, Inc.
Two Midtown Plaza
1360 Peachtree St. NE, Ste. 1430
Atlanta, GA 30309
(404)873-2166
Fax: (404)873-2158

State Street Bank & Trust Co.
3414 Peachtree Rd. NE, Ste. 1010
Atlanta, GA 30326
(404)364-9500
Fax: (404)261-4469

UPS Strategic Enterprise Fund
55 Glenlake Pkwy. NE
Atlanta, GA 30328
(404)828-8814
Fax: (404)828-8088
E-mail: jcacyce@ups.com
Website: http://www.ups.com/sef/
sef_home

Wachovia
191 Peachtree St. NE, 26th Fl.
Atlanta, GA 30303

(404)332-1000
Fax: (404)332-1392
Website: http://www.wachovia.com/wca

Brainworks Ventures
4243 Dunwoody Club Dr.
Chamblee, GA 30341
(770)239-7447

First Growth Capital Inc.
Best Western Plaza, Ste. 105
PO Box 815
Forsyth, GA 31029
(912)781-7131

Financial Capital Resources, Inc.
21 Eastbrook Bend, Ste. 116
Peachtree City, GA 30269
(404)487-6650

Hawaii

HMS Hawaii Management Partners
Davies Pacific Center
841 Bishop St., Ste. 860
Honolulu, HI 96813
(808)545-3755
Fax: (808)531-2611

Idaho

Sun Valley Ventures
160 Second St.
Ketchum, ID 83340
(208)726-5005
Fax: (208)726-5094

Illinois

Open Prairie Ventures
115 N. Neil St., Ste. 209
Champaign, IL 61820
(217)351-7000
Fax: (217)351-7051
E-mail: inquire@openprairie.com
Website: http://www.openprairie.com

ABN AMRO Private Equity
208 S. La Salle St., 10th Fl.
Chicago, IL 60604
(312)855-7079
Fax: (312)553-6648
Website: http://www.abnequity.com

Alpha Capital Partners, Ltd.
122 S. Michigan Ave., Ste. 1700
Chicago, IL 60603
(312)322-9800
Fax: (312)322-9808
E-mail: acp@alphacapital.com

Ameritech Development Corp.
30 S. Wacker Dr., 37th Fl.
Chicago, IL 60606
(312)750-5083
Fax: (312)609-0244

Apex Investment Partners
225 W. Washington, Ste. 1450
Chicago, IL 60606
(312)857-2800
Fax: (312)857-1800
E-mail: apex@apexvc.com
Website: http://www.apexvc.com

Arch Venture Partners
8725 W. Higgins Rd., Ste. 290
Chicago, IL 60631
(773)380-6600
Fax: (773)380-6606
Website: http://www.archventure.com

The Bank Funds
208 South LaSalle St., Ste. 1680
Chicago, IL 60604
(312)855-6020
Fax: (312)855-8910

Batterson Venture Partners
303 W. Madison St., Ste. 1110
Chicago, IL 60606-3309
(312)269-0300
Fax: (312)269-0021
Website: http://www.battersonvp.com

William Blair Capital Partners, L.L.C.
222 W. Adams St., Ste. 1300
Chicago, IL 60606
(312)364-8250
Fax: (312)236-1042
E-mail: privateequity@wmblair.com
Website: http://www.wmblair.com

Bluestar Ventures
208 South LaSalle St., Ste. 1020
Chicago, IL 60604
(312)384-5000
Fax: (312)384-5005
Website: http://www.bluestarventures.com

The Capital Strategy Management Co.
233 S. Wacker Dr.
Box 06334
Chicago, IL 60606
(312)444-1170

DN Partners
77 West Wacker Dr., Ste. 4550
Chicago, IL 60601
(312)332-7960
Fax: (312)332-7979

Dresner Capital Inc.
29 South LaSalle St., Ste. 310
Chicago, IL 60603
(312)726-3600
Fax: (312)726-7448

Eblast Ventures LLC
11 South LaSalle St., 5th Fl.
Chicago, IL 60603
(312)372-2600
Fax: (312)372-5621
Website: http://www.eblastventures.com

Essex Woodlands Health Ventures, L.P.
190 S. LaSalle St., Ste. 2800
Chicago, IL 60603
(312)444-6040
Fax: (312)444-6034
Website: http://www.essexwood
lands.com

First Analysis Venture Capital
233 S. Wacker Dr., Ste. 9500
Chicago, IL 60606
(312)258-1400
Fax: (312)258-0334
Website: http://www.firstanalysis.com

Frontenac Co.
135 S. LaSalle St., Ste.3800
Chicago, IL 60603
(312)368-0044
Fax: (312)368-9520
Website: http://www.frontenac.com

GTCR Golder Rauner, LLC
6100 Sears Tower
Chicago, IL 60606
(312)382-2200
Fax: (312)382-2201
Website: http://www.gtcr.com

High Street Capital LLC
311 South Wacker Dr., Ste. 4550
Chicago, IL 60606
(312)697-4990
Fax: (312)697-4994
Website: http://www.highstr.com

IEG Venture Management, Inc.
70 West Madison
Chicago, IL 60602
(312)644-0890
Fax: (312)454-0369
Website: http://www.iegventure.com

JK&B Capital
180 North Stetson, Ste. 4500
Chicago, IL 60601
(312)946-1200
Fax: (312)946-1103

E-mail: gspencer@jkbcapital.com
Website: http://www.jkbcapital.com

Kettle Partners L.P.
350 W. Hubbard, Ste. 350
Chicago, IL 60610
(312)329-9300
Fax: (312)527-4519
Website: http://www.kettlevc.com

Lake Shore Capital Partners
20 N. Wacker Dr., Ste. 2807
Chicago, IL 60606
(312)803-3536
Fax: (312)803-3534

LaSalle Capital Group Inc.
70 W. Madison St., Ste. 5710
Chicago, IL 60602
(312)236-7041
Fax: (312)236-0720

Linc Capital, Inc.
303 E. Wacker Pkwy., Ste. 1000
Chicago, IL 60601
(312)946-2670
Fax: (312)938-4290
E-mail: bdemars@linccap.com

Madison Dearborn Partners, Inc.
3 First National Plz., Ste. 3800
Chicago, IL 60602
(312)895-1000
Fax: (312)895-1001
E-mail: invest@mdcp.com
Website: http://www.mdcp.com

**Mesirow Private Equity Investments
Inc.**
350 N. Clark St.
Chicago, IL 60610
(312)595-6950
Fax: (312)595-6211
Website: http://www.meisrow
financial.com

Mosaix Ventures LLC
1822 North Mohawk
Chicago, IL 60614
(312)274-0988
Fax: (312)274-0989
Website: http://www.mosaix
ventures.com

Nesbitt Burns
111 West Monroe St.
Chicago, IL 60603
(312)416-3855
Fax: (312)765-8000
Website: http://www.harrisbank.com

Polestar Capital, Inc.
180 N. Michigan Ave., Ste. 1905
Chicago, IL 60601
(312)984-9090
Fax: (312)984-9877
E-mail: wl@polestarvc.com
Website: http://www.polestarvc.com

Prince Ventures (Chicago)
10 S. Wacker Dr., Ste. 2575
Chicago, IL 60606-7407
(312)454-1408
Fax: (312)454-9125

Prism Capital
444 N. Michigan Ave.
Chicago, IL 60611
(312)464-7900
Fax: (312)464-7915
Website: http://www.prismfund.com

Third Coast Capital
900 N. Franklin St., Ste. 700
Chicago, IL 60610
(312)337-3303
Fax: (312)337-2567
E-mail: manic@earthlink.com
Website: http://www.third
coastcapital.com

Thoma Cressey Equity Partners
4460 Sears Tower, 92nd Fl.
233 S. Wacker Dr.
Chicago, IL 60606
(312)777-4444
Fax: (312)777-4445
Website: http://www.thomacressey.com

Tribune Ventures
435 N. Michigan Ave., Ste. 600
Chicago, IL 60611
(312)527-8797
Fax: (312)222-5993
Website: http://www.tribuneventures.com

Wind Point Partners (Chicago)
676 N. Michigan Ave., Ste. 330
Chicago, IL 60611
(312)649-4000
Website: http://www.wppartners.com

Marquette Venture Partners
520 Lake Cook Rd., Ste. 450
Deerfield, IL 60015
(847)940-1700
Fax: (847)940-1724
Website: http://www.marquette
ventures.com

Duchossois Investments Limited, LLC
845 Larch Ave.
Elmhurst, IL 60126

(630)530-6105
Fax: (630)993-8644
Website: http://www.duchtec.com

Evanston Business Investment Corp.
1840 Oak Ave.
Evanston, IL 60201
(847)866-1840
Fax: (847)866-1808
E-mail: t-parkinson@nwu.com
Website: http://www.ebic.com

Inroads Capital Partners L.P.
1603 Orrington Ave., Ste. 2050
Evanston, IL 60201-3841
(847)864-2000
Fax: (847)864-9692

The Cerulean Fund/WGC Enterprises
1701 E. Lake Ave., Ste. 170
Glenview, IL 60025
(847)657-8002
Fax: (847)657-8168

Ventana Financial Resources, Inc.
249 Market Sq.
Lake Forest, IL 60045
(847)234-3434

Beecken, Petty & Co.
901 Warrenville Rd., Ste. 205
Lisle, IL 60532
(630)435-0300
Fax: (630)435-0370
E-mail: hep@bpcompany.com
Website: http://www.bpcompany.com

Allstate Private Equity
3075 Sanders Rd., Ste. G5D
Northbrook, IL 60062-7127
(847)402-8247
Fax: (847)402-0880

KB Partners
1101 Skokie Blvd., Ste. 260
Northbrook, IL 60062-2856
(847)714-0444
Fax: (847)714-0445
E-mail: keith@kbpartners.com
Website: http://www.kbpartners.com

Transcap Associates Inc.
900 Skokie Blvd., Ste. 210
Northbrook, IL 60062
(847)753-9600
Fax: (847)753-9090

**Graystone Venture Partners, L.L.C. /
Portage Venture Partners**
One Northfield Plaza, Ste. 530
Northfield, IL 60093

(847)446-9460
Fax: (847)446-9470
Website: http://www.portage
ventures.com

Motorola Inc.
1303 E. Algonquin Rd.
Schaumburg, IL 60196-1065
(847)576-4929
Fax: (847)538-2250
Website: http://www.mot.com/mne

Indiana

Irwin Ventures LLC
500 Washington St.
Columbus, IN 47202
(812)373-1434
Fax: (812)376-1709
Website: http://www.irwinventures.com

Cambridge Venture Partners
4181 East 96th St., Ste. 200
Indianapolis, IN 46240
(317)814-6192
Fax: (317)944-9815

CID Equity Partners
One American Square, Ste. 2850
Box 82074
Indianapolis, IN 46282
(317)269-2350
Fax: (317)269-2355
Website: http://www.cidequity.com

Gazelle Techventures
6325 Digital Way, Ste. 460
Indianapolis, IN 46278
(317)275-6800
Fax: (317)275-1101
Website: http://www.gazellevc.com

Monument Advisors Inc.
Bank One Center/Circle
111 Monument Circle, Ste. 600
Indianapolis, IN 46204-5172
(317)656-5065
Fax: (317)656-5060
Website: http://www.monumentadv.com

MWV Capital Partners
201 N. Illinois St., Ste. 300
Indianapolis, IN 46204
(317)237-2323
Fax: (317)237-2325
Website: http://www.mwvcapital.com

First Source Capital Corp.
100 North Michigan St.
PO Box 1602
South Bend, IN 46601

(219)235-2180
Fax: (219)235-2227

Iowa

Allsop Venture Partners
118 Third Ave. SE, Ste. 837
Cedar Rapids, IA 52401
(319)368-6675
Fax: (319)363-9515

InvestAmerica Investment Advisors, Inc.
101 2nd St. SE, Ste. 800
Cedar Rapids, IA 52401
(319)363-8249
Fax: (319)363-9683

Pappajohn Capital Resources
2116 Financial Center
Des Moines, IA 50309
(515)244-5746
Fax: (515)244-2346
Website: http://www.pappajohn.com

Berthel Fisher & Company Planning Inc.
701 Tama St.
PO Box 609
Marion, IA 52302
(319)497-5700
Fax: (319)497-4244

Kansas

Enterprise Merchant Bank
7400 West 110th St., Ste. 560
Overland Park, KS 66210
(913)327-8500
Fax: (913)327-8505

Kansas Venture Capital, Inc. (Overland Park)
6700 Antioch Plz., Ste. 460
Overland Park, KS 66204
(913)262-7117
Fax: (913)262-3509
E-mail: jdalton@kvci.com

Child Health Investment Corp.
6803 W. 64th St., Ste. 208
Shawnee Mission, KS 66202
(913)262-1436
Fax: (913)262-1575
Website: http://www.chca.com

Kansas Technology Enterprise Corp.
214 SW 6th, 1st Fl.
Topeka, KS 66603-3719
(785)296-5272
Fax: (785)296-1160

E-mail: ktec@ktec.com
Website: http://www.ktec.com

Kentucky

Kentucky Highlands Investment Corp.
362 Old Whitley Rd.
London, KY 40741
(606)864-5175
Fax: (606)864-5194
Website: http://www.khic.org

Chrysalis Ventures, L.L.C.
1850 National City Tower
Louisville, KY 40202
(502)583-7644
Fax: (502)583-7648
E-mail: bobsany@chrysalisventures.com
Website: http://www.chrysalis
ventures.com

Humana Venture Capital
500 West Main St.
Louisville, KY 40202
(502)580-3922
Fax: (502)580-2051
E-mail: gemont@humana.com
George Emont, Director

Summit Capital Group, Inc.
6510 Glenridge Park Pl., Ste. 8
Louisville, KY 40222
(502)332-2700

Louisiana

Bank One Equity Investors, Inc.
451 Florida St.
Baton Rouge, LA 70801
(504)332-4421
Fax: (504)332-7377

Advantage Capital Partners
LLE Tower
909 Poydras St., Ste. 2230
New Orleans, LA 70112
(504)522-4850
Fax: (504)522-4950
Website: http://www.advantagecap.com

Maine

CEI Ventures / Coastal Ventures LP
2 Portland Fish Pier, Ste. 201
Portland, ME 04101
(207)772-5356
Fax: (207)772-5503
Website: http://www.ceiventures.com

Commwealth Bioventures, Inc.
4 Milk St.
Portland, ME 04101

(207)780-0904
Fax: (207)780-0913

Maryland

Annapolis Ventures LLC
151 West St., Ste. 302
Annapolis, MD 21401
(443)482-9555
Fax: (443)482-9565
Website: http://www.annapolis
ventures.com

Delmag Ventures
220 Wardour Dr.
Annapolis, MD 21401
(410)267-8196
Fax: (410)267-8017
Website: http://www.delmag
ventures.com

Abell Venture Fund
111 S. Calvert St., Ste. 2300
Baltimore, MD 21202
(410)547-1300
Fax: (410)539-6579
Website: http://www.abell.org

ABS Ventures (Baltimore)
1 South St., Ste. 2150
Baltimore, MD 21202
(410)895-3895
Fax: (410)895-3899
Website: http://www.absventures.com

Anthem Capital, L.P.
16 S. Calvert St., Ste. 800
Baltimore, MD 21202-1305
(410)625-1510
Fax: (410)625-1735
Website: http://www.anthemcapital.com

Catalyst Ventures
1119 St. Paul St.
Baltimore, MD 21202
(410)244-0123
Fax: (410)752-7721

Maryland Venture Capital Trust
217 E. Redwood St., Ste. 2200
Baltimore, MD 21202
(410)767-6361
Fax: (410)333-6931

New Enterprise Associates (Baltimore)
1119 St. Paul St.
Baltimore, MD 21202
(410)244-0115
Fax: (410)752-7721
Website: http://www.nea.com

T. Rowe Price Threshold Partnerships
100 E. Pratt St., 8th Fl.
Baltimore, MD 21202
(410)345-2000
Fax: (410)345-2800

Spring Capital Partners
16 W. Madison St.
Baltimore, MD 21201
(410)685-8000
Fax: (410)727-1436
E-mail: mailbox@springcap.com

Arete Corporation
3 Bethesda Metro Ctr., Ste. 770
Bethesda, MD 20814
(301)657-6268
Fax: (301)657-6254
Website: http://www.arete-microgen.com

Embryon Capital
7903 Sleaford Place
Bethesda, MD 20814
(301)656-6837
Fax: (301)656-8056

Potomac Ventures
7920 Norfolk Ave., Ste. 1100
Bethesda, MD 20814
(301)215-9240
Website: http://www.potomac
ventures.com

Toucan Capital Corp.
3 Bethesda Metro Center, Ste. 700
Bethesda, MD 20814
(301)961-1970
Fax: (301)961-1969
Website: http://www.toucancapital.com

Kinetic Ventures LLC
2 Wisconsin Cir., Ste. 620
Chevy Chase, MD 20815
(301)652-8066
Fax: (301)652-8310
Website: http://www.kineticventures.com

Boulder Ventures Ltd.
4750 Owings Mills Blvd.
Owings Mills, MD 21117
(410)998-3114
Fax: (410)356-5492
Website: http://www.boulderventures.com

Grotech Capital Group
9690 Deereco Rd., Ste. 800
Timonium, MD 21093
(410)560-2000
Fax: (410)560-1910
Website: http://www.grotech.com

Massachusetts

Adams, Harkness & Hill, Inc.
60 State St.
Boston, MA 02109
(617)371-3900

Advent International
75 State St., 29th Fl.
Boston, MA 02109
(617)951-9400
Fax: (617)951-0566
Website: http://www.adventiner
national.com

American Research and Development
30 Federal St.
Boston, MA 02110-2508
(617)423-7500
Fax: (617)423-9655

Ascent Venture Partners
255 State St., 5th Fl.
Boston, MA 02109
(617)270-9400
Fax: (617)270-9401
E-mail: info@ascentvp.com
Website: http://www.ascentvp.com

Atlas Venture
222 Berkeley St.
Boston, MA 02116
(617)488-2200
Fax: (617)859-9292
Website: http://www.atlasventure.com

Axxon Capital
28 State St., 37th Fl.
Boston, MA 02109
(617)722-0980
Fax: (617)557-6014
Website: http://www.axxoncapital.com

**BancBoston Capital/BancBoston
Ventures**
175 Federal St., 10th Fl.
Boston, MA 02110
(617)434-2509
Fax: (617)434-6175
Website: http://
www.bancbostoncapital.com

Boston Capital Ventures
Old City Hall
45 School St.
Boston, MA 02108
(617)227-6550
Fax: (617)227-3847
E-mail: info@bcv.com
Website: http://www.bcv.com

Boston Financial & Equity Corp.
20 Overland St.
PO Box 15071
Boston, MA 02215
(617)267-2900
Fax: (617)437-7601
E-mail: debbie@bfec.com

Boston Millennia Partners
30 Rowes Wharf
Boston, MA 02110
(617)428-5150
Fax: (617)428-5160
Website: http://www.millennia
partners.com

Bristol Investment Trust
842A Beacon St.
Boston, MA 02215-3199
(617)566-5212
Fax: (617)267-0932

Brook Venture Management LLC
50 Federal St., 5th Fl.
Boston, MA 02110
(617)451-8989
Fax: (617)451-2369
Website: http://www.brookventure.com

Burr, Egan, Deleage, and Co. (Boston)
200 Clarendon St., Ste. 3800
Boston, MA 02116
(617)262-7770
Fax: (617)262-9779

Cambridge/Samsung Partners
One Exeter Plaza
Ninth Fl.
Boston, MA 02116
(617)262-4440
Fax: (617)262-5562

Chestnut Street Partners, Inc.
75 State St., Ste. 2500
Boston, MA 02109
(617)345-7220
Fax: (617)345-7201
E-mail: chestnut@chestnutp.com

Claflin Capital Management, Inc.
10 Liberty Sq., Ste. 300
Boston, MA 02109
(617)426-6505
Fax: (617)482-0016
Website: http://www.claflincapital.com

Copley Venture Partners
99 Summer St., Ste. 1720
Boston, MA 02110
(617)737-1253
Fax: (617)439-0699

Corning Capital / Corning Technology Ventures
121 High Street, Ste. 400
Boston, MA 02110
(617)338-2656
Fax: (617)261-3864
Website: http://www.corningventures.com

Downer & Co.
211 Congress St.
Boston, MA 02110
(617)482-6200
Fax: (617)482-6201
E-mail: cdowner@downer.com
Website: http://www.downer.com

Fidelity Ventures
82 Devonshire St.
Boston, MA 02109
(617)563-6370
Fax: (617)476-9023
Website: http://www.fidelityventures.com

Greylock Management Corp. (Boston)
1 Federal St.
Boston, MA 02110-2065
(617)423-5525
Fax: (617)482-0059

Gryphon Ventures
222 Berkeley St., Ste.1600
Boston, MA 02116
(617)267-9191
Fax: (617)267-4293
E-mail: all@gryphoninc.com

Halpern, Denny & Co.
500 Boylston St.
Boston, MA 02116
(617)536-6602
Fax: (617)536-8535

Harbourvest Partners, LLC
1 Financial Center, 44th Fl.
Boston, MA 02111
(617)348-3707
Fax: (617)350-0305
Website: http://www.hvpllc.com

Highland Capital Partners
2 International Pl.
Boston, MA 02110
(617)981-1500
Fax: (617)531-1550
E-mail: info@hcp.com
Website: http://www.hcp.com

Lee Munder Venture Partners
John Hancock Tower T-53
200 Clarendon St.
Boston, MA 02103

(617)380-5600
Fax: (617)380-5601
Website: http://www.leemunder.com

M/C Venture Partners
75 State St., Ste. 2500
Boston, MA 02109
(617)345-7200
Fax: (617)345-7201
Website: http://www.mcventure
partners.com

Massachusetts Capital Resources Co.
420 Boylston St.
Boston, MA 02116
(617)536-3900
Fax: (617)536-7930

Massachusetts Technology Development Corp. (MTDC)
148 State St.
Boston, MA 02109
(617)723-4920
Fax: (617)723-5983
E-mail: jhodgman@mtdc.com
Website: http://www.mtdc.com

New England Partners
One Boston Place, Ste. 2100
Boston, MA 02108
(617)624-8400
Fax: (617)624-8999
Website: http://www.nepartners.com

North Hill Ventures
Ten Post Office Square
11th Fl.
Boston, MA 02109
(617)788-2112
Fax: (617)788-2152
Website: http://www.northhill
ventures.com

OneLiberty Ventures
150 Cambridge Park Dr.
Boston, MA 02140
(617)492-7280
Fax: (617)492-7290
Website: http://www.oneliberty.com

Schroder Ventures
Life Sciences
60 State St., Ste. 3650
Boston, MA 02109
(617)367-8100
Fax: (617)367-1590
Website: http://www.shroderventures.com

Shawmut Capital Partners
75 Federal St., 18th Fl.
Boston, MA 02110

(617)368-4900
Fax: (617)368-4910
Website: http://www.shawmutcapital.com

Solstice Capital LLC
15 Broad St., 3rd Fl.
Boston, MA 02109
(617)523-7733
Fax: (617)523-5827
E-mail: solticecapital@solcap.com

Spectrum Equity Investors
One International Pl., 29th Fl.
Boston, MA 02110
(617)464-4600
Fax: (617)464-4601
Website: http://www.spectrumequity.com

Spray Venture Partners
One Walnut St.
Boston, MA 02108
(617)305-4140
Fax: (617)305-4144
Website: http://www.sprayventure.com

The Still River Fund
100 Federal St., 29th Fl.
Boston, MA 02110
(617)348-2327
Fax: (617)348-2371
Website: http://www.stillriverfund.com

Summit Partners
600 Atlantic Ave., Ste. 2800
Boston, MA 02210-2227
(617)824-1000
Fax: (617)824-1159
Website: http://www.summitpartners.com

TA Associates, Inc. (Boston)
High Street Tower
125 High St., Ste. 2500
Boston, MA 02110
(617)574-6700
Fax: (617)574-6728
Website: http://www.ta.com

TVM Techno Venture Management
101 Arch St., Ste. 1950
Boston, MA 02110
(617)345-9320
Fax: (617)345-9377
E-mail: info@tvmvc.com
Website: http://www.tvmvc.com

UNC Ventures
64 Burough St.
Boston, MA 02130-4017
(617)482-7070
Fax: (617)522-2176

Venture Investment Management Company (VIMAC)
177 Milk St.
Boston, MA 02190-3410
(617)292-3300
Fax: (617)292-7979
E-mail: bzeisig@vimac.com
Website: http://www.vimac.com

MDT Advisers, Inc.
125 Cambridge Park Dr.
Cambridge, MA 02140-2314
(617)234-2200
Fax: (617)234-2210
Website: http://www.mdtai.com

TTC Ventures
One Main St., 6th Fl.
Cambridge, MA 02142
(617)528-3137
Fax: (617)577-1715
E-mail: info@ttcventures.com

Zero Stage Capital Co. Inc.
101 Main St., 17th Fl.
Cambridge, MA 02142
(617)876-5355
Fax: (617)876-1248
Website: http://www.zerostage.com

Atlantic Capital
164 Cushing Hwy.
Cohasset, MA 02025
(617)383-9449
Fax: (617)383-6040
E-mail: info@atlanticcap.com
Website: http://www.atlanticcap.com

Seacoast Capital Partners
55 Ferncroft Rd.
Danvers, MA 01923
(978)750-1300
Fax: (978)750-1301
E-mail: gdeli@seacoastcapital.com
Website: http://www.seacoast
capital.com

Sage Management Group
44 South Street
PO Box 2026
East Dennis, MA 02641
(508)385-7172
Fax: (508)385-7272
E-mail: sagemgt@capecod.net

Applied Technology
1 Cranberry Hill
Lexington, MA 02421-7397
(617)862-8622
Fax: (617)862-8367

Royalty Capital Management
5 Downing Rd.
Lexington, MA 02421-6918
(781)861-8490

Argo Global Capital
210 Broadway, Ste. 101
Lynnfield, MA 01940
(781)592-5250
Fax: (781)592-5230
Website: http://www.gsmcapital.com

Industry Ventures
6 Bayne Lane
Newburyport, MA 01950
(978)499-7606
Fax: (978)499-0686
Website: http://
www.industryventures.com

Softbank Capital Partners
10 Langley Rd., Ste. 202
Newton Center, MA 02459
(617)928-9300
Fax: (617)928-9305
E-mail: clax@bvc.com

Advanced Technology Ventures (Boston)
281 Winter St., Ste. 350
Waltham, MA 02451
(781)290-0707
Fax: (781)684-0045
E-mail: info@atvcapital.com
Website: http://www.atvcapital.com

Castile Ventures
890 Winter St., Ste. 140
Waltham, MA 02451
(781)890-0060
Fax: (781)890-0065
Website: http://www.castileventures.com

Charles River Ventures
1000 Winter St., Ste. 3300
Waltham, MA 02451
(781)487-7060
Fax: (781)487-7065
Website: http://www.crv.com

Comdisco Venture Group (Waltham)
Totton Pond Office Center
400-1 Totten Pond Rd.
Waltham, MA 02451
(617)672-0250
Fax: (617)398-8099

Marconi Ventures
890 Winter St., Ste. 310
Waltham, MA 02451
(781)839-7177

Fax: (781)522-7477
Website: http://www.marconi.com

Matrix Partners
Bay Colony Corporate Center
1000 Winter St., Ste.4500
Waltham, MA 02451
(781)890-2244
Fax: (781)890-2288
Website: http://www.matrix
partners.com

North Bridge Venture Partners
950 Winter St. Ste. 4600
Waltham, MA 02451
(781)290-0004
Fax: (781)290-0999
E-mail: eta@nbvp.com

Polaris Venture Partners
Bay Colony Corporate Ctr.
1000 Winter St., Ste. 3500
Waltham, MA 02451
(781)290-0770
Fax: (781)290-0880
E-mail: partners@polarisventures.com
Website: http://www.polar
isventures.com

Seaflower Ventures
Bay Colony Corporate Ctr.
1000 Winter St. Ste. 1000
Waltham, MA 02451
(781)466-9552
Fax: (781)466-9553
E-mail: moot@seaflower.com
Website: http://www.seaflower.com

Ampersand Ventures
55 William St., Ste. 240
Wellesley, MA 02481
(617)239-0700
Fax: (617)239-0824
E-mail: info@ampersandventures.com
Website: http://www.ampersand
ventures.com

Battery Ventures (Boston)
20 William St., Ste. 200
Wellesley, MA 02481
(781)577-1000
Fax: (781)577-1001
Website: http://www.battery.com

Commonwealth Capital Ventures, L.P.
20 William St., Ste.225
Wellesley, MA 02481
(781)237-7373
Fax: (781)235-8627
Website: http://www.ccvlp.com

Fowler, Anthony & Company
20 Walnut St.
Wellesley, MA 02481
(781)237-4201
Fax: (781)237-7718

Gemini Investors
20 William St.
Wellesley, MA 02481
(781)237-7001
Fax: (781)237-7233

Grove Street Advisors Inc.
20 William St., Ste. 230
Wellesley, MA 02481
(781)263-6100
Fax: (781)263-6101
Website: http://www.groves
treetadvisors.com

Mees Pierson Investeringsmaat B.V.
20 William St., Ste. 210
Wellesley, MA 02482
(781)239-7600
Fax: (781)239-0377

Norwest Equity Partners
40 William St., Ste. 305
Wellesley, MA 02481-3902
(781)237-5870
Fax: (781)237-6270
Website: http://www.norwestvp.com

Bessemer Venture Partners (Wellesley Hills)
83 Walnut St.
Wellesley Hills, MA 02481
(781)237-6050
Fax: (781)235-7576
E-mail: travis@bvpny.com
Website: http://www.bvp.com

Venture Capital Fund of New England
20 Walnut St., Ste. 120
Wellesley Hills, MA 02481-2175
(781)239-8262
Fax: (781)239-8263

Prism Venture Partners
100 Lowder Brook Dr., Ste. 2500
Westwood, MA 02090
(781)302-4000
Fax: (781)302-4040
E-mail: dwbaum@prismventure.com

Palmer Partners LP
200 Unicorn Park Dr.
Woburn, MA 01801
(781)933-5445
Fax: (781)933-0698

Michigan

Arbor Partners, L.L.C.
130 South First St.
Ann Arbor, MI 48104
(734)668-9000
Fax: (734)669-4195
Website: http://www.arborpartners.com

EDF Ventures
425 N. Main St.
Ann Arbor, MI 48104
(734)663-3213
Fax: (734)663-7358
E-mail: edf@edfvc.com
Website: http://www.edfvc.com

White Pines Management, L.L.C.
2401 Plymouth Rd., Ste. B
Ann Arbor, MI 48105
(734)747-9401
Fax: (734)747-9704
E-mail: ibund@whitepines.com
Website: http://www.whitepines.com

Wellmax, Inc.
3541 Bendway Blvd., Ste. 100
Bloomfield Hills, MI 48301
(248)646-3554
Fax: (248)646-6220

Venture Funding, Ltd.
Fisher Bldg.
3011 West Grand Blvd., Ste. 321
Detroit, MI 48202
(313)871-3606
Fax: (313)873-4935

Investcare Partners L.P. / GMA Capital LLC
32330 W. Twelve Mile Rd.
Farmington Hills, MI 48334
(248)489-9000
Fax: (248)489-8819
E-mail: gma@gmacapital.com
Website: http://www.gmacapital.com

Liberty Bidco Investment Corp.
30833 Northwestern Highway, Ste. 211
Farmington Hills, MI 48334
(248)626-6070
Fax: (248)626-6072

Seaflower Ventures
5170 Nicholson Rd.
PO Box 474
Fowlerville, MI 48836
(517)223-3335
Fax: (517)223-3337
E-mail: gibbons@seaflower.com
Website: http://www.seaflower.com

Ralph Wilson Equity Fund LLC
15400 E. Jefferson Ave.
Gross Pointe Park, MI 48230
(313)821-9122
Fax: (313)821-9101
Website: http://www.Ralph
WilsonEquityFund.com
J. Skip Simms, President

Minnesota

Development Corp. of Austin
1900 Eighth Ave., NW
Austin, MN 55912
(507)433-0346
Fax: (507)433-0361
E-mail: dca@smig.net
Website: http://www.spamtownusa.com

Northeast Ventures Corp.
802 Alworth Bldg.
Duluth, MN 55802
(218)722-9915
Fax: (218)722-9871

Medical Innovation Partners, Inc.
6450 City West Pkwy.
Eden Prairie, MN 55344-3245
(612)828-9616
Fax: (612)828-9596

St. Paul Venture Capital, Inc.
10400 Vicking Dr., Ste. 550
Eden Prairie, MN 55344
(612)995-7474
Fax: (612)995-7475
Website: http://www.stpaulvc.com

Cherry Tree Investments, Inc.
7601 France Ave. S, Ste. 150
Edina, MN 55435
(612)893-9012
Fax: (612)893-9036
Website: http://www.cherrytree.com

Shared Ventures, Inc.
6550 York Ave. S
Edina, MN 55435
(612)925-3411

Sherpa Partners LLC
5050 Lincoln Dr., Ste. 490
Edina, MN 55436
(952)942-1070
Fax: (952)942-1071
Website: http://www.sherpapartners.com

Affinity Capital Management
901 Marquette Ave., Ste. 1810
Minneapolis, MN 55402
(612)252-9900

Fax: (612)252-9911
Website: http://www.affinitycapital.com

Artesian Capital
1700 Foshay Tower
821 Marquette Ave.
Minneapolis, MN 55402
(612)334-5600
Fax: (612)334-5601
E-mail: artesian@artesian.com

Coral Ventures
60 S. 6th St., Ste. 3510
Minneapolis, MN 55402
(612)335-8666
Fax: (612)335-8668
Website: http://www.coralventures.com

Crescendo Venture Management, L.L.C.
800 LaSalle Ave., Ste. 2250
Minneapolis, MN 55402
(612)607-2800
Fax: (612)607-2801
Website: http://www.crescendo
ventures.com

Gideon Hixon Venture
1900 Foshay Tower
821 Marquette Ave.
Minneapolis, MN 55402
(612)904-2314
Fax: (612)204-0913

Norwest Equity Partners
3600 IDS Center
80 S. 8th St.
Minneapolis, MN 55402
(612)215-1600
Fax: (612)215-1601
Website: http://www.norwestvp.com

Oak Investment Partners (Minneapolis)
4550 Norwest Center
90 S. 7th St.
Minneapolis, MN 55402
(612)339-9322
Fax: (612)337-8017
Website: http://www.oakinv.com

Pathfinder Venture Capital Funds (Minneapolis)
7300 Metro Blvd., Ste. 585
Minneapolis, MN 55439
(612)835-1121
Fax: (612)835-8389
E-mail: jahrens620@aol.com

U.S. Bancorp Piper Jaffray Ventures, Inc.
800 Nicollet Mall, Ste. 800
Minneapolis, MN 55402

(612)303-5686
Fax: (612)303-1350
Website: http://www.paperjaffrey
ventures.com

The Food Fund, Ltd. Partnership
5720 Smatana Dr., Ste. 300
Minnetonka, MN 55343
(612)939-3950
Fax: (612)939-8106

Mayo Medical Ventures
200 First St. SW
Rochester, MN 55905
(507)266-4586
Fax: (507)284-5410
Website: http://www.mayo.edu

Missouri

Bankers Capital Corp.
3100 Gillham Rd.
Kansas City, MO 64109
(816)531-1600
Fax: (816)531-1334

Capital for Business, Inc. (Kansas City)
1000 Walnut St., 18th Fl.
Kansas City, MO 64106
(816)234-2357
Fax: (816)234-2952
Website: http://
www.capitalforbusiness.com

De Vries & Co. Inc.
800 West 47th St.
Kansas City, MO 64112
(816)756-0055
Fax: (816)756-0061

InvestAmerica Venture Group Inc. (Kansas City)
Commerce Tower
911 Main St., Ste. 2424
Kansas City, MO 64105
(816)842-0114
Fax: (816)471-7339

Kansas City Equity Partners
233 W. 47th St.
Kansas City, MO 64112
(816)960-1771
Fax: (816)960-1777
Website: http://www.kcep.com

Bome Investors, Inc.
8000 Maryland Ave., Ste. 1190
St. Louis, MO 63105
(314)721-5707
Fax: (314)721-5135

Website: http://www.gateway
ventures.com

Capital for Business, Inc. (St. Louis)
11 S. Meramac St., Ste. 1430
St. Louis, MO 63105
(314)746-7427
Fax: (314)746-8739
Website: http://www.capitalfor
business.com

Crown Capital Corp.
540 Maryville Centre Dr., Ste. 120
Saint Louis, MO 63141
(314)576-1201
Fax: (314)576-1525
Website: http://www.crown-
cap.com

Gateway Associates L.P.
8000 Maryland Ave., Ste. 1190
St. Louis, MO 63105
(314)721-5707
Fax: (314)721-5135

Harbison Corp.
8112 Maryland Ave., Ste. 250
Saint Louis, MO 63105
(314)727-8200
Fax: (314)727-0249

Heartland Capital Fund, Ltd.
PO Box 642117
Omaha, NE 68154
(402)778-5124
Fax: (402)445-2370
Website: http://www.heartland
capitalfund.com

Odin Capital Group
1625 Farnam St., Ste. 700
Omaha, NE 68102
(402)346-6200
Fax: (402)342-9311
Website: http://www.odincapital.com

Nevada

Edge Capital Investment Co. LLC
1350 E. Flamingo Rd., Ste. 3000
Las Vegas, NV 89119
(702)438-3343
E-mail: info@edgecapital.net
Website: http://www.edgecapital.net

The Benefit Capital Companies Inc.
PO Box 542
Logandale, NV 89021
(702)398-3222
Fax: (702)398-3700

Millennium Three Venture Group LLC
6880 South McCarran Blvd., Ste. A-11
Reno, NV 89509
(775)954-2020
Fax: (775)954-2023
Website: http://www.m3vg.com

New Jersey

Alan I. Goldman & Associates
497 Ridgewood Ave.
Glen Ridge, NJ 07028
(973)857-5680
Fax: (973)509-8856

CS Capital Partners LLC
328 Second St., Ste. 200
Lakewood, NJ 08701
(732)901-1111
Fax: (212)202-5071
Website: http://www.cs-capital.com

Edison Venture Fund
1009 Lenox Dr., Ste. 4
Lawrenceville, NJ 08648
(609)896-1900
Fax: (609)896-0066
E-mail: info@edisonventure.com
Website: http://www.edisonventure.com

Tappan Zee Capital Corp. (New Jersey)
201 Lower Notch Rd.
PO Box 416
Little Falls, NJ 07424
(973)256-8280
Fax: (973)256-2841

The CIT Group/Venture Capital, Inc.
650 CIT Dr.
Livingston, NJ 07039
(973)740-5429
Fax: (973)740-5555
Website: http://www.cit.com

Capital Express, L.L.C.
1100 Valleybrook Ave.
Lyndhurst, NJ 07071
(201)438-8228
Fax: (201)438-5131
E-mail: niles@capitalexpress.com
Website: http://www.capitalexpress.com

Westford Technology Ventures, L.P.
17 Academy St.
Newark, NJ 07102
(973)624-2131
Fax: (973)624-2008

Accel Partners
1 Palmer Sq.
Princeton, NJ 08542

(609)683-4500
Fax: (609)683-4880
Website: http://www.accel.com

Cardinal Partners
221 Nassau St.
Princeton, NJ 08542
(609)924-6452
Fax: (609)683-0174
Website: http://www.cardinal
healthpartners.com

Domain Associates L.L.C.
One Palmer Sq., Ste. 515
Princeton, NJ 08542
(609)683-5656
Fax: (609)683-9789
Website: http://www.domainvc.com

Johnston Associates, Inc.
181 Cherry Valley Rd.
Princeton, NJ 08540
(609)924-3131
Fax: (609)683-7524
E-mail: jaincorp@aol.com

Kemper Ventures
Princeton Forrestal Village
155 Village Blvd.
Princeton, NJ 08540
(609)936-3035
Fax: (609)936-3051

Penny Lane Parnters
One Palmer Sq., Ste. 309
Princeton, NJ 08542
(609)497-4646
Fax: (609)497-0611

Early Stage Enterprises L.P.
995 Route 518
Skillman, NJ 08558
(609)921-8896
Fax: (609)921-8703
Website: http://www.esevc.com

MBW Management Inc.
1 Springfield Ave.
Summit, NJ 07901
(908)273-4060
Fax: (908)273-4430

BCI Advisors, Inc.
Glenpointe Center W.
Teaneck, NJ 07666
(201)836-3900
Fax: (201)836-6368
E-mail: info@bciadvisors.com
Website: http://www.bci
partners.com

Demuth, Folger & Wetherill / DFW Capital Partners
Glenpointe Center E., 5th Fl.
300 Frank W. Burr Blvd.
Teaneck, NJ 07666
(201)836-2233
Fax: (201)836-5666
Website: http://www.dfwcapital.com

First Princeton Capital Corp.
189 Berdan Ave., No. 131
Wayne, NJ 07470-3233
(973)278-3233
Fax: (973)278-4290
Website: http://www.lytellcatt.net

Edelson Technology Partners
300 Tice Blvd.
Woodcliff Lake, NJ 07675
(201)930-9898
Fax: (201)930-8899
Website: http://www.edelsontech.com

New Mexico

Bruce F. Glaspell & Associates
10400 Academy Rd. NE, Ste. 313
Albuquerque, NM 87111
(505)292-4505
Fax: (505)292-4258

High Desert Ventures, Inc.
6101 Imparata St. NE, Ste. 1721
Albuquerque, NM 87111
(505)797-3330
Fax: (505)338-5147

New Business Capital Fund, Ltd.
5805 Torreon NE
Albuquerque, NM 87109
(505)822-8445

SBC Ventures
10400 Academy Rd. NE, Ste. 313
Albuquerque, NM 87111
(505)292-4505
Fax: (505)292-4528

Technology Ventures Corp.
1155 University Blvd. SE
Albuquerque, NM 87106
(505)246-2882
Fax: (505)246-2891

New York

New York State Science & Technology Foundation
Small Business Technology Investment Fund
99 Washington Ave., Ste. 1731
Albany, NY 12210

(518)473-9741
Fax: (518)473-6876

Rand Capital Corp.
2200 Rand Bldg.
Buffalo, NY 14203
(716)853-0802
Fax: (716)854-8480
Website: http://www.randcapital.com

Seed Capital Partners
620 Main St.
Buffalo, NY 14202
(716)845-7520
Fax: (716)845-7539
Website: http://www.seedcp.com

Coleman Venture Group
5909 Northern Blvd.
PO Box 224
East Norwich, NY 11732
(516)626-3642
Fax: (516)626-9722

Vega Capital Corp.
45 Knollwood Rd.
Elmsford, NY 10523
(914)345-9500
Fax: (914)345-9505

Herbert Young Securities, Inc.
98 Cuttermill Rd.
Great Neck, NY 11021
(516)487-8300
Fax: (516)487-8319

Sterling/Carl Marks Capital, Inc.
175 Great Neck Rd., Ste. 408
Great Neck, NY 11021
(516)482-7374
Fax: (516)487-0781
E-mail: stercrlmar@aol.com
Website: http://www.serling
carlmarks.com

Impex Venture Management Co.
PO Box 1570
Green Island, NY 12183
(518)271-8008
Fax: (518)271-9101

Corporate Venture Partners L.P.
200 Sunset Park
Ithaca, NY 14850
(607)257-6323
Fax: (607)257-6128

Arthur P. Gould & Co.
One Wilshire Dr.
Lake Success, NY 11020
(516)773-3000
Fax: (516)773-3289

Dauphin Capital Partners
108 Forest Ave.
Locust Valley, NY 11560
(516)759-3339
Fax: (516)759-3322
Website: http://www.dauphincapital.com

550 Digital Media Ventures
555 Madison Ave., 10th Fl.
New York, NY 10022
Website: http://www.550dmv.com

Aberlyn Capital Management Co., Inc.
500 Fifth Ave.
New York, NY 10110
(212)391-7750
Fax: (212)391-7762

Adler & Company
342 Madison Ave., Ste. 807
New York, NY 10173
(212)599-2535
Fax: (212)599-2526

Alimansky Capital Group, Inc.
605 Madison Ave., Ste. 300
New York, NY 10022-1901
(212)832-7300
Fax: (212)832-7338

Allegra Partners
515 Madison Ave., 29th Fl.
New York, NY 10022
(212)826-9080
Fax: (212)759-2561

The Argentum Group
The Chyrsler Bldg.
405 Lexington Ave.
New York, NY 10174
(212)949-6262
Fax: (212)949-8294
Website: http://www.argentum
group.com

Axavision Inc.
14 Wall St., 26th Fl.
New York, NY 10005
(212)619-4000
Fax: (212)619-7202

Bedford Capital Corp.
18 East 48th St., Ste. 1800
New York, NY 10017
(212)688-5700
Fax: (212)754-4699
E-mail: info@bedfordnyc.com
Website: http://www.bedfordnyc.com

Bloom & Co.
950 Third Ave.

New York, NY 10022
(212)838-1858
Fax: (212)838-1843

Bristol Capital Management
300 Park Ave., 17th Fl.
New York, NY 10022
(212)572-6306
Fax: (212)705-4292

Citicorp Venture Capital Ltd. (New York City)
399 Park Ave., 14th Fl.
Zone 4
New York, NY 10043
(212)559-1127
Fax: (212)888-2940

CM Equity Partners
135 E. 57th St.
New York, NY 10022
(212)909-8428
Fax: (212)980-2630

Cohen & Co., L.L.C.
800 Third Ave.
New York, NY 10022
(212)317-2250
Fax: (212)317-2255
E-mail: nlcohen@aol.com

Cornerstone Equity Investors, L.L.C.
717 5th Ave., Ste. 1100
New York, NY 10022
(212)753-0901
Fax: (212)826-6798
Website: http://www.cornerstone-equity.com

CW Group, Inc.
1041 3rd Ave., 2nd fl.
New York, NY 10021
(212)308-5266
Fax: (212)644-0354
Website: http://www.cwventures.com

DH Blair Investment Banking Corp.
44 Wall St., 2nd Fl.
New York, NY 10005
(212)495-5000
Fax: (212)269-1438

Dresdner Kleinwort Capital
75 Wall St.
New York, NY 10005
(212)429-3131
Fax: (212)429-3139
Website: http://www.dresdnerkb.com

East River Ventures, L.P.
645 Madison Ave., 22nd Fl.

New York, NY 10022
(212)644-2322
Fax: (212)644-5498

Easton Hunt Capital Partners
641 Lexington Ave., 21st Fl.
New York, NY 10017
(212)702-0950
Fax: (212)702-0952
Website: http://www.eastoncapital.com

Elk Associates Funding Corp.
747 3rd Ave., Ste. 4C
New York, NY 10017
(212)355-2449
Fax: (212)759-3338

EOS Partners, L.P.
320 Park Ave., 22nd Fl.
New York, NY 10022
(212)832-5800
Fax: (212)832-5815
E-mail: mfirst@eospartners.com
Website: http://www.eospartners.com

Euclid Partners
45 Rockefeller Plaza, Ste. 3240
New York, NY 10111
(212)218-6880
Fax: (212)218-6877
E-mail: graham@euclidpartners.com
Website: http://www.euclidpartners.com

Evergreen Capital Partners, Inc.
150 East 58th St.
New York, NY 10155
(212)813-0758
Fax: (212)813-0754

Exeter Capital L.P.
10 E. 53rd St.
New York, NY 10022
(212)872-1172
Fax: (212)872-1198
E-mail: exeter@usa.net

Financial Technology Research Corp.
518 Broadway
Penthouse
New York, NY 10012
(212)625-9100
Fax: (212)431-0300
E-mail: fintek@financier.com

4C Ventures
237 Park Ave., Ste. 801
New York, NY 10017
(212)692-3680
Fax: (212)692-3685
Website: http://www.4cventures.com

Fusient Ventures
99 Park Ave., 20th Fl.
New York, NY 10016
(212)972-8999
Fax: (212)972-9876
E-mail: info@fusient.com
Website: http://www.fusient.com

Generation Capital Partners
551 Fifth Ave., Ste. 3100
New York, NY 10176
(212)450-8507
Fax: (212)450-8550
Website: http://www.genpartners.com

Golub Associates, Inc.
555 Madison Ave.
New York, NY 10022
(212)750-6060
Fax: (212)750-5505

Hambro America Biosciences Inc.
650 Madison Ave., 21st Floor
New York, NY 10022
(212)223-7400
Fax: (212)223-0305

Hanover Capital Corp.
505 Park Ave., 15th Fl.
New York, NY 10022
(212)755-1222
Fax: (212)935-1787

Harvest Partners, Inc.
280 Park Ave, 33rd Fl.
New York, NY 10017
(212)559-6300
Fax: (212)812-0100
Website: http://www.harvpart.com

Holding Capital Group, Inc.
10 E. 53rd St., 30th Fl.
New York, NY 10022
(212)486-6670
Fax: (212)486-0843

Hudson Venture Partners
660 Madison Ave., 14th Fl.
New York, NY 10021-8405
(212)644-9797
Fax: (212)644-7430
Website: http://www.hudsonptr.com

IBJS Capital Corp.
1 State St., 9th Fl.
New York, NY 10004
(212)858-2018
Fax: (212)858-2768

InterEquity Capital Partners, L.P.
220 5th Ave.
New York, NY 10001

(212)779-2022
Fax: (212)779-2103
Website: http://www.interequity-capital.com

The Jordan Edmiston Group Inc.
150 East 52nd St., 18th Fl.
New York, NY 10022
(212)754-0710
Fax: (212)754-0337

Josephberg, Grosz and Co., Inc.
633 3rd Ave., 13th Fl.
New York, NY 10017
(212)974-9926
Fax: (212)397-5832

J.P. Morgan Capital Corp.
60 Wall St.
New York, NY 10260-0060
(212)648-9000
Fax: (212)648-5002
Website: http://www.jpmorgan.com

The Lambda Funds
380 Lexington Ave., 54th Fl.
New York, NY 10168
(212)682-3454
Fax: (212)682-9231

Lepercq Capital Management Inc.
1675 Broadway
New York, NY 10019
(212)698-0795
Fax: (212)262-0155

Loeb Partners Corp.
61 Broadway, Ste. 2400
New York, NY 10006
(212)483-7000
Fax: (212)574-2001

Madison Investment Partners
660 Madison Ave.
New York, NY 10021
(212)223-2600
Fax: (212)223-8208

MC Capital Inc.
520 Madison Ave., 16th Fl.
New York, NY 10022
(212)644-0841
Fax: (212)644-2926

**McCown, De Leeuw and Co.
(New York)**
65 E. 55th St., 36th Fl.
New York, NY 10022
(212)355-5500
Fax: (212)355-6283
Website: http://www.mdcpartners.com

Morgan Stanley Venture Partners
1221 Avenue of the Americas, 33rd Fl.
New York, NY 10020
(212)762-7900
Fax: (212)762-8424
E-mail: msventures@ms.com
Website: http://www.msvp.com

Nazem and Co.
645 Madison Ave., 12th Fl.
New York, NY 10022
(212)371-7900
Fax: (212)371-2150

Needham Capital Management, L.L.C.
445 Park Ave.
New York, NY 10022
(212)371-8300
Fax: (212)705-0299
Website: http://www.needhamco.com

Norwood Venture Corp.
1430 Broadway, Ste. 1607
New York, NY 10018
(212)869-5075
Fax: (212)869-5331
E-mail: nvc@mail.idt.net
Website: http://www.norven.com

Noveltek Venture Corp.
521 Fifth Ave., Ste. 1700
New York, NY 10175
(212)286-1963

Paribas Principal, Inc.
787 7th Ave.
New York, NY 10019
(212)841-2005
Fax: (212)841-3558

Patricof & Co. Ventures, Inc. (New York)
445 Park Ave.
New York, NY 10022
(212)753-6300
Fax: (212)319-6155
Website: http://www.patricof.com

The Platinum Group, Inc.
350 Fifth Ave, Ste. 7113
New York, NY 10118
(212)736-4300
Fax: (212)736-6086
Website: http://www.platinumgroup.com

Pomona Capital
780 Third Ave., 28th Fl.
New York, NY 10017
(212)593-3639
Fax: (212)593-3987
Website: http://www.pomonacapital.com

Prospect Street Ventures
10 East 40th St., 44th Fl.
New York, NY 10016
(212)448-0702
Fax: (212)448-9652
E-mail: wkohler@prospectstreet.com
Website: http://www.prospectstreet.com

Regent Capital Management
505 Park Ave., Ste. 1700
New York, NY 10022
(212)735-9900
Fax: (212)735-9908

Rothschild Ventures, Inc.
1251 Avenue of the Americas, 51st Fl.
New York, NY 10020
(212)403-3500
Fax: (212)403-3652
Website: http://www.nmrothschild.com

Sandler Capital Management
767 Fifth Ave., 45th Fl.
New York, NY 10153
(212)754-8100
Fax: (212)826-0280

Siguler Guff & Company
630 Fifth Ave., 16th Fl.
New York, NY 10111
(212)332-5100
Fax: (212)332-5120

Spencer Trask Ventures Inc.
535 Madison Ave.
New York, NY 10022
(212)355-5565
Fax: (212)751-3362
Website: http://www.spencertrask.com

Sprout Group (New York City)
277 Park Ave.
New York, NY 10172
(212)892-3600
Fax: (212)892-3444
E-mail: info@sproutgroup.com
Website: http://www.sproutgroup.com

US Trust Private Equity
114 W.47th St.
New York, NY 10036
(212)852-3949
Fax: (212)852-3759
Website: http://www.ustrust.com/
privateequity

Vencon Management Inc.
301 West 53rd St., Ste. 10F
New York, NY 10019
(212)581-8787
Fax: (212)397-4126
Website: http://www.venconinc.com

Venrock Associates
30 Rockefeller Plaza, Ste. 5508
New York, NY 10112
(212)649-5600
Fax: (212)649-5788
Website: http://www.venrock.com

Venture Capital Fund of America, Inc.
509 Madison Ave., Ste. 812
New York, NY 10022
(212)838-5577
Fax: (212)838-7614
E-mail: mail@vcfa.com
Website: http://www.vcfa.com

Venture Opportunities Corp.
150 E. 58th St.
New York, NY 10155
(212)832-3737
Fax: (212)980-6603

Warburg Pincus Ventures, Inc.
466 Lexington Ave., 11th Fl.
New York, NY 10017
(212)878-9309
Fax: (212)878-9200
Website: http://www.warburgpincus.com

Wasserstein, Perella & Co. Inc.
31 W. 52nd St., 27th Fl.
New York, NY 10019
(212)702-5691
Fax: (212)969-7879

Welsh, Carson, Anderson, & Stowe
320 Park Ave., Ste. 2500
New York, NY 10022-6815
(212)893-9500
Fax: (212)893-9575

Whitney and Co. (New York)
630 Fifth Ave. Ste. 3225
New York, NY 10111
(212)332-2400
Fax: (212)332-2422
Website: http://www.jhwitney.com

Winthrop Ventures
74 Trinity Place, Ste. 600
New York, NY 10006
(212)422-0100

The Pittsford Group
8 Lodge Pole Rd.
Pittsford, NY 14534
(716)223-3523

Genesee Funding
70 Linden Oaks, 3rd Fl.
Rochester, NY 14625
(716)383-5550
Fax: (716)383-5305

Gabelli Multimedia Partners
One Corporate Center
Rye, NY 10580
(914)921-5395
Fax: (914)921-5031

Stamford Financial
108 Main St.
Stamford, NY 12167
(607)652-3311
Fax: (607)652-6301
Website: http://www.stamford
financial.com

Northwood Ventures LLC
485 Underhill Blvd., Ste. 205
Syosset, NY 11791
(516)364-5544
Fax: (516)364-0879
E-mail: northwood@northwood.com
Website: http://www.north
woodventures.com

Exponential Business Development Co.
216 Walton St.
Syracuse, NY 13202-1227
(315)474-4500
Fax: (315)474-4682
E-mail: dirksonn@aol.com
Website: http://www.exponential-ny.com

Onondaga Venture Capital Fund Inc.
714 State Tower Bldg.
Syracuse, NY 13202
(315)478-0157
Fax: (315)478-0158

Bessemer Venture Partners (Westbury)
1400 Old Country Rd., Ste. 109
Westbury, NY 11590
(516)997-2300
Fax: (516)997-2371
E-mail: bob@bvpny.com
Website: http://www.bvp.com

Ovation Capital Partners
120 Bloomingdale Rd., 4th Fl.
White Plains, NY 10605
(914)258-0011
Fax: (914)684-0848
Website: http://www.ovation
capital.com

North Carolina

Carolinas Capital Investment Corp.
1408 Biltmore Dr.
Charlotte, NC 28207
(704)375-3888
Fax: (704)375-6226

First Union Capital Partners
1st Union Center, 12th Fl.
301 S. College St.
Charlotte, NC 28288-0732
(704)383-0000
Fax: (704)374-6711
Website: http://www.fucp.com

Frontier Capital LLC
525 North Tryon St., Ste. 1700
Charlotte, NC 28202
(704)414-2880
Fax: (704)414-2881
Website: http://www.frontierfunds.com

Kitty Hawk Capital
2700 Coltsgate Rd., Ste. 202
Charlotte, NC 28211
(704)362-3909
Fax: (704)362-2774
Website: http://www.kittyhawk
capital.com

Piedmont Venture Partners
One Morrocroft Centre
6805 Morisson Blvd., Ste. 380
Charlotte, NC 28211
(704)731-5200
Fax: (704)365-9733
Website: http://www.piedmontvp.com

Ruddick Investment Co.
1800 Two First Union Center
Charlotte, NC 28282
(704)372-5404
Fax: (704)372-6409

The Shelton Companies Inc.
3600 One First Union Center
301 S. College St.
Charlotte, NC 28202
(704)348-2200
Fax: (704)348-2260

Wakefield Group
1110 E. Morehead St.
PO Box 36329
Charlotte, NC 28236
(704)372-0355
Fax: (704)372-8216
Website: http://www.wakefiel
dgroup.com

Aurora Funds, Inc.
2525 Meridian Pkwy., Ste. 220
Durham, NC 27713
(919)484-0400
Fax: (919)484-0444
Website: http://www.aurora
funds.com

Intersouth Partners
3211 Shannon Rd., Ste. 610
Durham, NC 27707
(919)493-6640
Fax: (919)493-6649
E-mail: info@intersouth.com
Website: http://www.intersouth.com

Geneva Merchant Banking Partners
PO Box 21962
Greensboro, NC 27420
(336)275-7002
Fax: (336)275-9155
Website: http://www.geneva
merchantbank.com

The North Carolina Enterprise Fund, L.P.
3600 Glenwood Ave., Ste. 107
Raleigh, NC 27612
(919)781-2691
Fax: (919)783-9195
Website: http://www.ncef.com

Ohio

Senmend Medical Ventures
4445 Lake Forest Dr., Ste. 600
Cincinnati, OH 45242
(513)563-3264
Fax: (513)563-3261

The Walnut Group
312 Walnut St., Ste. 1151
Cincinnati, OH 45202
(513)651-3300
Fax: (513)929-4441
Website: http://www.thewal
nutgroup.com

Brantley Venture Partners
20600 Chagrin Blvd., Ste. 1150
Cleveland, OH 44122
(216)283-4800
Fax: (216)283-5324

Clarion Capital Corp.
1801 E. 9th St., Ste. 1120
Cleveland, OH 44114
(216)687-1096
Fax: (216)694-3545

Crystal Internet Venture Fund, L.P.
1120 Chester Ave., Ste. 418
Cleveland, OH 44114
(216)263-5515
Fax: (216)263-5518
E-mail: jf@crystalventure.com
Website: http://www.crystal
venture.com

Key Equity Capital Corp.
127 Public Sq., 28th Fl.
Cleveland, OH 44114
(216)689-3000
Fax: (216)689-3204
Website: http://www.keybank.com

Morgenthaler Ventures
Terminal Tower
50 Public Square, Ste. 2700
Cleveland, OH 44113
(216)416-7500
Fax: (216)416-7501
Website: http://www.morgenthaler.com

National City Equity Partners Inc.
1965 E. 6th St.
Cleveland, OH 44114
(216)575-2491
Fax: (216)575-9965
E-mail: nccap@aol.com
Website: http://www.nccapital.com

Primus Venture Partners, Inc.
5900 LanderBrook Dr., Ste. 2000
Cleveland, OH 44124-4020
(440)684-7300
Fax: (440)684-7342
E-mail: info@primusventure.com
Website: http://www.primusventure.com

Banc One Capital Partners (Columbus)
150 East Gay St., 24th Fl.
Columbus, OH 43215
(614)217-1100
Fax: (614)217-1217

Battelle Venture Partners
505 King Ave.
Columbus, OH 43201
(614)424-7005
Fax: (614)424-4874

Ohio Partners
62 E. Board St., 3rd Fl.
Columbus, OH 43215
(614)621-1210
Fax: (614)621-1240

Capital Technology Group, L.L.C.
400 Metro Place North, Ste. 300
Dublin, OH 43017
(614)792-6066
Fax: (614)792-6036
E-mail: info@capitaltech.com
Website: http://www.capitaltech.com

Northwest Ohio Venture Fund
4159 Holland-Sylvania R., Ste. 202
Toledo, OH 43623
(419)824-8144

Fax: (419)882-2035
E-mail: bwalsh@novf.com

Oklahoma

Moore & Associates
1000 W. Wilshire Blvd., Ste. 370
Oklahoma City, OK 73116
(405)842-3660
Fax: (405)842-3763

Chisholm Private Capital Partners
100 West 5th St., Ste. 805
Tulsa, OK 74103
(918)584-0440
Fax: (918)584-0441
Website: http://www.chisholmvc.com

Davis, Tuttle Venture Partners (Tulsa)
320 S. Boston, Ste. 1000
Tulsa, OK 74103-3703
(918)584-7272
Fax: (918)582-3404
Website: http://www.davistuttle.com

RBC Ventures
2627 E. 21st St.
Tulsa, OK 74114
(918)744-5607
Fax: (918)743-8630

Oregon

Utah Ventures II LP
10700 SW Beaverton-Hillsdale Hwy.,
Ste. 548
Beaverton, OR 97005
(503)574-4125
E-mail: adishlip@uven.com
Website: http://www.uven.com

Orien Ventures
14523 SW Westlake Dr.
Lake Oswego, OR 97035
(503)699-1680
Fax: (503)699-1681

OVP Venture Partners (Lake Oswego)
340 Oswego Pointe Dr., Ste. 200
Lake Oswego, OR 97034
(503)697-8766
Fax: (503)697-8863
E-mail: info@ovp.com
Website: http://www.ovp.com

Oregon Resource and Technology Development Fund
4370 NE Halsey St., Ste. 233
Portland, OR 97213-1566
(503)282-4462
Fax: (503)282-2976

Shaw Venture Partners
400 SW 6th Ave., Ste. 1100
Portland, OR 97204-1636
(503)228-4884
Fax: (503)227-2471
Website: http://www.shawventures.com

Pennsylvania

Mid-Atlantic Venture Funds
125 Goodman Dr.
Bethlehem, PA 18015
(610)865-6550
Fax: (610)865-6427
Website: http://www.mavf.com

Newspring Ventures
100 W. Elm St., Ste. 101
Conshohocken, PA 19428
(610)567-2380
Fax: (610)567-2388
Website: http://www.news
printventures.com

Patricof & Co. Ventures, Inc.
455 S. Gulph Rd., Ste. 410
King of Prussia, PA 19406
(610)265-0286
Fax: (610)265-4959
Website: http://www.patricof.com

Loyalhanna Venture Fund
527 Cedar Way, Ste. 104
Oakmont, PA 15139
(412)820-7035
Fax: (412)820-7036

Innovest Group Inc.
2000 Market St., Ste. 1400
Philadelphia, PA 19103
(215)564-3960
Fax: (215)569-3272

Keystone Venture Capital Management Co.
1601 Market St., Ste. 2500
Philadelphia, PA 19103
(215)241-1200
Fax: (215)241-1211
Website: http://www.keystonevc.com

Liberty Venture Partners
2005 Market St., Ste. 200
Philadelphia, PA 19103
(215)282-4484
Fax: (215)282-4485
E-mail: info@libertyvp.com
Website: http://www.libertyvp.com

Penn Janney Fund, Inc.
1801 Market St., 11th Fl.
Philadelphia, PA 19103

(215)665-4447
Fax: (215)557-0820

Philadelphia Ventures, Inc.
The Bellevue
200 S. Broad St.
Philadelphia, PA 19102
(215)732-4445
Fax: (215)732-4644

Birchmere Ventures Inc.
2000 Technology Dr.
Pittsburgh, PA 15219-3109
(412)803-8000
Fax: (412)687-8139
Website: http://www.birchmerevc.com

CEO Venture Fund
2000 Technology Dr., Ste. 160
Pittsburgh, PA 15219-3109
(412)687-3451
Fax: (412)687-8139
E-mail: ceofund@aol.com
Website: http://www.ceoventure
fund.com

Innovation Works Inc.
2000 Technology Dr., Ste. 250
Pittsburgh, PA 15219
(412)681-1520
Fax: (412)681-2625
Website: http://www.innovation
works.org

Keystone Minority Capital Fund L.P.
1801 Centre Ave., Ste. 201
Williams Sq.
Pittsburgh, PA 15219
(412)338-2230
Fax: (412)338-2224

Mellon Ventures, Inc.
One Mellon Bank Ctr., Rm. 3500
Pittsburgh, PA 15258
(412)236-3594
Fax: (412)236-3593
Website: http://www.mellon
ventures.com

Pennsylvania Growth Fund
5850 Ellsworth Ave., Ste. 303
Pittsburgh, PA 15232
(412)661-1000
Fax: (412)361-0676

Point Venture Partners
The Century Bldg.
130 Seventh St., 7th Fl.
Pittsburgh, PA 15222
(412)261-1966
Fax: (412)261-1718

Cross Atlantic Capital Partners
5 Radnor Corporate Center, Ste. 555
Radnor, PA 19087
(610)995-2650
Fax: (610)971-2062
Website: http://www.xacp.com

Meridian Venture Partners (Radnor)
The Radnor Court Bldg., Ste. 140
259 Radnor-Chester Rd.
Radnor, PA 19087
(610)254-2999
Fax: (610)254-2996
E-mail: mvpart@ix.netcom.com

TDH
919 Conestoga Rd., Bldg. 1, Ste. 301
Rosemont, PA 19010
(610)526-9970
Fax: (610)526-9971

Adams Capital Management
500 Blackburn Ave.
Sewickley, PA 15143
(412)749-9454
Fax: (412)749-9459
Website: http://www.acm.com

S.R. One, Ltd.
Four Tower Bridge
200 Barr Harbor Dr., Ste. 250
W. Conshohocken, PA 19428
(610)567-1000
Fax: (610)567-1039

Greater Philadelphia Venture Capital Corp.
351 East Conestoga Rd.
Wayne, PA 19087
(610)688-6829
Fax: (610)254-8958

PA Early Stage
435 Devon Park Dr., Bldg. 500, Ste. 510
Wayne, PA 19087
(610)293-4075
Fax: (610)254-4240
Website: http://www.paearlystage.com

The Sandhurst Venture Fund, L.P.
351 E. Constoga Rd.
Wayne, PA 19087
(610)254-8900
Fax: (610)254-8958

TL Ventures
700 Bldg.
435 Devon Park Dr.
Wayne, PA 19087-1990
(610)975-3765
Fax: (610)254-4210
Website: http://www.tlventures.com

Rockhill Ventures, Inc.
100 Front St., Ste. 1350
West Conshohocken, PA 19428
(610)940-0300
Fax: (610)940-0301

Puerto Rico

Advent-Morro Equity Partners
Banco Popular Bldg.
206 Tetuan St., Ste. 903
San Juan, PR 00902
(787)725-5285
Fax: (787)721-1735

North America Investment Corp.
Mercantil Plaza, Ste. 813
PO Box 191831
San Juan, PR 00919
(787)754-6178
Fax: (787)754-6181

Rhode Island

Manchester Humphreys, Inc.
40 Westminster St., Ste. 900
Providence, RI 02903
(401)454-0400
Fax: (401)454-0403

Navis Partners
50 Kennedy Plaza, 12th Fl.
Providence, RI 02903
(401)278-6770
Fax: (401)278-6387
Website: http://www.navis
partners.com

South Carolina

Capital Insights, L.L.C.
PO Box 27162
Greenville, SC 29616-2162
(864)242-6832
Fax: (864)242-6755
E-mail: jwarner@capitalinsights.com
Website: http://www.capitalin
sights.com

Transamerica Mezzanine Financing
7 N. Laurens St., Ste. 603
Greenville, SC 29601
(864)232-6198
Fax: (864)241-4444

Tennessee

Valley Capital Corp.
Krystal Bldg.
100 W. Martin Luther King Blvd.,
Ste. 212

Chattanooga, TN 37402
(423)265-1557
Fax: (423)265-1588

Coleman Swenson Booth Inc.
237 2nd Ave. S
Franklin, TN 37064-2649
(615)791-9462
Fax: (615)791-9636
Website: http://
www.colemanswenson.com

Capital Services & Resources, Inc.
5159 Wheelis Dr., Ste. 106
Memphis, TN 38117
(901)761-2156
Fax: (907)767-0060

Paradigm Capital Partners LLC
6410 Poplar Ave., Ste. 395
Memphis, TN 38119
(901)682-6060
Fax: (901)328-3061

SSM Ventures
845 Crossover Ln., Ste. 140
Memphis, TN 38117
(901)767-1131
Fax: (901)767-1135
Website: http://www.ssm
ventures.com

Capital Across America L.P.
501 Union St., Ste. 201
Nashville, TN 37219
(615)254-1414
Fax: (615)254-1856
Website: http://
www.capitalacrossamerica.com

Equitas L.P.
2000 Glen Echo Rd., Ste. 101
PO Box 158838
Nashville, TN 37215-8838
(615)383-8673
Fax: (615)383-8693

Massey Burch Capital Corp.
One Burton Hills Blvd., Ste. 350
Nashville, TN 37215
(615)665-3221
Fax: (615)665-3240
E-mail: tcalton@masseyburch.com
Website: http://www.masseyburch.com

Nelson Capital Corp.
3401 West End Ave., Ste. 300
Nashville, TN 37203
(615)292-8787
Fax: (615)385-3150

Texas

Phillips-Smith Specialty Retail Group
5080 Spectrum Dr., Ste. 805 W
Addison, TX 75001
(972)387-0725
Fax: (972)458-2560
E-mail: pssrg@aol.com
Website: http://www.phillips-smith.com

Austin Ventures, L.P.
701 Brazos St., Ste. 1400
Austin, TX 78701
(512)485-1900
Fax: (512)476-3952
E-mail: info@ausven.com
Website: http://www.austinventures.com

The Capital Network
3925 West Braker Lane, Ste. 406
Austin, TX 78759-5321
(512)305-0826
Fax: (512)305-0836

Techxas Ventures LLC
5000 Plaza on the Lake
Austin, TX 78746
(512)343-0118
Fax: (512)343-1879
E-mail: bruce@techxas.com
Website: http://www.techxas.com

Alliance Financial of Houston
218 Heather Ln.
Conroe, TX 77385-9013
(936)447-3300
Fax: (936)447-4222

Amerimark Capital Corp.
1111 W. Mockingbird, Ste. 1111
Dallas, TX 75247
(214)638-7878
Fax: (214)638-7612
E-mail: amerimark@amcapital.com
Website: http://www.amcapital.com

AMT Venture Partners / AMT Capital Ltd.
5220 Spring Valley Rd., Ste. 600
Dallas, TX 75240
(214)905-9757
Fax: (214)905-9761
Website: http://www.amtcapital.com

Arkoma Venture Partners
5950 Berkshire Lane, Ste. 1400
Dallas, TX 75225
(214)739-3515
Fax: (214)739-3572
E-mail: joelf@arkomavp.com

Capital Southwest Corp.
12900 Preston Rd., Ste. 700
Dallas, TX 75230
(972)233-8242
Fax: (972)233-7362
Website: http://
www.capitalsouthwest.com

Dali, Hook Partners
One Lincoln Center, Ste. 1550
5400 LBJ Freeway
Dallas, TX 75240
(972)991-5457
Fax: (972)991-5458
E-mail: dhook@hookpartners.com
Website: http://www.hookpartners.com

HO2 Partners
Two Galleria Tower
13455 Noel Rd., Ste. 1670
Dallas, TX 75240
(972)702-1144
Fax: (972)702-8234
Website: http://www.ho2.com

Interwest Partners (Dallas)
2 Galleria Tower
13455 Noel Rd., Ste. 1670
Dallas, TX 75240
(972)392-7279
Fax: (972)490-6348
Website: http://www.interwest.com

Kahala Investments, Inc.
8214 Westchester Dr., Ste. 715
Dallas, TX 75225
(214)987-0077
Fax: (214)987-2332

MESBIC Ventures Holding Co.
2435 North Central Expressway, Ste. 200
Dallas, TX 75080
(972)991-1597
Fax: (972)991-4770
Website: http://www.mvhc.com

North Texas MESBIC, Inc.
9500 Forest Lane, Ste. 430
Dallas, TX 75243
(214)221-3565
Fax: (214)221-3566

Richard Jaffe & Company, Inc,
7318 Royal Cir.
Dallas, TX 75230
(214)265-9397
Fax: (214)739-1845

Sevin Rosen Management Co.
13455 Noel Rd., Ste. 1670
Dallas, TX 75240

(972)702-1100
Fax: (972)702-1103
E-mail: info@srfunds.com
Website: http://www.srfunds.com

Stratford Capital Partners, L.P.
300 Crescent Ct., Ste. 500
Dallas, TX 75201
(214)740-7377
Fax: (214)720-7393
E-mail: stratcap@hmtf.com

Sunwestern Investment Group
12221 Merit Dr., Ste. 935
Dallas, TX 75251
(972)239-5650
Fax: (972)701-0024

Wingate Partners
750 N. St. Paul St., Ste. 1200
Dallas, TX 75201
(214)720-1313
Fax: (214)871-8799

Buena Venture Associates
201 Main St., 32nd Fl.
Fort Worth, TX 76102
(817)339-7400
Fax: (817)390-8408
Website: http://www.buenaventure.com

The Catalyst Group
3 Riverway, Ste. 770
Houston, TX 77056
(713)623-8133
Fax: (713)623-0473
E-mail: herman@thecatalystgroup.net
Website: http://www.thecatalyst
group.net

Cureton & Co., Inc.
1100 Louisiana, Ste. 3250
Houston, TX 77002
(713)658-9806
Fax: (713)658-0476

Davis, Tuttle Venture Partners (Dallas)
8 Greenway Plaza, Ste. 1020
Houston, TX 77046
(713)993-0440
Fax: (713)621-2297
Website: http://www.davistuttle.com

Houston Partners
401 Louisiana, 8th Fl.
Houston, TX 77002
(713)222-8600
Fax: (713)222-8932

Southwest Venture Group
10878 Westheimer, Ste. 178

Houston, TX 77042
(713)827-8947
(713)461-1470

AM Fund
4600 Post Oak Place, Ste. 100
Houston, TX 77027
(713)627-9111
Fax: (713)627-9119

Ventex Management, Inc.
3417 Milam St.
Houston, TX 77002-9531
(713)659-7870
Fax: (713)659-7855

MBA Venture Group
1004 Olde Town Rd., Ste. 102
Irving, TX 75061
(972)986-6703

First Capital Group Management Co.
750 East Mulberry St., Ste. 305
PO Box 15616
San Antonio, TX 78212
(210)736-4233
Fax: (210)736-5449

The Southwest Venture Partnerships
16414 San Pedro, Ste. 345
San Antonio, TX 78232
(210)402-1200
Fax: (210)402-1221
E-mail: swvp@aol.com

Medtech International Inc.
1742 Carriageway
Sugarland, TX 77478
(713)980-8474
Fax: (713)980-6343

Utah

First Security Business Investment Corp.
15 East 100 South, Ste. 100
Salt Lake City, UT 84111
(801)246-5737
Fax: (801)246-5740

Utah Ventures II, L.P.
423 Wakara Way, Ste. 206
Salt Lake City, UT 84108
(801)583-5922
Fax: (801)583-4105
Website: http://www.uven.com

Wasatch Venture Corp.
1 S. Main St., Ste. 1400
Salt Lake City, UT 84133
(801)524-8939

Fax: (801)524-8941
E-mail: mail@wasatchvc.com

Vermont

North Atlantic Capital Corp.
76 Saint Paul St., Ste. 600
Burlington, VT 05401
(802)658-7820
Fax: (802)658-5757
Website: http://www.north
atlanticcapital.com

Green Mountain Advisors Inc.
PO Box 1230
Quechee, VT 05059
(802)296-7800
Fax: (802)296-6012
Website: http://www.gmtcap.com

Virginia

Oxford Financial Services Corp.
Alexandria, VA 22314
(703)519-4900
Fax: (703)519-4910
E-mail: oxford133@aol.com

Continental SBIC
4141 N. Henderson Rd.
Arlington, VA 22203
(703)527-5200
Fax: (703)527-3700

Novak Biddle Venture Partners
1750 Tysons Blvd., Ste. 1190
McLean, VA 22102
(703)847-3770
Fax: (703)847-3771
E-mail: roger@novakbiddle.com
Website: http://www.novakbiddle.com

Spacevest
11911 Freedom Dr., Ste. 500
Reston, VA 20190
(703)904-9800
Fax: (703)904-0571
E-mail: spacevest@spacevest.com
Website: http://www.spacevest.com

Virginia Capital
1801 Libbie Ave., Ste. 201
Richmond, VA 23226
(804)648-4802
Fax: (804)648-4809
E-mail: webmaster@vacapital.com
Website: http://www.vacapital.com

Calvert Social Venture Partners
402 Maple Ave. W
Vienna, VA 22180

(703)255-4930
Fax: (703)255-4931
E-mail: calven2000@aol.com

Fairfax Partners
8000 Towers Crescent Dr., Ste. 940
Vienna, VA 22182
(703)847-9486
Fax: (703)847-0911

Global Internet Ventures
8150 Leesburg Pike, Ste. 1210
Vienna, VA 22182
(703)442-3300
Fax: (703)442-3388
Website: http://www.givinc.com

Walnut Capital Corp. (Vienna)
8000 Towers Crescent Dr., Ste. 1070
Vienna, VA 22182
(703)448-3771
Fax: (703)448-7751

Washington

Encompass Ventures
777 108th Ave. NE, Ste. 2300
Bellevue, WA 98004
(425)486-3900
Fax: (425)486-3901
E-mail: info@evpartners.com
Website: http://www.encom
passventures.com

Fluke Venture Partners
11400 SE Sixth St., Ste. 230
Bellevue, WA 98004
(425)453-4590
Fax: (425)453-4675
E-mail: gabelein@flukeventures.com
Website: http://www.flukeventures.com

Pacific Northwest Partners SBIC, L.P.
15352 SE 53rd St.
Bellevue, WA 98006
(425)455-9967
Fax: (425)455-9404

Materia Venture Associates, L.P.
3435 Carillon Pointe
Kirkland, WA 98033-7354
(425)822-4100
Fax: (425)827-4086

OVP Venture Partners (Kirkland)
2420 Carillon Pt.
Kirkland, WA 98033
(425)889-9192
Fax: (425)889-0152
E-mail: info@ovp.com
Website: http://www.ovp.com

Digital Partners
999 3rd Ave., Ste. 1610
Seattle, WA 98104
(206)405-3607
Fax: (206)405-3617
Website: http://www.digitalpartners.com

Frazier & Company
601 Union St., Ste. 3300
Seattle, WA 98101
(206)621-7200
Fax: (206)621-1848
E-mail: jon@frazierco.com

Kirlan Venture Capital, Inc.
221 First Ave. W, Ste. 108
Seattle, WA 98119-4223
(206)281-8610
Fax: (206)285-3451
Website: http://www.kirlanventure.com

Phoenix Partners
1000 2nd Ave., Ste. 3600
Seattle, WA 98104
(206)624-8968
Fax: (206)624-1907

Voyager Capital
800 5th St., Ste. 4100
Seattle, WA 98103
(206)470-1180
Fax: (206)470-1185
E-mail: info@voyagercap.com
Website: http://www.voyagercap.com

Northwest Venture Associates
221 N. Wall St., Ste. 628
Spokane, WA 99201
(509)747-0728
Fax: (509)747-0758
Website: http://www.nwva.com

Wisconsin

Venture Investors Management, L.L.C.
University Research Park
505 S. Rosa Rd.
Madison, WI 53719
(608)441-2700
Fax: (608)441-2727
E-mail: roger@ventureinvestors.com
Website: http://www.venture
investers.com

Capital Investments, Inc.
1009 West Glen Oaks Lane, Ste. 103
Mequon, WI 53092
(414)241-0303
Fax: (414)241-8451
Website: http://
www.capitalinvestmentsinc.com

Future Value Venture, Inc.
2745 N. Martin Luther King
Dr., Ste. 204
Milwaukee, WI 53212-2300
(414)264-2252
Fax: (414)264-2253
E-mail: fvvventures@aol.com
William Beckett, President

Lubar and Co., Inc.
700 N. Water St., Ste. 1200
Milwaukee, WI 53202
(414)291-9000
Fax: (414)291-9061

GCI
20875 Crossroads Cir., Ste. 100
Waukesha, WI 53186
(262)798-5080
Fax: (262)798-5087

Glossary of Small Business Terms

Absolute liability
Liability that is incurred due to product defects or negligent actions. Manufacturers or retail establishments are held responsible, even though the defect or action may not have been intentional or negligent.

ACE
See Active Corps of Executives

Accident and health benefits
Benefits offered to employees and their families in order to offset the costs associated with accidental death, accidental injury, or sickness.

Account statement
A record of transactions, including payments, new debt, and deposits, incurred during a defined period of time.

Accounting system
System capturing the costs of all employees and/or machinery included in business expenses.

Accounts payable
See Trade credit

Accounts receivable
Unpaid accounts which arise from unsettled claims and transactions from the sale of a company's products or services to its customers.

Active Corps of Executives (ACE)
A group of volunteers for a management assistance program of the U.S. Small Business Administration; volunteers provide one-on-one counseling and teach workshops and seminars for small firms.

ADA
See Americans with Disabilities Act

Adaptation
The process whereby an invention is modified to meet the needs of users.

Adaptive engineering
The process whereby an invention is modified to meet the manufacturing and commercial requirements of a targeted market.

Adverse selection
The tendency for higher-risk individuals to purchase health care and more comprehensive plans, resulting in increased costs.

Advertising
A marketing tool used to capture public attention and influence purchasing decisions for a product or service. Utilizes various forms of media to generate consumer response, such as flyers, magazines, newspapers, radio, and television.

Age discrimination
The denial of the rights and privileges of employment based solely on the age of an individual.

Agency costs
Costs incurred to insure that the lender or investor maintains control over assets while allowing the borrower or entrepreneur to use them. Monitoring and information costs are the two major types of agency costs.

Agribusiness
The production and sale of commodities and products from the commercial farming industry.

America Online
An online service which is accessible by computer modem. The service features Internet access, bulletin boards, online periodicals, electronic mail, and other services for subscribers.

Americans with Disabilities Act (ADA)
Law designed to ensure equal access and opportunity to handicapped persons.

Annual report
Yearly financial report prepared by a business that adheres to the requirements set forth by the Securities and Exchange Commission (SEC).

Antitrust immunity
Exemption from prosecution under antitrust laws. In the transportation industry, firms with antitrust immunity are permitted under certain conditions to set schedules and sometimes prices for the public benefit.

Applied research
Scientific study targeted for use in a product or process.

Asians
A minority category used by the U.S. Bureau of the Census to represent a diverse group that includes Aleuts, Eskimos, American Indians, Asian Indians, Chinese, Japanese, Koreans, Vietnamese, Filipinos, Hawaiians, and other Pacific Islanders.

Assets
Anything of value owned by a company.

Audit
The verification of accounting records and business procedures conducted by an outside accounting service.

Average cost
Total production costs divided by the quantity produced.

Balance Sheet
A financial statement listing the total assets and liabilities of a company at a given time.

Bankruptcy
The condition in which a business cannot meet its debt obligations and petitions a federal district court either for reorganization of its debts (Chapter 11) or for liquidation of its assets (Chapter 7).

Basic research
Theoretical scientific exploration not targeted to application.

Basket clause
A provision specifying the amount of public pension funds that may be placed in investments not included on a state's legal list (see separate citation).

BBS
See Bulletin Board Service

BDC
See Business development corporation

Benefit
Various services, such as health care, flextime, day care, insurance, and vacation, offered to employees as part of a hiring package. Typically subsidized in whole or in part by the business.

BIDCO
See Business and industrial development company

Billing cycle
A system designed to evenly distribute customer billing throughout the month, preventing clerical backlogs.

Birth
See Business birth

Blue chip security
A low-risk, low-yield security representing an interest in a very stable company.

Blue sky laws
A general term that denotes various states' laws regulating securities.

Bond
A written instrument executed by a bidder or contractor (the principal) and a second party (the surety or sureties) to assure fulfillment of the principal's obligations to a third party (the obligee or government) identified in the bond. If the principal's obligations are not met, the bond assures payment to the extent stipulated of any loss sustained by the obligee.

Bonding requirements
Terms contained in a bond (see separate citation).

Bonus
An amount of money paid to an employee as a reward for achieving certain business goals or objectives.

Brainstorming
A group session where employees contribute their ideas for solving a problem or meeting a company objective without fear of retribution or ridicule.

Brand name
The part of a brand, trademark, or service mark that can be spoken. It can be a word, letter, or group of words or letters.

Bridge financing

A short-term loan made in expectation of intermediateterm or long-term financing. Can be used when a company plans to go public in the near future.

Broker

One who matches resources available for innovation with those who need them.

Budget

An estimate of the spending necessary to complete a project or offer a service in comparison to cash-on-hand and expected earnings for the coming year, with an emphasis on cost control.

Bulletin Board Service (BBS)

An online service enabling users to communicate with each other about specific topics.

Business and industrial development company (BIDCO)

A private, for-profit financing corporation chartered by the state to provide both equity and long-term debt capital to small business owners (see separate citations for equity and debt capital).

Business birth

The formation of a new establishment or enterprise. The appearance of a new establishment or enterprise in the Small Business Data Base (see separate citation).

Business conditions

Outside factors that can affect the financial performance of a business.

Business contractions

The number of establishments that have decreased in employment during a specified time.

Business cycle

A period of economic recession and recovery. These cycles vary in duration.

Business death

The voluntary or involuntary closure of a firm or establishment. The disappearance of an establishment or enterprise from the Small Business Data Base (see separate citation).

Business development corporation (BDC)

A business financing agency, usually composed of the financial institutions in an area or state, organized to assist in financing businesses unable to obtain assistance through normal channels; the risk is spread among various members of the business development corporation, and interest rates may vary somewhat from those charged by member institutions. A venture capital firm in which shares of ownership are publicly held and to which the Investment Act of 1940 applies.

Business dissolution

For enumeration purposes, the absence of a business that was present in the prior time period from any current record.

Business entry

See Business birth

Business ethics

Moral values and principles espoused by members of the business community as a guide to fair and honest business practices.

Business exit

See Business death

Business expansions

The number of establishments that added employees during a specified time.

Business failure

Closure of a business causing a loss to at least one creditor.

Business format franchising

The purchase of the name, trademark, and an ongoing business plan of the parent corporation or franchisor by the franchisee.

Business license

A legal authorization issued by municipal and state governments and required for business operations.

Business name

Enterprises must register their business names with local governments usually on a "doing business as" (DBA) form. (This name is sometimes referred to as a "fictional name.") The procedure is part of the business licensing process and prevents any other business from using that same name for a similar business in the same locality.

Business norms

See Financial ratios

Business permit
See Business license

Business plan
A document that spells out a company's expected course of action for a specified period, usually including a detailed listing and analysis of risks and uncertainties. For the small business, it should examine the proposed products, the market, the industry, the management policies, the marketing policies, production needs, and financial needs. Frequently, it is used as a prospectus for potential investors and lenders.

Business proposal
See Business plan

Business service firm
An establishment primarily engaged in rendering services to other business organizations on a fee or contract basis.

Business start
For enumeration purposes, a business with a name or similar designation that did not exist in a prior time period.

Cafeteria plan
See Flexible benefit plan

Capacity
Level of a firm's, industry's, or nation's output corresponding to full practical utilization of available resources.

Capital
Assets less liabilities, representing the ownership interest in a business. A stock of accumulated goods, especially at a specified time and in contrast to income received during a specified time period. Accumulated goods devoted to production. Accumulated possessions calculated to bring income.

Capital expenditure
Expenses incurred by a business for improvements that will depreciate over time.

Capital gain
The monetary difference between the purchase price and the selling price of capital. Capital gains are taxed at a rate of 28% by the federal government.

Capital intensity
The relative importance of capital in the production process, usually expressed as the ratio of capital to labor but also sometimes as the ratio of capital to output.

Capital resource
The equipment, facilities and labor used to create products and services.

Caribbean Basin Initiative
An interdisciplinary program to support commerce among the businesses in the nations of the Caribbean Basin and the United States. Agencies involved include: the Agency for International Development, the U.S. Small Business Administration, the International Trade Administration of the U.S. Department of Commerce, and various private sector groups.

Catastrophic care
Medical and other services for acute and long-term illnesses that cost more than insurance coverage limits or that cost the amount most families may be expected to pay with their own resources.

CDC
See Certified development corporation

CD-ROM
Compact disc with read-only memory used to store large amounts of digitized data.

Certified development corporation (CDC)
A local area or statewide corporation or authority (for profit or nonprofit) that packages U.S. Small Business Administration (SBA), bank, state, and/or private money into financial assistance for existing business capital improvements. The SBA holds the second lien on its maximum share of 40 percent involvement. Each state has at least one certified development corporation. This program is called the SBA 504 Program.

Certified lenders
Banks that participate in the SBA guaranteed loan program (see separate citation). Such banks must have a good track record with the U.S. Small Business Administration (SBA) and must agree to certain conditions set forth by the agency. In return, the SBA agrees to process any guaranteed loan application within three business days.

Champion
An advocate for the development of an innovation.

Channel of distribution
The means used to transport merchandise from the manufacturer to the consumer.

Chapter 7 of the 1978 Bankruptcy Act
Provides for a court-appointed trustee who is responsible for liquidating a company's assets in order to settle outstanding debts.

Chapter 11 of the 1978 Bankruptcy Act
Allows the business owners to retain control of the company while working with their creditors to reorganize their finances and establish better business practices to prevent liquidation of assets.

Closely held corporation
A corporation in which the shares are held by a few persons, usually officers, employees, or others close to the management; these shares are rarely offered to the public.

Code of Federal Regulations
Codification of general and permanent rules of the federal government published in the Federal Register.

Code sharing
See Computer code sharing

Coinsurance
Upon meeting the deductible payment, health insurance participants may be required to make additional health care cost-sharing payments. Coinsurance is a payment of a fixed percentage of the cost of each service; copayment is usually a fixed amount to be paid with each service.

Collateral
Securities, evidence of deposit, or other property pledged by a borrower to secure repayment of a loan.

Collective ratemaking
The establishment of uniform charges for services by a group of businesses in the same industry.

Commercial insurance plan
See Underwriting

Commercial loans
Short-term renewable loans used to finance specific capital needs of a business.

Commercialization
The final stage of the innovation process, including production and distribution.

Common stock
The most frequently used instrument for purchasing ownership in private or public companies. Common stock generally carries the right to vote on certain corporate actions and may pay dividends, although it rarely does in venture investments. In liquidation, common stockholders are the last to share in the proceeds from the sale of a corporation's assets; bondholders and preferred shareholders have priority. Common stock is often used in firstround start-up financing.

Community development corporation
A corporation established to develop economic programs for a community and, in most cases, to provide financial support for such development.

Competitor
A business whose product or service is marketed for the same purpose/use and to the same consumer group as the product or service of another.

Computer code sharing
An arrangement whereby flights of a regional airline are identified by the two-letter code of a major carrier in the computer reservation system to help direct passengers to new regional carriers.

Consignment
A merchandising agreement, usually referring to secondhand shops, where the dealer pays the owner of an item a percentage of the profit when the item is sold.

Consortium
A coalition of organizations such as banks and corporations for ventures requiring large capital resources.

Consultant
An individual that is paid by a business to provide advice and expertise in a particular area.

Consumer price index
A measure of the fluctuation in prices between two points in time.

Consumer research
Research conducted by a business to obtain information about existing or potential consumer markets.

Continuation coverage
Health coverage offered for a specified period of time to employees who leave their jobs and to their widows, divorced spouses, or dependents.

Contractions
See Business contractions

Convertible preferred stock
A class of stock that pays a reasonable dividend and is convertible into common stock (see separate citation). Generally the convertible feature may only be exercised after being held for a stated period of time. This arrangement is usually considered second-round financing when a company needs equity to maintain its cash flow.

Convertible securities
A feature of certain bonds, debentures, or preferred stocks that allows them to be exchanged by the owner for another class of securities at a future date and in accordance with any other terms of the issue.

Copayment
See Coinsurance

Copyright
A legal form of protection available to creators and authors to safeguard their works from unlawful use or claim of ownership by others. Copyrights may be acquired for works of art, sculpture, music, and published or unpublished manuscripts. All copyrights should be registered at the Copyright Office of the Library of Congress.

Corporate financial ratios
The relationship between key figures found in a company's financial statement expressed as a numeric value. Used to evaluate risk and company performance. Also known as Financial averages, Operating ratios, and Business ratios.

Corporation
A legal entity, chartered by a state or the federal government, recognized as a separate entity having its own rights, privileges, and liabilities distinct from those of its members.

Cost containment
Actions taken by employers and insurers to curtail rising health care costs; for example, increasing

employee cost sharing (see separate citation), requiring second opinions, or preadmission screening.

Cost sharing
The requirement that health care consumers contribute to their own medical care costs through deductibles and coinsurance (see separate citations). Cost sharing does not include the amounts paid in premiums. It is used to control utilization of services; for example, requiring a fixed amount to be paid with each health care service.

Cottage industry
Businesses based in the home in which the family members are the labor force and family-owned equipment is used to process the goods.

Credit Rating
A letter or number calculated by an organization (such as Dun & Bradstreet) to represent the ability and disposition of a business to meet its financial obligations.

Customer service
Various techniques used to ensure the satisfaction of a customer.

Cyclical peak
The upper turning point in a business cycle.

Cyclical trough
The lower turning point in a business cycle.

DBA
See Business name

Death
See Business death

Debenture
A certificate given as acknowledgment of a debt (see separate citation) secured by the general credit of the issuing corporation. A bond, usually without security, issued by a corporation and sometimes convertible to common stock.

Debt
Something owed by one person to another. Financing in which a company receives capital that must be repaid; no ownership is transferred.

Debt capital
Business financing that normally requires periodic interest payments and repayment of the principal within a specified time.

Debt financing
See Debt capital

Debt securities
Loans such as bonds and notes that provide a specified rate of return for a specified period of time.

Deductible
A set amount that an individual must pay before any benefits are received.

Demand shock absorbers
A term used to describe the role that some small firms play by expanding their output levels to accommodate a transient surge in demand.

Demographics
Statistics on various markets, including age, income, and education, used to target specific products or services to appropriate consumer groups.

Demonstration
Showing that a product or process has been modified sufficiently to meet the needs of users.

Deregulation
The lifting of government restrictions; for example, the lifting of government restrictions on the entry of new businesses, the expansion of services, and the setting of prices in particular industries.

Desktop Publishing
Using personal computers and specialized software to produce camera-ready copy for publications.

Disaster loans
Various types of physical and economic assistance available to individuals and businesses through the U.S. Small Business Administration (SBA). This is the only SBA loan program available for residential purposes.

Discrimination
The denial of the rights and privileges of employment based on factors such as age, race, religion, or gender.

Diseconomies of scale
The condition in which the costs of production increase faster than the volume of production.

Dissolution
See Business dissolution

Distribution
Delivering a product or process to the user.

Distributor
One who delivers merchandise to the user.

Diversified company
A company whose products and services are used by several different markets.

Doing business as (DBA)
See Business name

Dow Jones
An information services company that publishes the Wall Street Journal and other sources of financial information.

Dow Jones Industrial Average
An indicator of stock market performance.

Earned income
A tax term that refers to wages and salaries earned by the recipient, as opposed to monies earned through interest and dividends.

Economic efficiency
The use of productive resources to the fullest practical extent in the provision of the set of goods and services that is most preferred by purchasers in the economy.

Economic indicators
Statistics used to express the state of the economy. These include the length of the average work week, the rate of unemployment, and stock prices.

Economically disadvantaged
See Socially and economically disadvantaged

Economies of scale
See Scale economies

EEOC
See Equal Employment Opportunity Commission

8(a) Program
A program authorized by the Small Business Act that directs federal contracts to small businesses owned and

operated by socially and economically disadvantaged individuals.

Electronic mail (e-mail)
The electronic transmission of mail via phone lines.

E-mail
See Electronic mail

Employee leasing
A contract by which employers arrange to have their workers hired by a leasing company and then leased back to them for a management fee. The leasing company typically assumes the administrative burden of payroll and provides a benefit package to the workers.

Employee tenure
The length of time an employee works for a particular employer.

Employer identification number
The business equivalent of a social security number. Assigned by the U.S. Internal Revenue Service.

Enterprise
An aggregation of all establishments owned by a parent company. An enterprise may consist of a single, independent establishment or include subsidiaries and other branches under the same ownership and control.

Enterprise zone
A designated area, usually found in inner cities and other areas with significant unemployment, where businesses receive tax credits and other incentives to entice them to establish operations there.

Entrepreneur
A person who takes the risk of organizing and operating a new business venture.

Entry
See Business entry

Equal Employment Opportunity Commission (EEOC)
A federal agency that ensures nondiscrimination in the hiring and firing practices of a business.

Equal opportunity employer
An employer who adheres to the standards set by the Equal Employment Opportunity Commission (see separate citation).

Equity
The ownership interest. Financing in which partial or total ownership of a company is surrendered in exchange for capital. An investor's financial return comes from dividend payments and from growth in the net worth of the business.

Equity capital
See Equity; Equity midrisk venture capital

Equity financing
See Equity; Equity midrisk venture capital

Equity midrisk venture capital
An unsecured investment in a company. Usually a purchase of ownership interest in a company that occurs in the later stages of a company's development.

Equity partnership
A limited partnership arrangement for providing start-up and seed capital to businesses.

Equity securities
See Equity

Equity-type
Debt financing subordinated to conventional debt.

Establishment
A single-location business unit that may be independent (a single-establishment enterprise) or owned by a parent enterprise.

Establishment and Enterprise Microdata File
See U.S. Establishment and Enterprise Microdata File

Establishment birth
See Business birth

Establishment Longitudinal Microdata File
See U.S. Establishment Longitudinal Microdata File

Ethics
See Business ethics

Evaluation
Determining the potential success of translating an invention into a product or process.

Exit
See Business exit

Experience rating
See Underwriting

Export
A product sold outside of the country.

Export license
A general or specific license granted by the U.S. Department of Commerce required of anyone wishing to export goods. Some restricted articles need approval from the U.S. Departments of State, Defense, or Energy.

Failure
See Business failure

Fair share agreement
An agreement reached between a franchisor and a minority business organization to extend business ownership to minorities by either reducing the amount of capital required or by setting aside certain marketing areas for minority business owners.

Feasibility study
A study to determine the likelihood that a proposed product or development will fulfill the objectives of a particular investor.

Federal Trade Commission (FTC)
Federal agency that promotes free enterprise and competition within the U.S.

Federal Trade Mark Act of 1946
See Lanham Act

Fictional name
See Business name

Fiduciary
An individual or group that hold assets in trust for a beneficiary.

Financial analysis
The techniques used to determine money needs in a business. Techniques include ratio analysis, calculation of return on investment, guides for measuring profitability, and break-even analysis to determine ultimate success.

Financial intermediary
A financial institution that acts as the intermediary between borrowers and lenders. Banks, savings and loan associations, finance companies, and venture capital companies are major financial intermediaries in the United States.

Financial ratios
See Corporate financial ratios; Industry financial ratios

Financial statement
A written record of business finances, including balance sheets and profit and loss statements.

Financing
See First-stage financing; Second-stage financing; Thirdstage financing

First-stage financing
Financing provided to companies that have expended their initial capital, and require funds to start full-scale manufacturing and sales. Also known as First-round financing.

Fiscal year
Any twelve-month period used by businesses for accounting purposes.

504 Program
See Certified development corporation

Flexible benefit plan
A plan that offers a choice among cash and/or qualified benefits such as group term life insurance, accident and health insurance, group legal services, dependent care assistance, and vacations.

FOB
See Free on board

Format franchising
See Business format franchising; Franchising

401(k) plan
A financial plan where employees contribute a percentage of their earnings to a fund that is invested in stocks, bonds, or money markets for the purpose of saving money for retirement.

Four Ps
Marketing terms referring to Product, Price, Place, and Promotion.

Franchising
A form of licensing by which the owner-the franchisor- distributes or markets a product, method, or service through affiliated dealers called franchisees. The product, method, or service being marketed is identified by a brand name, and the franchisor

maintains control over the marketing methods employed. The franchisee is often given exclusive access to a defined geographic area.

Free on board (FOB)
A pricing term indicating that the quoted price includes the cost of loading goods into transport vessels at a specified place.

Frictional unemployment
See Unemployment

FTC
See Federal Trade Commission

Fulfillment
The systems necessary for accurate delivery of an ordered item, including subscriptions and direct marketing.

Full-time workers
Generally, those who work a regular schedule of more than 35 hours per week.

Garment registration number
A number that must appear on every garment sold in the U.S. to indicate the manufacturer of the garment, which may or may not be the same as the label under which the garment is sold. The U.S. Federal Trade Commission assigns and regulates garment registration numbers.

Gatekeeper
A key contact point for entry into a network.

GDP
See Gross domestic product

General obligation bond
A municipal bond secured by the taxing power of the municipality. The Tax Reform Act of 1986 limits the purposes for which such bonds may be issued and establishes volume limits on the extent of their issuance.

GNP
See Gross national product

Good Housekeeping Seal
Seal appearing on products that signifies the fulfillment of the standards set by the Good Housekeeping Institute to protect consumer interests.

Goods sector
All businesses producing tangible goods, including agriculture, mining, construction, and manufacturing businesses.

GPO
See Gross product originating

Gross domestic product (GDP)
The part of the nation's gross national product (see separate citation) generated by private business using resources from within the country.

Gross national product (GNP)
The most comprehensive single measure of aggregate economic output. Represents the market value of the total output of goods and services produced by a nation's economy.

Gross product originating (GPO)
A measure of business output estimated from the income or production side using employee compensation, profit income, net interest, capital consumption, and indirect business taxes.

HAL
See Handicapped assistance loan program

Handicapped assistance loan program (HAL)
Low-interest direct loan program through the U.S. Small Business Administration (SBA) for handicapped persons. The SBA requires that these persons demonstrate that their disability is such that it is impossible for them to secure employment, thus making it necessary to go into their own business to make a living.

Health maintenance organization (HMO)
Organization of physicians and other health care professionals that provides health services to subscribers and their dependents on a prepaid basis.

Health provider
An individual or institution that gives medical care. Under Medicare, an institutional provider is a hospital, skilled nursing facility, home health agency, or provider of certain physical therapy services.

Hispanic
A person of Cuban, Mexican, Puerto Rican, Latin American (Central or South American), European Spanish, or other Spanish-speaking origin or ancestry.

HMO
See Health maintenance organization

Home-based business
A business with an operating address that is also a residential address (usually the residential address of the proprietor).

Hub-and-spoke system
A system in which flights of an airline from many different cities (the spokes) converge at a single airport (the hub). After allowing passengers sufficient time to make connections, planes then depart for different cities.

Human Resources Management
A business program designed to oversee recruiting, pay, benefits, and other issues related to the company's work force, including planning to determine the optimal use of labor to increase production, thereby increasing profit.

Idea
An original concept for a new product or process.

Import
Products produced outside the country in which they are consumed.

Income
Money or its equivalent, earned or accrued, resulting from the sale of goods and services.

Income statement
A financial statement that lists the profits and losses of a company at a given time.

Incorporation
The filing of a certificate of incorporation with a state's secretary of state, thereby limiting the business owner's liability.

Incubator
A facility designed to encourage entrepreneurship and minimize obstacles to new business formation and growth, particularly for high-technology firms, by housing a number of fledgling enterprises that share an array of services, such as meeting areas, secretarial services, accounting, research library, on-site financial and management counseling, and word processing facilities.

Independent contractor
An individual considered self-employed (see separate citation) and responsible for paying Social Security taxes and income taxes on earnings.

Indirect health coverage
Health insurance obtained through another individual's health care plan; for example, a spouse's employersponsored plan.

Industrial development authority
The financial arm of a state or other political subdivision established for the purpose of financing economic development in an area, usually through loans to nonprofit organizations, which in turn provide facilities for manufacturing and other industrial operations.

Industry financial ratios
Corporate financial ratios averaged for a specified industry. These are used for comparison purposes and reveal industry trends and identify differences between the performance of a specific company and the performance of its industry. Also known as Industrial averages, Industry ratios, Financial averages, and Business or Industrial norms.

Inflation
Increases in volume of currency and credit, generally resulting in a sharp and continuing rise in price levels.

Informal capital
Financing from informal, unorganized sources; includes informal debt capital such as trade credit or loans from friends and relatives and equity capital from informal investors.

Initial public offering (IPO)
A corporation's first offering of stock to the public.

Innovation
The introduction of a new idea into the marketplace in the form of a new product or service or an improvement in organization or process.

Intellectual property
Any idea or work that can be considered proprietary in nature and is thus protected from infringement by others.

Glossary

Internal capital
Debt or equity financing obtained from the owner or through retained business earnings.

Internet
A government-designed computer network that contains large amounts of information and is accessible through various vendors for a fee.

Intrapreneurship
The state of employing entrepreneurial principles to nonentrepreneurial situations.

Invention
The tangible form of a technological idea, which could include a laboratory prototype, drawings, formulas, etc.

IPO
See Initial public offering

Job description
The duties and responsibilities required in a particular position.

Job tenure
A period of time during which an individual is continuously employed in the same job.

Joint marketing agreements
Agreements between regional and major airlines, often involving the coordination of flight schedules, fares, and baggage transfer. These agreements help regional carriers operate at lower cost.

Joint venture
Venture in which two or more people combine efforts in a particular business enterprise, usually a single transaction or a limited activity, and agree to share the profits and losses jointly or in proportion to their contributions.

Keogh plan
Designed for self-employed persons and unincorporated businesses as a tax-deferred pension account.

Labor force
Civilians considered eligible for employment who are also willing and able to work.

Labor force participation rate
The civilian labor force as a percentage of the civilian population.

Labor intensity
The relative importance of labor in the production process, usually measured as the capital-labor ratio; i.e., the ratio of units of capital (typically, dollars of tangible assets) to the number of employees. The higher the capital-labor ratio exhibited by a firm or industry, the lower the capital intensity of that firm or industry is said to be.

Labor surplus area
An area in which there exists a high unemployment rate. In procurement (see separate citation), extra points are given to firms in counties that are designated a labor surplus area; this information is requested on procurement bid sheets.

Labor union
An organization of similarly-skilled workers who collectively bargain with management over the conditions of employment.

Laboratory prototype
See Prototype

LAN
See Local Area Network

Lanham Act
Refers to the Federal Trade Mark Act of 1946. Protects registered trademarks, trade names, and other service marks used in commerce.

Large business-dominated industry
Industry in which a minimum of 60 percent of employment or sales is in firms with more than 500 workers.

LBO
See Leveraged buy-out

Leader pricing
A reduction in the price of a good or service in order to generate more sales of that good or service.

Legal list
A list of securities selected by a state in which certain institutions and fiduciaries (such as pension funds, insurance companies, and banks) may invest. Securities not on the list are not eligible for investment. Legal lists typically restrict investments to high quality securities meeting certain specifications. Generally, investment is

limited to U.S. securities and investment-grade blue chip securities (see separate citation).

Leveraged buy-out (LBO)
The purchase of a business or a division of a corporation through a highly leveraged financing package.

Liability
An obligation or duty to perform a service or an act. Also defined as money owed.

License
A legal agreement granting to another the right to use a technological innovation.

Limited partnerships
See Venture capital limited partnerships

Liquidity
The ability to convert a security into cash promptly.

Loans
See Commercial loans; Disaster loans; SBA direct loans; SBA guaranteed loans; SBA special lending institution categories Local Area Network (LAN) Computer networks contained within a single building or small area; used to facilitate the sharing of information.

Local development corporation
An organization, usually made up of local citizens of a community, designed to improve the economy of the area by inducing business and industry to locate and expand there. A local development corporation establishes a capability to finance local growth.

Long-haul rates
Rates charged by a transporter in which the distance traveled is more than 800 miles.

Long-term debt
An obligation that matures in a period that exceeds five years.

Low-grade bond
A corporate bond that is rated below investment grade by the major rating agencies (Standard and Poor's, Moody's).

Macro-efficiency
Efficiency as it pertains to the operation of markets and market systems.

Managed care
A cost-effective health care program initiated by employers whereby low-cost health care is made available to the employees in return for exclusive patronage to program doctors.

Management Assistance Programs
See SBA Management Assistance Programs

Management and technical assistance
A term used by many programs to mean business (as opposed to technological) assistance.

Mandated benefits
Specific treatments, providers, or individuals required by law to be included in commercial health plans.

Market evaluation
The use of market information to determine the sales potential of a specific product or process.

Market failure
The situation in which the workings of a competitive market do not produce the best results from the point of view of the entire society.

Market information
Data of any type that can be used for market evaluation, which could include demographic data, technology forecasting, regulatory changes, etc.

Market research
A systematic collection, analysis, and reporting of data about the market and its preferences, opinions, trends, and plans; used for corporate decision-making.

Market share
In a particular market, the percentage of sales of a specific product.

Marketing
Promotion of goods or services through various media.

Master Establishment List (MEL)
A list of firms in the United States developed by the U.S. Small Business Administration; firms can be selected by industry, region, state, standard metropolitan statistical area (see separate citation), county, and zip code.

Maturity
The date upon which the principal or stated value of a bond or other indebtedness becomes due and payable.

Medicaid (Title XIX)

A federally aided, state-operated and administered program that provides medical benefits for certain low income persons in need of health and medical care who are eligible for one of the government's welfare cash payment programs, including the aged, the blind, the disabled, and members of families with dependent children where one parent is absent, incapacitated, or unemployed.

Medicare (Title XVIII)

A nationwide health insurance program for disabled and aged persons. Health insurance is available to insured persons without regard to income. Monies from payroll taxes cover hospital insurance and monies from general revenues and beneficiary premiums pay for supplementary medical insurance.

MEL

See Master Establishment List

MESBIC

See Minority enterprise small business investment corporation

MET

See Multiple employer trust

Metropolitan statistical area (MSA)

A means used by the government to define large population centers that may transverse different governmental jurisdictions. For example, the Washington, D.C. MSA includes the District of Columbia and contiguous parts of Maryland and Virginia because all of these geopolitical areas comprise one population and economic operating unit.

Mezzanine financing

See Third-stage financing

Micro-efficiency

Efficiency as it pertains to the operation of individual firms.

Microdata

Information on the characteristics of an individual business firm.

Mid-term debt

An obligation that matures within one to five years.

Midrisk venture capital

See Equity midrisk venture capital

Minimum premium plan

A combination approach to funding an insurance plan aimed primarily at premium tax savings. The employer self-funds a fixed percentage of estimated monthly claims and the insurance company insures the excess.

Minimum wage

The lowest hourly wage allowed by the federal government.

Minority Business Development Agency

Contracts with private firms throughout the nation to sponsor Minority Business Development Centers which provide minority firms with advice and technical assistance on a fee basis.

Minority Enterprise Small Business Investment Corporation (MESBIC)

A federally funded private venture capital firm licensed by the U.S. Small Business Administration to provide capital to minority-owned businesses (see separate citation).

Minority-owned business

Businesses owned by those who are socially or economically disadvantaged (see separate citation).

Mom and Pop business

A small store or enterprise having limited capital, principally employing family members.

Moonlighter

A wage-and-salary worker with a side business.

MSA

See Metropolitan statistical area

Multi-employer plan

A health plan to which more than one employer is required to contribute and that may be maintained through a collective bargaining agreement and required to meet standards prescribed by the U.S. Department of Labor.

Multi-level marketing

A system of selling in which you sign up other people to assist you and they, in turn, recruit others to help them. Some entrepreneurs have built successful companies on this concept because the main focus of their activities is their product and product sales.

Multimedia
The use of several types of media to promote a product or service. Also, refers to the use of several different types of media (sight, sound, pictures, text) in a CD-ROM (see separate citation) product.

Multiple employer trust (MET)
A self-funded benefit plan generally geared toward small employers sharing a common interest.

NAFTA
See North American Free Trade Agreement

NASDAQ
See National Association of Securities Dealers Automated Quotations

National Association of Securities Dealers Automated Quotations
Provides price quotes on over-the-counter securities as well as securities listed on the New York Stock Exchange.

National income
Aggregate earnings of labor and property arising from the production of goods and services in a nation's economy.

Net assets
See Net worth

Net income
The amount remaining from earnings and profits after all expenses and costs have been met or deducted. Also known as Net earnings.

Net profit
Money earned after production and overhead expenses (see separate citations) have been deducted.

Net worth
The difference between a company's total assets and its total liabilities.

Network
A chain of interconnected individuals or organizations sharing information and/or services.

New York Stock Exchange (NYSE)
The oldest stock exchange in the U.S. Allows for trading in stocks, bonds, warrants, options, and rights that meet listing requirements.

Niche
A career or business for which a person is well-suited. Also, a product which fulfills one need of a particular market segment, often with little or no competition.

Nodes
One workstation in a network, either local area or wide area (see separate citations).

Nonbank bank
A bank that either accepts deposits or makes loans, but not both. Used to create many new branch banks.

Noncompetitive awards
A method of contracting whereby the federal government negotiates with only one contractor to supply a product or service.

Nonmember bank
A state-regulated bank that does not belong to the federal bank system.

Nonprofit
An organization that has no shareholders, does not distribute profits, and is without federal and state tax liabilities.

Norms
See Financial ratios

North American Free Trade Agreement (NAFTA)
Passed in 1993, NAFTA eliminates trade barriers among businesses in the U.S., Canada, and Mexico.

NYSE
See New York Stock Exchange

Occupational Safety & Health Administration (OSHA)
Federal agency that regulates health and safety standards within the workplace.

Optimal firm size
The business size at which the production cost per unit of output (average cost) is, in the long run, at its minimum.

Organizational chart
A hierarchical chart tracking the chain of command within an organization.

OSHA
See Occupational Safety & Health Administration

Overhead
Expenses, such as employee benefits and building utilities, incurred by a business that are unrelated to the actual product or service sold.

Owner's capital
Debt or equity funds provided by the owner(s) of a business; sources of owner's capital are personal savings, sales of assets, or loans from financial institutions.

P & L
See Profit and loss statement

Part-time workers
Normally, those who work less than 35 hours per week. The Tax Reform Act indicated that part-time workers who work less than 17.5 hours per week may be excluded from health plans for purposes of complying with federal nondiscrimination rules.

Part-year workers
Those who work less than 50 weeks per year.

Partnership
Two or more parties who enter into a legal relationship to conduct business for profit. Defined by the U.S. Internal Revenue Code as joint ventures, syndicates, groups, pools, and other associations of two or more persons organized for profit that are not specifically classified in the IRS code as corporations or proprietorships.

Patent
A grant made by the government assuring an inventor the sole right to make, use, and sell an invention for a period of 17 years.

PC
See Professional corporation

Peak
See Cyclical peak

Pension
A series of payments made monthly, semiannually, annually, or at other specified intervals during the lifetime of the pensioner for distribution upon retirement. The term is sometimes used to denote the portion of the retirement allowance financed by the employer's contributions.

Pension fund
A fund established to provide for the payment of pension benefits; the collective contributions made by all of the parties to the pension plan.

Performance appraisal
An established set of objective criteria, based on job description and requirements, that is used to evaluate the performance of an employee in a specific job.

Permit
See Business license

Plan
See Business plan

Pooling
An arrangement for employers to achieve efficiencies and lower health costs by joining together to purchase group health insurance or self-insurance.

PPO
See Preferred provider organization

Preferred lenders program
See SBA special lending institution categories

Preferred provider organization (PPO)
A contractual arrangement with a health care services organization that agrees to discount its health care rates in return for faster payment and/or a patient base.

Premiums
The amount of money paid to an insurer for health insurance under a policy. The premium is generally paid periodically (e.g., monthly), and often is split between the employer and the employee. Unlike deductibles and coinsurance or copayments, premiums are paid for coverage whether or not benefits are actually used.

Prime-age workers
Employees 25 to 54 years of age.

Prime contract
A contract awarded directly by the U.S. Federal Government.

Private company
See Closely held corporation

Private placement
A method of raising capital by offering for sale an investment or business to a small group of investors (generally avoiding registration with the Securities and Exchange Commission or state securities registration agencies). Also known as Private financing or Private offering.

Pro forma
The use of hypothetical figures in financial statements to represent future expenditures, debts, and other potential financial expenses.

Proactive
Taking the initiative to solve problems and anticipate future events before they happen, instead of reacting to an already existing problem or waiting for a difficult situation to occur.

Procurement
A contract from an agency of the federal government for goods or services from a small business.

Prodigy
An online service which is accessible by computer modem. The service features Internet access, bulletin boards, online periodicals, electronic mail, and other services for subscribers.

Product development
The stage of the innovation process where research is translated into a product or process through evaluation, adaptation, and demonstration.

Product franchising
An arrangement for a franchisee to use the name and to produce the product line of the franchisor or parent corporation.

Production
The manufacture of a product.

Production prototype
See Prototype

Productivity
A measurement of the number of goods produced during a specific amount of time.

Professional corporation (PC)
Organized by members of a profession such as medicine, dentistry, or law for the purpose of conducting their professional activities as a corporation. Liability of a member or shareholder is limited in the same manner as in a business corporation.

Profit and loss statement (P & L)
The summary of the incomes (total revenues) and costs of a company's operation during a specific period of time. Also known as Income and expense statement.

Proposal
See Business plan

Proprietorship
The most common legal form of business ownership; about 85 percent of all small businesses are proprietorships. The liability of the owner is unlimited in this form of ownership.

Prospective payment system
A cost-containment measure included in the Social Security Amendments of 1983 whereby Medicare payments to hospitals are based on established prices, rather than on cost reimbursement.

Prototype
A model that demonstrates the validity of the concept of an invention (laboratory prototype); a model that meets the needs of the manufacturing process and the user (production prototype).

Prudent investor rule or standard
A legal doctrine that requires fiduciaries to make investments using the prudence, diligence, and intelligence that would be used by a prudent person in making similar investments. Because fiduciaries make investments on behalf of third-party beneficiaries, the standard results in very conservative investments. Until recently, most state regulations required the fiduciary to apply this standard to each investment. Newer, more progressive regulations permit fiduciaries to apply this standard to the portfolio taken as a whole, thereby allowing a fiduciary to balance a portfolio with higher-yield, higher-risk investments. In states with more progressive regulations, practically every type of security is eligible for inclusion in the portfolio of investments made by a fiduciary, provided

Glossary

that the portfolio investments, in their totality, are those of a prudent person.

Public equity markets
Organized markets for trading in equity shares such as common stocks, preferred stocks, and warrants. Includes markets for both regularly traded and nonregularly traded securities.

Public offering
General solicitation for participation in an investment opportunity. Interstate public offerings are supervised by the U.S. Securities and Exchange Commission (see separate citation).

Quality control
The process by which a product is checked and tested to ensure consistent standards of high quality.

Rate of return
The yield obtained on a security or other investment based on its purchase price or its current market price. The total rate of return is current income plus or minus capital appreciation or depreciation.

Real property
Includes the land and all that is contained on it.

Realignment
See Resource realignment

Recession
Contraction of economic activity occurring between the peak and trough (see separate citations) of a business cycle.

Regulated market
A market in which the government controls the forces of supply and demand, such as who may enter and what price may be charged.

Regulation D
A vehicle by which small businesses make small offerings and private placements of securities with limited disclosure requirements. It was designed to ease the burdens imposed on small businesses utilizing this method of capital formation.

Regulatory Flexibility Act
An act requiring federal agencies to evaluate the impact of their regulations on small businesses before the regulations are issued and to consider less burdensome alternatives.

Research
The initial stage of the innovation process, which includes idea generation and invention.

Research and development financing
A tax-advantaged partnership set up to finance product development for start-ups as well as more mature companies.

Resource mobility
The ease with which labor and capital move from firm to firm or from industry to industry.

Resource realignment
The adjustment of productive resources to interindustry changes in demand.

Resources
The sources of support or help in the innovation process, including sources of financing, technical evaluation, market evaluation, management and business assistance, etc.

Retained business earnings
Business profits that are retained by the business rather than being distributed to the shareholders as dividends.

Revolving credit
An agreement with a lending institution for an amount of money, which cannot exceed a set maximum, over a specified period of time. Each time the borrower repays a portion of the loan, the amount of the repayment may be borrowed yet again.

Risk capital
See Venture capital

Risk management
The act of identifying potential sources of financial loss and taking action to minimize their negative impact.

Routing
The sequence of steps necessary to complete a product during production.

S corporations
See Sub chapter S corporations

Glossary *(vertical, right margin)*

SBA
See Small Business Administration

SBA direct loans
Loans made directly by the U.S. Small Business Administration (SBA); monies come from funds appropriated specifically for this purpose. In general, SBA direct loans carry interest rates slightly lower than those in the private financial markets and are available only to applicants unable to secure private financing or an SBA guaranteed loan.

SBA 504 Program
See Certified development corporation

SBA guaranteed loans
Loans made by lending institutions in which the U.S. Small Business Administration (SBA) will pay a prior agreed-upon percentage of the outstanding principal in the event the borrower of the loan defaults. The terms of the loan and the interest rate are negotiated between theborrower and the lending institution, within set parameters.

SBA loans
See Disaster loans; SBA direct loans; SBA guaranteed loans; SBA special lending institution categories

SBA Management Assistance Programs
Classes, workshops, counseling, and publications offered by the U.S. Small Business Administration.

SBA special lending institution categories
U.S. Small Business Administration (SBA) loan program in which the SBA promises certified banks a 72-hour turnaround period in giving its approval for a loan, and in which preferred lenders in a pilot program are allowed to write SBA loans without seeking prior SBA approval.

SBDB
See Small Business Data Base

SBDC
See Small business development centers

SBI
See Small business institutes program

SBIC
See Small business investment corporation

SBIR Program
See Small Business Innovation Development Act of 1982

Scale economies
The decline of the production cost per unit of output (average cost) as the volume of output increases.

Scale efficiency
The reduction in unit cost available to a firm when producing at a higher output volume.

SCORE
See Service Corps of Retired Executives

SEC
See Securities and Exchange Commission

SECA
See Self-Employment Contributions Act

Second-stage financing
Working capital for the initial expansion of a company that is producing, shipping, and has growing accounts receivable and inventories. Also known as Second-round financing.

Secondary market
A market established for the purchase and sale of outstanding securities following their initial distribution.

Secondary worker
Any worker in a family other than the person who is the primary source of income for the family.

Secondhand capital
Previously used and subsequently resold capital equipment (e.g., buildings and machinery).

Securities and Exchange Commission (SEC)
Federal agency charged with regulating the trade of securities to prevent unethical practices in the investor market.

Securitized debt
A marketing technique that converts long-term loans to marketable securities.

Seed capital
Venture financing provided in the early stages of the innovation process, usually during product development.

Self-employed person
One who works for a profit or fees in his or her own business, profession, or trade, or who operates a farm.

Self-Employment Contributions Act (SECA)
Federal law that governs the self-employment tax (see separate citation).

Self-employment income
Income covered by Social Security if a business earns a net income of at least $400.00 during the year. Taxes are paid on earnings that exceed $400.00.

Self-employment retirement plan
See Keogh plan

Self-employment tax
Required tax imposed on self-employed individuals for the provision of Social Security and Medicare. The tax must be paid quarterly with estimated income tax statements.

Self-funding
A health benefit plan in which a firm uses its own funds to pay claims, rather than transferring the financial risks of paying claims to an outside insurer in exchange for premium payments.

Service Corps of Retired Executives (SCORE)
Volunteers for the SBA Management Assistance Program who provide one-on-one counseling and teach workshops and seminars for small firms.

Service firm
See Business service firm

Service sector
Broadly defined, all U.S. industries that produce intangibles, including the five major industry divisions of transportation, communications, and utilities; wholesale trade; retail trade; finance, insurance, and real estate; and services.

Set asides
See Small business set asides

Short-haul service
A type of transportation service in which the transporter supplies service between cities where the maximum distance is no more than 200 miles.

Short-term debt
An obligation that matures in one year.

SIC codes
See Standard Industrial Classification codes

Single-establishment enterprise
See Establishment

Small business
An enterprise that is independently owned and operated, is not dominant in its field, and employs fewer than 500 people. For SBA purposes, the U.S. Small Business Administration (SBA) considers various other factors (such as gross annual sales) in determining size of a business.

Small Business Administration (SBA)
An independent federal agency that provides assistance with loans, management, and advocating interests before other federal agencies.

Small Business Data Base
A collection of microdata (see separate citation) files on individual firms developed and maintained by the U.S. Small Business Administration.

Small business development centers (SBDC)
Centers that provide support services to small businesses, such as individual counseling, SBA advice, seminars and conferences, and other learning center activities. Most services are free of charge, or available at minimal cost.

Small business development corporation
See Certified development corporation

Small business-dominated industry
Industry in which a minimum of 60 percent of employment or sales is in firms with fewer than 500 employees.

Small Business Innovation Development Act of 1982
Federal statute requiring federal agencies with large extramural research and development budgets to allocate a certain percentage of these funds to small research and development firms. The program, called the Small Business Innovation Research (SBIR) Program, is designed to stimulate technological innovation and make greater use of small businesses in meeting national innovation needs.

Small business institutes (SBI) program
Cooperative arrangements made by U.S. Small Business Administration district offices and local colleges and

universities to provide small business firms with graduate students to counsel them without charge.

Small business investment corporation (SBIC)
A privately owned company licensed and funded through the U.S. Small Business Administration and private sector sources to provide equity or debt capital to small businesses.

Small business set asides
Procurement (see separate citation) opportunities required by law to be on all contracts under $10,000 or a certain percentage of an agency's total procurement expenditure.

Smaller firms
For U.S. Department of Commerce purposes, those firms not included in the Fortune 1000.

SMSA
See Metropolitan statistical area

Socially and economically disadvantaged
Individuals who have been subjected to racial or ethnic prejudice or cultural bias without regard to their qualities as individuals, and whose abilities to compete are impaired because of diminished opportunities to obtain capital and credit.

Sole proprietorship
An unincorporated, one-owner business, farm, or professional practice.

Special lending institution categories
See SBA special lending institution categories

Standard Industrial Classification (SIC) codes
Four-digit codes established by the U.S. Federal Government to categorize businesses by type of economic activity; the first two digits correspond to major groups such as construction and manufacturing, while the last two digits correspond to subgroups such as home construction or highway construction.

Standard metropolitan statistical area (SMSA)
See Metropolitan statistical area

Start-up
A new business, at the earliest stages of development and financing.

Start-up costs
Costs incurred before a business can commence operations.

Start-up financing
Financing provided to companies that have either completed product development and initial marketing or have been in business for less than one year but have not yet sold their product commercially.

Stock
A certificate of equity ownership in a business.

Stop-loss coverage
Insurance for a self-insured plan that reimburses the company for any losses it might incur in its health claims beyond a specified amount.

Strategic planning
Projected growth and development of a business to establish a guiding direction for the future. Also used to determine which market segments to explore for optimal sales of products or services.

Structural unemployment
See Unemployment

Sub chapter S corporations
Corporations that are considered noncorporate for tax purposes but legally remain corporations.

Subcontract
A contract between a prime contractor and a subcontractor, or between subcontractors, to furnish supplies or services for performance of a prime contract (see separate citation) or a subcontract.

Surety bonds
Bonds providing reimbursement to an individual, company, or the government if a firm fails to complete a contract. The U.S. Small Business Administration guarantees surety bonds in a program much like the SBA guaranteed loan program (see separate citation).

Swing loan
See Bridge financing

Target market
The clients or customers sought for a business' product or service.

Targeted Jobs Tax Credit
Federal legislation enacted in 1978 that provides a tax credit to an employer who hires structurally unemployed individuals.

Tax number
A number assigned to a business by a state revenue department that enables the business to buy goods without paying sales tax.

Taxable bonds
An interest-bearing certificate of public or private indebtedness. Bonds are issued by public agencies to finance economic development.

Technical assistance
See Management and technical assistance

Technical evaluation
Assessment of technological feasibility.

Technology
The method in which a firm combines and utilizes labor and capital resources to produce goods or services; the application of science for commercial or industrial purposes.

Technology transfer
The movement of information about a technology or intellectual property from one party to another for use.

Tenure
See Employee tenure

Term
The length of time for which a loan is made.

Terms of a note
The conditions or limits of a note; includes the interest rate per annum, the due date, and transferability and convertibility features, if any.

Third-party administrator
An outside company responsible for handling claims and performing administrative tasks associated with health insurance plan maintenance.

Third-stage financing
Financing provided for the major expansion of a company whose sales volume is increasing and that is breaking even or profitable. These funds are used for further plant expansion, marketing, working capital, or development of an improved product. Also known as Third-round or Mezzanine financing.

Time deposit
A bank deposit that cannot be withdrawn before a specified future time.

Time management
Skills and scheduling techniques used to maximize productivity.

Trade credit
Credit extended by suppliers of raw materials or finished products. In an accounting statement, trade credit is referred to as "accounts payable."

Trade name
The name under which a company conducts business, or by which its business, goods, or services are identified. It may or may not be registered as a trademark.

Trade periodical
A publication with a specific focus on one or more aspects of business and industry.

Trade secret
Competitive advantage gained by a business through the use of a unique manufacturing process or formula.

Trade show
An exhibition of goods or services used in a particular industry. Typically held in exhibition centers where exhibitors rent space to display their merchandise.

Trademark
A graphic symbol, device, or slogan that identifies a business. A business has property rights to its trademark from the inception of its use, but it is still prudent to register all trademarks with the Trademark Office of the U.S. Department of Commerce.

Translation
See Product development

Treasury bills
Investment tender issued by the Federal Reserve Bank in amounts of $10,000 that mature in 91 to 182 days.

Treasury bonds
Long-term notes with maturity dates of not less than seven and not more than twenty-five years.

Treasury notes
Short-term notes maturing in less than seven years.

Trend
A statistical measurement used to track changes that occur over time.

Trough
See Cyclical trough

UCC
See Uniform Commercial Code

UL
See Underwriters Laboratories

Underwriters Laboratories (UL)
One of several private firms that tests products and processes to determine their safety. Although various firms can provide this kind of testing service, many local and insurance codes specify UL certification.

Underwriting
A process by which an insurer determines whether or not and on what basis it will accept an application for insurance. In an experience-rated plan, premiums are based on a firm's or group's past claims; factors other than prior claims are used for community-rated or manually rated plans.

Unfair competition
Refers to business practices, usually unethical, such as using unlicensed products, pirating merchandise, or misleading the public through false advertising, which give the offending business an unequitable advantage over others.

Unfunded accrued liability
The excess of total liabilities, both present and prospective, over present and prospective assets.

Unemployment
The joblessness of individuals who are willing to work, who are legally and physically able to work, and who are seeking work. Unemployment may represent the temporary joblessness of a worker between jobs (frictional unemployment) or the joblessness of a worker whose skills are not suitable for jobs available in the labor market (structural unemployment).

Uniform Commercial Code (UCC)
A code of laws governing commercial transactions across the U.S., except Louisiana. Their purpose is to bring uniformity to financial transactions.

Uniform product code (UPC symbol)
A computer-readable label comprised of ten digits and stripes that encodes what a product is and how much it costs. The first five digits are assigned by the Uniform Product Code Council, and the last five digits by the individual manufacturer.

Unit cost
See Average cost

UPC symbol
See Uniform product code

U.S. Establishment and Enterprise Microdata (USEEM) File
A cross-sectional database containing information on employment, sales, and location for individual enterprises and establishments with employees that have a Dun & Bradstreet credit rating.

U.S. Establishment Longitudinal Microdata (USELM) File
A database containing longitudinally linked sample microdata on establishments drawn from the U.S. Establishment and Enterprise Microdata file (see separate citation).

U.S. Small Business Administration 504 Program
See Certified development corporation

USEEM
See U.S. Establishment and Enterprise Microdata File

USELM
See U.S. Establishment Longitudinal Microdata File

VCN
See Venture capital network

Venture capital
Money used to support new or unusual business ventures that exhibit above-average growth rates, significant potential for market expansion, and are in need of additional financing to sustain growth or further research and development; equity or equity-type financing traditionally provided at the

Glossary

commercialization stage, increasingly available prior to commercialization.

Venture capital company

A company organized to provide seed capital to a business in its formation stage, or in its first or second stage of expansion. Funding is obtained through public or private pension funds, commercial banks and bank holding companies, small business investment corporations licensed by the U.S. Small Business Administration, private venture capital firms, insurance companies, investment management companies, bank trust departments, industrial companies seeking to diversify their investment, and investment bankers acting as intermediaries for other investors or directly investing on their own behalf.

Venture capital limited partnerships

Designed for business development, these partnerships are an institutional mechanism for providing capital for young, technology-oriented businesses. The investors' money is pooled and invested in money market assets until venture investments have been selected. The general partners are experienced investment managers who select and invest the equity and debt securities of firms with high growth potential and the ability to go public in the near future.

Venture capital network (VCN)

A computer database that matches investors with entrepreneurs.

WAN

See Wide Area Network

Wide Area Network (WAN)

Computer networks linking systems throughout a state or around the world in order to facilitate the sharing of information.

Withholding

Federal, state, social security, and unemployment taxes withheld by the employer from employees' wages; employers are liable for these taxes and the corporate umbrella and bankruptcy will not exonerate an employer from paying back payroll withholding. Employers should escrow these funds in a separate account and disperse them quarterly to withholding authorities.

Workers' compensation

A state-mandated form of insurance covering workers injured in job-related accidents. In some states, the state is the insurer; in other states, insurance must be acquired from commercial insurance firms. Insurance rates are based on a number of factors, including salaries, firm history, and risk of occupation.

Working capital

Refers to a firm's short-term investment of current assets, including cash, short-term securities, accounts receivable, and inventories.

Yield

The rate of income returned on an investment, expressed as a percentage. Income yield is obtained by dividing the current dollar income by the current market price of the security. Net yield or yield to maturity is the current income yield minus any premium above par or plus any discount from par in purchase price, with the adjustment spread over the period from the date of purchase to the date of maturity.

Index